DISTRIBUTED SYSTEMS

INTERNATIONAL COMPUTER SCIENCE SERIES

Consulting editors   **A D McGettrick**   University of Strathclyde

J van Leeuwen   University of Utrecht

SELECTED TITLES IN THE SERIES

DISTRIBUTED SYSTEMS

Concepts and Design

George F. Coulouris
Queen Mary and Westfield College, University of London
Harlequin Limited

Jean Dollimore
Queen Mary and Westfield College, University of London

ADDISON-WESLEY
PUBLISHING
COMPANY

Wokingham, England · Reading, Massachusetts · Menlo Park, California · New York
Don Mills, Ontario · Amsterdam · Bonn · Sydney · Singapore
Tokyo · Madrid · San Juan · Milan · Paris · Mexico City · Seoul · Taipei

The programs in this book have been included for their instructional value. They have been tested with care but are not guaranteed for any particular purpose. The publisher does not offer any warranties or representations, nor does it accept any liabilities with respect to the programs.

Many of the designations used by manufacturers and sellers to distinguish their products are claimed as trademarks. Addison-Wesley has made every attempt to supply trademark information about manufacturers and their products mentioned in this book. A list of the trademark designations and their owners appears on p. xii.

Cover designed by Crayon Design of Henley-on-Thames and printed by The Riverside Printing Co. (Reading) Ltd.
Typeset by the University of London Computer Centre from PostScript files prepared by the authors.
Printed and bound in Great Britain by The Bath Press, Avon.
First printed in 1988. Reprinted 1989, 1990, 1991 (twice) and 1993.

British Library Cataloguing in Publication Data
Coulouris, George F.
    Distributed systems : concepts and design
    — (International computer science
    series).
    1. Distributed computer systems
    I. Title   II. Dollimore, Jean
    III. Series
    004'.36

    ISBN 0–201–18059–6

Library of Congress Cataloging in Publication Data
Coulouris, George F.
    Distributed systems.

    (International computer science series)
    Bibliography: p.
    Includes index.
    1. Electronic data processing—Distributed processing.   I. Dollimore, Jean.
II. Title.   III. Series.
QA76.9.D5C68   1988   004'.36   88–24192
ISBN 0–201–18059–6

To Anna, Jason, Julian, Rachel and Susan

Preface

Distributed systems are already used in many fields of computer application and their benefits are sought whenever a new application or a replacement system is planned. Networking enables systems to be designed to serve geographically dispersed groups of users or organizations; distributed processing enables systems and applications to be based on several computers, with processing and other system responsibilities distributed amongst them.

The term 'distributed system' has been applied to so wide a range of multi-computer and multiprocessor computer systems of differing designs and goals that its usage has become somewhat devalued. In Chapter 1 we distinguish the network-based or loosely-coupled systems with which we are primarily concerned in this book from other kinds of multi-computer and multiprocessor systems. We identify **transparency** as the most important characteristic of properly-designed distributed systems.

Transparency has several aspects: for the *user* it offers a unified interface to a networked collection of computer systems, providing access to programs and data objects located in any of the computers in the network using the same names and operations regardless of their location. For the *system manager* it offers flexibility of configuration, allowing systems to be expanded or contracted by the addition or subtraction of computers and avoiding the total replacement of the existing hardware that is commonly undertaken when centralized systems have reached the limits of their capacity. For the *application programmer* it avoids the need to program communication operations explicitly, providing instead a range of interfaces to remote services enabling application programs to access files, devices and system resources wherever they are located. For the *system programmer* it offers the possibility of **open** systems to which new services can be added without any need to rebuild or even restart the existing system software.

System software is required in all computer systems in order to provide a uniform interface or platform for application programs to rest on. The system software conceals low-level details of the specific hardware, implementing a set of generic services for filing, input/output and resource allocation. It also controls access to system resources and protects users' private data against accidental or intentional interference. Traditionally these functions have all been performed in a single software component – the operating system. The advent of high-speed computer networks and the demand for integrated distributed systems has coincided with the development of better structures for conventional operating systems, allowing them to be built as a collection of inter-communicating software modules or processes each performing a well-defined function, such as file management, resource allocation or task scheduling. This approach was first adopted as early as 1970 (e.g. by Brinch Hansen [1970]) in the construction of operating systems for single computers. A further step was taken with the development of open systems; these provide facilities for system modules to be added, offering services to other programs. In such systems the boundary between the operating system and the programs developed by users is less rigid, allowing the system to be viewed as an extensible set of software resources and services.

A key element of these approaches to operating systems is the use of asynchronous processes, communicating only by message passing, to represent system modules. This avoids the problems of synchronization that arise when data objects are shared between asynchronous tasks running in a single address space. For example, Tanenbaum [1987] has developed MINIX – a relatively simple but complete UNIX-like operating system for the IBM PC – with the filing system and the memory manager treated as autonomous processes communicating only by message passing with the remainder of the system.

Similar software structures are used in distributed systems. The use of message passing as the basic mechanism for communication between cooperating software components is a natural consequence of the use of computer networks to link the co-operating components. The open approach to system structure is particularly appropriate in distributed systems, allowing the software to be extended by users, just as the hardware resources can be extended by the connection of additional computers to the network.

There are many problems that must be solved in order to construct useful and efficient distributed systems. Our aim in this book is to identify those problems, to describe the main approaches and solutions to them that have emerged to date, and to illustrate these approaches by descriptions of the facilities offered by some practical distributed systems. The state-of-the-art in distributed systems products follows close behind the testing of theory and design by the development of experimental systems. In this book we have chosen to describe the facilities and behaviour of such experimental systems when they provide the best examples of the principles that we are seeking to illustrate.

We have focussed on the design of general-purpose distributed systems (sometimes referred to as 'distributed operating systems', although this label seems inappropriate to us) and have given less attention to the design of distributed applications, in the belief that concepts and principles that are effective in building general-purpose systems are likely to be helpful in more specific contexts too. Designers of distributed applications need a sound understanding of distributed system software since their work is likely to be much enhanced by its appropriate use.

We have, however, obtained the authors' permission to reprint a milestone paper on the design of a distributed application – describing the Grapevine system developed at the Xerox Palo Alto Research Center in 1979–82. This provides an excellent counterpoint to the remainder of the book, illustrating the use of many of the ideas presented in the context of a specific application that was developed without the benefit of much distributed system software support.

We have not attempted to cover the topics of distributed system management, performance monitoring and evaluation, load balancing, configuration control or system maintenance. We note that these topics are now beginning to receive attention in the distributed systems literature and we look forward to the inclusion of the results of recent and future work in this area in the next edition.

Organization and intended usage

This book is intended to provide an introduction to the concepts and design principles used in the construction of distributed computer systems. We assume only that the reader has a knowledge of programming, of elementary computer architecture and of the facilities offered by a general-purpose operating system such as UNIX. Courses on computer networks and operating systems are not necessary pre-requisites, since we include a discussion of the essential topics from computer networks in Chapter 3 and the operating systems techniques mentioned are explained as they arise.

Although the book is based on material used by the authors for teaching a course on distributed systems at Masters level, it includes material that should make it suitable for teaching in the second or third year of undergraduate courses in computer science and for self-study by those with a background of the type outlined above.

A treatment of distributed systems based on the book might form a one-year course, providing an alternative to the conventional operating systems courses found in many computer science curricula. Alternatively, it can be used as a supplementary text for courses on computer networks or operating systems.

The book proceeds from the architectural foundations of distributed systems through networks, file servers including transaction handling, replication and security issues and concludes with descriptions of the design and the facilities offered in some specific systems. This sequence should be suitable for courses on distributed systems or for self-study covering the subject as a whole, but there are several valid alternatives to a simple 'front-to-back' reading for readers wishing to approach distributed systems from a specific perspective. The following gives an indication of some themes that may be studied by reading the chapters mentioned:

- For an overview of distributed systems and an understanding of their scope and potential benefits, the reader should peruse Chapters 1 and 2, Chapters 10 and 11 and Appendix 2.
- Chapter 3 gives enough background on computer networks for the reader to appreciate the impact that the network technology has on the design of the systems software and the applications. Chapter 4 discusses remote

procedure calling systems, the most important type of network protocol used in most distributed software.

- Chapters 5, 6, 7 and 8 and 10 (especially Sections 10.3, 10.5 and 10.6) should provide a good understanding of the design of file servers for distributed systems.
- Chapters 2, 3 (especially Sections 3.1, 3.3 and 3.4), 9 and 10 (especially Sections 10.1, 10.2, 10.4 and 10.7–10.9) give a system manager's or a system user's view of distributed systems.

The use of boxed text in the book requires a short explanation. The boxes contain definitions of system interfaces, especially the various interfaces required in file servers. The definitions are enclosed in numbered boxes for ease of identification and reference. The definitions take the form of procedure headings in a notation explained in Chapter 5 and a short textual description of the actions of each procedure.

We have also included a few short programs and excerpts from programs, written in Modula-2. We have used Modula-2 because of the facilities that it provides for the separate specification of program modules and their interfaces. The programs are sufficiently simple that readers with a knowledge of Pascal, C or a related language should have little difficulty in following them.

Acknowledgements

This book has evolved from two teaching activities that we have undertaken during the past six years.

1. In collaboration with colleagues at Queen Mary College we have taught a course (of about 30 hours) on Distributed Computer Systems as a part of a Master of Science degree course in Computer Science at QMC. The course, which includes most of the topics covered in the book, was a test-bed for much of the material. It was first taught in 1982, in seminar style, based on the relatively few research papers on distributed systems available at that time, and has been taught each year since then, using in the latter years a combination of research literature sources and the developing material that now forms this book. We are grateful to the colleagues with whom we collaborated in the presentation of the course, especially Allan Davison and Colin Low, and to other colleagues in the Department of Computer Science for sharing in and encouraging the use of seminar teaching, enabling the teachers to explore the literature while teaching the course, sometimes at the expense of an imperfect presentation to the students. We are grateful to the students who participated in this exploration for their enthusiasm and their patience.

2. In December 1985 we were invited to present a condensed version of the same course to a group of Master's students and staff at Peking University, China. It was for that course that much of the material in this book was first prepared in something like its present form, and we are extremely grateful to

Peking University, the staff of the Department of Computer Science and particularly to our host and colleague there Professor Chen Baojue, for making it possible for us to teach the course to a gifted class of students and for providing us with the initial stimulus to organize the material.

We should like to thank the following people and organizations for the particular contributions mentioned: Jean Bacon of the Cambridge University Computer Laboratory was a most thorough and constructive reviewer, providing us with essential feedback on the first draft. Tom Berson wrote an outline and contributed some of the text for Chapter 9. Allan Davison first suggested and organized the MSc course on distributed systems at Queen Mary College; without his enthusiasm and energy we should never have got started. Colin Low originated the approach to levels of transparency used in Chapter 2 and provided some insights on computer networks that inform Chapter 3. William Roberts provided the drawing of the QMC Computer Science network used in Figure 1.6. The Addison-Wesley staff, especially Simon Plumtree, encouraged us at many difficult times. The authors of the excellent Grapevine paper [Birrell et al.1982] and the editors of the Communications of the ACM gave permission to reprint their paper.

We should also like to thank the following for helping in various ways: David Ashton, Ben Bacarisse, Robert Bradshaw, Keith Clarke, Jo Marks, Jim Mitchell, Sape Mullender, Andy Tanenbaum and Sylvia Wilbur. Finally, we should like to thank the Department of Computer Science at Queen Mary College for the use of facilities to prepare the camera-ready copy of the book†, and all of the staff and students for encouragement during the many months that it took us.

George Coulouris   Electronic mail *george@dcs.qmw.ac.uk*
Jean Dollimore   Electronic mail: *jean@dcs.qmw.ac.uk*
July 1988

We should like to thank Harry Porter, Portland State University, Portland, Oregon, for bringing to our attention a significant error (in earlier printings) in our treatment in Section 7.3.3 of version control using timestamps.

GFC and JD
April 1990

---

† The text of the book was edited on an Apple Macintosh II and formatted using *troff* on a UNIX system. The diagrams were prepared on the Macintosh II using CricketDraw and were merged with the text using the excellent *psfig* package distributed by the University of Pennsylvania. The resulting PostScript files were proofed on an Apple LaserWriter and subsequently transferred via the JANET network to a Linotronic typesetter at the University of London Computer Centre for the production of camera-ready pages at a resolution of 1270 dots per inch.

Contents

Chapter 1
An Introduction to Distributed Systems

This chapter introduces and defines distributed computer systems and discusses the factors that have led to their current widespread use. We describe the main components and attributes of general-purpose distributed systems:

- workstations and servers
- information sharing
- transparency

We give a brief outline of the historical development of distributed systems and conclude the chapter with a discussion of their main advantages and drawbacks.

1.1 Scope

This book is concerned with the design and construction of general-purpose distributed computer systems. These are systems based on a set of separate computers that are capable of autonomous operation, linked by a computer network. General-purpose distributed systems are designed to enable the individual computers of which they are composed to use shared resources in the network, providing computing facilities that are at least as flexible and widely-applicable as conventional, centralized or 'mainframe' computers. Users of a distributed system are given the impression that they are using a single, integrated computing facility, although the facility is actually provided by more than one computer and the computers may be in different locations.

The shared resources needed to provide an integrated computing service are provided by some of the computers in the network and are accessed by system software that runs in all of the computers, using the network to coordinate their work and to transfer data between them. Distributed systems of this type are known as **loosely-coupled systems** to distinguish them from the other kinds of computer system that can lay claim to the title 'distributed', but the 'loosely-coupled' prefix is commonly dropped and we shall not use it except where ambiguity would otherwise occur.

The other, more tightly-coupled kinds of distributed computing system are reviewed briefly in Section 1.1.2. Their goals are different. They are so called because they exploit multiple processing units, often sharing a single memory or address space, to achieve high performance in a computer system that is otherwise centralized.

1.1.1 Loosely-coupled systems

Loosely-coupled distributed systems are particularly effective in exploiting the power and flexibility of single-user computers or **workstations**, enabling them to access shared data and resources located in other **server** computers via high-speed local networks (Figure 1.1).

This simple model, defined in terms of a network linking just two types of computer system, is known as the **workstation/server model.** Most of the distributed systems currently in general use conform to this widely-adopted model – the Xerox distributed system [Lampson et al. 1981] is an early example, and networks of Sun workstations are currently widely in use. We introduce these and other examples of the workstation-server model later in this chapter.

The concepts and techniques for the construction of loosely-coupled systems described in this book can be used in networks of computers with a variety of hardware and software configurations. The computers may be either single- or multi-user systems. Current developments in loosely-coupled distributed systems go beyond the workstation/server model, aiming to provide more power than a single workstation can offer to each user. In Chapter 2 we define the characteristics of the workstation/server model and two other architectural models for loosely-coupled systems. Some examples are: Locus [Popek and Walker

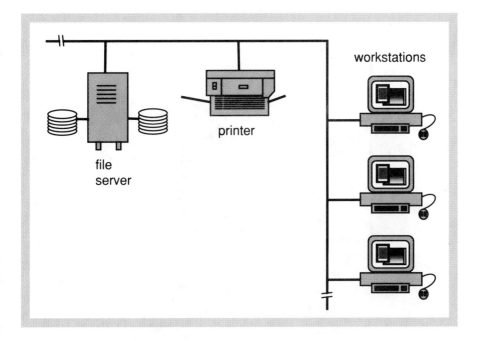

Figure 1.1 A small distributed system.

1985], Amoeba [Mullender 1985], the Cambridge Distributed Computing System [Needham and Herbert 1982], Vax cluster [Digital Equipment Corporation 1987, Kronenberg et al. 1985]. Most of these systems will be described in detail in later chapters of the book.

Workstations □   The number of available single-user computers designed for use as workstations is increasing rapidly. Most of them have similar processing power and memory capacities to current 32-bit minicomputers. Many also have high-resolution graphical displays integrated with them in a manner that is particularly effective for high-performance interactive graphical applications.

A workstation is a computer designed for a single user, with sufficient processing power and memory to run users' application programs. Although workstations can provide their users with a substantial amount of dedicated computing power, many of the benefits of multi-user systems are absent unless the workstation is part of a distributed system with shared files and other services. The key features of current workstations include (see Figure 1.2):

- a high-resolution screen (with approximately 1000 by 800 pixels in monochrome or colour) and support for rapid display of text and graphics;
- a *mouse*, used for pointing at windows, icons, menus and other objects on the screen and for input to graphical programs;
- a 32-bit microprocessor with at least 2 Mbytes of RAM;

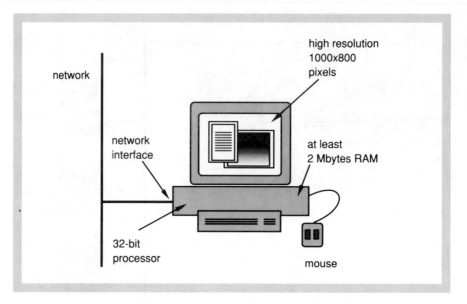

Figure 1.2 A workstation.

- physical parameters appropriate for location on the user's desk – that is, they are small and relatively quiet;
- an interface to a local network, the dominant network technology being the Ethernet.

The UNIX operating system is still widely used in workstations although it was originally designed for use as a timesharing system on multi-user computers. UNIX supports concurrent user processes, each of which may have a large address space. Concurrently active processes share the limited memory space of a single computer. Each time a process takes over a page of memory from another temporarily suspended process, the original contents of the page are copied to disk storage and a page belonging to the new process is copied in from disk. This is called *paging*. We shall discuss operating systems that are designed to be more suitable for use in workstations in Chapter 2.

The need for disk storage depends on the operating system used and on the availability and speed of access to a file server. Workstations are supplied with a range of options for disk storage.

In distributed systems that include file servers, *diskless* workstations can be used. This brings a reduction in the cost of each workstation, but can produce heavy loads on the file server and on the network. When an operating system such as UNIX is used in a diskless workstation, the largest part of the disk traffic is caused by paging. It is currently popular to create small working environments in which about five diskless workstations share a file server. An alternative is to have workstations with small local disks (e.g. 20 Mbytes), used for paging, temporary files and some executable application programs.

A workstation may have a wide range of other peripheral devices connected to it, including printers, plotters and other more specialized devices. In distributed systems, benefits are derived from sharing such devices between several workstations. The most obvious benefit is the saving in cost to be obtained by sharing a single device between many users. But the benefits to be obtained through the sharing of stored data can be greater.

Information sharing □   Users of centralized computer systems are so accustomed to the benefits of information sharing that they may easily overlook its significance. The benefits of shared access to a single filing system with files containing databases, programs, documentation and other information were first recognized with the emergence of multi-access or timesharing systems in the early 1960s – CTSS [Corbato et al. 1962], Multics [Organick 1972], UNIX [Bourne 1982] – and have been regarded ever since as a standard feature of multi-user computer systems.

For example, all of the users of multi-user computers who are engaged in program development work can share the same program development tools, with a single copy of the compilers, procedure libraries, editors and debugging aids. Whenever a new development tool or a new release of a compiler is installed, all of the users obtain access to it. When software developers work as a team, software modules developed by one member of the team can very easily be made available to other members simply by authorizing them to access it.

Similar benefits derive from the sharing of data in commercial applications. For example, in the use of an on-line database to manage the reservation of seats on aircraft, it is essential that all of the booking clerks in different booking offices should share a single database of flight records showing the seats already reserved.

Users of single-user workstations do not automatically obtain the benefits of data sharing in the same way as users of timesharing systems. To obtain the same benefits, workstations must be connected to networks that include file servers with substantial amounts of shared disk storage. The file servers must provide facilities for application programs running in the workstations to share data, while maintaining appropriate protection against unauthorized access and against hardware and software failures. Most importantly, when several application programs are accessing and updating the same data concurrently, there must be provision for synchronization of the reading and updating of the data. The design and construction of software systems to provide all of these functions (**file services**) will be considered in some detail in Chapters 5–8 of this book. These and several other types of service will be a major topic in this book.

1.1.2 Other kinds of distributed computing system

In this book we are concerned exclusively with loosely-coupled distributed systems. Some other kinds of computing systems are often referred to as 'distributed'. These are compared with loosely-coupled systems in Figure 1.3.

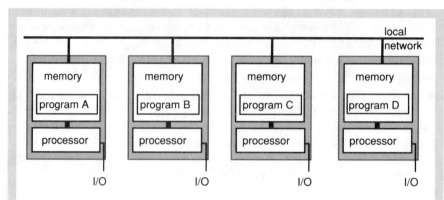

A loosely-coupled distributed system

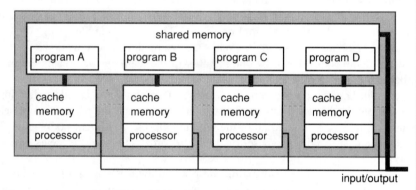

A tightly-coupled multiprocessor system

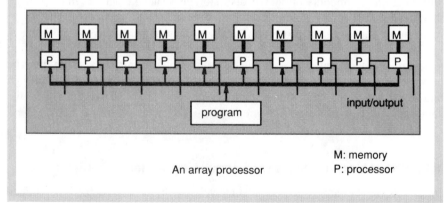

An array processor

M: memory
P: processor

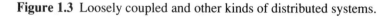

Figure 1.3 Loosely coupled and other kinds of distributed systems.

Tightly-coupled multiprocessor systems □   Figure 1.3 shows a tightly-coupled system. This type of system integrates a number of processors into an integrated hardware system under the control of a single operating system. The operating system allocates processors and memory space to users' tasks and allows them to run concurrently. The hardware environment includes a shared memory or a very high-speed connection between several separate processor/memory systems with a unified virtual addressing system. The use of shared memory or a shared virtual address space enables the users' tasks to communicate with each other and with the operating system through shared variables and tables as in conventional single-processor, multiprocess systems.

In tightly-coupled systems with shared memory the number of processors that can be usefully deployed is limited by the memory bandwidth. Multi-processor mainframe computers with a small, fixed number of processors organized in tightly-coupled fashion have been available from most major computer suppliers for several years; for a very early example, there is the CDC6600 [Thornton 1970]. Early work on the principles of tightly-coupled systems was undertaken in a number of experimental systems including C.MMP [Wulf et al. 1972, 1974], CM* [Jones et al. 1977], CYBA-M [Aspinall 1984] and Iliffe's P-N machine [Iliffe 1982].

More recently a number of multiprocessor systems with a large, variable number of processing units [Sequent 1986] offer up to 32 processors sharing a single memory and address space. The problems of memory bandwidth contention are reduced by associating a relatively large cache memory with each processor.

Array processors □   An array processor is analogous to a conventional computer with a large number of arithmetic and logic units linked in a regular array. They can be used to perform matrix calculations and other regular operations in parallel on arrays of data. Some examples are the ICL DAP [Reddaway 1973, Hockney and Jesshope 1986], Illiac 4 [Barnes 1968, Bouknight et al. 1981] and Connection Machine [Hillis 1985]. The distinguishing characteristic of such machines is that the entire array of processors obeys a single stream of instructions, some of the instructions being applied to many data items distributed throughout the array of processing units. We illustrate an array processor in Figure 1.3, showing only a few components, but an array processor, for example a DAP, could consist of 32×32 components. These so-called single-instruction, multiple-data (or SIMD) computers are extremely useful for achieving high processing speeds when processing large regular sets of data, but they are not intended to address the problems of geographical distribution or those arising from the need for concurrent execution of many independent tasks.

Other parallel architectures □   There are a number of novel architectures based on variations of the tightly-coupled model; for example, the *dataflow* architecture [Dennis 1974, Treleaven et al. 1982] and more recent parallel functional architectures [Darlington and Reeves 1981]. These are designed to make computations faster by processing them in parallel. Unlike array processors, the dataflow architecture is designed to exploit irregular parallelism at the machine instruction level. Computations are broken down into a form that allows potentially concurrent executions to execute simultaneously. For example, in calculating the sum of two squares, the two squares may be calculated in parallel and the addition waits for its operands to be available.

The reader is referred to Chambers et al. [1984] and Duce [1984] for descriptions of some recent research aimed at exploring the design and application of a wide of range of distributed systems, including examples of each of the types described above.

1.2 Motivations and definitions

The distinction between distributed systems and centralized ones is not precisely defined; the definition of a distributed system is based on several characteristics. In this section we intend to outline the technical needs and the economic pressures that have led to the emergence of distributed systems and to identify their main characteristics.

Factors leading to distributed systems □   We can identify a number of factors and trends which, taken together, have led to the emergence of loosely-coupled distributed systems.

- The cost of VLSI processor and memory components has fallen dramatically and is continuing to do so.
- High-speed computer network technologies are now widely available at moderate cost.
- The interactive service obtained from large centralized computer services is often of poor quality with long, unpredictable response times, restricted user interfaces and difficulty in configuring the hardware and software to users' needs.
- Increasingly diverse application facilities are required by users – for example to perform network-based communication, complex information retrieval, multi-font text processing, interactive graphics and highly-interactive user interfaces.

These developments have rendered *Grosch's Law* [Grosch 1953, Siewiorek et al. 1981] largely irrelevant as a basis for planning computer systems that are to be used for interactive computing. Grosch's Law states that the processing capacity of a computer system is roughly proportional to the square of its cost. It was originally formulated on the basis of Grosch's observation of the computer marketplace in the 1960s and is often cited as a pragmatic rule-of-thumb providing some guidance for estimating the economies of scale for computer systems.

Thus Grosch's Law predicts that a single computer system priced at $1 million is more powerful than two systems priced at $500 000 each or four systems at $250 000. Such predictions are generally correct for comparisons between mainframe systems but the falling cost of hardware tends to favour computer systems consisting of many processors and memory units. When we consider personal computers and workstations, Grosch's law fails: a single minicomputer such as a Digital Equipment Corporation Vax could cost from $250 000 to $500 000 and would be rated at 2–10 MIPS (million instructions per second). At the time of writing, Sun-3 or Apple Macintosh-2 workstations can be purchased for around $5 000–$10 000 and are rated at 2–3 MIPS.

Whether Grosch's Law holds or not, changes in users' priorities have reduced the relevance of comparisons based on raw processing power. Computers are used for a widening range of tasks by an increasing population of new users. Users' needs have shifted towards applications that demand rapid graphical interaction between the user and the program. This requires dedicated single-user computing resources. In addition, the increasing variety of the application functions required by users tends to increase the system overheads involved in supporting many users simultaneously on a computer with a single processor and memory.

It is often argued that a timeshared computer is the most economical way to provide interactive computing facilities to a number of users. The argument is based on the fact that the cost of the basic hardware is shared between the users; it is valid only when the processing and memory resources required to support each user are a fraction of the resources available in the shared computer. When the total demand for resources exceeds those available, even for a short time, the users may not be able to proceed with their work.

Speed of response to user input (keyboard or mouse actions) is critical to the usability of interactive programs. Many interactive programs require all of the processing resource of a single-processor computer to handle each user input and produce the corresponding changes on the screen. The necessary speed of response can only be achieved on single-user systems. Window systems and much of the application software used in computer-aided design, office work, document preparation and typesetting are highly interactive and use high-resolution graphical displays and mouse pointing as input.

In single-user systems response times are rapid and consistent because only one interactive process is running at any time. This is so even when several windows are visible on the screen because the user is unable to interact with more than one application at a time. We shall return to these topics in Chapter 2.

Defining characteristics of distributed systems □   There is no single characteristic or rule that distinguishes distributed systems. LeLann [1981] discusses aims and objectives for distributed systems and notes some defining characteristics. He gives extensibility, increased availability and better resource sharing as the most important objectives. Amongst the other defining characteristics that he mentions are the existence of a multiplicity of similar components, interconnected processing elements, 'transparency', the absence of hierarchic control structures and the existence of processes with disjoint address spaces communicating via explicit message passing.

The authors of the ANSA Reference Manual [ANSA 1987] define the consequences of distribution in terms of *separation* and *transparency*. The separation of components is an inherent property of distributed systems. Its consequences include the need for communication and for explicit system management and integration techniques. Separation allows the truly parallel execution of programs, the containment of component faults and recovery from faults without disruption of the whole system, the use of isolation and interlocks as a method of enforcing security and protection policies, and the incremental growth or contraction of the system through the addition or subtraction of components.

Transparency is defined as the concealment of separation from the user and the application programmer, so that the system is perceived as a whole rather than as a collection of independent components. The implications of transparency are a major influence on the design of the system software.

ANSA [1987] identifies eight forms of transparency:

- *Access transparency* enables local and remote files and other objects to be accessed using identical operations.
- *Location transparency* enables objects to be accessed without knowledge of their location.
- *Concurrency transparency* enables several users or application programs to operate concurrently on shared data without interference between them.
- *Replication transparency* enables multiple instances of files and other data to be used to increase reliability and performance without knowledge of the replicas by users or application programs.
- *Failure transparency* enables the concealment of faults, allowing users and application programs to complete their tasks despite the failure of hardware or software components.
- *Migration transparency* allows the movement of objects within a system without affecting the operation of users or application programs.
- *Performance transparency* allows the system to be reconfigured to improve performance as loads vary.
- *Scaling transparency* allows the system and applications to expand in scale without change to the system structure or the application algorithms.

This book is largely concerned with the exposition of techniques and mechanisms by which these various forms of transparency can be achieved. The reader should retain them in mind. They will be of assistance in identifying the motivations for many of the techniques described throughout the book.

1.3 Historical development

The motivations for distributed systems identified in the last section first became apparent in the early 1970s, a few years after the emergence of minicomputers, which in some instances were used as single-user computers for software development and interactive graphical applications. But the necessary hardware and software to make single-user computers fully effective, and the communication facilities to enable them to be used in a cooperative fashion, were absent. The earliest developments, and many of the most significant ones, were made at the Xerox Palo Alto Research Centre (known as *Xerox PARC*) in the period 1971–1980. These included the development of single-user workstations, servers, and a high-speed local network.

1.3.1 The Alto workstation

In the early 1970s the research team working at Xerox PARC initiated a project to build an experimental computing environment based on single-user computers. The goals of the project were derived from previous experience with interactive graphical applications on minicomputers with integrated graphical displays used as single-user computers. This experience had demonstrated the superiority of the single-user approach for applications involving interactive graphics and other highly interactive tasks. The advantages of single-user systems were (1) the dedicated processing power, enabling application programs to maintain an interactive dialogue with the user without interruption; and (2) the direct connection of the display screen to the memory, enabling programs to display and modify information on the screen almost instantaneously.

The first workstation developed was the *Alto*, designed at Xerox PARC in the period 1971–1973. Altos came into general use as personal computer systems at Xerox PARC in 1973 [Thacker et al. 1981]. The main features of the Alto were:

- a high-resolution monochrome display (875 lines of 680 pixels),
- a mouse with three buttons and a keyboard,
- between 128 kbytes and 512 kbytes of main memory,
- a 2.5 Mbyte cartridge disk,
- a microprogrammable processor used to support microcoded emulators for instruction sets, display of raster graphics and input/output device handling,
- an interface to the Ethernet local network, also developed at Xerox PARC and described in Chapter 3 of this book.

The Alto's microprogrammable processor performed simple operations on 16-bit words in 400 nanoseconds. It was used to implement instruction sets specifically designed to support high-level programming [Johnson and Wick 1982]. In describing the use of an Alto as a file server, Mitchell and Dion [1982] quote the performance when executing Mesa programs as about 0.25 MIPS. The microprogrammable architecture was important in achieving the flexibility and performance needed for interactive graphical applications in low-cost hardware. The cost and complexity were reduced because the control of input/output devices and the generation of the screen display were supported by microcoded tasks rather than by separate hardware controllers.

The Alto was used in a wide range of experimental applications. These included integrated program development systems for a number of advanced programming languages, for example InterLisp [Teitelman and Masinter 1981], Smalltalk [Goldberg 1983], and Mesa [Mitchell et al. 1979]. They also included a variety of office system application prototypes including multi-font document editing, as in, for example, the Bravo editor [Card et al. 1983], diagram preparation, document filing and electronic messaging [Birrell et al. 1982].

Subsequently, office system products including the Xerox Star system [Smith et al. 1982] were based on these prototypes. Substantial advances in the user interface were made possible by the workstation approach. Many of these were developed on the Alto at Xerox PARC and adopted by the Apple Corporation for use in the Macintosh personal computer.

1.3.2 Other workstations

In general, the hardware model that was pioneered in the Alto has been retained and enhanced in the many workstations that have followed it, although there have been substantial changes in the processor architecture and technology and in memory capacity.

The microprogrammable architecture adopted for the Alto has persisted in some workstations designed for research work and advanced graphical applications. Examples include the Three Rivers/ICL Perq computer [Loveluck 1982] and the Xerox Dorado – a high-performance successor to the Alto also developed at Xerox PARC [Lampson and Pier 1980, Clark et al. 1981]. The processors in the Alto, the Dorado and the Perq were constructed using a substantial number of high-speed integrated circuits. But the demand for low-cost workstations and the development of single-chip 16- and 32- bit microprocessors with performance that exceeded the Alto and good support for virtual memory resulted in their adoption and in availability of workstations at much lower costs. Examples include the Sun Microsystems Sun-2 and Sun-3 workstations, the Apollo Domain DN300 and DN600 workstations and the Apple Macintosh II, all based on the Motorola 68000 and 68020 processors, and the UK-manufactured Whitechapel MG1 and MG200 based on the National Semiconductor 32000 series of processors. These second- and third-generation workstations have speeds in the range 1–3 MIPS.

The expanding market for workstations and the demand for workstation performance higher than can be achieved with the industry-standard 32-bit microprocessors has stimulated the development of RISC (*R*educed *I*nstruction *Set C*omputer) processors. As their name implies, RISC processors have much simpler instruction sets, designed to meet the needs of the code generators in compilers for the most commonly-used programming languages without encumbering the processor design with many complex instructions that are seldom used. This can be seen as a reversion to the microprogrammable processor architecture of the Alto and the Dorado, but with a single processor chip.

The advantages of the RISC approach are that the design is more easily translated to silicon in very large-scale circuits (i.e. with very small individual components). This enables a faster instruction execution rate, since the performance of silicon circuits is inversely related to the *square* of the component size. The performance of RISC-based workstations (e.g. Sun 4, Whitechapel MG10, Acorn ARM) is in the 4–10 MIPS range, and the manufacturers have discussed plans for workstations with speeds up to 100 MIPS.

1.3.3 Xerox distributed systems

The stand-alone use of Alto computers was insufficient for many of the applications for which the workstations were intended to be used. For program development there was a need to share the source and object code of programs. For office applications there was a need to share documents and other files, to provide communication with other users and to provide access to high-quality printers. The Alto was therefore used as the basis for several experimental servers developed at Xerox PARC.

These included a series of distributed filing systems [Lampson 1981c], culminating in the Xerox Distributed File System (XDFS) [Mitchell and Dion 1982, Mitchell 1985]. This file service provided clients – processes in other computers in the network that used the file service – with facilities to store and access data in files in a manner similar to the filing systems found in most conventional operating systems, but using numeric file identifiers to refer to files, rather than text names. The mapping of text names onto file identifiers was provided as another component of the system called the **directory service**. An application program with a text name for a file could therefore be a client of both the directory service and the file service. It would use the directory service to map a file name to a file identifier and it would use the file service to read or write data to the file with that identifier. The directory service was also a client of the file service, storing its mappings in the file service.

Because the files stored by the file service were potentially accessible to all of the computers in the network, it was necessary to incorporate access control facilities to ensure that only authorized users could access the files and concurrency control measures to ensure that updates by different clients to the same file were properly sequenced. The Xerox Distributed File Service will be referred to frequently in this book and is described in detail in Chapter 10.

1.3.4 Other distributed system developments before 1980

As with workstations, the pioneering development of file server and distributed system software at Xerox PARC has had a substantial influence on subsequent developments, but there was a substantial body of other research done before 1980 that has had an equally important impact on subsequent developments.

Amongst those discussed in this book are: the Cambridge Distributed Computing System (CDCS), the Apollo Domain system, the Newcastle Connection and Locus. Figure 1.4 is a table showing the dates of completion and other important characteristics of these and other systems discussed in this book. The architectural models quoted in the column headed *Architectural model* are defined in Chapter 2.

1.3.5 Distributed system developments after 1980

There has been a rapid expansion of research and development activity, for example the Accent, Mach, Amoeba, Argus, V-system and Chorus research projects and the Sun NFS-based product development. All of these systems are

	Organization	Network	Architectural model	Computers	Discussed in chapter	Operational	
Xerox DS	Xerox PARC	Ethernet & Xerox internet	w'station/server	Xerox Alto	1, 2, 10	1977	See Cedar and Grapevine for subsequent development.
CDCS	Cambridge Univ.	Cambridge Ring	processor pool	LSI-4, M68000	2, 10	1979	See Mayflower, below, for subsequent development.
Locus	UCLA	Ethernet	integrated	Vax, IBM PC	10	1980	Emulates UNIX.
Apollo Domain	Apollo Comp.	token ring	integrated	Apollo workstations	10	1980	Largest existing configuration: 1800 workstations.
Newcastle Connection	Newcastle Univ.	various	integrated	various	2	1980	A predecessor of the Sun NFS system.
Grapevine	Xerox PARC	Ethernet & Xerox internet	n/a	Xerox Alto	11	1981	Distributed, replicated application-oriented database. Superseded by Clearinghouse, a Xerox product.
Cedar	Xerox PARC	Ethernet	w'station/server	Xerox Dorado & Dandelion	2, 4	1982	A research environment for the development of office and personal systems.
V-system	Stanford Univ.	Ethernet	w'station/server	Vax, Sun	2	1982	Experimental system. Interworks with UNIX.
Argus	MIT	not available	w'station/server	n/a	4, 10	1983	A research project to develop an integrated programming language and system based on CLU.
Amoeba	Vrije Univ., Amsterdam	Ethernet	hybrid	Vax, M68000 & others	2, 10	1984	A research project on the use of *capabilities* in distributed systems. Interworks with UNIX.
Unix BSD4.2 with Sun NFS	Sun Micro.	Ethernet	integrated	Vax, Sun, & others	1, 10	1985	A widely-used distributed UNIX system.
Mach	CMU	Ethernet	—	Vax + others	2,4,10	1986	Operating system kernel for distributed systems. Runs Unix. Successor to CMU Accent system.
Chorus	Chorus systèmes, Paris, France	Ethernet	—	Sun3 Bull/SPS7	2	1988	Operating system kernel to support distributed systems. Runs UNIX.
Mayflower	Cambridge Univ.	Cambridge Ring & Ethernet	hybrid	Vax, Sun, Xerox w'stations	4	1987	A language-based research project based on CLU.

Figure 1.4 Distributed systems discussed in this book.

discussed later in the book and references to the literature on them will be quoted there. The early projects at Xerox and elsewhere have continued, for example in Grapevine and Cedar at Xerox PARC and in Mayflower at Cambridge University. The file servers whose design is discussed in this book are shown in Figure 1.5.

	Transparency						Cooperating servers	Discussed in chapters
	access	location	concur-rency	repli-cation	failure	migration		
XDFS Xerox PARC	yes	yes	yes	no	yes	no	yes	1, 7, 10
CDFS Cambridge Univ.	yes	no	yes	no	yes	no	no	6, 7, 10
Newcastle Connection Newcastle Univ.	yes	no	no	no	no	no	yes	2
Locus file system UCLA	yes	yes	yes	yes	yes	yes	yes	10
Apollo Domain Apollo computers	yes	yes	yes	no	no	yes	yes	10
Amoeba FUSS Vrije Univ., Amsterdam	yes	yes	yes	yes	yes	no	yes	7, 10
Sun NFS Sun microsystems	yes	yes	no	no	no	no	yes	1, 10

Figure 1.5 File servers discussed in this book.

The file servers are classified according to the degree of transparency they achieve. The meaning of transparency for files may be interpreted as follows:

- *Location transparency:* file names may be used without knowing the location of files.
- *Concurrency transparency:* several users may use the same file or group of files at the same time without causing inconsistency in the files.
- *Failure transparency:* even if a client or server crashes during operations on files or groups of files, the files will remain in a consistent state.

Some of the distributed systems are designed to provide a file service based on a group of cooperating servers; these are indicated in the last column.

1.3.6 UNIX-based distributed systems

Although research in distributed systems has been in progress for several years, many distributed systems currently in use have evolved in an environment consisting of multi-user computers and workstations with traditional operating systems such as UNIX linked by a network. We therefore outline here what has been achieved with distributed UNIX systems, bearing in mind the transparency goals mentioned earlier.

Distributed UNIX systems □ A common practice is to have a network of multi-user computers and workstations running the BSD 4.2 UNIX† with or without *network file service* software. This version of UNIX provides the conventional

---

† BSD 4.2 UNIX is the extended version of the UNIX operating system that is distributed by University of California at Berkeley.

UNIX operating system in each separate computer with its own hierarchical file naming scheme and password file. In addition it contains facilities for communication between processes in separate computers, allowing files to be transferred from one computer to another, processes to be run in other computers and users to login to remote computers. But the user must name the remote computer when copying files, running processes and logging in.

BSD 4.2 UNIX can be extended by installing network file service software, such as the Sun Network File System (NFS) [Sun 1987a]. This allows any computer in the network to export the names of any of its filestores, allowing them to be mapped as a part of the file name space in other computers. The actual mapping is accomplished by an extended version of the UNIX *mount* operation, allowing a remote file system to appear as a part of the directory hierarchy in the machine performing the *mount* operation. The network file system software in the computer that has mounted remote file stores intercepts the read, write and other file operations that refer to remote files and maps these references to the correct files in the remote computer. To perform the operations, it communicates with a process in the remote computer, requesting it to perform the operations. Although NFS does not provide a global naming scheme for all files, it does allow users and programs to name files in remote computers in the same way as those in the local computer. A simple file server can be simulated by designating a computer to store shared files. The NFS software in the server computer exports a filestore containing the names of all of the shared files. All of the computers that are potential clients can *mount* the shared filestore.

Another recent development is the Sun Yellow Pages system, discussed in Section 8.4. This is an extension of Sun NFS that allows a network of UNIX systems to maintain consistent databases of names and attributes. The system is used to maintain consistent password files and system configuration files in large networks of workstations and multi-user computers.

Transparency in NFS □   When computers run NFS, normal UNIX application programs can access files without making any changes to allow for a distributed environment. A substantial degree of transparency is provided, in that it provides uniform naming for local and remote files and the file access functions are the same for both. However, UNIX systems do not provide concurrency transparency for files and Sun NFS is no exception to this.

Replication transparency and the other forms of transparency mentioned are not present in NFS. The main limitations of NFS are those of UNIX.

An example of NFS in use □   Figure 1.6 shows the distributed system environment in the Computer Science Department at Queen Mary College London as it is at the time of writing. We include this as an illustration of the type of distributed UNIX system we have just described. The illustration shows a commonly used local area network – an Ethernet with three connected sections containing about 40 Whitechapel MG1s used for undergraduate teaching together with a number of other computers used by the staff of the department. BSD 4.2 UNIX and Sun NFS run in almost all of the computers and the role of file server is

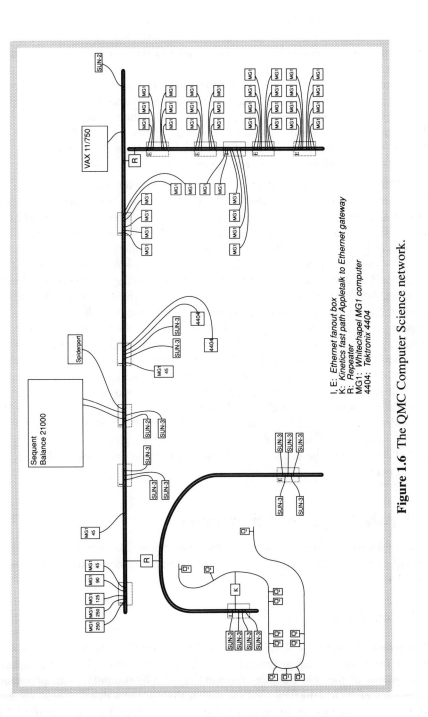

Figure 1.6 The QMC Computer Science network.

played by the Sequent, the Vax and some of the Suns. The network is connected to a wide area network via the Vax. The Vax is also used for serving files containing source programs and manual pages to most of the computers in the network.

The student workstations have small disks (20 Mbytes) that are used for swapping and temporary files. The commonly used executable programs such as editors and compilers are copied to the workstation disks each night by broadcasting them over the network. However, any student may make use of any workstation and therefore student files are not stored on the workstation disks. Instead of this, they are stored in file servers.

Hierarchically controlled systems □   There are many computer systems in commercial use that are described as distributed. It sometimes appears as though almost any computer application that involves the use of a computer network may be deemed to qualify for the name 'distributed' in the marketplace. Which of them is truly distributed in the sense we have defined above?

We mentioned above that LeLann's characterization of distributed systems excludes hierarchic control structures. In many existing applications where a network system is used only for a single application, a quite rigidly defined hierarchical control structure has been used; for example, the communication systems used in on-line data processing by banks, airlines, cash-machine (auto-teller) systems, etc. [Champine 1977]. In such systems a single computer controls the operation of a network of computers linked to it. The network of computers is controlled by the applications software in a hierarchic fashion with the central computer at the apex of the hierarchy. Such systems would be more accurately described as network-based than as distributed.

Most network-based applications could be designed and implemented more easily using general-purpose distributed systems principles, but to date very few have been because the distributed systems components were not available to the developers.

1.4 Advantages and drawbacks

The following are some of the advantages and drawbacks that users and system managers can expect to derive from the replacement of conventional systems by distributed ones.

1.4.1 Advantages

Predictable response □   Distributed systems are particularly attractive to users whose tasks are diverse, interactive, and require significant processing capacity but are not of the 'big number-crunching' type. Workstations with processing capacities of up to 10 MIPS are available at the time of writing. The dedication of this processing power to support a single user ensures a rapid response when performing most interactive tasks.

Extensibility □   The manager of a distributed system is able to extend the system as the demand for service grows without replacing any of the existing components. The smallest practical distributed system might consist of two workstations and a file server. The largest might have several hundred workstations and several file servers, print servers and other special-purpose servers. Further workstations and servers can be added as required to meet operational demands or to add new facilities. The limiting parameter is the network bandwidth, since each active workstation adds to the communication load on the network. Current local networks have been demonstrated to have the capacity to support up to several hundred workstations.

Sharing of resources □   Consider the problem of resource sharing in an environment that includes several computers. If the computers are all a part of a single distributed system, peripherals such as printers and disks can be shared between all of the computers on the network. If they are not linked each computer must have its own peripherals. For example, in a distributed system each workstation may have no disk storage or only a small disk (10–20 Mbytes) for temporary storage. Access to permanent files on a large disk can be provided to all of the workstations by a single file server. A single printer may be shared in a similar way by the provision of a print server.

Replication □   High reliability and rapid access to stored information can be achieved by maintaining several copies of data in different server computers. The design and use of systems for replication are discussed in Chapter 8.

Continued availability □   When one of the components in a distributed system fails most of the work in progress need not be interrupted. Only the work that was using the failed component must be moved. For example, a user may move to another workstation if the one being used breaks down. Similarly, a file service can be restarted on another computer when the computer it runs on has failed. File services that are represented on more than one computer can be used even after one server fails.

1.4.2 Drawbacks

Loss of flexibility in the allocation of memory and processing resources □   In a centralized computer system or a tightly-coupled multiprocessor system all of the processor and memory resources are available for allocation by the operating system in any manner required by the current workload. In distributed systems, the processor and memory capacity of the workstations determine the largest task that can be performed.

Dependence on network performance and reliability □   Failure of the local network causes the service to users to be interrupted. Overloading of the network degrades the performance and responsiveness to the users. Much effort has gone into the design of reliable and fault-tolerant networks. Network failures occur very infrequently in practice but this remains a theoretical drawback.

Security weaknesses □ To achieve extensibility, many of the software interfaces in distributed systems are made available to clients. Any client that has access to the basic communication service can also access the interfaces to servers. Such an open architecture is attractive to system developers, but software security measures are needed to protect the services against intentional or accidental violation of access control and privacy constraints. For example, workstation software cannot be trusted to perform tasks such as authenticating users.

Recent work on software security, data encryption and capability-based access control offer appropriate solutions. Techniques for the control of access to files are introduced in Chapter 5 and Chapter 9 deals with protection and security methods in distributed systems.

1.5 Summary

In a distributed system, processing activities may be located in more than one computer and the computers communicate over a network in order to perform joint tasks.

Workstations provide users with local processing power enabling them to perform interactive tasks more effectively than in a timeshared system. In distributed systems, workstation users can share information and other resources available in the network. File servers are computers running software to enable workstation users to share information and to store and retrieve their personal files.

The availability of cheap hardware has shifted the emphasis from making the maximum use of resources as in timesharing systems to the provision of systems that provide a good working environment for human users.

The design of distributed systems is concerned with making the separation of components transparent to both application programs and users. Many aspects of transparency relate to the naming and access to shared data provided by file servers and to the provision of replicated copies of data. The Sun NFS system illustrates a system that is widely used and provides access and location transparency. It does not provide concurrency, failure or replication transparency.

The main advantages of distributed systems are responsiveness to users, extensibility, the ability to share information and resources and continued availability. The main drawbacks are related to the difficulties of making private information secure and that the failure of single components within a system that is still running can produce new sorts of error modes.

EXERCISES

1.1 Describe three important advantages of a distributed computer system as compared with a timesharing system.

1.2 Describe some of the consequences that could arise when one computer in a distributed system fails and the rest continue to run:
   (a) if the computer is a workstation,
   (b) if the computer is a file server.

1.3 A department already has a Vax multi-user computer, a few workstations and a number of terminals, but is planning to extend its computing resources. Make the case for installing a local area network and buying a number of workstations rather than buying another Vax and a few more terminals.

1.4 A laboratory contains a number of networked workstations for use by various groups of students. Any particular student comes to the laboratory from time to time and does not necessarily always expect to use the same workstation. How do you suggest that the students files should be stored:
   (a) if the workstation has a small hard disk (e.g. 20 Mbytes),
   (b) if the workstation has a floppy disk drive, but no hard disk?

The following exercises should not be regarded as a test of the knowledge gained from this chapter; they are intended to encourage the reader to think more generally about some of the issues that are relevant to the design of distributed computer systems.

1.5 In the distributed system described in question 1.4, the UNIX operating system is used and students must login when they arrive. The login program uses a password file to check the users' passwords. Describe the advantages and disadvantages of keeping the password file:
   (a) on a hard disk attached to each workstation,
   (b) on a file server.
In the case that the password file is stored in a file server, there may be quite a bottleneck when the students arrive for a class. Can you suggest any solution to this problem? If your solution requires replication of the password file, describe how the various copies might be made consistent.

1.6 Describe the main tasks of a file server. Do you think a file server should offer parts of files or just entire files? How does the service you describe compare with file access in UNIX?

1.7 In this question you should assume that workstations and servers communicate by sending messages directly to one another. Describe the contents of a message sent by an application program to request data from a file server. Describe the contents of the message the file server sends back. How do you think a file server will cope if several workstations send messages simultaneously?

1.8 Describe three different classes of information that are shared by users or application programs in a conventional computer. Describe situations relating to your examples, in which several processes may access data concurrently. Are any of these situations likely to lead to inconsistency in the stored data? If the same classes of data are stored in a file server and application programs run in workstations, do you think that the problems of inconsistency are likely to be more or less severe?

1.9 Describe briefly how an electronic mail program delivers personal mail in a single multi-user computer. Suggest how such a program should be modified to work in a distributed system.

1.10 Describe briefly how an electronic bulletin board program might store the messages in a single multi-user computer. Suggest how such a program should be modified to work in a distributed system.

1.11 In the distributed system shown in Figure 1.4, the Vax computer is used as a server of manual pages. Users at any computer may read the manuals by using the *man* command and the NFS software makes requests for the information from the server. Which of the sorts of transparency are present in this service? Describe how such a service could be made more transparent to failures of the Vax computer.

1.12 Explain why workstation software cannot be trusted to carry out tasks related to the security of a distributed system.

Chapter 2
Architecture and Design Goals

In this chapter we introduce the three main architectural models that have been used in distributed systems; the *workstation/server model*, the *processor pool model* and the *integrated model* and discuss goals for distributed system design: *transparency, consistency* and *effectiveness*.

We consider the system software requirements for distributed systems, introducing topics that will be discussed in depth in later chapters and describing some approaches used in existing systems.

2.1 Introduction

An architectural description of a system defines the main components of the system, their purposes and the relationships between them. Architectural descriptions are used by designers in many technical disciplines where the complexity of the system renders the use of detailed descriptions of all of the components inconvenient. They enable design to proceed in a top-down manner, with the goals and intentions of the design identified at an early stage. Architectural descriptions are also useful after the design stage because they provide concise descriptions of the design goals, rules and guidelines according to which a system is constructed.

The architecture of a distributed system identifies the main hardware and software components and modules of the system and defines the relationships between them. Important aspects of this are the types of computers used, their locations in the network and the locations at which system programs and application programs are executed. We shall call this the architectural model. In Section 2.2 we describe the three main architectural models for distributed systems that have emerged to date: the *workstation/server* model, the *processor pool* model and the *integrated* model.

All of the architectural models discussed are based on the use of modular, distributed system software. The development of distributed systems has benefited substantially from the software engineering notions of software modularity, layering and data abstraction; these notions are used to structure the system software for a distributed environment.

The operating system in a conventional computer system provides several important services to application programs. These include:

- file system management and file access facilities,
- peripheral device handling,
- user authentication and access control (i.e. login facilities),
- memory and processor resource allocation,
- creation and scheduling of processes.

In centralized systems these tasks are usually performed by a single software component called the *operating system kernel*, but in distributed systems these system services may well be located in several separate computers and must therefore be performed by separate software components.

All of the tasks performed by conventional operating systems are required in distributed systems and in addition each computer must also include software to support communication on a local network. However, the use of a separate computer for each system task and the separate execution of application and system programs that is a characteristic of the workstation/server model simplifies the resource management software and reduces system overheads in both the servers and the workstations, since it is no longer necessary to share a single processor and memory between all of these activities. For example, the software responsible for the allocation of memory and processor resources within a single-user workstation is rarely concerned with sharing of resources between competing users and can be much simplified in comparison to a multi-user minicomputer or mainframe system. The use of servers for system tasks such as file handling and printing also simplifies the system software needed in workstations.

2.2 Architectural models

In this section we discuss three architectural models for distributed systems. The models are intended as an aid to classifying and analysing the properties of distributed systems. Tanenbaum and van Renesse [1985] have surveyed recent work on distributed operating systems using a similar architectural classification with some further variations. In Chapter 10 we will describe several existing distributed systems and indicate how they fit the architectural models given here.

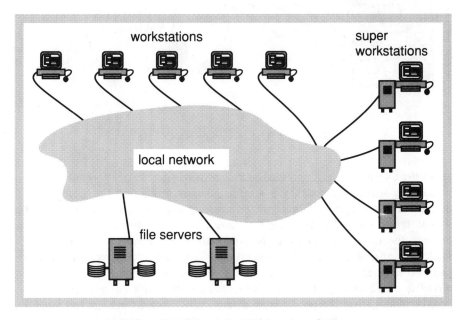

Figure 2.1 The workstation/server model.

The majority of distributed systems in use and under development are based on the *workstation/server* model (Figure 2.1). In this model each user is provided with a single-user computer, known as a workstation. Application programs are executed in the users' workstations. The need for workstations is based primarily on user interface requirements in application tasks. Other factors affecting the division of tasks include the need to share data between users and applications, leading to a need for shared file servers and directory servers; and to share expensive peripheral devices such as high-quality printers, plotters, tape drives and document scanners, leading to a need for specialized device servers.

In the pure *processor pool* model (Figure 2.2) programs are executed in a set of computers managed as a processor service. Users are provided with terminals

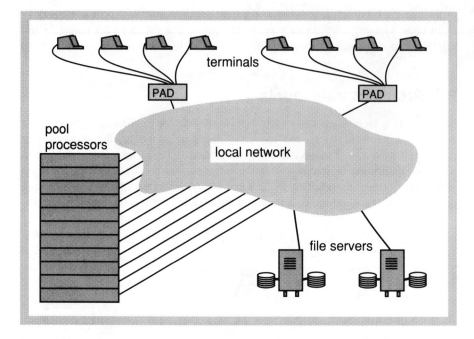

Figure 2.2 The processor pool model.

rather than workstations, connected to the network via terminal concentrators and interacting with programs via a terminal access protocol. The model has a number of advantages, but the restricted mode of user interaction imposed by the use of terminals rather than workstations is a substantial drawback. But in practice the distinction between the workstation/server and the processor pool model is not a sharp one, since workstations are now widely available and are included in most network systems, so a *hybrid model* has emerged. The hybrid model is based on the workstation/server model, but with the addition of some pool computers that can be allocated dynamically for tasks that are too large for workstations or tasks that require several computers concurrently.

The *integrated* model (Figure 2.3) brings many of the advantages of distributed systems to heterogeneous networks containing single-user and multi-user computers. In this model each computer is provided with appropriate software to enable it to perform both the role of server and the role of application processor. The system software located in each computer is similar to an operating system for a centralized multi-user system, with the addition of networking software.

2.2.1 The workstation/server model

The workstation/server model was introduced in Chapter 1; Figure 1.1 shows a simple workstation/server network. A more elaborate workstation/server

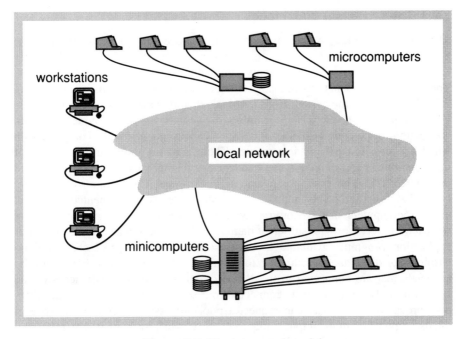

Figure 2.3 The integrated model.

configuration is shown in Figure 2.1. The workstations may be of several different types. For example, some standard workstations and some higher-performance *super workstations* as shown in Figure 2.1. Each workstation provides the computing power to execute application programs and to support a graphical user interface for a single user, but many applications require access to shared files, such as programs, databases, bulletin boards, software libraries and user documentation, and to other shared resources such as wide-area network gateways, printers and magnetic tapes.

The workstations are integrated by the use of communication software enabling them all to access the same set of servers. The servers provide access to shared devices, files and other networked resources. These provide simple sharing of hardware devices such as printers, access to shared data through file servers and several other services that are designed to replace the functions of a centralized operating system. For example, an authentication service is usually provided to validate user identities and authorize them to use system resources and a network gateway service is often provided, offering access to wide-area networks for all of the workstations on a local network.

There are many specific examples of workstation/server systems based on a variety of commercially-developed hardware and software. We discuss the original Xerox implementation in Section 1.2.1 and some current distributed products and experimental systems are described in Chapter 10.

2.2.2 The processor pool model

The first distributed system based on the processor pool model was the Cambridge Distributed Computing System developed in the Computer Laboratory at Cambridge University, England [Needham and Herbert 1982]. There were no workstations in the system as it was originally constructed (Figure 2.2). Users access the system from terminals that are attached to the network via PAD computers. The PADs are simple server computers that provide a network connection (discussed in Chapter 3) between each terminal and the computer with which the user is currently interacting. There are also a substantial number of microcomputers and minicomputers attached to the network (the *pool processors* in Figure 2.2). The pool processors in the original Cambridge system were General Automation LSI4s, and these were subsequently supplemented by a bank of microcomputers using Motorola M68000 processors. The pool processors consist of a processor with sufficient memory to load and run any of the system or application programs available in the system. The pool processors have no terminals or disks attached directly to them but users can access them from the terminals that are connected to the PAD computers. When a user accesses the system initially the terminal is connected to a server that manages and allocates pool processors. The user can request a pool processor, specifying the type of microcomputer or minicomputer required. If a pool processor of the requested type is available it is allocated to the user for exclusive use until the 'session' is terminated. Another server called the *ancilla* can then be requested to load the pool processor with a program.

The program that is loaded could be any program designed to operate using the services in the Cambridge Distributed Computing System. It is often a conventional operating system adapted to work in the distributed environment (for example, the TRIPOS operating system, a simple portable operating system developed for use on a number of minicomputers at Cambridge University [Richards et al. 1979] was adapted for this purpose). Once an operating system has been loaded into the user's pool processor, the user can interact directly with it from the terminal, issuing commands to load and execute programs, access and manipulate files or perform any of the other functions that the operating system provides. The user can continue to work with the same operating system for the duration of the session, or invoke the *ancilla* again to load a new operating system.

Other services provided included a file server and a number of others including a *name server*, a *boot server* (providing a facility to load executable programs from the file server into pool processors), a *time server* (giving the time of day) and a *printer server* (providing facilities for printing files on printers attached to the server). Pool processors are used to run the server software that performs many of these services, but the file servers are based on minicomputers with directly-connected disk storage.

The resulting system is more effective than the workstation/server model in several ways:

- *Utilization of resources*: The number of computers required to support a user population of a given size is a function of the maximum number of users *simultaneously logged in*, whereas in the workstation/server model there is a need for a considerably larger number of computers because some workstations are physically inaccessible to users who wish to use the system (e.g. locked in the offices of absent colleagues).
- *Flexibility*: The system's services can be expanded without installing any more computers; pool processors can be allocated to act as extra servers to carry any additional load arising from an increased user population or to provide new services.
- *Compatibility*: Existing application programs and system software designed for use in centralized systems can be used with only limited changes, whereas specially-constructed application programs are needed to exploit the graphical capabilities of the workstations in workstation/server systems.
- *Heterogeneous processors*: A variety of computers can be used as pool processors, providing users with access to computers with different order codes and performance characteristics and enabling the processing power of the system to be upgraded by replacing or adding to the pool processors.

Despite these advantages, the processor pool model does not satisfy the needs of high-performance interactive programs, especially when graphics are used in the application or when a window system is used. The problem is the speed of communication needed between the application program and the terminal. The performance requirements for graphical applications are defined in Section 2.3.2 below, where it is shown that even when a terminal is connected to a host computer via a high-bandwidth local network the speed at which graphical data can be transferred to the screen is too slow for many interactive tasks.

The hybrid case □   At least one system has been developed that includes a pool of processors within a workstation/server system. The Amoeba system, developed by Mullender and Tanenbaum [1986] as a research project on distributed systems at the Vrije (Free) University, Amsterdam, is an example of this hybrid type of system (Figure 2.4). This approach offers many of the advantages of both models. Users can use highly interactive or graphical application programs on workstations, while a variety of pool processors of different types and performances are available to run programs for which the workstations are not suitable or to perform tasks that require more than one processor.

The Amoeba system model includes some workstations for interactive use, some pool processors and a variety of servers. A number of geographically separate Amoeba systems can be connected by gateways.

An operating system kernel has been designed for use in all of the computers in an Amoeba system. The use of the pool processors is organized by a *loader server* and a *process server*. Pool processors are allocated dynamically: when a client program such as a command interpreter needs to create and run a new process it contacts the loader server to get information about the program to be run, such as the type of computer needed and the store requirements; the loader

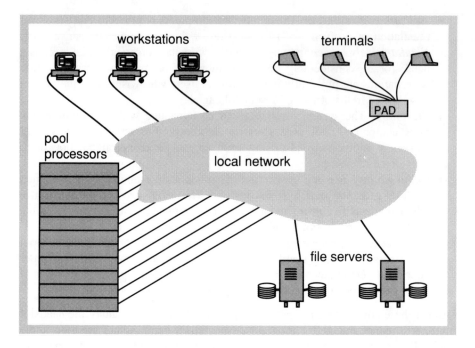

Figure 2.4 The hybrid model.

also provides the program code, initialized data and stack. The client then supplies these values of the code, data and stack to the process server. The process server selects a pool processor and creates a new process using the values of the code and data supplied. It returns a reference to the new process in the form of a *capability* (discussed in Section 2.4) to allow the client to interact with the process.

The Amoeba system has been implemented and used at the Vrije University, Amsterdam with 24 pool processors based on Motorola 68010 processing units. There is a procedure library that emulates the UNIX system functions, allowing UNIX programs to run on Amoeba. There are a number of utilities including compilers, editors and shells. A file server called FUSS (Free University Storage System), supporting file recovery and atomic transactions based on file versions, has also been developed for Amoeba. This will be discussed further in Chapters 7 and 10.

We can now summarize the advantages of the hybrid approach:

- *Matching processing resources to users' needs*: When a user needs to run a program that does not fit the workstation (it might be too large, too slow, or require a different order code), a pool processor can be used to run the program with its input and output directed to the workstation.
- *Concurrent execution*: The user need not be restricted to just one pool processor; programs and tasks that involve a heavy processing load can be allocated several pool processors. For example, when compiling a multi-

segment program one (or more) pool processors could be allocated to compile each segment.

- *Access via terminals*: The use of terminals is not excluded as it is from the workstation/server model. Users may access the system from workstations or from terminals.

2.2.3 The integrated model

The operating systems used in centralized multi-user computers interpret file names and user names relative to the local filing system and run programs using the local processor, memory and other resources. When several such systems are connected by a local network, the operating system in each computer is generally extended to allow users in one computer to copy files between computers and to run processes in other computers. When this is done the separate local name spaces remain; the user must refer to files and other objects by quoting the name of the computer in which the object resides as well as the local name of the object.

At a more ambitious level, a set of computers can be managed by a single distributed operating system that makes them appear to the users as a single computing system. The Locus system [Popek and Walker 1985], developed at the University of California at Los Angeles, is an example of a UNIX-like distributed operating system for linked multi-user and other computers. Systems like Locus provide an **integrated** distributed environment in which each computer has a high degree of autonomy but computers may share data using a global naming scheme. The computers may be workstations or multi-user computers, but each one runs a complete set of standard software and deals with its own applications and services, for example the file service. When a program is to be executed the system decides on a computer in which to run it (with a bias towards the computer issuing the request to execute the program), locates the executable program file and loads it into the selected computer. In such systems programs can read and write the contents of files without regard to their location. File names are global, allowing users on any computer in the system to refer to them using the same naming scheme. The mapping from user names to identifiers used in deciding ownership and access permission for files is also uniform throughout the system.

The Locus system is described more fully in Chapter 10. Although Locus and some other examples of this class of system have been developed and used in prototype form, they have not been widely adopted. A simpler approach was adopted in the Newcastle Connection [Brownbridge et al. 1982]. This is a direct modification of the UNIX operating system allowing programs to use the UNIX file operations (e.g. *read* and *write*) to refer to any files in a networked collection of UNIX systems. This is accomplished by extending the file and directory naming hierarchy upwards to include a root node above the individual filestores in the various computers in the network. A pathname therefore begins with a string that identifies a computer followed by the conventional pathname for a file within the filestore on that computer. This provides a global name space for files, but the names of files are not independent of their location in the network.

Current practice in the use of networked UNIX systems is based on the Sun NFS already mentioned in Secton 1.3.6 and described in detail in Section 10.3. This approach includes many of the features of Locus and the Newcastle Connection. The names of files are independent of their location; each client computer can select parts of remote filing systems that it wishes to have access to. The approach is described more fully in Chapter 10.

2.3 Design goals

The main goal for the designer of a distributed system is to make the effect of distribution *transparent* to the user; users should have a view of the system as whole; they should not normally need to be aware of the locations of hardware and software components from which the system is constructed. In addition, the system should execute tasks for its users *consistently* and *effectively*. These three aspects of the design of a distributed system are discussed in the next three sections.

It will assist our discussion to distinguish four kinds of work done by a distributed system. The user-level tasks performed by a distributed system are defined by application programs (i.e. programs that perform computations, edit documents, retrieve information from databases, process data, etc.), but the work done to perform these tasks can be considered under the four headings:

1. executing application programs,
2. managing the user interface on behalf of application programs, i.e. acquiring keyboard and mouse input and displaying information on the workstation or terminal screen,
3. accessing shared resources on behalf of application programs (e.g. files, printers),
4. communicating with external systems and processes on behalf of application programs (e.g. using wide-area networks, handling real-time events).

The allocation of these four types of work within a local network is strongly related to the architectural model adopted. In the workstation/server model, each application program is executed in the workstation of the user who has invoked it; in the processor pool model each application is executed in a dedicated pool processor; in the integrated model applications run in shared multi-user systems or workstations.

The allocation of the system tasks involved in (2), (3) and (4) is more varied and the system software components that perform these activities are defined as separate server processes running in workstations, in separate server computers or in multi-user systems. In the workstation/server and the processor pool model, the aim is to separate system activities and application activities and to run them in separate computers, but even in the integrated model there is some separation. This is generally related to the use of resources such as gateways and printers and to provide shared information, for example in the form of databases.

2.3.1 Location transparency

The term *transparency* refers to several aspects of the design of a distributed system.

In Section 1.3 we identified eight forms of transparency in distributed systems. Here we are concerned primarily with *location transparency* because it is the form of transparency that is most strongly affected by the architecture of the system. We can distinguish three levels of location transparency that have been achieved in local computer networks.

Level 0 □ At this level the user sees separate computer systems that are able to communicate in specific ways. Usually there are facilities for remote login, file transfers and remote execution of programs. These network applications are supported by network system software that provides reliable message-based communication between computers in the network. More specific protocols are defined in the application programs for the above facilities; these protocols are widely used and either are actual international standards [CCITT 1981] or regarded as *de facto* standards [DOD 1980].

Many of the networks that operate at this level are composed of heterogeneous computer systems, running different operating systems, or different versions of the same operating system. Networks based on different versions of UNIX are a common example; although many versions of UNIX support a network filing system, the standard versions of AT & T UNIX and of Berkeley BSD UNIX did not do so until very recently, and the use of networking was limited to remote login, remote execution, and file copying between networked UNIX systems.

Level 1 □ At this level there are some some application programs that conceal the multi-computer environment. When using these applications users are not aware that more than one computer may be cooperating to provide the service they use. The functionality of such applications is free of any constraints due to the distributed nature of the underlying system. The applications are constructed as fully distributed systems with server processes providing location-independent access to specific shared data, and client processes interacting with users and accessing the shared data on their behalf.

As an almost trivial example, in the UNIX 4.2 BSD system there are some simple distributed services. One is called *remote who*. This service will display the names and locations of the users logged in on all of the machines in the network. The results are identical, no matter where the service is invoked.

Electronic mail addressing is another example of a level 1 distributed application. The recipients of communication in electronic mail are users and bulletin boards. In many electronic mail systems the end-point is specified as *recipient@organization*. But in some mail systems, instead of the recipient's *organization* the network address of a specific computer must be used; this method of addressing mail destroys the location transparency of mail addressing, since a user may change the computer used to receive mail without any change in his or her organizational status. Grapevine [Birrell et al. 1982] is a distributed local and wide-area mail system that manages the delivery of messages to mailboxes on any one of a large number of computers while maintaining a high degree of location transparency as well as most of the other forms of transparency identified in Section 1.3. Grapevine is described fully in Chapter 11.

Transparency at Level 1 calls for more sophisticated application-level protocols and these have yet to be fully standardized, although substantial progress has been made towards the standardization of mail and office document communication [CCITT 1984]. In the absence of standards, the task of porting of re-implemented distributed services onto new computers is open ended. In a network of heterogeneous computer systems, it is inevitable that there will be a mix of services. Some will be at Level 0, some at Level 1.

Level 2 □   At this level the servers provide general-purpose network-wide services to share data and hardware resources, concealing the multicomputer environment from application programs. Application programs can be constructed without any need to take account of the location of the shared data and resources. Unless programmers choose to work without the support of the general-purpose services they need never be aware of the way in which hardware is configured because the services provide system-wide services.

File servers are the most common example of Level 2 components at present. The Sun Network File System (NFS) is such a system component. It enables application programs to operate on files without regard to the locations of the files. The Locus distributed system was designed to provide transparency not only for file access but for the execution of application programs.

Other Level 2 services are emerging to meet the need for transparency in the connection between application programs and the user. For example, window servers such as X Windows and NeWS (discussed in the next section) provide graphical operations in windows that may be located on a screen in a local or a remote computer without change to the application program.

2.3.2 Consistency

The behaviour of a computer system as seen by its users must be predictable. The system should be designed so that the data stored in files or databases and the information displayed on screens remains valid for any sequence of external and internal events. We shall discuss the causes of inconsistency in files and databases and user interfaces in the next two sections. Other causes of inconsistency such as communication failure will be discussed in later chapters.

Independent failure modes □   Such problems can also arise in centralized systems, but inconsistency caused by hardware or software failure is more likely to occur in distributed systems because the failure of a computer or a part of the network can leave other computers still running. When several computers are used to produce an effect, such as a modification to a set of data, and one of them fails or becomes inaccessible, the resulting effect may be partial, whereas the failure of centralized systems is usually total; the system 'crashes' stopping all programs and thus preventing further changes to data stored on disks, etc.

This characteristic, often referred to as *independent failure modes*, must be considered throughout the design of distributed systems.

Database consistency □   It is important to ensure that related changes to a database are performed in a strict sequence, with each change completed before the next begins. A problem arises in applications that involve simultaneous access to a database by several independent processes. A second problem arises when total or partial failures of the system software, workstations, servers, or the network itself occur during changes to a database.

To achieve database consistency distributed systems should include provision for both concurrent updating of databases and recovery from system failure. Some solutions to these problems are described in Chapter 7.

For an example of the second problem, consider a distributed system that supports a conventional tree-structured file directory structure, in which the directories containing the file names are stored in one server and the file contents are stored in another. Inconsistency between the directories and the files can occur unless the servers organize their operations very carefully. Failure of the directory server might leave the file server still running, successfully creating new files in response to requests to do so from application programs, but the names of the new files would not be recorded in a directory.

User interface consistency □   There are many issues to be considered in the design of the user interface for an interactive program; most are outside the scope of this book† but we should consider here the effect of distributed resources and possible communication delays on the responsiveness of interactive programs. This is an issue of consistency: whenever a user performs an input action such as a key depression or a mouse click in an interactive program the screen becomes temporarily inconsistent with the user's model of the program's state. The program then processes the user's input and performs the necessary operations to update the screen. Unless the input is processed and the changes are transmitted to the screen quickly enough to give the user the impression of an instantaneous change the user becomes aware of the screen inconsistency.

This *interactive delay* is the sum of two times: T_1, the time to process the input and compute the changes needed to update the screen image, and T_2, the time to transmit the changes to the screen and alter the screen image.

In multi-user computer systems T_1 varies throughout the day because fixed central processing resources are shared between a changing set of users and tasks. In most distributed system architectures T_1 is constant because a separate workstation is available to each user. This characteristic of distributed systems has been described very well by James Morris at the University of California at Berkeley in the epithet: "The nicest thing about workstations is that they don't run faster at night."

---

† The reader is referred to Card et al. [1983] and Pfaff [1985] for further discussion of human aspects of the user interface, and to Salmon and Slater [1987] for a discussion of graphical techniques in the user interface.

To obtain the smallest possible interactive delay we must also consider the time T_2 taken to transmit changes to the screen and to alter the screen image. In many interactive applications the changes are large, as for example when a page is turned in a text editor; or input events may occur in rapid succession, as for example when a displayed object is moved by *dragging* it with the mouse. For page turning, the screen should be updated at a rate of at least 4 frames per second for optimum user satisfaction; and when dragging and similar interactive techniques are used the screen must be updated at a rate of about 20 frames per second for smooth animation. Let us consider the effect on T_2 (i.e. the time to transmit changes to the screen) of three alternative system architectures:

- For a conventional terminal linked to a host computer by a communication system (i.e. a direct serial link or virtual circuit in a local network) the communication time is determined by the speed of the link, and the time to alter the screen image is determined by the performance of the terminal. Conventional terminals do not perform well in interactive situations that require rapid changes to the screen image because their serial links are of relatively low speed and their facilities for graphical operations are extremely limited.

- An obvious step is to replace the conventional terminal by a workstation with a screen whose image is mapped directly to *pixels* stored in local memory and to link the workstation to the host computer by a high-bandwidth local network. The workstation takes responsibility for maintaining the screen image, and the host computer processes the user's input and sends commands to the workstation to update the screen image. Unfortunately this straightforward and apparently promising change of architecture does not always produce the required performance. The screen of a typical workstation contains 1000×1000 pixels and an Ethernet packet has a maximum length of 1500 bytes. About 85 packets must be transmitted to replace the entire image on a monochrome screen with 1-bit pixels or about 700 packets for a colour screen with 8-bit pixels. In a 10 MHz network the theoretical minimum time to transmit this amount of data is 0.1 second for monochrome screens and 0.8 second for colour screens. In practice, packet overheads and network latency will increase these times by at least a factor of two. Comparison of these times with the optimum interactive performance figures for page-turning and dragging given above shows that they are not acceptable.

- The remaining option is to transfer to the workstation the entire task of processing user input and updating the screen. The network is no longer involved in the process and the interactive delay is determined only by the processing speed of the workstation and the speed of access to the screen for programs running in the workstation. For workstations whose screens are directly mapped in memory, the screen can be updated at memory speeds. For workstations based on current microprocessor and memory hardware, the resulting speed of screen updating is adequate for most interactive tasks.

Our analysis of the factors causing interactive delay in application programs indicates that the technical requirements for minimizing this delay are best met by personal workstations of the sort we defined in Chapter 1. Personal workstations that are able to execute most of the commonly used interactive application programs, such as word processing, compilation and simple graphics have been adopted as a key component in many distributed systems. But there are of course many applications that are not very interactive and some may require larger processing resources than the personal workstation can provide. Pool processors can be used very effectively for such applications.

Window servers □ In the processor pool architecture the processors that execute application programs are separate from the users' workstations. Application programs must use the network to cause changes on the screens of the workstations. This model clearly suffers from the problem of interactive delay outlined above, but the X Windows and Sun NeWS window systems [Scheifler and Gettys 1986, Sun 1987b, Stern 1987] provide a partial solution for this and other situations in which the application is remote from the display. In these systems a process in the workstation acts as a *window server* and application programs, which may be running in other computers, are clients of the window server. Clients make service requests to the window server in order to update the display. The quantity of information that passes between applications and window server can be considerably less than the number of pixels on the screen. This is achieved by building the window server with a procedural interface that supports high-level graphical operations. We describe the characteristics of X Windows and Sun NeWS more fully in Section 2.4.3.

2.3.3 Effectiveness

Factors – other than the traditional performance criteria of processor speed and memory capacity – that influence the effectiveness of a distributed system for its users include:

Speed of response □ In centralized systems the response to interaction experienced by users is often slow and irregular, depending on the total load caused by all of the users. In a distributed system a separate computer can be allocated to each user to execute all of his or her tasks producing a faster and more regular response to user interaction.

Extensibility □ An important goal in designing a distributed system is to provide a system structure that is suitable for both large and small configurations. The smallest useful configuration might have five computers and the largest five hundred. The number of users could span a similar range. Not only must the system be capable of substantial growth, but such growth must not disrupt the operation of the system. It is not practical to interrupt the work of five hundred users to add a workstation to the system for the five hundred and first user, or to add a file server when the disk capacity of the current file server is exceeded.

Reliability, fault tolerance and recoverability □   The design of computer
systems so that they recover automatically from hardware or software failures has
traditionally been restricted to systems used in certain specialized applications
where the extra cost of hardware duplication and software checkpointing were
acceptable. Distributed systems offer some resilience against hardware failure as
an automatic consequence of their architecture. The failure of a single
workstation interrupts the work of a single user but does not affect the service
provided to other users. Even the failure of a server computer may not have a
critical impact on the service to users if there are several instances of the same
service running in the system, as is often the case for the most common services,
such as printing and filing. In the case of filing, files must be replicated in a
number of servers to gain this sort of advantage; replication is discussed in
Chapter 8.

The design of software that can recover the data stored permanently in files
to a consistent state after a 'crash' of a client or a server program has perhaps
been the subject of more research than any other aspect of distributed systems
design. The results of that research can be seen in the *transaction-based file
servers* that have been developed by several research teams and are beginning to
appear as products.

Transaction-based file servers are constructed to provide a guarantee that
they will either perform all of the set of changes to files specified as constituting a
transaction by a client program; or, if the file server is prevented from doing so
by a client or server crash during the transaction, the files will be left completely
unchanged. Chapter 7 discusses the principles upon which transaction-based
filing systems are based, and Chapter 10 contains descriptions of several practical
implementations.

2.4 System software requirements

What system software is needed in workstations and server computers in place of
the operating system of conventional computers? In Section 2.1 we have pointed
out that services such as user authentication, filing, printing and device handling
that are provided as a part of the operating system in centralized computer
systems are implemented in distributed systems by separate software components,
generally running in different computers. In later chapters of this book we
discuss the design and implementation of server software to support a range of
file-based services, replacing the filing system and other file-based facilities
provided by the operating system in centralized systems. This section discusses
the requirements for a *system kernel* to support the client programs that are
executed in workstations and the server programs that are executed in server
computers.

The system software in workstations can be simpler than the system kernel
in a conventional operating system. The storage, retrieval and naming of files and
the identification and authentication of users can be performed by servers, so the
software to perform these functions need not be present in workstations. In

addition, memory management and the scheduling of processor utilization are potentially simpler in a single-user workstation than in a multi-user system. In each server, there is typically only a single service program, although it may have several tasks to enable the server to provide a service to several clients concurrently.

When a process creates another process, the parent and child process may either (1) share some or all of their variables and other data or (2) have entirely independent address spaces. Processes that share all of their address space with their parent process are often called **lightweight processes** because the sharing substantially reduces the time required to create a process or to change the process that is currently active.

On the other hand, networking software must be present in each workstation and each server with full support for communication between client and server processes. Networking software will be described in Chapters 3 and 4.

The UNIX approach □   BSD 4.2 UNIX is currently the industry standard operating system for workstations. The UNIX kernel supports concurrent processes in disjoint virtual address spaces. They therefore are not lightweight in the sense defined above. Interprocess communication within and between computers is provided by *sockets* in the BSD 4.2 version; these are described in Chapter 4. When UNIX is used in distributed systems it is usually the operating system for both workstations and servers.

The BSD 4.2 version requires 500 to 1000 kbytes of random access memory for the operating system code, working memory and buffers, including a complete set of filing system functions and other functions needed for a multi-user system. Many of the language systems and application programs used with the UNIX system are very large. Although several processes may share the same binary program, individual procedures cannot be shared, so, for example, when UNIX is used in workstations each application program must include a copy of the procedures needed to interface with the window manager and the network libraries. This often occupies 200 to 500 kbytes of memory. Because the virtual address spaces of processes are disjoint, the virtual address map must be re-loaded whenever control is switched between processes. This and other system overheads involved in a change of process results in delays that can become significant in comparison to the required interactive response time.

A workstation running UNIX will perform at considerably less than its full potential both in terms of speed of interaction and availability of memory. However UNIX is widely used for compatibility and availability reasons. We shall show how a remote procedure call mechanism can be built, both in the UNIX environment and in terms of lightweight processes, in Section 4.8.

Lightweight kernels □   A simpler system kernel providing lightweight processes and interprocess communication is a better basis for building workstation software. Server software may also be built on such a basis. If the same system kernel is used in both workstations and server computers, a module such as a file service may be run in any convenient computer – even in a workstation if necessary.

If the user interface is to allow users to switch attention between application tasks, at least one process is required to support each of these tasks. The processes in a single workstation may cooperate, passing data from one application to another or between an application and the window system. The ability to run a number of concurrent processes is therefore valuable. Servers also require a number of cooperating processes to listen for service calls and to execute their tasks.

The system software must support this cooperation with appropriate facilities for concurrent processes, interprocess communication and synchronization. In contrast to UNIX processes, the processes in a workstation or server should be lightweight in the sense that they can be quickly created and switched. Lightweight processes can be implemented as threads of control sharing a single name space in a high-level language, using fork and join operations, as for example in Mesa [Lampson and Redell 1980]; or as separate high-level language processes communicating by message passing, as for example in occam [INMOS 1983] and CSP [Hoare 1978]. In the latter case, processes on the same computer may actually share memory 'behind the scenes' to speed up message passing between processes. In the next section we describe a number of systems that include lightweight processes.

2.4.1 Open systems

A distributed computer system should provide for an open-ended set of services. There may be many different services and alternative versions of the same type of service – for example, different file naming and access functions appropriate to workstations offering their users UNIX-like facilities on the one hand and MS/DOS-like facilities on the other. Each client program selects and loads into its execution environment interfaces to the services needed for a particular application.

This requires an 'open' software structure in workstations and server computers; that is, one that provides access to a set of services that is variable and can be extended. Lampson and Sproull [1979] have described an *open operating system* as one 'offering a variety of facilities, any of which the user may reject, accept, modify or extend'. System software is required in workstations and server computers to schedule the execution of tasks in client and server programs and to enable them to communicate with one another.

The kernel in conventional systems □ In conventional systems, the code that implements the services such as filing and input/output, resource management, scheduling and creation of processes and interprocess communication is executed in a single address space (the 'kernel'), together with the lower-level functions needed to support these services. The kernel in conventional systems makes use of *threads* – concurrent processes sharing a single address space – to perform the tasks associated with the various services it provides. System tables and data structures are accessible to all of the threads because the threads share a single kernel address space. Without the multiple threads and sharing of data between them, many of the facilities provided by the kernel could not be constructed.

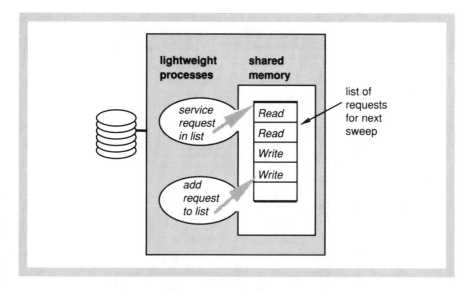

Figure 2.5 Threads performing elevator algorithm.

As an illustration of the need for concurrency in the implementation of services provided by an operating system kernel, consider the part of the system that reads and writes blocks of data on disk drives in response to requests from user programs. The work of accessing a particular disk drive is usually organized according to an 'elevator algorithm' illustrated in Figure 2.5. This is a method for optimizing the sequence in which read and write requests are performed to allow the disks to be accessed by regular sweeps of the disk heads. The requests arriving while one sweep is performed are placed in a list for processing in the next sweep. The list of requests is ordered according to the positions of the blocks to which they refer. There are two concurrent tasks, one moving the disk heads and performing the access requests and the other receiving requests and placing them in an ordered list. The threads performing these two tasks share the memory space in which the lists of requests are stored. Their use of the shared memory must be managed to ensure that only one thread accesses any list at a time. The topic of synchronization in the use of shared memory is described in full detail in Peterson and Silberschatz [1985].

The distributed case □ Many of the services in a distributed system provide similar facilities to those built into the kernel of a conventional operating system. The requirement for 'openness' in the distributed case means that they are provided in a different way – by server programs. But the server programs have a similar structure; for example, to construct file servers a disk block service would be needed and this might well use the elevator algorithm as outlined above. To construct such services for distributed systems, multiple threads and shared data structures are needed in the server computers.

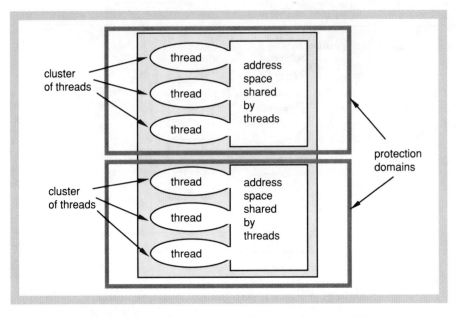

Figure 2.6 A cluster of threads in a protection domain.

Similarly, in workstations there may be several application programs running in different windows. The window system provides the user with a facility to switch attention between the contexts. The application programs and the window system may be constructed either as discrete processes, each with a separate address space, or as single threads in a shared address space, allowing them to share access to the screen buffer. If processes with disjoint address spaces are used, the kernel must include some special support for the window system.

When a shared address space is used, programs must rely on data typing in the programming language used to provide the necessary protection of their private data.

2.4.2 Protection domains

Each process makes use of a collection of resources such as areas of memory, files and ports (communication channels to be discussed in Section 3.4). The resources belonging to a process need some form of protection against the actions of other processes in the same computer. There are different ways of protecting these resources – for example, memory may be protected by addressing hardware; files and ports may be protected by the use of **capabilities**. A capability is a reference or name that acts as a token providing access to a resource or data object. When a process possesses the capability for a resource or data object it is allowed access to it.

The collection of objects that a process may access is called a **protection domain**; each process executes within a protection domain, allowing it to access only the resources defined by that domain. Domains may be disjoint or they may overlap, allowing processes to share the use of resources.

We have discussed the use of lightweight processes or *threads* with shared memory as a desirable component of a kernel. When threads are used in a cooperative task and require access to the same resources, it make sense to include them in the same protection domain. A **cluster** is a group of threads that executes within a protection domain as illustrated in Figure 2.6. That is, the threads within a cluster share access to memory, ports and files, introducing a two-tier process structure with a cluster of threads running concurrently in each protection domain.

When threads run in a computer with a single processor, they can only run one at a time and must take turns, but in a shared memory multiprocessor the kernel could be designed to allow several threads to run concurrently.

We will now describe briefly how clusters of threads are used in several kernels that have been designed for use in distributed systems. We discuss these systems here as concrete examples of concepts that will be developed and used later in the book. At the first reading, the reader may choose to omit some of these.

Amoeba □   The Amoeba system is built from *clusters* and *threads*. A cluster is a group of threads sharing an address space. A thread is capable of independent execution and communicates with other threads using shared memory. Each of the threads within a cluster runs until it is blocked by an external event, such as input or output, and at that point another thread is resumed.

Clusters of threads are useful for constructing servers; when some of them are listening for client calls, the others are able to proceed. A file server in order to read and write files for clients must access a disk and this will cause the thread to block, but other threads in the cluster can continue to do useful work.

Amoeba's design philosophy is to work with a minimum kernel and to build services outside the kernel, with a protection system based on capabilities. Each capability contains a reference to the corresponding resource or data object and acts as a security 'key' without which the user cannot access the object. The use of capabilities to control access to files in a shared file server is discussed in Chapter 5. In Amoeba, the use of capabilities supports the security needed to run servers at user level rather than as a privileged part of the system, making it possible to provide a wide range of varying services.

The V-kernel □   The V-kernel [Cheriton 1984, Cheriton and Zwaenpoel 1985], developed at Stanford University, is the basis for a distributed workstation/server system (called the V-System) running on Sun workstations on an Ethernet. The design is described in terms of two analogies.

The first analogy is that the kernel is a *software backplane* that provides a base for building and configuring systems. It consists of lightweight processes and interprocess communication (IPC). New services are 'plugged in' and communicate with other processes using the IPC provided in the kernel and their internal design is invisible to the rest of the system.

The second analogy is the *free market analogy*: servers provide services and clients communicate with servers to request and receive services. The design of clients and servers is completely unconstrained apart from the protocols for IPC. In contrast to the free market model, a single machine operating system acts as a *centrally planned economy* in which 'resources are controlled and allocated by a benign dictator'.

The V-kernel runs in each workstation and is based on clusters (called *teams* in V) of threads, that can be dynamically created and destroyed and share an address space. Application tasks can be programmed using concurrent threads and there are two main advantages over a UNIX program: (1) if a blocking call, for example for input/output, occurs, one thread can wait while another thread continues to work, whereas in UNIX the entire process is blocked, (2) there is only one method of communication between processes – by sending messages implemented by memory sharing when processes are in a single machine and by network communication when they are not, whereas, in UNIX, kernel threads communicate via shared memory and user processes must use pipes.

The Mach kernel □ The Mach kernel is being developed at Carnegie Mellon University [Rashid 1986]. It is a successor to the Accent project [Rashid and Robertson 1981], and is intended as a basis for development of distributed systems that include multiprocessors. The Mach kernel provides multiple clusters (called *tasks* in Mach), multiple threads of execution within each cluster and synchronous message-based interprocess communication via ports using capabilities to refer to ports. Different operating systems can be built on top of the kernel, which may be extended by user programs. The emulations for Accent and UNIX are currently available.

A cluster consists of a large virtual address space, has access to several ports and is a framework in which a number of threads carry out computations. A thread can execute independently, and the threads within a cluster share the memory and ports belonging to that cluster. The cluster is the unit of protection and the threads within a cluster are not protected from one another. The thread is the unit of scheduling, and threads may be created, suspended, resumed or terminated. In a parallel processor, multiple threads from one cluster may run at the same time as one another, within the address space of the cluster. A cluster may also be created, suspended, resumed or terminated. The scheduling of threads within a cluster is subservient to that of the whole cluster.

The Cedar programming environment □ Cedar, developed at Xerox PARC [Teitelman 1984, Donahue 1985] to exploit new high-performance workstations such as the Dorado, is a direct descendant from the earlier work on the Alto workstation and the Mesa language. The aims of the project were: to build an integrated programming environment for building experimental programs; to support concurrent execution of independent applications sharing low-level resources and higher-level components; to combine strong typing with the interpretive symbolic power of InterLisp or Smalltalk.

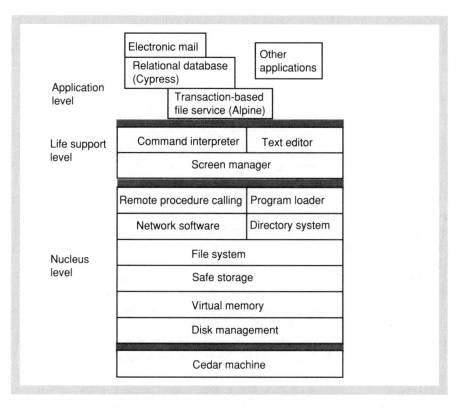

Figure 2.7 Software dependencies in Cedar.

All programming in Cedar uses the Cedar language supported by a microcoded virtual machine. The language is a procedural language derived from Mesa and has lightweight processes, shared variables, modules and monitors. The functionality of modules is defined by interface specifications. The checking of types and the binding of procedure names in the interfaces is normally performed at program load time, but there is provision for programmers to leave some bindings to be completed at run-time. In addition it has heap storage with automatic garbage collection – referred to as 'safe storage'.

The resulting system is an open one, based on a collection of program modules sharing the address space of the machine, in which there is no distinction between operating system procedures and other procedures. The modules of Cedar are arranged into layers and the procedures in each layer can call only procedures in the same layer or lower ones, allowing application programs to choose components at any level. Any program can use as many of the available components as it needs.

A program is 'configured' by the compilation system from a specification of how a set of modules should be combined. The support modules of the Cedar system are arranged in layers with the ones with the least dependencies at the bottom. The 'nucleus' or kernel includes safe storage, filing and remote procedure calling. The next level up – the 'life support' module – contains the basic facilities for program development such as a text editor, a screen manager and command interpreters. The top level contains applications like text processing, interactive graphics, a transaction-based file service and electronic mail.

The Chorus system □   The Chorus operating system is UNIX-compatible and is based on a small kernel [Rozier and Martins 1987], with facilities for building distributed operating systems and small real-time systems and has been under development since 1980 at INRIA and Chorus Systèmes in Paris, France.

The Chorus kernel provides clusters (called *actors* in Chorus), threads and ports. Threads execute concurrently within a cluster, and communicate with each other using shared memory if they reside within the same cluster. Threads are scheduled by the kernel, which also provides primitives for synchronization and allocation of priorities to threads. Threads may be scheduled to run concurrently in a single processor or in parallel in different processors of a shared-memory multiprocessor.

Ports are communication channels that are used for the exchange of messages between threads of different clusters, independently of their location.

A complete distributed system is built on top of the Chorus kernel as a set of system servers (clusters). A UNIX system has been built with UNIX process manager, file manager and terminal manager implemented as external clusters. As in Amoeba, the objects managed by the servers are protected by capabilities.

SOS □   SOS [Shapiro 1986a, 1986b] is an object-oriented operating system, designed to support distributed application programs. Instead of relating protection domains to the address spaces in computers, SOS treats them as a separate abstraction.

There are two types of protection domain called *contexts* and *groups*. A context is a set of objects within a single computer that are accessed using threads with shared memory that may communicate freely with one another. A group is a collection of interrelated objects in the same or different computer that may provide a service. Communication between groups is strictly controlled.

When a client needs to gain access to a remote object, for example a service, it requests a lightweight process to act as a *proxy* for accessing the remote object. Proxies are processes in the client's environment that provide access to a remote resource with the particular access rights appropriate to that client. Proxies are built at run-time by the remote service, specifically for that client, and are migrated into the client's context by an 'acquaintance' service. The proxy allows controlled communication between two domains: the client's context and a remote service. Any access to the service is by local invocation of the proxy. The proxy is the sole interface between the client and the resource.

2.4.3 File services

In distributed systems servers perform many of the functions related to the sharing of information and hardware resources that would be performed within the operating system of a centralized computer system. The sharing of information requires that it be stored permanently and reliably in a location conveniently accessible to all of its users, with an agreed scheme for the naming and ownership of the shared information objects.

In conventional multi-user computer systems the sharing of information is supported by the provision of a filing system on local disks with a single naming scheme. The ownership of files is based on a globally-defined set of user identifiers issued at login time to each user after authentication of their identity by the familiar password mechanism. In distributed systems the storage and naming of files and the user authentication service must be separate from the workstations, in computers that are accessible to all workstations. Similarly, shared hardware resources such as printers must be attached to server computers and shared indirectly, through the use of services that control them.

Probably the most important server in any distributed system is the one that enables programs to access files on a shared disk, but there is a wide range of possibilities for the service functions offered by such servers. The simplest servers of this kind are those that are now commonplace in networks of low-cost microcomputers, offering simple emulation on a shared hard disk of the floppy-disk filing functions normally provided by microcomputer operating systems. The servers most commonly found in current workstation-based networks provide an emulation of the UNIX filing system functions, with remote access to the UNIX filestores mounted on workstations or servers. There are a number of server software packages that support such facilities, the most widely used being the Sun NFS system, already mentioned in Section 2.2.1 and described in greater detail in Chapter 10.

More sophisticated file servers have been developed in a number of research projects. Several of these are described in Chapter 10. They are designed to improve the reliability and consistency of shared files by the provision of facilities to update files atomically and mechanisms for the recovery of files after system failures. Many of these are modular in structure and support a number of levels of service enabling client programs to choose the level of service appropriate for a particular application. The most important levels of service are outlined below and are fully described in Chapters 5 to 7.

- *Block service level*: The service functions at this level provide facilities to allocate disk blocks to a client process, to read and write data in disk blocks and to release blocks for re-use. The client process retains responsibility for the maintenance of the mappings between *file identifiers* and disk blocks. The block service is normally implemented on a server computer with one or more large disk drives.
- *File service level*: The next level maintains the mapping between *file identifiers* and disk blocks. The service functions provide facilities to create and remove files and to read and write sequences of bytes within them. The file service can be located on the same computer as the block service or in a different computer. More than one file service could be provided, possibly with different representations for files in each, sharing the disk space on a single block server.

- *Directory service level*: The mapping of user-friendly *text names* for files to the *file identifiers* used by the file service is provided by the directory service. The mapping need be performed only once for each file used by a client process. Subsequently, the client may make many accesses to a file, but these are always in terms of the *file identifier*. The use of this mapping is sufficiently infrequent to make the provision of a separate mapping service an effective option. Directories, giving the mappings from *text names* to *file identifiers* are stored as tables in files on the file server. The design and implementation of file servers and directory servers are discussed in detail in Chapters 5 and 6.
- *Transaction service level*: The synchronization of access when several processes are altering data in the same file requires another layer of software to ensure that all the necessary changes are made, and that they occur in a consistent sequence. The functions of a transaction service are discussed in detail in Chapter 7.

2.4.4 Window servers

The need for window servers arises from the requirement to share workstation screens between local and remote processes, allowing a workstation user to interact with some local and some remote applications or, in the case of a processor pool architecture, allowing the user to interact with graphical applications from a workstation that runs a window server but no application programs.

Historically, the window systems used in workstations and personal computers have been a purely local software component, a set of library procedures shared between applications or a set of functions within the workstation operating system. The responsibility of a window system or *window manager* in a workstation is to perform all of the output to the screen and to direct input from the mouse and the keyboard to the appropriate application. It provides facilities for application programs to display text and graphics in windows and it may include specific support for standard interactive techniques such as menu selection, dragging of graphical objects to new positions and rubber-band-like line drawing.

Windows are areas of the workstation screen that behave like separate screens. The window system maintains this illusion, generating and changing the screen image as the windows are moved or changed in size. It displays objects in the windows on request from application programs, clipping each object to the boundary of the window in which it is displayed or scrolling the window if the application so requests. Windows are particularly useful in providing users with a view of the state of several applications tasks. Each application task may be represented by a process that uses one or more windows. There is a *current window* through which the user interacts with one of the application tasks. The user can switch attention from one task to another by selecting a new current window.

Window servers have a similar software structure to those of other servers; the clients for window servers are interactive application programs, which may be running on the same computer as the window server or a different one. In both cases, message-based communication is used to transmit requests from clients to the window server. In X Windows [Scheifler and Gettys 1986, Stern 1987] this is takes the form of remote procedures calls. X provides a fixed service interface that can be called in the C language to create and manipulate windows, to draw a variety of graphical objects in them and to accept user input.

NeWS [Sun 1987b] provides a service, together with the ability to send the definitions of new procedures to be added to the service. The application program sends sequences of program text containing descriptions of graphical operations in a high-level language (*PostScript* [Adobe 1986]). The program texts transmitted to the NeWS server may include procedure definitions as well as commands to perform graphical operations, so that, for example, the entire sequence of actions needed to enable a user to 'drag' an object from one part of the screen to another can be downloaded to the server as a procedure in PostScript, so that when it is invoked no communication with the application program is needed until the dragged object reaches its final destination on the screen.

The communication overheads associated with the use of a remote window server could be quite high, but in both X Windows and NeWS great care has been taken to minimize them. In particular, the requests from clients to the window servers are 'batched', retaining requests in the client until some small interval of time has elapsed (e.g. 1/20th of a second to maintain an acceptable rate of interaction with the user), taking advantage of the human perceptual latency. This form of optimization in the communication between clients and servers is only possible where a client's requests to a server are not expected to return results; fortunately most graphical output operations do not need to deliver results – their effect is simply to modify the display. A normal remote procedure call cannot be used for this form of client–server communication because it causes the client to block awaiting a reply; so a simple message-based protocol is used instead.

2.4.5 Naming and location of services

We have summarized a number of services that may be present in a distributed system. The procedures within a service are grouped together in a *service interface* – we shall discuss this in more detail in Chapter 4. Each of the services may be represented by one or more instances of an interface existing in a number of different computers. The locations of service interfaces are accessed using *transport addresses*, that is, the network addresses of software ports that can accessed via the *transport layer* of the network software. (See Chapter 3 for a more detailed explanation.) A client that needs to make a request to a service must be able to obtain the transport address of an instance of the service's interface. To achieve this, a *binding operation* must be performed; that is, a service name must be translated to the transport address of an appropriate instance of the service interface.

A simple way would be for the transport address of a service interface to be included in the code of each client program (e.g. when the client program is compiled). This is too static; distributed systems should be configurable, that is, it should be possible to add, move or remove servers as necessary. But the client programs would have to be modified and re-compiled whenever one of these changes occurs. This is an aspect of transparency; client programs should be independent of the locations of the services they use. Even in centralized operating systems access to operating system functions by user programs is indirect; *function identifiers* are used, and these are translated to memory locations by the operating system on each function call, rather than compile the memory locations of the system functions directly into the user programs. This approach is adopted to make user programs independent of the memory layout of the operating system in any particular computer.

In distributed systems the names and transport addresses of the currently available service interfaces are recorded in a *name server* (also called a *binder*). A name server maps *text names* to network transport addresses for all of the text names that have been *registered* with it. So any server that offers a service interface must first register its text name with the name service. A client process wishing to call a procedure in a service interface presents the text name of the service in an enquiry to the name server. The name server looks up the text name and returns the transport address. The client records the transport address as the *identifier* for the service. Whenever the client needs to transmit a request to the service, it uses the identifier.

We are left with the problem: how do clients obtain the transport address of the binder? One solution adopted, for example, in the Cambridge Distributed Computing System is to keep the binder at a fixed network address. This is the only network address that may be compiled into client software, but for reliability reasons it is helpful to have more than one name server. If this is done, the network transport addresses of all of them should be known to clients and they can each be tried in turn if the first fails to respond.

A more commonly-used solution is for the remote procedure calling software, or in some cases the operating system, in each computer to obtain the address of the binder when it starts up and to verify it periodically, or if there is evidence of problems in communicating with the binder. If broadcast communication is available within the local network, the location of the binder may be found by broadcasting an enquiry message in a form that only the binder accepts. The binder responds with its location. In the absence of broadcast communication, polling over a range of possible transport address addresses might be used.

2.5 Summary

We have covered a lot of ground in this chapter. We have described the three main architectural models: workstation/server, processor pool and integrated. These models are intended to be used as aids in understanding the hardware and software organization of distributed systems; not to exclude other models. In practice there are many systems that combine the models we have described.

We have defined and discussed a set of design goals for distributed systems; some of them directly related to the performance of a system but many of them, such as user interface consistency and extensibility, related more to the quality of a system as perceived by its users.

We have begun to discuss the implementation of distributed systems by identifying the requirements for system software in a distributed system and discussing the merits of a number of approaches. Of these, the discussion on lightweight processes and the design of system kernels to support them is perhaps the most significant factor in the success of most of the distributed systems that have been developed to date.

EXERCISES

2.1   Explain the terms *server* and *service*. Describe the functions of a file service, directory service, block service, print service and authentication service.

2.2   Describe how pool processors are used in a distributed system, mentioning the benefits that can be derived from them.

2.3   The table below shows ways of choosing components in a distributed system corresponding to three of our architectural models.

Workstations	Servers	Pool processors
included	included	included
	included	included
included		included

Label each row with the name of the appropriate architectural model. Describe where application programs are executed in each case and discuss the advantages and disadvantages of each model.

2.4   Describe the integrated architectural model and explain where the functions described in the previous three exercises are performed in a distributed system with this model.

2.5   Compare the implications for the user interface of each of the architectural models. Describe the function of a window server.

2.6   Explain the significance of *independent failure modes* in a distributed system and give some examples of problems they could give rise to.

2.7 Give arguments for building the file system outside the kernel in an operating system designed for a distributed system with workstations and servers and explain the term 'open operating system'.

2.8 Discuss the benefits to be derived from the use of lightweight processes in the operating system kernel (a) in a workstation, (b) in a server.

2.9 Describe the levels of protection for memory, files and ports that can be provided by organizing processes as clusters of lightweight processes or threads.

2.10 Describe the function of a *name server* and explain how it might be used by other services, for example a file service.

Chapter 3
Networks and Protocols

This chapter summarizes the principles of wide-area and local computer networks and describes three important local network technologies.

Local networks provide the primary means of communication between the components of a distributed system. Some distributed systems are designed to operate across internetworks consisting of several local networks linked by a wide-area network. Wide-area networking concepts are important because their development preceded that of local networks and many of the concepts and techniques of wide-area networking are used in both classes of network.

The performance and reliability requirements of distributed systems differ substantially from those of other applications of computer networks. We define these requirements and discuss their impact on the design of network protocols for distributed systems.

53

3.1 Introduction

Historically, computer networks were developed to meet a variety of needs for data communication both locally and over wide areas, with differing performance and reliability requirements. Distributed systems rely entirely on computer networks for the communication of data and control information between the computers of which they are composed and they require high levels of network performance and reliability. To understand the performance requirements, let us consider the communication between a client and a server.

A request for service from a client to a server generally involves the transmission of messages in each direction to transfer the request to the server and to return the reply to the client. Until the messages have been transmitted, the client must wait. Thus the rate of progress of the client's work depends upon the speed and responsiveness of the network. Figure 3.1 shows in simple form the sequence of actions by the client, the network and the server when a request is processed.

Client	Network	Server
sends request for service		
waits for reply	transmitting request	
.		receives request
.		executes request
.		sends reply
.	transmits reply	
receives reply and continues		

Figure 3.1 The sequence of client–server communication.

For distributed systems to be competitive with centralized systems the time taken for communication between client and server should be comparable with, or less than, the time to perform the service requested. Anything longer would limit the responsiveness of individual client programs and the overall performance of the distributed system. This leads to a requirement to transmit requests in 0.1 to 10 msec for most kinds of server. If the service request is to a file server (e.g. to read or write a file block or to create a new file) the messages containing requests and replies might for example be 1000 bytes in length.

Current wide-area networks operate at transmission rates in the range 2 to 100 kHz (i.e. kbits per second), giving minimum transmission times for a 1000 byte message in the range 4 sec down to 80 msec, but storage and switching delays at each node in the network through which a message passes mean that we must multiply the basic transmission time by the number of network nodes traversed. These calculations rule wide-area networks out of serious consideration as a basis for the construction of distributed systems, although they are useful in a subsidiary role, linking local networks in larger groupings (called **internetworks**).

Current local networks are able to transmit data at rates in the range 0.2 to 10 MHz (Mbits per second) in working systems, with experimental networks running at speeds of up to 100 MHz. These transmission rates do not take conflicting communication traffic or any protocol or software overheads into account, but they give some indication of the potential performance of lightly-loaded local networks, giving basic transmission times for a 1000 byte message in the range 40 msec down to 800 μsec (in working systems) or 80 μsec (in experimental networks).

The topologies used in local networks mean that there are no storage or switching delays and the *latency* (that is, the delay between issuing a command to transmit a message and the start of transmission) in most lightly-loaded local networks is small (less than 1 msec), although the software in the sending and receiving hosts may add delays of up to 10 msec if they have operating systems that do not support lightweight processes.

The above calculations suggest that local networks with transmission speeds above 1 MHz should offer acceptable performance for use in lightly-loaded distributed systems and that 10 MHz offers a reasonable capacity to support systems that generate substantial traffic. These conjectured requirements are in line with the performance of current local networks, and experience with them tends to support our conjectures.

Despite these unfavourable performance comparisons between wide-area and local networks, it is important to have a knowledge of the principles on which both types of network are designed because many of the principles and much of the terminology are applicable to both.

Wide-area networks □   A wide-area network consists of a collection of communication circuits linking special-purpose computer systems, known as **Packet Switching Exchanges (PSEs)** (originally used in the ARPA network with the name **Interface Message Processor (IMP)**). A PSE is located at each node in the network (see Figure 3.2). PSEs are dedicated to the task of data communication. They send and receive packets of data through the network on behalf of other computers.

The PSEs operate the network by forwarding the packets from one PSE to another along the route from source to destination. They are responsible for defining the route taken by each packet. This mode of network operation is referred to as **store-and-forward** communication, because every packet of data is stored temporarily by each PSE along its route before it is forwarded to another PSE. Store-and-forward network systems can be used for computer-to-computer communication over any distance where circuits exist to carry the packets.

Computers that use a network to send and receive data are called **hosts**. Hosts are normally located close to a PSE and connected directly to it. They pass packets of data to the PSEs for transmission through the network to other hosts and receive packets from the PSEs that are addressed to them.

The packet-switching method involves inevitable delays. Each packet arriving at a node in the network is stored by a PSE for the time that it requires to decide on the route for the next stage in its journey and then to re-transmit the packet along a circuit to the next node. Each of these delays is of the order of a

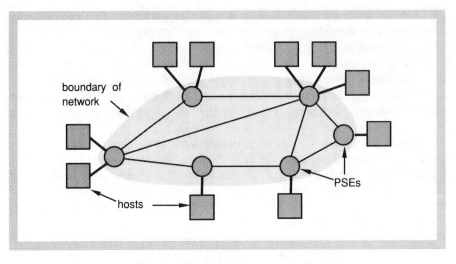

Figure 3.2 A wide-area network.

few milliseconds. As a consequence, message transmission times are relatively long and may depend upon the route taken by each message. Short messages are transmitted in 100 to 200 msec in typical wide-area networks. If satellite channels† are used or the route is complex, involving many PSEs, the transmission time for a short message may be as long as 500 msec.

Wide-area networks have been in use since 1965 using a variety of types of communication link including:

1. private and leased telephone circuits,
2. public switched telephone circuits,
3. fibre-optic and other wide-band circuits,
4. satellite communication channels.

The circuits are normally owned and managed by a *carrier company* and leased to user organizations. The carriers are telecommunication companies whose main business is the provision of telephone services and other analogue telecommunication services. Although fibre-optic links and satellite channels have very high bandwidths, the bandwidth is normally subdivided to provide many circuits. Circuits that are available for wide-area networks at an economic cost typically provide data transmission speeds in the range from 2400 bits per second to 64 kbits per second.

The advent and growth of wide-area computer networking has led to the provision by carrier companies of public **digital network services**. These services offer packet-switched data transmission facilities using wide-area networking technology. There are now many such wide-area packet-switching

---

† Satellite transmission necessarily incurs a delay because the *time of flight* of an electronic signal to an orbiting synchronous satellite and back to ground is of the order of 200 msec.

network services – the DARPA network was an early example that has led to many commercial derivatives in the United States. In Europe, there is the PSS network in Great Britain, and the TRANSPAC network in France, and there are plans to link these national networks.

Historically, wide-area networks were developed to link widely-distributed computers for simple data transmission tasks. They were used primarily for the connection of interactive terminals to remote host computers, the transfer of entire files (file transfer) and batch-processing jobs (remote job entry) between computers, the transmission of electronic mail and to gather data and issue commands in geographically distributed systems (e.g. command and control systems). Generally, these tasks do not require very high transmission speeds and have little need to synchronize the activities of several computers.

It should by now be apparent that wide-area networks do not offer the speeds of communication required for distributed systems. Local-area networks have been designed to avoid the delays inherent in packet-switching and routing and it is they that have been exploited to provide the communication functions required in distributed systems.

An apparent consequence of this observation is that distributed computer systems can be distributed only over relatively small local areas. This certainly is the case at present, but it should be noted that the switching delays and the low data rates found in wide-area networks are not inevitable. Some experimental wide-area distributed systems have been developed using satellite channels and wide-band ground links [Leslie et al. 1984], and these developments together with improvements in the speed of packet-switching computers may eventually result in the feasibility of wide-area distributed systems.

Local networks □   Local networks use dedicated communication circuits, normally on a single site extending at most over a few kilometres. Messages are transmitted directly from the source computer to the destination computer without intermediate storage or processing. There are no PSEs in local networks; instead, the host computers are collectively responsible for the management of traffic on the network using special-purpose hardware interfaces to transmit and receive the data on the network circuits. The mode of operation is based on **broadcast communication** rather than the store-and-forward mode used in wide-area networks. That is, each packet is transmitted to all of the computers in the network and each computer is responsible for identifying and receiving the packets that are addressed to it.

With all broadcast-mode communication the network is a shared channel, and only one sender at a time can use it to transmit data. This leads to conflicts between senders that must be resolved within the network hardware or software and if communication traffic is heavy it means that the effective transmission rate seen by an individual host is reduced because the network is not always available for transmission. Fortunately, the traffic that is typically generated in distributed systems does not impose a high or continuous load on local networks, so the effective transmission rate is usually comparable to the basic network transmission rate.

Local networks have been the subject of much development work since the early 1970s and a number of network technologies have emerged with adequate performance to support distributed systems. Standardization work by the Institute of Electrical and Electronics Engineers has resulted in the adoption of four different local network technologies as American National Standards [IEEE 1983, 1985d], partially unified by the use of common address and data field formats [IEEE 1985c].

The Ethernet, originally developed at Xerox PARC in the early 1970s, has been adopted as a United States Standard [IEEE 1985a] and is the most widely used local network technology for distributed systems. It is based on broadcasting over a simple passive circuit, with a single high-speed cable linking all of the computers using the network. The Cambridge Ring developed at Cambridge University in the mid-1970s exemplifies another class of local network, known as a **slotted ring**, in which all of the computers in the network are linked in a ring structure and data is transmitted in small fixed-size packets by passing it from station to station around the ring. Another ring network technology, known as a **token ring**, can accommodate larger, variable-size packets, and has been adopted as IEEE standard 802.5 and by IBM and some other manufacturers for linking personal computer and workstation products [IEEE 1985b]. We describe the main attributes of all three types of local network in Section 3.3.

Internetwork □   There is a clear need for distributed systems to operate over areas wider than local networks can cover. This need has been met to a limited extent by the integration of local and wide-area networking technologies to produce *internetworks*, using a wide-area network to link several local networks. Internetworks are also useful as means to increase the capacity of distributed systems beyond the limited number of host connections and traffic capacity of a single local network.

The performance of the resulting network is not homogeneous, so the design of distributed system software or applications that work successfully in an internetwork must take the differences in performance into account. In addition there must be a transport protocol that is applicable throughout the network. The DARPA TCP/IP protocols [Postel 1980, Hinden et al. 1983] and the Xerox PUP protocol [Boggs et al. 1980] are the most widely-used internetwork protocols.

3.2 Computer networking principles

3.2.1 Packets

In almost all computer networks the logical unit of information transmission is a **message** – a sequence of data items of arbitrary length. Before a message can be transmitted it must be subdivided into **packets**. The simplest form of packet is a sequence of binary data elements (e.g. an array of bits or bytes) of restricted length, together with addressing information sufficient to identify the source and destination points in the network. A length restriction is applied to data packets:

1. so that each station in a network can allocate buffer storage sufficient to hold the largest possible packet;
2. to ensure that the network can be shared between stations wishing to communicate without excessive delays due to the pre-emption of circuits for the transmission of long messages.

The task of dividing the messages into a number of packets before transmission and re-assembling them at the receiving station is performed in a network software module called the **transport layer**. The transport layer must be used, directly or indirectly, by all programs wishing to transmit or receive messages.

3.2.2 Protocols

The term **protocol** is used to refer to a set of precisely-defined rules and conventions used for communication between similar software modules running on the different computers in a network. An important part of the definition of a protocol is the format of the data accepted and transmitted across the network by the software that supports the protocol. For example, a **transport protocol** transmits messages of any length from a source to a destination. The protocol specifies the format of the messages and of the source and destination addresses. Programs wishing to transmit such messages can issue calls to the transport layer software module, passing it a message in the specified format. The transport layer software then concerns itself with the decomposition of the message into a form that can be communicated via another, lower-level protocol. It divides each message into a number of packets and calls upon a **network layer** software module in the same computer to transmit the packets to the destination.

Network software is arranged in a hierarchy of layers. Each layer is represented by a software module in every host computer in the network. In wide-area networks the lower layers, up to the network layer, must also be represented in the PSEs, since it is the network layer that routes packets through the network to their destinations. A layer can be thought of as a program or process that communicates directly with the corresponding process in the another computer in the network but in reality, as we have seen in the previous paragraph, the data is not transmitted directly between the protocol programs at each level. Instead, each layer of network software communicates with the layers above and below, accepting data in the specified format from the layer above it and applying transformations to it before passing it for further processing to the layer below. Similarly the converse transformations are applied to data received from the layer below before it is passed to the layer above.

Thus each layer provides a service to the layer above it and enhances the service provided by the layer below it. The lowest layer is the **physical layer** and it is this which transmits the data through the circuits of the network. At the destination, the data is processed and passed upwards through the hierarchy of software modules until it is in a form in which it can be passed to the intended recipient program.

The definitions of the layers and their protocols has been an area of intensive research and standardization for more than 15 years. One particular seven-layer model has been adopted as a reference model for network software by the International Standards Organization (ISO). The model has been named the *Reference Model for Open Systems Interconnection*; hence it is known as the **ISO OSI reference model**. We shall summarize the ISO model here in order to introduce its concepts and terminology for later use. There are many sources for more detail on this standard [Tanenbaum 1981a, 1981b, Halsall 1988, Stallings 1985] giving full descriptions of the ISO OSI reference model as a basis for a comprehensive treatment of communication software for wide-area networks.

Although the ISO model was defined with wide-area networks in mind, it is a useful reference point in the design of network software in general. However, the ISO model is often unnecessarily elaborate for distributed systems based on local networks and, as we shall see in Section 3.4, simpler models are usually adopted in distributed systems work.

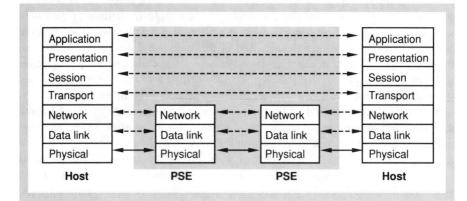

Figure 3.3 The ISO OSI reference model.

3.2.3 The ISO OSI reference model

Figure 3.3 shows the seven layers encompassed by the ISO OSI model and their hierarchical structure. The layers are described and the relevance of each to the implementation of distributed systems is discussed below. The layers are described in top-down fashion, since that is the point of view of the application system developer and, in this context, a distributed system is an application system.

Application layer □ The purpose of the model is to support communication between processes running in separate computers performing application tasks on behalf of their users. The range of possible applications is not restricted by the model. For each application or class of applications that requires network communication an application-level protocol will be required.

For example, a microcomputer may be connected via a network to a host computer simply as a terminal using terminal emulation application software. The terminal emulation application uses a *virtual terminal* application-level protocol to transmit the input from the keyboard to the operating system on the host computer and to receive data for display on the screen. The virtual terminal protocol software simply emulates the communication that would occur with a conventional terminal connected directly to the host.

As another example, when a user who is logged-in on one computer wishes to obtain a copy of a file that is stored on a remote computer, he or she requests the copy from the *file transfer* application software on his or her computer. The file transfer software on the user's computer communicates with a *file transfer process* on the remote computer using a *file transfer protocol* designed to communicate the name of the file required, the user's permission status and other details of the request. The file transfer process on the remote computer then uses other features of the file transfer protocol to transmit the contents of the file. Note that this is quite different from the task performed by file servers. A file transfer operation copies an entire file from the filestore of one computer to another, whereas a file server provides operations to access parts of a file remotely.

Since each application has different communication needs, the set of protocols for use at the application level is not defined in the ISO OSI model, but certain application level protocols, including virtual terminal, file transfer, electronic mail and remote job entry protocols have emerged as candidates for standardization [CCITT 1984].

Distributed systems are extensible; new applications and services are added as the need arises. The requirement for extensibility in this way was not envisaged in the formulation of the OSI model. No fixed or standard set of application-level protocols can meet the needs of all applications.

The solution adopted in many distributed system designs is to build the application software in terms of a single *remote procedure calling* protocol† (discussed in Chapter 4). The application layer can then be extended simply by the compilation of new procedures into the application software environment (i.e. the client and server software).

Presentation layer □ Data format conversions are needed to transfer data between computers because different data representations may be used. For example, the packing of bytes into machine words is performed differently in different manufacturers' hardware. As another example, the transfer of floating-point numerical data between computers requires a translation from the floating point format of the source computer to that of the destination computer.

---

† Remote procedure calling protocols are usually considered as application-level protocols and are defined as an extension to a programming language or languages. There is a proposed language-independent standard for remote procedure calling – the *X.410 Remote Operations Server* protocol [CCITT 1985b] – within the CCITT X.400 series of application-level protocol standards, but it may not be suitable for many distributed systems purposes.

The presentation layer software in each computer transforms data from the formats used in the computer it is running on into a set of standard network representations called **external data representations** (**EDR**) before transmission. Received data is transformed from the network representations into the local data formats. (It would be wasteful to do this if the sending and receiving hosts are of the same type, so some presentation-level protocols allow this to be flagged as a special case, not requiring conversion.) Standards for external data representation have been defined [CCITT 1985a].

In addition, there are other useful transformations to data that are independent of the particular communication needs of applications. For example:

- Data encryption is needed in many applications that handle confidential or secret data.
- Data compression is needed in networks that are slow or heavily loaded.

The presentation layer performs such systematic translations. The translations are transparent to the application layer. For example, if data compression is used, the presentation layer software at the transmitting station compresses each message that it is given by the application layer and passes the message in its compressed form to the session layer software. At the receiving station, the presentation layer unpacks the messages it receives and then passes them to the application layer.

When a remote procedure calling protocol is used, data is transferred between computers as the parameters and results of remote procedure calls. These may include any of the data types used in programming languages – integers, characters, arrays, records, etc., including user-defined data types. Translation is therefore required where language systems or application programs in the source and destination computers use different representations for these data types. Once again, this requirement goes well beyond the needs envisaged by the OSI model. Solutions to these problems will be discussed in Chapter 4.

Session layer □   The session layer is responsible for the establishment and maintenance of **virtual connections** between pairs of processes in different computers connected by a network. For example, a connection might be established to transfer a file between two computers or to enable a user to log in to a remote computer.

The session layer in the source computer is passed the name of a service in a call from the presentation or application layer and uses it to establish a virtual connection to a server process through the session layer in the destination computer. To get communication established between the processes in the source and destination computers a negotiation is required. Essentially, they must agree to communicate via a virtual connection. One of the processes makes known a name for a virtual connection. If a partner then requests a connection with the same name, agreement is taken to have occurred. A connection is established and is referenced by a **session identifier** in subsequent requests for data transmission from the presentation and application layers. The use of session identifiers provides a gain in efficiency, eliminating the need for the application layer to quote the destination address for each transmission; a more important gain is obtained in wide-area networks because they adopt a *virtual circuit* model for communication; the routing of data packets at intermediate points in the network can be inferred very simply from the session identifier.

In local networks the overheads associated with *connectionless* communication are minimal and the session layer is often omitted. In distributed systems using remote procedure calling in the client–server paradigm, a server process is always willing to communicate with new client processes. A session may be established for each client's communication with the server, but in a single local network the use of sessions for client–server communication is of little benefit, since routing does not occur.

Transport layer □ The transport layer's task is to provide a network-independent message transport service between pairs of network **ports** (also known as **sockets**). Ports are software-definable destination points for communication within a host computer. The transport layer is responsible for delivering messages to ports. The source and destination ports are defined by **transport addresses** composed of the network address of a host computer and a port identifier. In an internetwork, the transport layer is responsible for routing between networks, using transport addresses that are applicable throughout the internetwork; within a single network, routing is performed by the *network layer*.

In wide-area networks there are typically a small number of ports with fixed identifiers, each allocated to a given service such as remote login or file transfer. In a local network a process may create one or more ports through which it is willing to accept service requests. Clients obtain a port identifier from a name server and may then transmit requests to the server through any service port without further negotiation. There are two possible modes of communication that may be provided by the transport layer: **virtual circuit** and **datagram**.

In wide-area communication **virtual circuits** are generally used. A virtual circuit is a logical channel between an origin and destination address pair. The virtual circuit is implemented by the transport layer software in each host. It establishes the virtual circuits, maintains a table of the virtual circuits that are currently open and ensures the reliable transmission of sequences of messages over the virtual circuits.

The transport layer accepts messages of arbitrary length, segments them into packets and submits them to the network layer for transmission, re-assembling them at their destination. The routing algorithms used in the network layer may result in the arrival of the packets in a sequence that is different from the order in which they are sent. The transport layer records a sequence number in each packet and uses the sequence numbers to ensure that messages are reconstructed in the correct sequence.

In wide-area networking the transport layer does much of the donkey-work of communication. In particular:

- It translates transport addresses into addresses that are recognizable to the network layer for a specific network.
- It segments messages into packets of appropriate length for the network that is to be used and re-assembles them in the correct sequence at the destination.

- It ensures that messages are transferred reliably from the source to the destination, dealing with lost and duplicated messages by applying an acknowledgement scheme for individual packets – the transport layer software in the destination computer sends an acknowledgement packet to the transport layer in the source computer for each data packet that it receives. If no acknowledgement is received by the source within a specified time interval, the packet is re-transmitted.

In distributed systems based on local networks **datagram communication** is more commonly used. This refers to the transmission of messages between a sending and receiving process on a 'one-off' basis without establishing a prior connection.

The responsibilities of the transport layer can be very much lighter when datagram communication is used in local networks:

- In local networks, duplicate and out-of-order messages cannot arise, although messages may occasionally be lost. As we shall see in Section 3.3, the inherent reliability of the physical and data link layers in local networks makes such errors extremely unlikely but not impossible. The transport layer does not usually take responsibility for detecting and recovering them. Instead, checks and recovery procedures are applied in the application layer (see Saltzer et al. [1984] for a discussion of the merits of this approach).
- In most local network environments the length of datagram messages is restricted to the maximum packet length of the underlying network, so message segmentation is not required.
- The remaining responsibilities of the transport layer are concerned with addressing. The transport layer is still responsible for the implementation of port addresses that enable communication between software processes, whereas the network layer deals in hardware addresses.
- Where datagram communication extends across an internetwork composed of several local networks, the transport layer has responsibility for the routing of messages between networks.

In most distributed systems a remote procedure calling protocol is used for all client–server communication. This is built using datagram communication only, and takes responsibility for the detection and correction of errors and lost messages and for the segmentation of long messages.

Network layer □   The network layer transfers data packets in a specific network, using packet formats that are acceptable for transmission on that network. There is separate network layer software for each type of network. It accepts data packets from the transport layer in the network's standard packet format. The network layer takes responsibility for the transmission of each packet to its destination, using the services of the data link layer. In a wide-area network this involves the generation of a route from source to destination within the network, passing through as many PSEs as are necessary.

In a single local area network the network layer is largely redundant, since packets can be transmitted directly from any computer on the network to any other. So the network layer, if present, has little work to do.

Data link layer □   The data link layer is responsible for the error-free transmission of packets between computers that are directly connected. In wide-area networks the connections are between pairs of PSEs and between PSEs and hosts. In local networks, the data link layer is responsible for packet transmission between host computers.

The data link layer often includes mechanisms for error-detection and recovery mechanisms and flow control (see Tanenbaum [1981a] for a description of these functions), but, since it is only concerned with data transmission on individual network links, these mechanisms are often replicated at higher levels.

Physical layer □   As the name implies, the physical layer consists of the hardware that drives the network and the circuits themselves. It transmits sequences of binary data by analogue signalling, using amplitude or frequency modulation of electrical signals (on cable circuits), light signals (on fibre-optic circuits) or electromagnetic signals (on radio and microwave circuits). There is a trend towards the use of digital signalling in telecommunications, and this will reduce the complexity of the physical layer, although rates and signalling standards will continue to differ between public and local networks.

3.3 Local network technologies

Communication in local networks is achieved without the need for specialized computers dedicated to communication tasks. The host computers are connected directly to a network circuit by relatively simple interface hardware. The interface hardware and network driver software in each host can send and receive data at high speeds with low error rates and without switching delays, implementing the physical layer, the datalink layer and the network layer with a single protocol.

It is possible to provide relatively simple software in each computer that can perform the entire task of transmitting or receiving messages. These important characteristics of local networks give considerable advantages in cost, speed and reliability in comparison with wide-area networks.

The circuits used in local networks may be pairs of twisted wires, coaxial cables or optical fibres, capable of data transmission speeds ranging from 100 thousand to 100 million bits per second. Since all local networks are designed to provide direct communication between any two hosts, the topology used (ring, bus or branching bus) has relatively little influence on the behaviour as seen by the user. Virtually all successful high-speed local networks have been structured as either rings or buses (Figures 3.4 and 3.5).

In networks with a simple or branching bus topology there is a circuit composed of a single cable or a set of connected cables passing near all of the hosts on the network. When more than one cable is used the connections are made by **repeaters** – simple amplifying and connecting units that have no effects on the timing or logical behaviour of the network. The cable is passive, and each host has a *drop cable* connected to the main cable by a T-connection or *tap*. Data

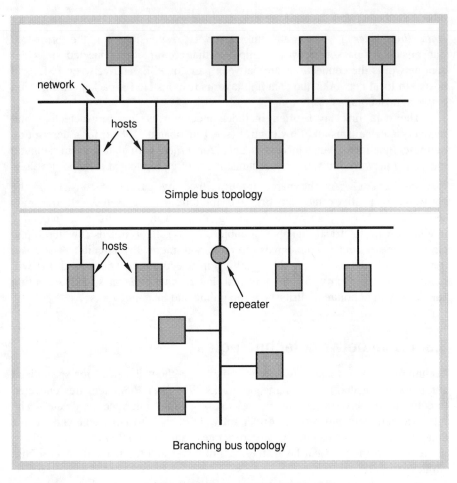

Figure 3.4 Bus topologies.

is transmitted by 'broadcasting' a signal on the cable as a single sequence of pulses. This form of signalling is analogous in some ways to the data bus systems that were originally developed to connect the parts of conventional computer systems together. The major difference between bus networks and the system buses used inside computer systems is that the latter are parallel buses allowing the transmission of 16 or 32 bits simultaneously and the transmission of data on them is scheduled by a central arbitration unit, whereas in bus-like local networks there are no centralized components and the use of the cable is scheduled by a distributed method of control involving cooperation between all the computers connected to the network. This has led to the description of such networks as **contention buses**, because all of the host computers needing to send a message at any time contend for the use of the cable.

In networks with a ring-like topology the cable is made up of separate links connecting adjacent stations. Data is transmitted in one direction around the ring

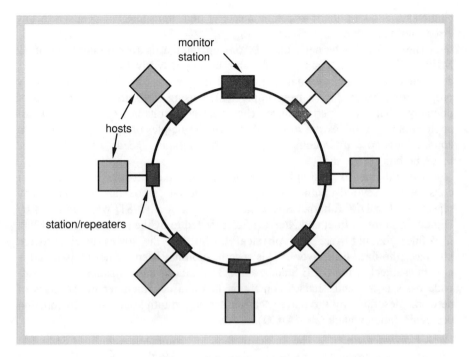

Figure 3.5 Ring topology.

by signalling between stations. Each node applies the signal it receives to the next section of cable. The data circulates around the ring until some station removes it from the circuit; the receiving station does this in some ring systems, but in others the data is allowed to complete a circular journey and is removed by the sending station. In most ring systems a **monitor station** is included to ensure that data does not circulate indefinitely (e.g. in case the sending station or the receiving station fails) and to perform other 'housekeeping' functions. Ring networks fall into several subclasses: slotted, register insertion, contention and token rings.

In the following sections we describe the method of operation of the Ethernet as the most important contention bus network and of two types of ring network. We will consider slotted rings, exemplified by the Cambridge Ring, and token rings, exemplified by the IEEE 802.5 specification for token rings. For further information on local networks the reader is referred to the introductory texts by Stallings [1984, 1987].

3.3.1 Ethernet

The Ethernet was developed at Xerox PARC in 1973 [Metcalfe and Boggs 1976, Shoch et al. 1982, 1985] as a part of the intensive programme of research carried out there on personal workstations and distributed systems. The Ethernet demonstrated the usefulness of high-speed local networks linking computers on a single site, allowing them to communicate at high transmission speeds with low error rates and without switching delays.

The standard Ethernet [IEEE 1985a] operates at a transmission rate of 10 MHz using low-loss coaxial cable and high-speed drivers in the computers connected to it; the original prototype Ethernet ran at 3 MHz and many proprietary networks have been implemented using the same basic method of operation with cost/performance characteristics suitable for a variety of applications. At the lowest cost level the same principles of operation are used to connect low-cost microcomputers with transmission speeds of 100 to 200 thousand bits per second.

The Ethernet is a simple or branching bus-like network using a circuit consisting of several continuous segments of low-loss coaxial cable linked by repeaters. The DIX Ethernet Specification [Xerox et al. 1981] was published by Digital Equipment, Intel and Xerox (often referred to by the initials DIX) in 1980. It defines the hardware (the **physical layer**) and the lowest-level software interface (the **data link layer**). This specification has been further revised and is now the subject of the IEEE Standard 802.3. Further standardization on a world-wide basis is in hand. It is a contention bus and is a member of the class of networks described by the phrase 'carrier sensing, multiple access with collision detection' (abbreviated: **CSMA/CD**).

Packet broadcasting □   The basic method of communication in CSMA/CD networks is by broadcasting packets of data on a cable that is accessible to all of the stations on the network. All stations are continually 'listening' to the cable for packets addressed to them. Any station wishing to transmit a message broadcasts one or more packets (called **frames** in the Ethernet Specification) on the cable. Each packet contains the address of the destination station, the address of the sending station and a variable-length sequence of bits representing the message to be transmitted. Data transmission proceeds at 10 million bits per second and packets† vary in length between 64 and 1518† bytes, so the time to transmit a packet on the Ethernet ranges from 50 μsec to 1.2 msec depending on its length.

Ethernet packet layout □
The packets transmitted by stations on the Ethernet have the following layout:

6 bytes	6 bytes	2 bytes	46 bytes ≤ length ≤ 1500 bytes	4 bytes
destination address	source address	type	data for transmission	frame check sequence

Apart from the destination and source addresses already mentioned, packets contain a type field, a data field and a frame check sequence. Note that the length of the packet is not transmitted‡. Instead, receiving stations detect the end of

---

†   1518 is an arbitrary value chosen to ensure that all hosts can allocate adequate buffer capacity to hold incoming packets. There are no technical obstacles to the use of longer packets.

‡   In the Standard Ethernet Specification [IEEE 1985a], the length of the data field *is* transmitted, in place of the type field.

transmission (there is a mandatory interval of 9.6 μsec between packets) and it is assumed that the last 4 bytes received constitute the frame check sequence.

The type field is used by the upper layers of protocol to distinguish packets of various types. The specification does not allow more than 1024 stations in a single Ethernet, but addresses occupy 6 bytes in order to allow all of the stations in a set of interconnected Ethernets to have unique addresses. Where Ethernets are connected by a wide-area network to form part of an internet, it is necessary to ensure that the addresses used throughout the internet are unique. This is achieved by registering each Ethernet that may be used as part of an internet with a central authority. The Xerox Corporation acts as such an authority for Ethernets, allocating separate ranges of 48-bit addresses to each **registered Ethernet**.

The data field contains all or part (if the message length exceeds 1500 bytes) of the message that is being transmitted. It is the only field whose length may vary between defined limits. The lower bound of 46 bytes on the packet length is necessary to ensure that collisions can be detected by all stations on the network.

The frame check sequence is a checksum generated and inserted by the sender and used to validate packets by the receiver. Packets with incorrect checksums are simply dropped by the datalink layer in the receiving station. This is an example of the potential unreliability of the simple datagram protocols used in local networks; to guarantee the transmission of a message, the application layer must use a protocol that acknowledges receipt of each packet and re-transmits any unacknowledged packets. The incidence of data corruption in local networks is so small that the use of this method of recovery when guaranteed delivery is required is perfectly acceptable.

Packet collisions □   Even in the relatively short time that it takes to transmit packets there is a finite probability that two stations on the network will attempt to transmit messages simultaneously. If a station attempts to transmit a packet without checking whether the cable is in use by other stations, a collision may occur.

The Ethernet has three mechanisms to deal with this possibility. The first is called **carrier sensing**; the interface hardware in each station listens for the presence of a signal (known as the **carrier** by analogy with radio broadcasting) in the cable. When a station wishes to transmit a packet, it waits until no signal is present in the cable and then begins to transmit.

Unfortunately, carrier sensing does not prevent all collisions. The possibility of collision remains due to the finite time τ taken for a signal inserted at a point in the cable (travelling at electronic speed: approximately 3×10^8 metres per second) to reach all other points. Consider two stations **A** and **B** that are ready to transmit packets at almost the same time. If **A** begins to transmit first, **B** can check and find no signal in the cable at any time $t < \tau$ after **A** has begun to transmit. **B** then begins to transmit, **interfering** with **A**'s transmission. Both **A**'s packet and **B**'s packet will be damaged by the interference.

The technique used to recover from such interference is called **collision detection**. Whenever a station is transmitting a packet through its hardware output port, it also listens on its input port and the two signals are compared. If they differ, then a collision has occurred. When this happens the station stops transmitting and produces a **jamming signal** on the cable to ensure that all stations recognize the collision. As we have already noted, a minimum packet length is necessary to ensure that collisions are always detected. If two stations transmit simultaneously from opposite ends of the network, they will not become aware of the collision for τ seconds. If the packets that they transmit take less than τ to be broadcast, the collision will not be noticed, since each sending station would not see the other packet until after it has finished transmitting its own, whereas stations at intermediate points would receive both packets simultaneously, resulting in data corruption.

After the jamming signal, all transmitting and listening stations cancel the current packet. The transmitting stations then have to try to transmit their packets again. A further difficulty now arises. If the stations involved in the collision all attempt to re-transmit their packets immediately after the jamming signal another collision will probably occur. To avoid this, a technique known as **back-off** is used. Each of the stations involved in a collision chooses to wait a time $n\tau$ before retransmitting. The value of n is a random integer chosen separately at each station and bounded by a constant L defined in the network software. If a further collision occurs, the value of L is doubled and the process is repeated if necessary for up to 10 attempts.

Finally, the interface hardware at the receiving station computes the check sequence and compares it with the check sum transmitted in the packet. If the comparison fails the packet is rejected (i.e. it is not transmitted). Using all of these techniques, the stations connected to the Ethernet are able to manage the use of the cable without any centralized control or synchronization.

Ethernet efficiency □   A single Ethernet may extend over distances of up to 2.5 km. For a 1 km cable the value of τ is less than 5 µsec and the probability of collisions is small enough to ensure a high efficiency. The Ethernet can achieve a channel utilization of between 80% and 95%, although the delays due to contention become noticeable when 50% utilization is exceeded. Because the loading is variable, it is impossible to *guarantee* the delivery of a given message within any fixed time, since the network might be fully loaded when the message is ready for transmission. But the *probability* of transferring the message with a given delay is as good as, or better than, other network technologies.

Empirical measurements of the performance of an Ethernet at Xerox PARC and reported by Shoch and Hupp [1980] confirm this analysis. In practice, Ethernets used in distributed systems are relatively lightly loaded. They operate for most of the time with no stations waiting to transmit and a channel utilization close to 1.

3.3.2 Cambridge Ring

The Cambridge Ring is a **slotted ring** network transmitting data at 10 MHz on circuits composed of two twisted pairs of conventional telephone wire. The Cambridge Ring was developed at Cambridge University in the 1970s and is widely used in Britain. At the data link level it transmits fixed-length **mini-**

packets between stations. Stations are connected to the network through **repeaters**. Each repeater normally passes to its output the stream of bits that it receives on its input. Since the repeaters are connected in a ring, with the output of one station connected to the input of the next, this ensures that the data travels around the ring in a specific direction, with only a small delay for transmission through each repeater†.

Repeaters that are connected to stations include *station logic* that handles the lowest level of protocol needed to support station-to-station data transmission.

Packet format □   At the data-link level the Cambridge Ring is designed to transmit fixed-length packets containing two bytes of data. The format of a minipacket is:

3 bits	8 bits	8 bits	16 bits	2 bits
control bits	destination address	source address	data for transmission	response bits

A typical ring has a total signal path sufficient to hold three or four minipackets. The minipackets circulate continuously, in a manner analogous to a train of railway wagons on a loop track. Stations wishing to transmit wait for an empty minipacket to pass and then fill the empty minipacket as it passes. The **control bits** comprise: a **preamble bit**, whose value is always 1 to mark the start of the minipacket, a **full/empty bit** and a **monitor bit**. The full/empty bit indicates whether or not the packet may be used by a station wishing to transmit. When a transmitting station fills an empty packet, it switches the full/empty bit to *full*, sets the two address fields to show the destination and source addresses for the message it wishes to transmit and loads the data bytes with the next two bytes of the message it is transmitting.

All stations watch for **full packets**. When one arrives at a station, the destination address in the packet is compared with the station's address. If the addresses match and the receiving station is ready to receive some data, the data bytes are copied into a buffer and the **response bits** are altered to show that the minipacket has been received at the destination. The minipacket then travels on, completing its journey back to the station that transmitted it. When it arrives there, the station sets the full/empty bit to *empty* and examines the response bits to discover whether the data was successfully received at the destination and compares the data bytes with those it transmitted to ensure that the packet was transmitted without error. If it was, the transmitting station attempts to send the next two bytes of its message in the same manner.

If the response bits indicate failure, the network software in the computer attached to the transmitting station is informed. If the destination was not ready to receive the data, the station logic in the transmitting station delays the action of informing the network software for a number of ring cycle times. This is to ensure

---

† The delay is approximately equal to the time for one bit to be received and transmitted by a repeater. Since the network operates at 10^7 bits per second, the delay at each repeater is 10^{-7} sec or 0.1 μsec.

that no station can hog the network by attempting to send the same packet continuously when the destination is not ready to receive it†.

There are features in the specification of the Cambridge Ring to ensure the reliable operation of the network, including a **monitor station**, which is responsible for ensuring that no packets remain full for more than one cycle of the ring, and that the appropriate number of empty packets are inserted into the Ring at start-up and remain there during operation.

We should note that data communication at the level we have described is performed by the network hardware in the Cambridge Ring and is similar to that defined at the data link layer in the ISO OSI model, leaving the construction of a more useful variable-length packet protocol and all higher levels of protocol for implementation (if required) in the network software.

As we have already seen, the lowest level of communication supported by the Ethernet implements a packet transport service, similar to the ISO network layer. The Cambridge Ring therefore requires an extra layer of network software for most types of data communication.

3.3.3 Comparison of Ethernet and Ring

The two types of network have approximately equal performance. The Cambridge Ring has a higher channel utilization under high loads and can provide a guarantee of service within a fixed time. The Ethernet provides higher performance for the transmission of large volumes of data under light loads.

In practice, both networks have been used for the construction of a variety of distributed computer systems. The differences in architecture are not evident above the lowest levels of network software.

However, there are operational differences. The Ring can be extended to almost any length, since the length of the total signal path is not critical, whereas the length of the Ethernet cable is limited by the need to keep the end-to-end signal delay short (below about 10 μsec) to reduce the probability of collisions. Because the Ring is composed of a number of separate circuit segments linking adjacent stations, the cable used to link each pair of stations may be different. This feature has been used to introduce fibre optic circuits for sections of Rings that extend over several kilometres.

For similar reasons, the Ring architecture can easily be extended to allow data transmission at speeds of up to 100 MHz or more, whereas in the Ethernet this would require an inconveniently large minimum packet length. In fact, an

---

† An analogy with the use of trains for the transport of freight may be helpful in understanding the operation of slotted rings such as the Cambridge Ring. The analogy has the packets as freight wagons that are permanently in motion around the ring (like a circular 'shuttle service') and the data as freight. The freight is dropped into the empty wagons at sending stations and the wagons are marked with the address of the destination. When the freight arrives at its destination it is removed (actually, the contents of ring packets are copied at their destination and then allowed to continue around the ring back to the sending station, which removes them, but here the analogy becomes a little strained!).

experimental fast ring has been developed at Cambridge University with a designed speed of 100 MHz [Hopper et al. 1986, Hopper and Needham 1988]. The Cambridge Fast Ring operates on principles similar to the original Cambridge Ring, but the size of minipackets has been increased to allow 40 bytes of data to be transported in each, partially overcoming the software overheads associated with minipackets which are one of the main drawbacks of the original Cambridge Ring.

Other drawbacks of the slotted ring technology are the need for a monitor station, making the reliability of the network dependent on the reliability of the monitor station and the further reliance on active elements to transmit packets from station to station.

3.3.4 Token ring

Token rings were explored early in the development of local network technologies [Farmer and Newhall 1969, Farber and Larson 1972, Pierce 1972] But their exploitation has been slower than that of the other local network technologies. Nevertheless, they have been used in several commercial products and IBM has adopted a token ring that conforms to the IEEE 802.5 Standard [IEEE 1985b] as a basis for distributed system products. As the name implies, token rings have a topology similar to slotted rings (see Figure 3.5) but, instead of the fixed-sized slots found in the Cambridge Ring, messages of almost any length can be transmitted as single packets. This is achieved with the help of a single permanently-circulating **token packet** which has a distinguished format.

To extend our freight train analogy to token rings, the token corresponds to a locomotive that circulates continuously. The locomotive is marked as 'busy' or 'free'. When there are no wagons attached it is free, otherwise it is busy. Wagons containing data can be attached to the locomotive whenever it passes a station if it is not already busy. When wagons are attached the locomotive is marked as busy and the destination address of wagons is marked on the locomotive. The destination station must detach the wagons as they pass and mark the locomotive as free.

A single token is used in most token rings. It circulates continuously and there is a monitor station that injects a free token if it is missing (to initialize the network and to guard against loss of the token when a station fails). In the IEEE Token Ring the token occupies 3 bytes and a single bit in the token is used to indicate whether it is busy or free. When the token is free, no other data circulates in the ring. When it is busy, the token is followed by a sequence of address and data field bytes. The formats of packets and tokens are shown below.

3 bytes	6 bytes	6 bytes	≤ 5000 bytes	4 bytes	1 byte	1 byte
token	destination address	source address	data for transmission	frame check sequence	end delimiter	frame status

A token has the following format:

1 byte	1 byte	1 byte
starting delimiter	access control	frame control

The *starting delimiter* byte has a fixed bit pattern that enables stations to recognize the start of a frame and synchronize to the data transmission rate. The 8 bits in the *access control* field are used to distinguish between busy and free tokens, to identify the priority of the frame that is being transmitted (3 bits) and to reserve the next free frame with a given priority (3 bits). The monitor station uses the eighth bit to help it to check that the ring is functioning correctly.

The operation of the token ring follows the pattern defined in our 'freight train' analogy. A station wishing to send a message checks the access control field and sets the busy bit if it is free. The source and destination address fields are inserted by the sending station, and the message data is appended to them, followed by the frame check sequence and the end delimiter. The destination station sets the access control field to free and removes all of the trailing fields from the token.

We will not detail the use of the priority and reservation bits in the access control field; their purpose is to enable a variety of regimes for sharing of the channel capacity amongst the stations on the network. One important consequence is that they can be used to ensure a fair distribution of the channel capacity amongst stations waiting to transmit messages, preventing the hogging of the available bandwidth by one or two stations.

The token ring enjoys the advantages of the Cambridge Ring cited above, but does not suffer from the drawbacks of small fixed-size packets (the packets may in principle be of almost any length; the limitation to 5000 bytes is a default value for a parameter that can be configured on a per-installation basis). The requirement for a monitor station is the most severe remaining drawback.

3.4 Protocols for distributed systems

As we have already indicated, a simplified version of the layered protocol model is needed for distributed systems. The goal is to enable client processes to communicate with server processes with the minimum of delay. The delays involved in the transmission of a message are composed of a **latency** – the overhead incurred in initiating the communication – and a **transmission time** proportional to the number of bits transmitted. For satisfactory performance, the total transmission time for short messages should be of the order of a few hundred microseconds or a few milliseconds rather than tens of milliseconds, and the data transmission rate should be at least 1 million bits per second.

To minimize the latency, transfers of control between software modules and copying of data between processes must be minimized. Much of the responsibility for acknowledgements, error detection, conversions between data representations, acknowledgement messages and error handling to ensure reliable communication can be handled at the application level – by the remote procedure calling software or by the client and server programs – reducing the protocol complexity and hence the overheads at lower levels. The very high reliability of communication in local networks makes this a realistic approach. In local networks no routing of packets is needed and the network layer of protocols that takes responsibility for this in the ISO model is redundant.

Hence a datagram transport-level protocol and a data link layer are sufficient to support the needs of most client–server based distributed systems. The resulting communication architecture is often referred to as a set of **lightweight protocols**.

3.4.1 Support for client–server communication

Chapter 4 describes the design and implementation of remote procedure calling software and discusses the advantages and limitations of its use. Remote procedure calling, or some variant of it is widely used for client–server communication in distributed systems and applications. We have illustrated, in Figure 3.1, the communication actions between clients and servers. Whether or not RPC is used, the format of the communication between clients and servers takes the form of exchanges of messages. The simplest form of exchange consists of a request message from a client to a server and a reply message from the server to the client. We shall see in Section 4.5 that more complex exchanges involving acknowledgement messages are needed when the request or the reply contains a large amount of data, as is often the case for file access requests. Our discussion here deals with the simple case†, but the addition of acknowledgement messages does not significantly alter the requirements.

Transport layer □   Direct support for remote procedure calling and similar request–reply exchanges can be provided by a message passing (or *datagram*) transport level protocol. Client processes send request messages to server processes and then wait for a reply and server processes accept request messages and send back reply messages. Each communication takes the form of a single message transmitted between two processes.

This form of communication can be supported by a transport-level module that provides two message communication primitives: *Send* and *Receive*, defined as follows. A call to the *Send* operation specifies the destination and a sequence of data items to be transmitted; a call to *Receive* specifies the source from which a message is expected and a memory space where the incoming message is to be stored. However, because servers should be prepared to receive request messages from many clients, the source in a *Receive* operation may be left unspecified by quoting a distinguished source address that represents 'any source'.

---

†   In some cases a reply is not necessary. For example, we have noted in Section 2.3.2 that a response is not needed for many window server operations, since their purpose is to change the workstation's screen.

Even in this simple form of message transmission there are a number of variations. The send and receive operations may be **blocking** or **non-blocking**. In blocking communication messages are not buffered; whenever a *Send* or a *Receive* is issued the sending or the receiving process is blocked until another process has arrived at the corresponding point in its sequence of execution so that the message can be transmitted. Note that the use of a blocking *Send* by a client does not result in the client waiting for a *reply* form the server, it merely causes the client to wait until a server is ready to *Receive* the message that the client wishes to send. The client's RPC software must then issue a blocking *Receive* to wait for the server's reply.

In non-blocking communication, messages are buffered and sending and receiving processes are not blocked. Whenever a *Send* is executed the message is copied to a buffer in the address space of the sending process and the process is then allowed to proceed. If a message transmission fails for any reason, the sending process is informed by an interrupt or signal. Similarly a receiving process proceeds with its program after issuing a *Receive*; it will then be interrupted whenever a message has been received and placed in a specified buffer.

In a system environment that supports multiple processes in a single processor, blocking communication has few disadvantages, and the simplicity of synchronizing communicating processes is a substantial advantage. Non-blocking communication appears to be more efficient, but it involves extra complexity in buffer management and introduces the difficulties associated with interrupt-controlled programs. If blocking communication is used as the basic transmission method, buffering may be added to provide the effect of non-blocking communication at the cost of adding an extra software layer where necessary. For example, in the case of window server functions that do not produce a reply (referred to above) there is a performance gain if clients can make several remote calls and they are transmitted in a single message; a message buffer is introduced in each client and clients are not blocked for the window server to receive each request.

An optimized transport layer □   When client–server exchanges are performed using *Send* and *Receive*, four transport-layer operations are invoked; two *Send* and two *Receive* operations. Amoeba [Mullender and Tanenbaum 1985] and Cheriton's V System [Cheriton 1984] have protocols designed to support the pattern of communication occurring in remote procedure calls more directly and hence to reduce the system software overheads, by introducing a trio of message communication primitives: *Request*, *GetRequest* and *SendReply*. *Request* takes a destination (the transport address of a server port), the identifier of the desired server function and a memory space where the reply is to be stored.

When *Request* is used by a client process the process is blocked until the server performs the requested function and transmits a reply message to the client process. These specially designed protocols automatically connect reply messages to the clients that sent the call message and they may also deal with numbering of messages so that duplicates may be recognized; whereas, if the simple *Send* and *Receive* operations are used, the connection must be done by

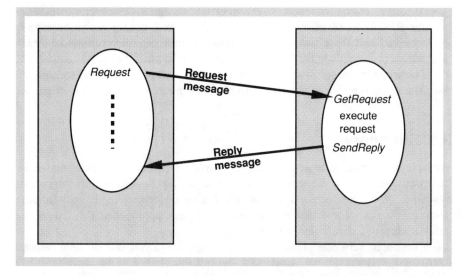

Figure 3.6 Transport primitives for remote procedure calls.

software at a level above the transport layer.

GetRequest is used by a server process to acquire service requests a shown in Figure 3.6. When the server has completed the requested action it uses *SendReply* to send the reply message. When the reply message is received by the client the original *Request* is unblocked, and execution of the client program continues. This set of transport layer primitives supports the the relationship of client to server well and entails only three calls to the transport layer software for each client–server exchange.

Network error handling □ Datagram communication is potentially unreliable – that is, network errors are not detected in the transport level software. The frequency of errors in local networks is so low that it is more appropriate to deal with the possibility of errors at the application level. When a datagram transport service is used for client–server communication, the RPC software must deal with the following failure modes:

- *Lost messages*: This aspect of the unreliability of datagrams could result in the non-delivery of the request message to the server or non-delivery of the reply message to the client. In both cases, the client is blocked indefinitely. A *timeout* primitive is typically provided to enable the client to terminate the wait for a reply message. A lost message could result, for example when a packet is dropped as the check sum is incorrect.

In internetworks the following may also occur:

- *Duplicate messages*: These are filtered out by the RPC software. Request messages and reply messages have a *request identifier* and a *message identifier*. These will be identical only in duplicated messages.

- *Messages out of sequence*: This property of datagrams causes no difficulties for RPC because clients are blocked after a call until a reply message is received and the client checks that the *request identifier* returned in each reply corresponds to the *request identifier* sent in the most recent request.
- *Damaged messages*: These are detected by the use of checksum techniques. The result is an RPC-generated program exception condition in the client.

3.5 Summary

We have not attempted to give a comprehensive treatment of computer networks; that would require a book in itself and there are several satisfactory texts available. We have focussed on the networking concepts and designs that are needed as a basis for distributed systems and have approached them from the point of view of a distributed system designer.

Computer networks have been developed for a variety of applications; distributed systems are an important application, but not the only one. In distributed systems most communication is client–server communication and high performance is needed because client–server interactions are frequent; they replace the *system calls* in centralized systems. Two performance parameters are important: transmission speed and latency.

Local area networks perform substantially better in both respects than wide-area networks, provided that the network software is tailored to the needs of distributed systems. In practice, all of the leading local network technologies (Ethernet, slotted ring, token ring) perform satisfactorily in distributed systems and there is little to choose between them. Their behaviour under heavy loads is different, but most distributed systems do not generate communication loads that exhibit these differences.

The main difference between wide-area and local networks is that packets are transmitted in a store-and-forward fashion along a selected route through the network in wide-area networks, whereas in local networks packets are transmitted from source to destination without routing. The networking principles described in Section 3.2 were established to meet a wide range of needs, primarily in wide-area network environments. They have to be modified for distributed systems – the requirements are simpler than for wide-area applications, but performance is more critical. We have outlined these requirements in Section 3.3 and they are discussed in detail in Chapter 4.

EXERCISES

3.1 Describe the way in which network software is arranged as a hierarchy of layers. How are peer-to-peer protocols used in this context, and what are their two main concerns?

3.2 The ISO OSI reference model has seven layers with the transport layer in the middle. Describe the task of the transport layer. Explain virtual circuits and datagrams.

3.3 Describe briefly the function of each of the three layers below the transport layer. Which of these layers are included in the hardware of the Ethernet, the Cambridge Ring and the Token Ring?

3.4 Describe datagram communication in local area networks. What errors can occur when unreliable datagrams are used in (a) local area networks, (b) internetworks?

3.5 Explain the reasons for using fewer than seven protocol layers in local area networks.

3.6 Describe the functions of the presentation layer and their relevance to remote procedure calling over a local area network.

3.7 Describe how the channel is acquired for transmission in the Ethernet, the Cambridge Ring and the Token Ring. What is the factor determining the time of waiting in each case? Is this time affected by the overall size of the network?

3.8 Describe the advantages and disadvantages of using an Ethernet when compared with the Cambridge Ring and the Token Ring. What additional advantage does the Token Ring have when compared with the Cambridge Ring?

3.9 Describe blocking and non-blocking communication. Explain the difficulties in implementing the latter. Explain the requirements for a kernel to be used in servers that must be able to receive incoming request messages as well as to perform service operations and send (blocking) reply messages.

3.10 Describe the transport level operations for sending and receiving messages. Describe, in terms of these, the sequence of operations performed by client and server when the former makes a remote procedure call to the latter.

3.11 Describe an optimization of the message passing operations that is suitable for remote procedure calling.

3.12 What are the advantages and disadvantages of applying encryption at a high level, for example in the application or presentation layer, and at a lower level, for example the datalink layer.

Chapter 4
Remote Procedure Calling

This chapter introduces the issues that arise in the use of remote procedure calls (RPCs) and describes several approaches to their implementation. The differences between ordinary procedure calls and RPCs are mainly due to the fact that the calling and the called procedure are in separate processes, usually in separate computers:

- Remote procedure calls and results are sent in messages between client and server.
- They are prone to the failure of one or other of the computers or processes and to communication failure.
- They have separate lifetimes and do not share the same address space.
- The calling process needs to locate the computer and process that will execute the RPC.

We discuss the use of interface definitions as a basis for separate compilation of clients and servers and describe the implementation of RPC mechanisms in two different kinds of system environment:

1. on top of an operating system that supports message passing between processes – taking a specific RPC software package designed for use in BSD 4.2 UNIX as an example;
2. with a server constructed as a set of lightweight processes in a system environment that supports message passing between host computers, but not between processes.

4.1 Introduction

In this chapter we discuss remote procedure calling as a mechanism for constructing distributed programs. A distributed computer system can be viewed as a set of software components running in a number of computers in a network. Users interact with application programs which may be clients of any of the services available in the network. The service programs may themselves be clients of other service programs. Such combinations of application programs and servers can be regarded as distributed programs.

The procedure call is a well-understood mechanism for communication within a program. In the design of conventional programs procedures play an important role in decomposing a program into separate components. Standardized components may also be included through the use of procedure libraries. Some programming languages also provide support for data abstraction by the use of modules or abstract data types. The construction of distributed programs requires similar mechanisms. The remote procedure call (RPC) is modelled on the local procedure call, but the called procedure is executed in a different process and usually a different computer from the caller. The use of remote procedure calling facilitates the building of distributed programs, removing concern for the communication mechanisms from the programs that use remote procedures, leaving only the fundamental difficulties of building distributed systems such as synchronization and independent failure of components (see Section 2.3.2) and the coexistence of independent execution environments. Application programs can make use of distributed services by calls to remote procedures by name without knowing their location thus allowing complete configurability of a distributed system in terms of the location of its components.

Conventional procedure calling □ We will first describe procedure calling as it occurs in non-distributed programs. When a procedure is called control is transferred to the sequence of instructions that constitutes the body of the procedure. The procedure body is executed in a newly-created execution environment that includes copies of the arguments given in the calling instruction. When the procedure has been executed, control returns to the calling point, possibly returning a result.

In most commonly-used procedural languages, including Pascal, Modula-2 and C, the environment in which a called procedure is executed is an extension of the environment in which the calling instruction was executed. This means that the procedure can modify the calling environment. It has access to the names of any global variables declared in the program and to any other data objects whose addresses were passed to it as arguments.

Parameters □ The uses of parameters in procedure calling can be classified as being for *input* or *output* purposes. In the former case, the purpose is to pass values into the execution environment of the procedure when it is called. In the latter, it is to transfer values from the execution environment back to the calling environment when it returns. Parameters used only for input can use the mechanism known as *call by value*, in which copies of arguments are transferred

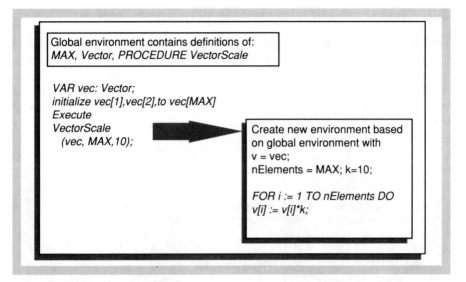

Figure 4.1 Environment diagram for local procedure call *VectorScale*.

```
TYPE   Vector = ARRAY [1..MAX] OF INTEGER;
VAR   vec:Vector;

PROCEDURE VectorScale(VAR v: Vector; nElements, k: INTEGER);
      VAR   i: CARDINAL;
BEGIN
      FOR i := 1 TO nElements DO v[i] := v[i]*k;
END VectorScale;

BEGIN
      (* initialize vec[1], vec[2], ... vec[MAX] *)
      VectorScale(vec, MAX, 10)
END Example.
```

Figure 4.2 *VectorScale* procedure.

to the procedure's execution environment. Parameters used for output normally use *call by reference*, in which the address of the argument is passed and the procedure accesses or modifies the values stored in the calling environment as shown in Figure 4.1, which shows the execution environment created when the program in Figure 4.2 calls the procedure *VectorScale*.

Some parameters are used for both input and output; they also require *call by reference*. The Modula-2 procedure to multiply each of the elements of a vector *v* by a factor *k* illustrates a typical use of reference parameters (denoted by the prefix *VAR* in Modula-2).

4.2 Characteristics of remote procedure calling

The idea behind remote procedure calls is simple: to allow a program to call procedures in a different computer or in a different address space in the same computer. The remote procedure call is sent in the form of a **request message** to a remote process that is able to receive the call, execute the procedure and send back a **reply message**. Figure 4.3 is an illustration of a remote procedure call from a process in one computer to a separate process in another computer.

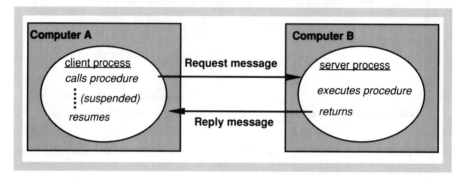

Figure 4.3 A remote procedure call.

For the most part, the semantics are analogous to local procedure calls – the calling program is suspended until the called procedure returns; the caller can pass arguments to the remote procedure and the procedure can return a result.

In contrast to local procedures, remote procedures cannot have access to any variables or data values in the calling program's environment, since the procedure is executed in an address space that is disjoint from the calling program's address space.

Parameters in remote procedure calls □ RPC systems provide for input and output parameters as follows: when a remote procedure call is made, the values of the input arguments are sent in the request message to the remote procedure and copied into its execution environment; when the remote procedure returns it sends back the values of the output arguments in the reply message and these are copied into the calling environment as shown in Figure 4.4.

The parameter *v* in the Modula-2 procedure *VectorScale* given in Figure 4.2 is used both as an input and an output parameter. If *VectorScale* were implemented as a remote procedure the corresponding argument value would have to be transferred in both directions. The parameters *nElements* and *k* are used only for *input*, so they need only be copied from the calling environment into the procedure's execution environment.

Conventional programs include functions or procedures that return results. The same is true of remote procedures. In practice, most remote procedures do return results and these are included in reply messages, together with the output arguments.

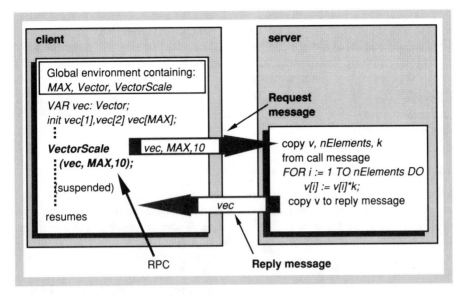

Figure 4.4 Environment diagram for remote procedure call *VectorScale*.

Arguments containing pointers □   As remote procedures are executed in a separate address space from their callers, it would be meaningless to pass addresses in arguments. Similarly, it is meaningless to pass argument values containing pointer structures (e.g. linked lists), since pointers are normally represented by memory addresses. In many RPC systems the programmer must avoid input or output arguments containing addresses.

Some RPC systems □   In a classic paper Birrell and Nelson [1984] describe the RPC mechanism they built for the Cedar programming environment, using datagram communication over the Xerox internet. They based their RPCs on the Mesa language [Mitchell et al. 1979] and aimed to make RPC as simple to use as ordinary procedure calls.

This work was preceded by the publication of Xerox Courier RPC [Xerox 1981], a standard intended to be used for building remote applications. Courier was used in the implementation of Clearinghouse, the successor to Grapevine (see Chapter 11). Courier is designed to be used for internetwork applications and is based on virtual circuits (Section 3.2.2) which do not satisfy the performance requirements for building distributed programs in local area networks.

The Argus language developed at MIT by Liskov and described in Section 10.3.1 is designed for the construction of distributed programs and remote procedure calls are integrated into the language. The Argus language is based on the CLU language developed earlier at MIT to support data abstraction. Argus provides **guardians** – these are modules that may be used to provide services and they are intended to be accessed by remote procedure call. The procedures in a guardian are called **handlers** and a call to a handler is automatically treated as a remote call.

Several RPC mechanisms have been built for use in UNIX systems. These include Courier RPC based on the Courier standard and Sun RPC on which Sun NFS (described in Chapter 1) is based. They also include the Admiral RPC system developed at University College London by Wilbur and Bacarisse [1987] and used as an example later in this chapter.

Clients and servers □   In this chapter, we will refer to the process that calls a remote procedure as a client and the process that executes the procedure as a server.

4.2.1 Marshalling arguments and results

Marshalling is the process of taking the arguments and results of a procedure call, assembling them into a form suitable for transmission across a network and disassembling them on arrival. For example, if the procedure *VectorScale* in Figure 4.2 is called as a remote procedure as follows:

     VectorScale(vector, 10, 25);

the arguments would be assembled in a flattened form, as shown in Figure 4.5 and sent in a request message. On arrival, the arguments are unflattened and interpreted as indicated by the parameter types in the procedure definition. The order and the method by which arguments are marshalled must be known by the client and server.

     Marshalling procedures for scalar data types, together with procedures to marshal compound types built from the scalar ones, are usually provided as a part of the RPC software, but some systems allow the programmer to define marshalling procedures for types that include pointers. For example, in Concurrent CLU, developed for use in the Cambridge Distributed Computer System [Bacon and Hamilton 1988], for user-defined types, the type definition must contain procedures for marshalling.

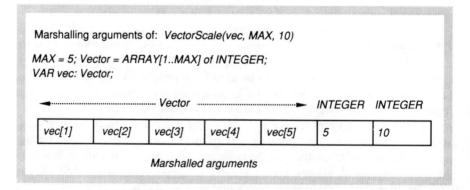

Figure 4.5 Marshalling the arguments of *VectorScale*.

     A list structure could be marshalled by converting it into a relative form from which the original form can be reconstructed on arrival. If the RPC implementation does not allow marshalling for pointer structures, then the programmer may provide mechanisms for marshalling but this is not very convenient.

4.2.2 Exception handling

When a server procedure discovers in the arguments supplied an error or an inconsistency that it cannot resolve, there must be a way for it to report this to the caller. For example, when using a file server a client might quote an invalid file identifier, or attempt to read beyond the end of a file. This falls under the general heading of *exception handling* and corresponds to a similar requirement in conventional operating systems to report exception conditions arising in system functions. In UNIX and other conventional operating systems, the system functions deliver a well-known value to indicate failure and further information about the type of error is reported in a variable inserted into the environment of the calling program. A similar method is often used in RPC systems designed for use with existing programming languages that have no exception handling mechanisms. This method requires the caller to test every return value and, in the case of failure, to request further information about the type of error.

The Xerox Courier RPC protocol defines an extension to conventional procedure semantics that enables an error report to be passed explicitly to the caller, instead of a result, as the response to the calling instruction. When a procedure is defined, input and output parameter types are specified and in addition an error report specification is given, containing the names used to identify the various types of error that may occur.

Some recent programming languages including CLU [Liskov et al. 1981] and Mesa provide language constructs for exception handling in which the expected result of a procedure is either a normal result or an exception consisting of a name describing the exception and sometimes some results. The exception handling mechanism consists of two parts, the **raising of exceptions** and their **handling procedures**. When an error occurs in a procedure, an exception is raised and the appropriate handling procedure is automatically executed in the caller's environment. We do not include a full explanation of exception handling in this book; the reader is referred to Liskov and Guttag [1986] for further information. The provision of exception handling saves the programmer from the need to test the result of each call and a similar facility may be provided in an RPC system. Birrell and Nelson [1984] provided exception handling in Cedar RPC based on the facilities in Mesa for notifying exceptions, in which the remote procedure can send an exception in a reply message; when it is received in the caller's process, the exception handling procedure is called.

4.2.3 Separate lifetime of client and server

In remote procedure calling the process that executes the call has an independent lifetime from that of the caller. There are two distinct cases:

1. An RPC execution process is created for each particular client or for each particular procedure call. For example, in Argus, a new process is created at the receiving guardian (server) to execute each handler (remote procedure) and several instances of the same handler may exist at the same time. When the handler procedure terminates, the systems kills the process.
2. The process that executes the calls runs continuously (e.g. as a service), repeatedly listening for request messages, executing the appropriate procedure and returning reply messages. A server that runs continuously may be called by any number of clients. In this case the static or global variables accessible during execution of the remote procedure are shared by all the callers.

If there is only a single server process, calls can only be serviced one at a time. However, if several concurrent processes are available, several calls can be served simultaneously but the server software must handle synchronization of access to any shared data that it uses in main memory or files.

In the Cedar environment, programs can create lightweight processes or threads that can share variables. In Cedar RPC, a single process is devoted to receiving request messages and a pool of worker processes is available for executing remote procedures. When a request message arrives it is handed on to an idle worker process that executes the procedure and returns the reply message.

4.2.4 RPC call semantics

A remote procedure call is completed if a request message goes from client to server and the corresponding reply message is successfully returned. However, successful completion is not guaranteed because messages may be lost† or one of the computers may fail. Any one of the following problems may arise:

1. The request message is lost.
2. The reply message is lost.
3. The server crashes and is re-started.
4. The client crashes and is re-started.

RPC mechanisms usually include timeouts to prevent clients waiting indefinitely for reply messages, and if there is a time out after (1) the remote procedure has not yet been called, after (2) it has been called, and after (3) and (4) it may have been called. The fifth possibility is that there has been no failure and the procedure may or may not yet have been called. This known as **maybe** call semantics, because clients cannot tell for sure whether remote procedures have been called or not.

To be sure that the remote procedure is called at least once, the client can try again repeatedly after timeouts until it either gets a reply or can tell that the server has failed. Eventually, when the RPC is completed, the client will not know how

---

†   We mentioned in Chapter 3 that datagrams are normally used for RPC messages and that their inherent unreliability can result in lost messages.

many times it has been called. This is called **at-least-once** call semantics.

Some operations can have the wrong effect if they are performed more than once. For example, an operation to increase a bank balance by $10 should only be performed once; if it were to be repeated, the balance could grow and grow! To allow the use of such non-repeatable operations, RPCs should be designed to be called exactly once. Birrell and Nelson guarantee in Cedar RPC that if the server does not crash and the client receives the result of a call, then the procedure has been called exactly once. Otherwise, an exception is reported and the procedure will have been called either once or not at all. This is known as **at-most-once** call semantics and is the one usually chosen in RPC implementations. However, if a server can be designed with repeatable operations in all of its remote procedures, then at-least-once call semantics may be acceptable.

4.2.5 Transparency of RPC

Birrell and Nelson aimed to make remote procedure calls as much like local procedure calls as possible and there is no distinction in syntax between a local and a remote procedure call. Procedure definitions are used to obtain the names and parameter types of remote procedures and the Cedar RPC software automatically provides the necessary calls to marshalling and message passing procedures for the client. However, arguments cannot contain pointers. Although request messages are retransmitted after a timeout, this is transparent to the caller and the duration of remote calls is unlimited provided the server is still running – to make them like local procedure calls.

RPCs are more vulnerable to failure than local calls, since they involve a network, another computer and another process. They consume much more time than local ones – the time taken to call a remote procedure is 100 to 1000 times greater than for a local call. Therefore it can be argued that programs that make use of remote procedures must handle errors that cannot occur in local procedure calls. An alternative philosophy, adopted for Concurrent CLU, is that RPC syntax should not be transparent and the language should be extended to make remote operations explicit to the programmer.

In discussing the design of RPC in Argus, Liskov and Scheifler [1982] say that although the RPC system should hide low-level details of message passing from the user, the possibility of long delay or failure should not be hidden from the caller. The caller should be able to cope with failures according to the demands of the application, possibly by terminating an RPC, and in that case it should have no effect. If clients are allowed to abort RPCs, this can have implications for the design of the server; an aborted RPC should have no effect whatsoever. This implies that even if the server has partially executed a procedure it should be able to restore things to how they were before the procedure was called.

4.2.6 User packages

In Chapter 2 we introduced the notion of client programs running in workstations making use of services provided by remote servers. We can now see that a service can be defined by a set of definitions of remote procedures or an **RPC interface definition**. But, both because of the differences between local and remote procedures and because a service should be defined at a level appropriate for the widest possible use, the RPC interface is not necessarily the most convenient for client programs.

Services are often supported by a **user package**; this is a library of conventional procedures that can be linked into application programs. The user package would typically be implemented as a part of the service it supports. Figure 4.6 shows the relationship between an application program, a user package and the RPC interface. The RPC software translates procedure calls and their arguments into messages, sends request messages to the server, receives reply messages and translates the latter to data values.

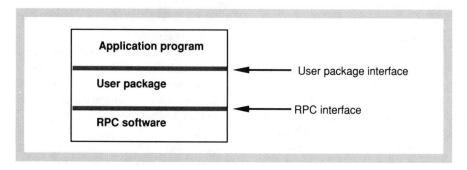

Figure 4.6 Levels in the client software.

The user package contains within it remote procedure calls to procedures in the server and presents to application programs a higher-level, convenient local procedural interface. This may be compared to UNIX, where input/output in C is done through a **standard input/output library** based on **system calls**. The user package corresponds to the former and the remote procedures in the interface correspond to the latter. Because remote calls can be concealed from application programs, the use of a user package has the additional advantage that the application programmer can be insulated from the extra notation and initialization involved in using remote procedures.

It may sometimes reduce the complexity of the remote service to put some of the server's functionality in the user package. But the procedures in the user package must only perform activities that can be safely handled outside the server without compromising the reliability or security of the service as seen by other clients. As we shall see in Chapter 9, when considering the security of a service in a distributed system it is useful to distinguish between trusted and untrusted software. In this sense, software such as the user package which runs in workstations is untrusted, since it may be intentionally or inadvertently modified.

We shall see in Chapter 8 that when a file service (or any other service) is based on a number of cooperating servers in separate computers, the user package can perform the task of locating a particular server. This makes the distribution of the service transparent to the user.

4.3 Interface definitions

An **RPC interface** defines those characteristics of the procedures provided by a server that are visible to the server's clients. The characteristics that must be defined include the names of the procedures and the types of their parameters. Each parameter should also be defined as *input*, *output* or both, to enable the RPC system to marshal the values of the arguments.

RPC systems include a notation for defining RPC interfaces as a basis for separate compilation and binding of client and server. An interface definition contains a list of procedure names, together with the types of their input and output arguments. Interface compilers can be designed to compile interfaces into a number of different languages enabling clients and servers written in different languages to communicate using remote procedure calls.

It is important to ensure that the input arguments passed and the output arguments expected in a remote procedure call match (in number and type) the input and output parameters of the called procedure. For conventional procedure calling in most programming languages these checks are performed by the compiler. In many recently-designed procedural languages (e.g. Modula-2, CLU, Mesa and Ada) the information about the parameters of procedures needed to perform the checks (in the case of conventional procedure calls) is given in a distinguished part of the program – called a *definition module* in Modula-2. A program may contain several definition modules and each definition module gives parameter specifications for a related group of procedures.

The definition and use of remote procedures in distributed systems requires a similar construct to ensure that the calls to remote procedures are consistent with the procedure definitions. RPC systems generally include an **interface language** to enable programmers to specify the RPC interfaces of services, although an RPC system that is part of a language that already includes a facility to specify interfaces, including the input and output properties of parameters, does not require a separate interface language – this was the case in Cedar RPC. However, a separate interface language is required when RPC is to be added to a language such as C or Pascal that has no facility for interface definition, or when the aim is to provide RPC between clients and servers in different language environments. Unfortunately, Modula-2 definition modules do not include definitions of the input and output properties of procedure parameters, so separate interface definitions are required for them.

Interface languages □ An interface language typically provides a number of scalar types, for example character, boolean, integer and real, together with facilities for defining structured types such as arrays, strings and records based on the scalar types. The notation is rich enough to define the parameters and results of procedure calls in languages that do not themselves have facilities for the separate definition of these properties of procedures. Figure 4.15 shows an interface definition in the Admiral interface language and is followed in Figure 4.16 by the corresponding procedure declarations in the C language.

An interface language can be defined to be applicable to a range of underlying procedural languages. For example, the Xerox Courier RPC interface language was originally specified for use with the Mesa programming language, but was subsequently published as the Courier standard and applied to both Mesa and to C. The Cedar RPC protocol using Mesa interfaces has also been implemented in both InterLisp and Smalltalk [Teitelman 1983], allowing applications running in entirely different environments to communicate with one another.

The Matchmaker interface language and compiler [Jones and Rashid 1986] is used in the Mach environment (see Section 2.4.1). It was designed to allow distributed programs to be built from multiple existing programming languages by using remote procedure calls. The Mach environment currently supports the languages Common Lisp, C, Ada and Pascal. Both clients and servers can be built in any of these languages.

4.3.1 Data abstraction

The ability to combine a group of procedures and variables in a module and to export only selected procedure names was introduced in programming languages such as Modula-2, CLU and Ada as a method for structuring programs. The idea underlying this technique for structuring programs is called *data abstraction*. The use of Modula-2 modules does not necessarily result in data abstraction, but if the procedures exported by a module are defined to provide a complete set of operations on a given class of data object, this is called an *abstract data type*. In distributed systems, a server may be viewed as defining one or more data abstractions. For example, a file server provides a complete set of operations on the class of objects called files.

DEFINITION MODULE FileReadWrite;
EXPORT QUALIFIED Write, Read, fileIdentifier;
TYPE fileIdentifier;   (defined in the corresponding implementation module *)*
PROCEDURE Write(F: fileIdentifier; position : CARDINAL;
*   data: ARRAY[1..MAX] of CHAR);*
PROCEDURE Read(F :fileIdentifier; position, length:CARDINAL;
*   VAR data:ARRAY[1..MAX] of CHAR);*
END FileReadWrite.

Figure 4.7 *FileReadWrite* module.

In many ways, RPC interface definitions for services in distributed systems are similar to module definitions. In Modula-2 the names of the procedures defined in a module are hidden from the other modules of a program unless they are explicitly *exported* and other modules can make use of the names exported by a given module by *importing* them. The requirements for remote procedure calling are quite similar although the caller and the remote procedure run in separate processes.

A definition module in Modula-2 for a part of a file service is shown in Figure 4.7. The objects whose names are exported from the definition module are made available to other modules whereas the implementation module that implements the procedures and gives the definitions of the exported type names is concealed from the other modules. Each module that uses the exported procedures will contain an *IMPORT* statement e.g.:

FROM FileReadWrite IMPORT Write, Read, fileIdentifier;

A definition in an RPC interface language has the same components as a Modula-2 *definition module* and the name of the RPC interface (corresponding to the name given in the *DEFINITION MODULE* statement) is exported to a binder when the server starts executing and is used at run-time for clients to obtain access to the relevant service via a binder.

4.3.2 Processing an interface definition

The interface definition may be used to produce the necessary marshalling operations, to ensure that request messages are dispatched to the appropriate procedure in the server and to enable the server to export and the client to import the interface. The interface definition may also be used to perform compile-time type checking in the client program by checking the calls to the remote procedures against the definitions in the interface definition; and to type check the server program by comparing the definitions of the procedures against the interface definition. When an interface language is used to enable programs in conventional languages to use RPCs, the interface definition is processed by an **interface compiler**.

Marshalling □ The definitions of the parameters of the procedures in an interface can be used to generate appropriate marshalling operations, one for each procedure defined in the interface. In clients, the marshalling operations assemble the input arguments in request messages and reconstruct the output arguments from incoming reply messages. In servers, the marshalling operations reconstruct the input arguments from incoming request messages and assemble output arguments in reply messages.

Dispatching □ Each procedure in an interface is given a unique procedure identifier (they are usually numbered 0, 1, 2 ... in order) and the procedure identifier is included in request messages. Servers include a 'dispatcher' that calls the procedure indicated by the procedure identifier in the incoming request message.

Imports and exports □   In server programs the name of the interface is exported and in client programs the interface is imported.

4.4 Binding

There are three aspects to the binding of remote procedure calls:

1. The client must locate a server that will execute the procedure. It would be impractical to bind the host address of a server into the client program at compilation time – the location of the server could then be changed only if every program that calls it were to be re-compiled.
2. The types of the arguments and results given by the client must conform to those expected by the remote procedure. These are resolved by using a common RPC interface when compiling the client and server programs.
3. As the client and server programs are compiled separately and often at different times, it is necessary to ensure that they are both compiled from the same RPC interface.

Using a binder □   The method normally used to deal with (1) and (3) is to make use of a **binder** as discussed in Section 2.4.5. This is a service that maintains a table of the names and locations of all currently exported services, together with a checksum to identify the version of the interface used at the time of export. The same service may run in several computers and we refer to these as **instances** of the service.

When an instance of a service starts executing, its interface is **exported**. This involves notifying the binder that it is available, by giving the name of the interface and the address of the process or computer it is running in, together with a checksum calculated from the interface. Servers can withdraw their own instances of services by notifying the binder. A typical service interface for a binder would include the procedures shown in Figure 4.8.

PROCEDURE Register(serviceName:String; location:Port; checkSum:integer)
    (* causes the binder to record an instance of a service in its table,
       together with a checksum *)
PROCEDURE Withdraw (serviceName:String; location:Port; checkSum:integer)
    (* causes the binder to remove an instance of the service from its table*)
PROCEDURE WhereIs (serviceName:String; checkSum:integer): Port
    (* the binder looks up the named service and returns its location
      if the checksum agrees with the one stored in its table *)

Figure 4.8 Binder interface.

When a client program starts, it can be bound to an instance of a service, by making one *WhereIs* request to a binder to discover its location. The interface checksum is used to ensure that the client and server have been compiled from the same interface definition. The client program continues to use the same instance of the service until it fails, at which point it may contact the binder and attempt to get a new binding. If there are several instances of a service, the binder may return them all and leave the client to select a particular one. An alternative strategy is for the binder to pick an instance at random.

Grapevine as a binder □ We discuss the Grapevine distributed database in detail in Chapter 11. Birrell and Nelson use Grapevine as the binder for Cedar RPCs. The Grapevine database is distributed in a large number of servers in the Xerox internet and is very reliable – it maintains at least three separate copies of each entry. Entries in the Grapevine database are not always updated immediately. This is acceptable for long-lived services, but applications that require frequently changing bindings would require a more dynamic form of binder.

The Grapevine database includes access controls that restrict who may export particular interface names. This makes it possible to prevent unauthorized software, for example in workstations, from masquerading as a service.

4.5 The RPC software

The software that supports remote procedure calling has three main tasks:

1. transmitting request messages and reply messages using a message passing protocol;
2. marshalling arguments and, in the server, dispatching calls to the requested procedure;
3. combining the RPC modules with client and server programs in conventional languages.

4.5.1 Message passing

Remote procedure calling mechanisms are usually built above transport layer datagrams, using the blocking *Send* and *Receive* operations described in Section 3.4. A message is passed successfully from sender to recipient only when a *Send* is paired with a *Receive*. We summarize the reasons for preferring datagrams to virtual circuits here:

1. RPC messages are generally short and the establishment of a connection is an undesirable overhead.
2. Server computers may need to serve a large number of clients and the storing of state information relating to connections is undesirable.
3. Local area networks are reliable.

Message passing module □ There is a message passing module in both the client and the server programs whose task is to deal with communication between them. Both the request and the reply message can be represented by a single record type as in Figure 4.9.

```
TYPE Message = RECORD
      messageType: {Request, Reply};
      requestId : INTEGER;   (* one per RPC *)
      messageId: INTEGER;    (* one per request message *)
      sourceAddress: Port;   (* or network address of client *)
      procedureId: INTEGER;
      arguments: flattenedList;
END;
```

Figure 4.9 Message structure.

The client generates a *messageId* for each request message and the server copies them into the corresponding reply messages. This enables clients to check that a reply message is the result of the current RPC, not from a delayed earlier call.

As we saw in Section 4.2.4 the client sometimes times out and retransmits a request. The client generates a *requestId* for each remote procedure call and puts the same one in each request message so that the server may recognize and filter out duplicates. To support at-most-once call semantics, servers keep records of all outstanding requests including those they are currently working on, and when a duplicate request message arrives they replace the *messageId* in the record with the latest one. However, a repeated request from a client could arrive after the server has sent the reply message, for example, if a reply message is lost, so servers also keep a record of the reply to the last request executed for each client so that they can if necessary retransmit the reply message.

```
VAR m:Message;
m.messageType:= Request;
m.requestId := MakeId();
m.messageId := MakeId();            (* MakeId – generates an id *)
m.sourceAddress:= 42.100.100.3; (* e.g. an internet address *)
m.procedureId:=0;                   (* Write = 0, Read = 1 *)
m.arguments:= {12345, 100, 5, "hello"}; (* flattened *)
```

Figure 4.10 Message data structure for *Write(12345, 100, 5, "hello")*.

The request message must specify the *procedureId* of the particular procedure to be executed – a small integer generated from the interface specification and the values of the input arguments in marshalled form in the field called *arguments*. The request message also includes the client's port or network address for use by the server when returning the reply message.

In the server's reply message *arguments* contains the output arguments in marshalled form. Figure 4.10 illustrates the values assigned to make an RPC to the procedure *Write* in the interface defined in Figure 4.6.

4.5.2 RPC exchange protocols

The *Send* and *Receive* operations defined in Section 3.4 are very basic in that they do not provide acknowledgement and are able to carry only a single datagram whose length is limited (e.g. to 1500 bytes in an Ethernet). They are used to transmit RPC *Request* and *Reply* messages when the input and output arguments can fit into a single datagram. Special acknowledgement messages are not required because a server's *Reply* message is regarded as an acknowledgement of the client's *Request* message. Similarly, a subsequent call from a client may be regarded as an acknowledgement of a server's *Reply* message.

This is known as the **RR** *request/reply* protocol and is useful for most RPCs and if timeouts and retries are used, but if duplicate request messages are not filtered out it provides at-least-once call semantics. However, servers can support at-most-once call semantics by keeping records (as shown in the previous section) that enable them to filter out duplicate request messages and to retransmit reply messages. In situations where a server has a large number of clients, this may result in servers needing to store large quantities of information. In some implementations, servers restrict the quantity of such data by discarding it after a limited period of time. A new protocol that requires clients to acknowledge the receipt of reply messages enables servers to discard such information when it is no longer needed.

RRA protocol □   Spector [1982] describes three protocols that are satisfactory for implementing various types of RPC:

- the *request* (**R**) protocol;
- the *request/reply* (**RR** – see above) protocol;
- the *request/reply/acknowledge-reply* (**RRA**) protocol.

The **R** protocol is used when there is no value to be returned from the procedure executed and the client requires no confirmation that the procedure has been executed, as for example in window servers. This provides **maybe** call semantics, requires no retransmission of request messages and is the least reliable form of RPC semantics. The client may proceed immediately after request messages as there is no need to wait for reply messages.

In the **RRA** protocol the client acknowledges the server's *Reply* messages. It also requires that the unique *messageId*s in *Request* messages must be ordered. The *Acknowledgement* message contains the *messageId* in the *Reply* message being acknowledged. This will be interpreted as acknowledging the receipt of all *Reply* messages with lower *messageId*s, so the loss of an acknowledgement message is harmless. The server is then free to delete all records relating to acknowledged *Reply* messages. The protocols are summarized in Figure 4.11.

Name	Messages sent by		
	Client	Server	Client
R	*Request*		
RR	*Request*	*Reply*	
RRA	*Request*	*Reply*	*Acknowledge-Reply*

Figure 4.11 RPC protocols.

Long messages □   The *Send* and *Receive* operations may not be regarded as adequate for use in RPC messages in which the arguments or results are too big to fit in a single datagram. For example, in a file server, quite large quantities of data may be transferred as input arguments to the *Write* operation or as output arguments of the *Read* operation. It can be argued that the application should arrange to transmit small amounts of data per call, but an alternative solution is to design a protocol on top of the *Send* and *Receive* operations for passing **multipackets**.

The term multipacket is used by Spector to refer to a message made up of a sequence of datagrams. Requests and replies that do not fit within a single datagram can be transmitted as multipackets. Multipackets may be implemented by using *Send* to transmit the components in sequence without acknowledgement or retransmission. In order to interleave multipackets with normal datagrams, each message has a component that indicates whether it is part of a multipacket. The recipient uses *Receive* to collects the parts of a multipacket.

External data representation □   In Section 3.2.3 we mentioned the special needs of RPC in the presentation layer. The input and output arguments transmitted in remote procedure calling can be data values of many different types and not all computers store even simple values such as integers and characters in the same order. In order to be able to exchange data values between any two computers, such values are converted to an agreed external data form before transmission and converted to the local form on receipt. For example, in UNIX interprocess communication, library procedures are provided to convert 16- or 32-bit values from local order to network order and back again. For communication between computers of the same type, the conversion to external data form may be omitted. When virtual circuits are used, pairs of computers may negotiate as to whether to use an external data representation.

The Courier standard defines a representation for the commonly used simple and structured data types including strings, arrays, sequences and records.

Figure 4.12 shows a request message in an external data representation in which the entire message consists of a sequence of 16-bit objects using a convention that a cardinal or integer occupies one object and that two characters also occupy an object. There would be a further convention to define which end of each object is the most significant bit and, when characters are packed, which of the pair comes first. In the example, the RPC interface definition of the procedure *Write* can be used to define the procedure for unmarshalling the sequence of objects.

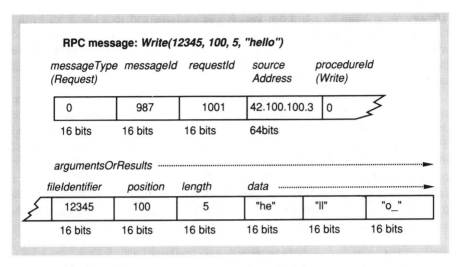

Figure 4.12 Request message for *Write(12345, 100, 5, "hello")*.

4.5.3 Interface compiler

An **interface compiler** may be used as a basis for integration of remote procedure calls into existing programming languages. It processes the interface specification in both the client and server programs. The interface compiler replaces each call to a remote procedure in the client program by a call to a **stub procedure**. This is a procedure in the client program that 'stands-in' for the remote procedure in the server program (Figure 4.13).

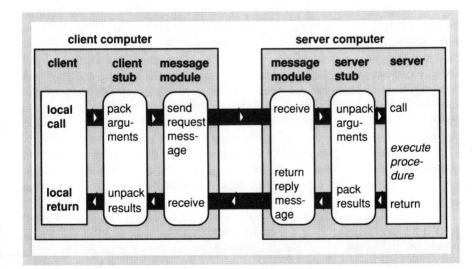

Figure 4.13 Stub procedures.

The interface compiler generates the stub procedures and includes them in the client program, one for each procedure in the interface specification. The task of a stub procedure is to marshal the arguments and to pack them up with the procedure identifier into a message, send the message to the server and then await the reply message, (un)marshal it and return the results.

When a server program is compiled, it too is processed by the interface compiler that checks the procedure definitions in the server against the interface specification and generates one stub procedure for each procedure in the interface. The server includes a 'dispatcher' that extracts procedure identifiers from request messages and calls the appropriate stub procedure. A server stub procedure obtains input arguments by (un)marshalling request messages, calls the appropriate server procedure, and when it returns marshals the output arguments (or in the case of failure an error report), making a reply message which it sends back to the client.

4.6 RPC in UNIX systems

UNIX was originally developed in the period 1969–74 [Ritchie and Thompson 1974]. Early versions of UNIX provided facilities for communication between concurrent processes within a single computer – user-level programs running concurrently in separate address spaces. But originally the only form of communication between processes was the *pipe* – an unnamed, unidirectional stream of bytes – and there was no support for networked communication. Pipes were designed as a method for linking chains of simple data-transforming programs (called *filters*) to make *pipelines* to perform more complex data transformations. The processes in a pipeline are created by a single *parent process* which also creates all of the pipes needed to connect them – no separate binding operation is required, so pipes are not named. The communication between the filter processes that make up a pipeline is a classic producer–consumer situation [Ben-Ari 1982], so pipes are defined as input/output streams without any explicit synchronization between the sending and receiving process. Even if pipes are extended to operate across a network they are not suitable for remote procedure calling and other distributed uses because delayed binding of processes to pipes is not possible and because stream communication does not support the synchronized sending and receiving of discrete messages.

The BSD 4.2 version of UNIX includes extended facilities for interprocess communication both across local and wide-area networks and within a single computer. The facilities were designed with the particular needs of client-server communication in mind.

Subsequently, several RPC systems were developed for use in networked BSD 4.2 UNIX systems (and the Courier RPC system, developed at the Xerox PARC for use in the Mesa and Cedar environments was converted for use in them). In UNIX Courier RPC, a Courier daemon listens on a well-known port for service requests and on receipt of each request message a new process is created to execute the remote procedure – in the absence of lightweight processes, this is a time-consuming operation.

The Sun NFS network file system is based on Sun RPC – intended to be used for remote procedure calling between UNIX kernels. Sun RPC uses the UDP datagram protocol (discussed below) for network communication and includes its own external data representation for machine-independent representation of the data objects sent in messages. The Admiral RPC system, described in Section 4.6.2, is also based on the UNIX BSD 4.2 interprocess communication facilities.

4.6.1 Interprocess communication in BSD 4.2 UNIX

The interprocess communication mechanism in BSD 4.2 UNIX is based on **socket** pairs [Berkeley 1981, Bach 1986]. A socket is a reference point to which messages may be sent and from which messages may be received; each socket has a protocol associated with it. Any process can create a socket for use in communication with another process; the socket enables messages to be mapped directly to the process. When a socket is created, a protocol must be specified – this may be *datagram* (using UDP – Unreliable Datagram Protocol) or *stream* (using TCP/IP – Transmission Control Protocol/Internet Protocol). The latter is reliable and sequenced.

For communication to take place between a pair of processes, each must create its own socket and the two sockets are used as a pair. One of the processes sends a message through its socket to a remote socket on which the other process is receiving; the remote socket must have a socket identifier before a message can be sent to it. For communication within one computer, sockets are referred to by pathnames like those used to refer to UNIX files and for communication between separate computers, sockets are referred to by an Internet address and a *port number* – a number for a socket that is unique within each host. We shall refer to both as **socket identifiers**. The process that has created a socket may associate an identifier with it by using the *bind* operation.

Datagram communication □ In order to send datagrams (which must consist of single network packets), a socket pair is identified each time a communication is made. This is achieved by the sending process using the identifier of the receiving socket each time it sends a message.

Any process, for example a server that plans to receive messages via its socket, must first bind an identifier to that socket and make the identifier known to potential clients. In an RPC system, each server creates a socket, binds an identifier to it and passes these, with its service interface name, to the RPC system binder. The RPC system binder binds service names to socket identifiers; this is *not* the same as what is done by the UNIX *bind* operation, which is local to each host and binds a socket identifier (i.e. an internet address and port number) to a socket. This is illustrated in Figure 4.14 in which the details of the arguments are simplified.

- The sending process uses the *sendto* operation with arguments specifying the socket through which the message is to be sent, the identifier of the destination socket and the message itself.

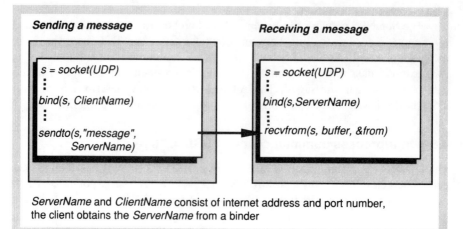

ServerName and *ClientName* consist of internet address and port number, the client obtains the *ServerName* from a binder

Figure 4.14 Sockets used for datagrams.

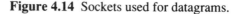

- The receiving process uses the *recvfrom* operation with arguments specifying the local socket on which to receive a message and memory locations in which to store the message and the identifier of the sending socket.

Both operations are blocking and communication occurs only when a *sendto* in one process and a *recvfrom* in another use the same pair of sockets. In client-server communication, there is no need for servers to have prior knowledge of clients' socket identifiers because the *recvfrom* operation supplies one with each message it receives.

Connection-based communication □ In order to use the reliable, sequenced or *stream* protocol, two processes must first establish a *connection* between their socket pair. A potential server creates a socket and binds an identifier to it; potential clients may then request connections to the server's socket. For communication between clients and servers, clients request connections and a *listening* server *accepts* them. When a connection is accepted, UNIX automatically creates a new socket and pairs it with the client's socket so that the server may continue listening for other clients' connection requests through the original socket. A connected pair of stream sockets can be used in subsequent stream communication until the connection is closed. Because the establishment of a connection in this way involves additional communication and processing activity, most UNIX RPC systems use connectionless, datagram communication. An exception is the UNIX version of the Courier RPC system. For further detail on the interprocess communication mechanisms in current UNIX systems, readers are referred to the book by Bach [1986] on the design of the UNIX system.

4.6.2 Admiral RPC

Admiral RPC, developed by Bacarisse and Wilbur at University College, London, runs with BSD 4.2 UNIX, using datagrams for message passing and the C programming language. It includes a purpose designed interface language and a simple binder.

Procedures are grouped together to form interfaces and one or more servers may export instances of the same interface. When a server starts execution it exports its interface to a binder and then runs for as long as required. During this time the server 'listens' for incoming calls and, when a call arrives, it executes the appropriate procedure and returns the reply. After this it returns to the task of listening. The interface is withdrawn from the binder when the server exits from its program.

Client programs may import any interface currently registered in the binder and make remote calls to the procedures it contains. An instance of an interface may be shared by several clients but normally only one call is executed at a time. If the designer of a service wants to serve several clients at the same time several instances of a service may be offered. Alternatively the server may create extra processes so that it can listen and execute procedures at the same time.

The RPC system consists of an interface language and a library of C procedures to be used in client and server programs.

RPC library □ The RPC library includes a number of procedures to marshal arguments, to send request or reply messages and to dispatch each call. We describe a few of them here. The following are used in server programs:

rpc_export(interface, name)
> causes the name of the interface to be registered with the binder. The interface will be withdrawn when the server process exits.

rpc_listen
> is used to wait for incoming calls. When a call arrives the appropriate procedure is called. The procedure *rpc_listen* also allows a server to use a timeout or to listen selectively for calls to one or more of the interfaces it has exported.

The following library procedures are used in the stub procedures generated by the interface compiler:

rpc_transact
> is used in client stub procedures to send a request message to the server and wait to receive the reply message.

rpc_return
> is used by server stub procedures to send the reply message.

rpc_source
> discovers the name of the caller's socket.

Interface language □ The interface language includes the definition of types, procedures, import and export statements. Client and server programs are written in C but the definition of an interface must be *included* in both. The client program must also include an *import* statement so that the interface language compiler will generate client stubs and the server program must include an *export* statement so that it will generate server stubs. The interface compiler is used to process both programs and produces C programs as output. Each C program is then compiled and linked with the RPC library.

Type definitions may be included to define parameter or result types of the procedures defined in the interface. The interface compiler translates type definitions to *typedefs* in the C programs generated. This enables the same type names to be used in the definition of procedures parameters in the server and definition of arguments in the client.

The interface language allows four base types: *byte*, *word*, *long* and *instance*. The first three correspond to 8, 16 and 32 bit integers in C programs. Variables of type *instance* are used to refer to instances of remote services. Arrays and structures may be defined in terms of the base types. The mode of use of parameters must be given and is denoted by arrows:

$\rightarrow$ means 'output',
$\leftarrow$ means 'input' (and this is the default mode when no indication is given),
$\leftrightarrow$ means that the parameter is used for both input and output.

The result delivered by a function is treated as an output parameter and its type must be specified, prefixed by $\rightarrow$.

An example □   Figure 4.15 shows the Admiral interface language definition for the *FileReadWrite* operations, corresponding to the interface given in Modula-2 in Figure 4.7.

---

interface Files;
type Buf is ref[size] byte;
Write(FileIdentifier:word; position:word; data←Buf; size:word)→word;
Read(FileIdentifier:word; position:word; data→Buf; size:word)→word;
end;

Figure 4.15 Files interface in Admiral RPC.

In this example the type *Buf* defines an array whose size is determined at run-time. Any procedure that has such a parameter must include the size as another parameter. In a call to the *Write* procedure the size is determined by the length of the data to be written to the file. The caller of the *Read* procedure provides a buffer for the file data in the output argument and the remote procedure is designed to read just that amount of data from the file.

Server program □   If the above interface is in a file called *files.i* then the server program for the *Files* interface takes the form shown in Figure 4.16. The *export main* declaration causes the interface compiler to automatically generate a main module that calls *rpc_export* and then loops repeatedly calling *rpc_listen* in each iteration. Alternatively, if *export main* is omitted, the server programmer can

```
#include "files.i"
export Files, main;
short integer Write(id, position, buf, size)
    short integer id, position,size;
    char *buf;
{    /* procedure body to perform file writing */
    .
    .
    .

}
short integer Read(id, position, buf, size)
    short integer id, position, size;
    char *buf;
{    /* procedure body to perform file reading */
    .
    .
    .

}
```

Figure 4.16 C program for server.

construct the main module of the server. The interface compiler also generates server stubs that are used when a request message arrives to unpack the arguments and invoke the *Read* and *Write* procedures.

Client program □   The client program would include:

```
#include "files.i"
import Files;
```

and calls to Read and Write e.g.

```
char buffer[1024];
Read(1, 20, buffer, 1024);
```

The interface compiler will generate a C stub procedure for each procedure defined in the interface, that is, for *Read* and *Write*. It will also generate a C structure defining the *Files* interface. As an example, the stub procedure for *Write* will set up a request message containing the arguments: *id, position, buffer* and *size*. It will call *rpc_transact* giving as argument the *Files* interface definition, the *procedureId* of the *Write* procedure (0) (*Read* is 1), the message and its size. When *rpc_transact* returns, the stub procedure copies the result into a local variable and returns it.

The stub generated for *Read* is similar except that, when *rpc_transact* returns, the data read from the file is sent in the reply message and eventually copied into the argument of *Read*.

Binding □   The Admiral system includes a binder to register interfaces. We have described above how a server calls *rpc_export* in order to register its interface with the binder. The name of the interface together with the internet address of the server is recorded in the binder. The binder runs on a selected host on the local area network and its internet address is compiled into the RPC software.

A client is automatically bound to a server the first time it makes a call to a procedure in a particular interface. When the client stub calls *rpc_transact* it supplies the name of the interface as argument. If this is the first use of this interface a call is made to the binder to discover the address of the server. There is no need to contact the binder in subsequent calls to procedures in the same interface.

4.7 Performance

In this section we quote some performance figures for remote procedure calling. For comparison, we note that a local procedure call requires about 0.01 to 0.1 msec.

Spector [1982] describes highly optimized remote procedure calling using a specially-designed transport protocol with microcoded support. He reports that a null remote procedure can be executed without microcoded support in about 4.8 msec and with microcode support in 0.15 msec using Alto computers and a 3 MHz Ethernet. Birrell and Nelson [1984] report for remote procedure calls based on a more generalized transport protocol. They quote times in the range 1 to 3.5 msec using a similar Ethernet without microcoded support, but using Dorado computers with an order of magnitude more performance than the Alto.

The results reported above should be regarded as optimum cases. It is interesting to consider the factors that contribute to the time taken to perform a remote procedure call. These are:

1. marshalling of arguments and results (packing and unpacking in both client and server);
2. transmission over the network in both directions;
3. time to execute the procedure in the server;
4. time to get service from the server. If the server consists of a single process then callers are effectively queued and the time depends on how busy the server is. If the server creates a new process for each call, then the time depends on process creation time. Another alternative is to have a pool of lightweight worker processes available to execute remote procedures.

Two implementations of remote procedure calling available for the UNIX operating system (Courier and Admiral) perform in the range 10 to 20 msec per call (with a single integer argument and result) on a Sun-2 and a 10 MHz Ethernet [Roberts 1985]. Admiral generally performed better than Courier. This could be attributed to the facts that Courier spawns a new UNIX process to service each call and uses TCP/IP for message passing, whereas Admiral has a single server process and uses datagram communication. Wilbur and Bacarisse quote for

Admiral 8 msec for a call to a null procedure plus about 0.013 msec per byte for transmission of arguments or results between Sun-3 workstations on a 10 MHz Ethernet.

They mention that the times (1), (3) and (4) above are quite significant and that when they moved from Sun-2 to Sun-3 workstations, the call time was reduced from 18 to 7.5 msec and the time per byte from 0.05 to 0.013 msec. Note that, in UNIX, the number of copies per request or reply message includes copying from the client program to the stub, from the stub to the kernel, and from the kernel to the network buffer with a similar number of copies on arrival.

The V-kernel (described in Section 2.4) was designed to achieve a very high rate of data transfer by reducing the number of copying operations and by the use of message passing primitives designed to support remote procedure interfaces. Cheriton [1984] quotes figures for RPC, between a pair of Sun-2 workstations over a 10 MHz Ethernet. A null procedure call takes 1.29 msec and an RPC with 1024 bytes of data takes about 5.8 msec.

4.8 Implementing RPC with lightweight processes

In UNIX the processes in a single computer have disjoint address spaces and therefore cannot communicate by the use of shared variables in memory. The mechanisms provided in UNIX for interprocess communication in a single computer (originally *pipes* and more recently *sockets*) are implemented by a two-stage copying method using memory within the operating system's kernel buffers. This results in a considerable performance penalty for programs making significant use of the interprocess communication facilities. For communication between processes in different computers, a similar method is used, but the data is transferred between the two kernels involved using the network transport layer. Only the kernel in each computer has direct access to the network transport layer. Calls to kernel functions from user-level programs are themselves relatively costly in processing time.

Although several distributed systems have been constructed from computers running versions of UNIX, the process model that it provides is not ideal. The very strong separation between the processes within a single computer is appropriate to a timesharing environment. In single-user workstations and servers, although applications must be adequately protected against software or system error, some layers of software other than what is found in a UNIX kernel may be trusted to share memory and other resources. This philosophy has been adopted in the workstation and server software for several recently-developed distributed systems – Cedar, Amoeba and V are described in Section 2.4 – resulting in a structure based on separate modules for each major system responsibility such as RPC and screen management. Only those modules relevant to a particular computer's task are loaded and applications access the relevant modules directly.

This section discusses the implementation of RPC facilities using lightweight processes (or threads) with shared memory and simple transport-layer operations that transfer datagrams between networked computers. Our treatment follows that of Lampson [1981a].

Building blocks □   We will assume that the client and server computers can be programmed in a language (such as Mesa) that includes concurrent lightweight processes with shared variables. We will assume that a network transport service is available that supports *Send* and *Receive* primitives for the transmission of messages between computers using addresses that do not distinguish between processes in a single computer. Therefore a single process in each computer receives all incoming messages and distributes them to other processes by using shared variables. Concurrent processes are required in a server because it should be able to execute remote procedures for several clients at once.

4.8.1 Monitors

The use of shared memory for communication between the processes within a single computer must be synchronized. The *monitor* construct developed by Hoare [1974] for the sharing of resources between concurrent processes is suitable for this purpose. Readers with a knowledge of the use of monitors to protect shared variables and of process synchronization using *signal* and *wait* can skip this section.

The lock and the semaphore [Ben-Ari 1982] are mechanisms that can be used to ensure that a set of processes is mutually excluded from using a resource, for example shared memory. The **monitor** is a programming construct that groups together a set of **shared variables**, a construct for **mutual exclusion** and a group of procedures that access the shared variables. Thus, a monitor consists of:

- Declarations of shared variables. These will include condition variables, described below.
- Definitions of **entry procedures**. These are procedures that can be called from outside the monitor and perform operations on the shared variables.
- There may be definitions of other procedures local to the monitor and variables that are not shared.

The term **entry procedure** refers to a procedure that may be called from outside the monitor in order to perform operations on the shared variables. The name entry procedure is taken from the Mesa programming language.

To ensure that all access to shared variables is synchronized, the entry procedures in a monitor should not access variables outside the monitor. The monitor enforces the following rules:

1. Only one process at a time can succeed in entering the monitor (i.e. calling one of its entry procedures). If a process is already using the monitor, other processes that make procedure calls are suspended until the monitor is free.
2. The entry procedures may be called by any process.
3. The shared variables in the monitor can be assigned and accessed only by the procedures in the monitor.

These rules guarantee mutual exclusion between a set of processes that use the shared variables in the monitor. Monitors have been implemented in Mesa and in Modula-2 by Wirth [1982] as well as in several other languages designed for concurrent programming.

Waiting for a monitor to be free □   We describe a process as 'entering a monitor' when it successfully calls an entry procedure and 'leaving a monitor' when the entry procedure returns. A process is 'in a monitor' between entering and leaving it. Only one process may be in a monitor at a time and therefore, when a process tries to enter a monitor at a time when another process is in the monitor, the first process is temporarily suspended.

Each monitor has a (possibly empty) queue of suspended processes to which processes can be appended before entering the monitor; whenever a process leaves a monitor, the process at the front of the queue is removed from the queue and resumes execution by entering the monitor.

There may be more than one instance of a particular type of monitor. For example, if there are several buffers being used, each buffer will have a separate instance of a monitor defined for handling buffers. Each instance of a monitor will have its own queue of suspended processes.

The mutual exclusion of processes from a monitor may be described in terms of semaphores. Suppose that for each instance of a monitor there is a semaphore (say S), whose initial value is 1, then when an entry procedure is called P(S) is executed, and on return from the procedure V(S) is executed.

Signals □   When processes collaborate in the use of shared variables, one process may depend on the action of another process in order for it to be sensible for it to continue. In this case, the first process should be able to suspend itself under a certain condition until another process that changes the condition causes it to resume.

Hoare defines a condition variable: this is a shared variable in a monitor – it relates to a condition that is necessary for a process to be able to continue execution. For example, in a buffer monitor there might be a pair of procedures – one to add a character and another to remove a character from the buffer. The condition 'not full' must be true before a character may be added to the buffer; 'not empty' must be true before a character may be removed from the buffer. A monitor should contain one condition variable for each separate condition of this sort.

The **condition variable** does not hold the value of the condition itself; it is used for communication between a process that wants to suspend itself and a process that can notify the suspended process to resume execution when the condition changes.

A process that cannot continue execution requests its own suspension by using the *wait* operation with a condition variable as argument.

Another process whose action causes the condition to change can notify the waiting process about the change by using the *sendSignal* operation (Hoare called this operation *signal*) with a condition variable as argument.

A condition variable is represented by a queue of processes that are currently waiting on the condition associated with it and is initially empty.

The effect of **wait**(s)

> where *s* is a condition variable
> is that the process executing the *wait* is suspended by being appended to the queue of processes for *s* and releases the mutual exclusion on the monitor.
> (The process will be resumed when another process executes *sendSignal(s)*.)

The effect of **sendSignal**(*s*)

> where *s* is a condition variable
> if any process is waiting on *s*, the process at the head of the queue for *s* is removed from the queue and resumed; else no effect.

As the execution of a *wait* by a process in a monitor releases the exclusion from other processes entering the monitor, another process will eventually enter the monitor, change the condition that determines the need to wait and *signal* on the same condition variable, thus releasing a waiting process. When a process resumes as a result of a *signal* it may assume that the condition it waits on has been fulfilled. This does, of course, require correct programming of the *signal* and *wait* in relation to the conditions.

At the stage that a process in a monitor *signals* and a *waiting* process is resumed, there appear to be two processes in the monitor, and the process that called the *signal* should be excluded whilst the resumed process is in the monitor. A simple solution to this problem is to stipulate that a *signal* must be the last operation of an entry procedure, so that the signalling process leaves the monitor as its next action. A more general solution is to make the rule that a process that signals in a monitor waits until the resumed process leaves the monitor.

The language Mesa has monitors with shared variables similar to those proposed by Hoare. The monitors in Mesa also include *condition variables* and a *wait* operation. The *sendSignal* operation is replaced by *notify*. This has different semantics – its meaning is that the waiting process will be resumed, but not necessarily immediately. For this reason, the resumed process must test the condition again, for some other process may meanwhile have changed it.

4.8.2 Implementing RPC using monitors

Server actions □   A server needs one *listening* process to receive request messages from clients and several processes to do the work: that is, to execute the procedures. A simple and efficient server model can be based on a pool of **worker processes** that are *Wait*ing for a signal indicating that work has arrived (see Figure 4.17). The listening process repeatedly calls *Receive* and puts a copy of each request message received into a queue of message buffers that it shares with the worker processes. It then *Signal*s to cause one of the waiting worker processes to resume execution. If all of the worker processes are busy, the signal will have no effect, but any request messages in the queue will be dealt with when a worker process completes its current job.

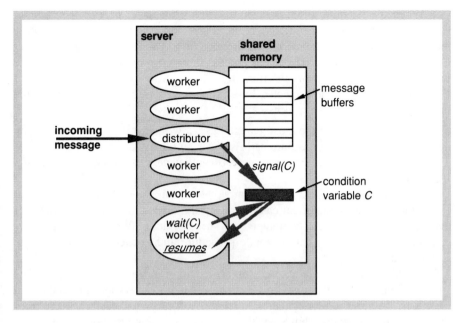

Figure 4.17 Listening process and worker processes.

When a worker process resumes execution it removes the first message from the queue of messages and executes the procedure called in it. It *Sends* the reply message to the the network address of the computer that made the call, obtaining this address from the *sourceAddress* field in the request message. See Figure 4.9 for the components of a message record. The worker process then takes the next request message from the queue, or, if the queue is empty, it uses *Wait* to suspend itself. The message buffers containing the queue of outstanding calls must be protected by a monitor, to ensure that the actions of adding calls by the listener and removing calls by workers are serialized.

Client actions □   The client uses a binder to obtain the address of a server and then sends request messages to it. In a client computer that has only one process, the client process blocks on a *Receive* until a return message arrives. In a computer that contains several client processes, there may be several remote procedure calls outstanding and a listening process is needed to receive the return messages and pass them to the correct clients. The unique *messageId* is copied from the request message to the reply message and enables the listening process to identify the client that originated the call.

The listening process and the client processes use shared memory to communicate. See Figure A1.1 in Appendix 1. The shared memory contains a set of *CallOut* records, one for each outstanding call. Clients create *CallOut* records to hold copies of request messages with their unique *messageId*s and a condition variable on which they *Wait*.

When the listening process receives a reply message, it finds the *CallOut* record with the same *messageId*, replaces the request message by the reply message and *signals* on the corresponding condition variable, causing the correct client process to resume. The client process then removes the *CallOut* message with the appropriate *messageId* from the shared *CallOut* record. The set of *CallOut* records must be protected by a monitor to serialize access to it by the listening process and client processes.

Symmetrical RPC □ In the most general case, a worker process in a server may need to make a remote procedure call itself, or, in other words, a server becomes a client of another server. For example, a **directory server** is usually a client of a file server.

The general case of remote procedure call is symmetrical between computers. In the symmetrical case, we drop the distinction between computers that provide services and computers that use services. We propose that any computer is able both to call a remote procedure and to execute a procedure in response to a remote call.

In this case, the client and server listening processes have the same specification. They act as **distributor** processes that *Receive* both call and return messages. In order to distinguish the two sorts of messages, each message must include a component that shows whether the message is a request or a reply.

Now that we make no distinction between client and server, each computer contains a distributor process, some worker processes and some client processes (that make the remote procedure calls). Appendix 1 contains a Modula-2 program illustrating the implementation of a symmetrical RPC mechanism as described in this section.

4.9 Summary

The remote procedure call can be used to build distributed programs in a way that is similar to the use of local procedure calling in conventional programs. An RPC is achieved by an exchange of request and reply messages between client and server containing the name of the procedure and its input or output arguments. Lightweight message passing protocols can enhance the performance of RPCs. The client that makes an RPC uses a binder to locate a server that has previously registered the service with that binder.

Interface specifications are required in RPC systems. Some languages, such as Mesa, include constructs for defining interfaces but purpose-designed interface languages are used either with languages such as C that are not adequate in this respect or when the RPC is to be designed for interworking between a number of different language systems.

The RPC call may be made transparently so that clients are not concerned with the details of message passing. The RPC is generally designed to have an at-most-once call semantics, and transparency can be achieved by an interface compiler producing stub procedures containing the implementation details. It can be argued that RPCs should not be entirely transparent as their semantics and performance differ from those of local procedure calls.

Remote procedure calling has been implemented in UNIX systems but the performance is limited both by the large amount of copying required and by the characteristics of UNIX processes. Considerably better performance can be achieved in systems that are based on lightweight processes with shared memory and specialized message passing protocols.

EXERCISES

4.1   Explain why a procedure designed to be used remotely cannot use global variables to communicate with the caller.

4.2   Discuss the problem of passing an argument containing a reference in a remote procedure call.

4.3   Consider a remote call to a *Read* operation that requests 1000 bytes of data from a file server. Estimate the time required to do the following:
    (a) transmit the RPC message and the reply message,
    (b) read the data from disk.

4.4   Give a list of error conditions that could occur during the remote *Read* call in the previous question:
    (a) due to the filing system (e.g. reading off the end of the file),
    (b) due to failure of the network or the computer running the server or the binder.

4.5   Describe the role of the *user package* in remote procedure calling.

4.6   Describe the tasks performed by the stub procedures:
    (a) in the client,
    (b) in the server.

4.7   Describe the contents of an RPC message, explaining the purpose of each component.

4.8   Explain how the caller of an RPC waits for a reply message.

4.9   Consider the effects of the unreliability of datagrams when a client makes two successive remote procedure calls to a server. Give a list of all possible message sequences, taking in to account lost messages and duplicated request messages. To simpilify this, assume that each message can be lost once only.

4.10   For each message sequence in your answer to the previous exercise, explain how the RPC software can ensure at-most-once call semantics.

4.11   The procedure *VectorScale* given in Section 4.1 is to be used as a remote procedure in a server. Describe how this procedure accesses the array belonging to the client.

4.12   Give two reasons why the C language cannot be used as an interface language.

4.13 Design a multipacket protocol using *Send* and *Receive*. Explain how the recipient recognizes that the component parts belong to the same multipacket, how the recipient recognizes the last packet of a multipacket and the effect of lost packets.

4.14 Use the Admiral interface language to define the interface of a server that performs the simple integer arithmetic operations (addition, subtraction, multiplication and division). Explain how this server can inform clients about errors such as division by zero and arithmetic overflow.

4.15 Explain why remote procedure call semantics may differ from the semantics of ordinary procedure calls and describe the meanings of 'maybe', 'at-least-once' and 'at-most-once' call semantics. Explain how each of these may be achieved.

4.16 Give three reasons why datagrams are generally preferred to connected communication for implementing RPCs. Explain why acknowledgement messages are not generally needed in implementing RPCs. Describe the RRA protocol and under what circumstances it might be adopted.

Chapter 5
File and Directory Services

In this chapter we define service functions for a basic file service and a basic directory service. The services are basic in the sense that they do not include all of the facilities found in conventional file systems. They provide primitive facilities in terms of which a wide range of file systems can be constructed.

They are intended to illustrate the principles involved in the construction of distributed filing systems in a modular fashion. If implemented they would constitute a basis on which a range of *user-level file services* could be constructed. Such user-level file services could be defined entirely from first principles, or they could emulate the file operations from any of a range of existing operating systems. We describe the construction of a hierarchic file system as an illustration.

5.1 Introduction

Most applications of computers use files for permanent storage of information. The **file** is an abstraction of a storage construct that is based on magnetic disks or other secondary storage media. Conventional operating systems include a **file system** that is concerned with the organization, storing, retrieval, naming, sharing and protection of files. File systems are designed to allow programs to use a set of operations that characterize the file abstraction and free them from concerns about the details of disk storage allocation and layout. Figure 5.1 shows a model of the sort of file system that is generally included in a conventional operating system. This model is similar to the one proposed by Madnick and Alsop [1969] in which a file system is constructed from a hierarchy of modules, in which each level depends only on levels below it.

At their simplest, files are defined as sequences of similar data items (e.g. 8-bit bytes) and file systems provide functions to read and write sub-sequences of data beginning at any point in a file. Some file systems provide facilities for creating and accessing files of records with more complex formats and with keyword-based indexes for locating records. Such facilities can be constructed as a layer of software at the application level in systems that do not provide them.

The file systems for centralized computer systems are designed to hold large numbers of files with facilities for creating, naming and deleting files. The naming of files is supported by the use of directories. The **directory** is an abstraction that is intended to provide a mapping between text names and references to files. These mappings are stored as files of a special type. To access files programs must open them, quoting their names. In many file systems directories may hold the names of other directories, leading to the familiar hierarchic file naming scheme found in UNIX and other operating systems. File systems also take responsibility for the sharing of files and **access control** – that

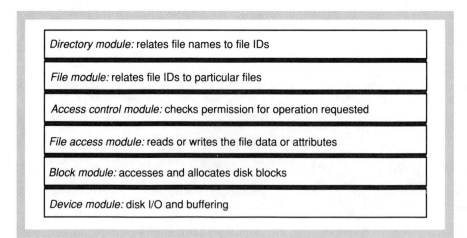

Figure 5.1 File system modules.

is, restricting access to authorized users and defining classes of access for each file (e.g. read-only, read-write, execute) for which users may be authorized.

A distributed **file service** is an essential component of a distributed system; it is needed to support shared information, to enable users to access files without copying them to their local workstation disk and if diskless workstations are used it is needed for all permanent data storage. In all distributed systems it makes a major contribution to the transparency of the system as seen by users because it offers a single integrated service accessible to users at every workstation. In addition other servers, for example the name server (or binder), the authentication server and the print server, can be implemented more easily if they can call upon the file service to provide permanent storage facilities.

File naming and the mapping from file names to file identifiers is usually handled by a separate service called the **directory service**. The directory service is normally a client of the file service and, in that case, its mappings are stored by the file service. The directory service can also take responsibility for access control by storing an **access list** for each file and withholding the file identifier from clients who are not authorized to access a particular file. An access list specifies which clients are allowed to perform each of the various operations, such as read or write, on a particular file.

The implementation of a file service may involve the coordinated use of software running in several computers, for example when files are stored in more than one computer. In the workstation/server model, the file service is offered by a set of one or more dedicated server computers. For example the Xerox Distributed File System (XDFS) was implemented on a cooperating set of server computers; whereas in the integrated model, for example Locus or Sun NFS, every computer contains the file service software. The set of operations offered by the file and directory services are usually implemented as remote procedure calls.

Programs that need to use a service will usually be written in terms of a **user package** that conceals the details of remote procedure calling (see Section 4.2.6). The functions in an RPC interface are designed to provide a minimal, consistent and complete set of operations, but they are not necessarily the most convenient to use (since a much larger set of functions with more specialized specifications would be required). The user package could for example convert the separate services offered by a file service and a directory service into a single facility resembling or even emulating precisely a conventional filing system such as the UNIX filing system.

5.2 Division of responsibilities

For reasons discussed in earlier chapters the division of system tasks into an appropriate modular structure is of even greater value in the development of distributed systems than in conventional ones. This consideration leads to a division of the functions of conventional file systems into a **block service**, a **file service** and a **directory service** as illustrated in Figure 5.2. The block service

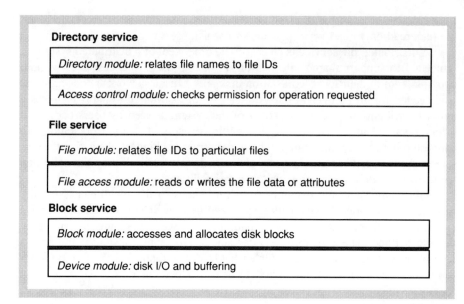

Figure 5.2 A distributed directory service, file service and block service.

deals with the allocation of disk blocks and provides operations for storing and retrieving data in them. We discuss the design of a block service in Chapter 6. The file service is concerned only with implementing operations on a set of files without concern for any structure or relationship between the files. This is sometimes termed a 'flat' file service.

In a flat file service, **unique file identifiers** (UFIDs) are used to refer to files in file service operations. UFIDs are usually long integers of a fixed length with no hierarchical structure, making it simple for the file server to map them to the data in the files. UFIDs must be chosen so that each file has a UFID that is unique amongst all of the files in a distributed system. A client program that possesses the appropriate UFID may call any of the functions of the file service to access or alter the contents of the file it refers to.

The division of responsibilities between file service and directory service is based upon the use of UFIDs for access to the contents of files. When a file is created the file service allocates a new UFID for it and the client may ask the directory service to record the UFID together with a text name. When a text name for a file has been recorded in this way, clients may subsequently obtain the UFID of the file by quoting its text name to the directory service.

Access control □   Shared file systems require some form of access control. File servers generally take one of two approaches to this problem. In the first approach, access control is based on **capabilities** (see Section 2.4.2) and access to a file depends entirely on the ability of a client to present a valid capability for it, rather than on the identity of the client. To maintain a reasonable degree of protection against unauthorized access, UFIDs that act as 'keys' or capabilities in this way should be impossible or at least very difficult to generate or counterfeit. We discuss the algorithm used to ensure UFIDs that are unique throughout a distributed system and difficult to counterfeit in Section 5.3.2.

The second approach is to use **identity-based** access control and requires each file to have an associated list of those users and services that are entitled to use it. The file server then needs to know the identity of the user or service on whose behalf the client is requesting a file operation in order to check the client's access rights.

The two approaches may be combined by applying identity-based access control when the client makes the first of a set of operations on a file or group of files. Clients that satisfy the check are given capabilities so that their future interaction with the file service is simplified. We use the combined approach in this chapter, but with identity-based access control in the directory service and capability-based access control in the file server. This frees the file server from any concerns about the identity of users and services, file ownership and access control lists, resulting in a simple design without unnecessary overheads for access to the majority of files that are not shared.

The task of the file service □   The main goal of a distributed file service is to offer filing facilities of at least the same generality as those found in non-distributed file systems. A simpler service could be constructed that for example supports only the transfer of entire files but this would be inadequate for general-purpose use; the performance overheads would be too great for clients needing to access only a small portion of a file nor could such a service be used to support an extended virtual memory for diskless clients as is done for example with CFS, the Cambridge File Server.

Birrell and Needham [1980], working on the design of CFS, discussed the requirements of a universal file server. They state:

> We would wish to have a simple, low-level, file server in order to share
> an expensive resource, namely a disk, whilst leaving us free to design
> the filing system most appropriate to a particular client, but we would
> wish also to have available a high-level system shared between clients.

As we shall see in Chapter 10, these were amongst the criteria adopted and successfully met in the design of the Cambridge File Server.

A file service that is to be used in such a wide variety of ways must offer a general-purpose, efficient set of operations. Files hold both *data* and *attributes*. The data generally consist of a simple sequence of items, accessible by simple operations that read or write portions of the sequence. The attributes hold information such as the length of the file, time of access, owner and access control lists which may be stored and read separately from the file data. The data in the file and the length of the file are intended to be accessed by ordinary users but the access control lists and other attributes are intended to be used by the directory service.

The task of the directory service □   In its simplest form a directory service provides a mapping between **text names** for files and their UFIDs. Text names are required because UFIDs would be an impossibly awkward (although theoretically possible) method of reference to files for human users. A set of mappings from text names to UFIDs is called a directory and there may be many directories. The translation from file name to UFID performed by the directory service replaces the *open* operation found in non-distributed systems. Once a client has an appropriate UFID, it may access the file it refers to, because our capability-based file server makes no check on the identity or access rights of the client when performing file operations.

The directory service therefore should ensure that UFIDs are not given to the wrong clients. Some file servers require a different form of UFID for each type of access (e.g. *Read, Write, Delete*), enabling them to reject requests, for example to delete a file by a client who has only been granted access to read the file. The directory service checks the identity of the client and the form of access requested against the access control list for the file in order to determine whether to issue a UFID.

Because the directory service is separate from the file service a variety of directory services can be designed and offered for use with a single file service, each supporting a different syntax and relationships between the text names for files. Thus a UNIX directory service could be constructed and used with a file service to provide a precise emulation of the UNIX file system. The same file service could be used with a different directory service to emulate almost any other file naming scheme (for example as in CP/M or MS/DOS) or to support some novel or specialized filing scheme.

The directory service itself can be decomposed. We shall define a basic level of service that creates, modifies and looks up text names in non-hierarchic directories and applies access control. Other levels of service can be constructed to parse text names, build directories into hierarchies or other structures and perform more complex searches.

File space management – a potential pitfall □   There is a potential pit into which neglected files may fall, never to be recovered. This arises when a file has not been entered into any directory (or when the name of a file has been removed from all directories) and the program responsible for creating the file (or the last program to hold a UFID for the file) terminates without explicitly deleting the file. Such a program might be termed 'delinquent' with respect to the file service, but such delinquency might well be a consequence of an unintentional error in a partially-debugged program.

It is not possible for a directory service to discover the existence of a file that has been lost in this way since its UFID is not in any directory. Because of our division of responsibilities between the file service and the directory service, the file service would have difficulty in determining that the file is no longer required since it has no knowledge of the format of directories – they are identical to any other file as far as the file service is concerned. This is especially so when several directory services, each with a different directory format, coexist in the same system as we have indicated might be desirable above.

A number of views can be, and have been, taken of this problem. In the Xerox XDFS file server it was ignored on the grounds that it is an infrequent occurrence [Mitchell 1982]. In the Cambridge File Server the directory service is more closely associated with the file service so that the pitfall is removed (see Chapter 10 for a discussion of how this was done). In the discussion of file server design that follows we shall ignore the issue. This approach is likely to be acceptable whenever the service calls to the file server are hidden from application programs by a user package that takes care to ensure that file names and identifiers are entered in directories as soon as files are created. However, this is not sufficient to ensure that there are no lost files, for a program may crash between the file operation that creates or deletes a file and the associated directory operation.

Mutable and immutable files □   The files provided in conventional operating systems are **mutable** files† – that is, for each file there is just one stored sequence that is altered by each update operation. The early file servers, such as XDFS and CFS and systems with an integrated model based on UNIX such as Sun NFS and Locus all provide mutable files.

Some more recent file servers (for example, the Cedar file system [Gifford et al. 1988]) provide **immutable** files. An immutable file cannot be modified once it has been created and each file is represented by a history of immutable versions. Rather than updating a file, a new version is created each time a change is made to the file contents and the old version is retained unchanged. In practice the use of storage may be reduced by keeping a record of the difference between versions. Old versions are retained on the disk only until the disk space is required for other purposes.

We shall describe servers that manage mutable files in this chapter; we return to the topic of file versions in Section 7.2.2.

5.3 The file service

We shall now define a set of operations for a flat file service. As a file contains both data and attributes, there are separate operations to deal with the data and the attributes. The length of a file is an attribute that is normally accessible to the same clients as the data in the file and is updated by the file service after writing or truncating the file. We will include operations on the length with the operations on file data. A discussion of the operations on the other attributes that are normally used by the directory service is deferred to the end of this section. Our definitions are illustrative of the operations to be found in current file servers.

Notation for service interface definitions □   We describe service interfaces by listing their procedures, giving a brief explanation of the action of each procedure. We make no distinction between output arguments and function

---

†   *Mutable* is defined as 'liable to change' and *immutable* as 'unchangeable' (*Concise Oxford Dictionary*).

Read(File, i, n) → (Data) — REPORTS (BadPosition)
> If *i* ≥ *1* and *i* ≤ *Length(File)*:
>> reads a sequence of up to *n* items in *File* starting at item *i* and returns the *Data* read.
> If *i* < *1* or *i* > *Length(File)*:
>> returns the empty sequence, reports an error.

Write(File, i, Data) — REPORTS (BadPosition)
> If *i* ≥ *1* and *i* ≤ *Length(File)*:
>> Writes a sequence of *Data* items to *File*, starting at item *i*, if necessary extending the file.
> If *i* > *Length(File)*: null operation, reports an error.

Length(File) → l
> returns the length of the file.

Truncate(File, l)
> If *l* < *Length(File)*: shortens the file to length *l*; else does nothing.

Create() → File
> creates a new file of length 0 and delivers a UFID for it.

Delete(File)
> removes the file from the file store.

Box 5.1   File service operations.

---

results, referring to both as 'results' returned by the procedure. We use the following notation for specifying the name of a procedure, its inputs and results and any error conditions (or exceptions) that may arise:

> *ProcedureName (argument1, argument2, ...) -> (result1, result2, ...)*
>   *— REPORTS (error1, error2, ...)*

The input parameters are listed in brackets after the name of the operation, the names of parameters following a naming convention introduced in the table below. The results are listed after the input parameters, separated from them by an arrow and have names chosen according to the same convention. Any exceptions or error conditions that may arise in a procedure are identified by the names listed after the word *REPORTS*.

In Box 5.1 the following parameter and result names are used:

File:	the UFID of a file
i, n:	integers (lower case letters)
Data:	a sequence of data items
BadPosition:	an error in *i*

For example, the procedure definition

> *Read (File, i, n) → (Data) — REPORTS (BadPosition)*

defines the procedure *Read* with three input arguments – the UFID of a file and two integers – and returns a sequence of data items as a result. It will report a

```
DEFINITION MODULE Files;
EXPORT QUALIFIED Read, Write, Length, Truncate, Create, Delete,
    ErrorType, Sequence, Seqptr, MAX, UFID, ErrorReport;

CONST MAX = 2048;
TYPE
    Sequence = RECORD
        l    : CARDINAL;
        s    : ARRAY[1..MAX] OF CHAR;
    END;
    Seqptr = POINTER TO Sequence;
    UFID   = CARDINAL;
    ErrorType = (NONE, READ, WRITE);
VAR
    ErrorReport: ErrorType;

PROCEDURE Read(File : UFID; i, n : CARDINAL) : Seqptr;
PROCEDURE Write(File : UFID; i : CARDINAL; Data : Seqptr);
PROCEDURE Length(File : UFID) : CARDINAL;
PROCEDURE Truncate(File : UFID; l : CARDINAL);
PROCEDURE Create() : UFID;
PROCEDURE Delete(File : UFID);
END Files.
```

Figure 5.3 File service interface defined in Modula-2.

BadPosition error if the argument i is outside the bounds of the file. All of the procedures in Box 5.1, except *Create*, would report an error for an invalid UFID, but these *REPORTS* are not shown. A UFID is invalid either if it is unknown in that server or if its form is inappropriate for the operation requested.

In Figure 5.3 and other examples in Modula-2, we show the error report being given to the calling client in a global variable named *ErrorReport*.

Operations on the file data □   Box 5.1 defines a set of operations for accessing and modifying the data in files and for creating and deleting files. The *Create* operation makes a new zero length file and returns a UFID for it. All the other file operations refer to files by UFIDs. The most important operations are those for reading and writing. The *Read* operation copies a sub-sequence of items from a file into a sequence that is returned to the client program. The *Write* operation copies a sequence of items from a sequence in the client program into a file, replacing a sub-sequence of the file or extending the file. Both the *Read* and *Write* operations require the position i of the start of a sub-sequence in the file to be specified. The *Delete* operation removes the data and attributes of a file. The *Length* operation returns the number of items in the file. It is sometimes necessary to shorten a file; *Truncate* does so.

```
MODULE CopyFile;
FROM InOut IMPORT WriteString, WriteLn;
FROM Files IMPORT Read, Write, Length, Truncate,
          UFID, ErrorType, MAX, ErrorReport;

PROCEDURE CopyFile(File1, File2 : UFID);
VAR
    i, l : CARDINAL;
BEGIN
    l := Length(File1);
    Truncate(File2, l);
    FOR i := 1 TO l BY MAX DO
        Write(File2, i, Read(File1, i, MAX));
    END;
    IF ErrorReport ≠ NONE THEN
        WriteString("CopyFile failed");
        WriteLn;
    END;
END CopyFile;
END CopyFile.
```

Figure 5.4 *CopyFile* **using file service operations.**

Example in Modula-2 □   Figure 5.3 shows a full set of declarations in Modula-2 for our file service procedures assuming that they operate only on files of characters, and that the transfers performed by *Read* and *Write* are limited to *MAX* characters. As a simple example illustrating the use of these operations, we can construct a procedure *CopyFile* to copy the contents of a file whose UFID is *F1* to a newly created file *F2*. If we suppose for the moment that *F1, F2* and *i* are declared appropriately, the task can be performed by a simple loop of the form:

```
F2 := Create();
FOR i := 1 TO Length(F1) BY MAX DO
    Write(F2, i, Read(F1, i, MAX));
END;
```

Figure 5.4 shows a more complete version of *CopyFile* in which it is assumed that the destination file, supplied as the second argument, already exists when the procedure is called. Note that the programs that we have shown so far do not refer to files by name and therefore would need to be embedded in a program that determines file identifiers from a directory to make them useful.

The definitions we have given for *Read* and *Write* differ only slightly from the similarly-named operations to be found in UNIX. In UNIX a **read-write pointer** is implicitly associated with each file while it is in use (see Bourne [1982], pp. 117–123). The *read* and *write* operations of UNIX do not include a starting position. The current position of the read-write pointer is taken as the starting position for each *read* or *write* operation. The read-write pointer is advanced to the end of the sub-sequence transferred by each *read* or *write*. In addition, the pointer can be explicitly re-positioned using an additional operation called *seek*.

Repeatable operations and stateless servers □   The file operations defined above have two properties that are important in the construction of distributed systems.

1. The operations are **repeatable**. That is to say, if an operation is executed more than once the effect is the same as for a single execution. We saw in Chapter 4 how communication errors, failure of computers and delays may lead to repeated executions of a single remote procedure call. If repeating an operation may have the wrong effect the server must prevent the repetition by implementing duplicate suppression. If operations are repeatable, there is no need for the overheads due to duplicate suppression. On the other hand, allowing operations to be repeated may lead to a degradation in performance, for example, if the overloading of a file server causes clients to timeout and repeat operations. The CFS file server relied on the use of repeatable operations whereas XDFS used both repeatable operations and duplicate suppression. The UNIX file access operations are not repeatable because the position of the read-write pointer is incremented by each operation.

2. **Stateless** file servers can be constructed around repeatable operations. The read-write pointer of UNIX is an example of state information. In a conventional operating system the kernel can hold a read-write pointer for each open file in a table for each process. However, if a file server does this on behalf of its clients, two unfortunate situations may arise. If a server crashes and then re-starts, the state information that it was holding may be lost and the client program might continue its task unaware of the crash, producing inconsistent results. Similarly when a client program crashes and then re-starts its task the server is left holding information that is wrong but cannot easily be withdrawn. Therefore operations that do not rely on stored state in the server can simplify the design of file servers.

Atomicity □   Simple stateless servers do not meet all application requirements. If the information in a file or set of related files may be updated concurrently by several client processes and there are consistency constraints requiring that an entire set of updates by a single client process is performed before another client process accesses the data, the server must be designed to provide the necessary support. Consider the following example in which a file is used to hold the balance of a bank account that is initially $100 and the following sequence of operations occurs:

1. Client A reads the balance.
2. Client B reads the balance.
3. Client A adds $10 to the balance and writes it back to the account.
4. Client B adds $20 to the balance and writes it back to the account.

The result is a balance of $120 and that is wrong. This is an illustration of what is known as the 'lost update' problem. A's update is lost because B overwrites it without seeing it. We return to this problem in Chapter 7. The operations of the two transactions should be performed in an order that produces sensible results. This could, for example, be achieved by recording a lock on the file containing the account while one of the clients is accessing it. The need to retain some state information (such as locks) during a sequence of data transfers to files re-appears as a part of the mechanism needed to support **atomic transactions** on files. But the state information needed to support atomic transactions is used only by the server and is removed as soon as the transaction has been completed or after a client or server crash. Chapter 7 is devoted to a discussion of such mechanisms including measures to maintain the consistency of files in the face of workstation and server crashes.

5.3.1 Operations on file attributes

We have defined a set of operations to create and delete files and to read and write data in them. In most conventional file systems there is some additional information associated with files, such as date of creation, date of last access and last modification, file type, file ownership and access lists, which is maintained by the file system. In our file service we associate with each file a collection of data values called **file attributes**. The file service regards the attributes as an uninterpreted sequence of bytes and is able to store and retrieve them, but is not responsible for their size, layout or contents.

GetAttributes(File) → Attr
     returns the file attributes for the file.
SetAttributes(File, Attr)
     sets the file attributes.

Box 5.2   File attribute operations.

The directory service determines the internal structure and the values stored in the attributes. An attribute has a record structure with the same layout for all files managed by a particular directory service. Typically its size will be a few hundred bytes. In the next section we shall consider the construction of a directory service that manages and controls access to a collection of files. The directory service is responsible for the attributes of files, changing the dates whenever a client requests access to a file, recording the type and ownership of each file and managing the access control lists. A single file service may manage several sets of files that are accessed through several directory services and the attribute records for each set of files may differ in size and layout. Box 5.2 defines two further file service operations to enable a directory service to store status information about each file.

5.3.2 The construction of UFIDs

UFIDs must be generated in a manner that ensures uniqueness and makes them difficult to forge. In general there may be several server computers cooperating to provide a file service so UFIDs must be unique amongst all of the computers in a distributed system. Even after the file associated with a given UFID value is deleted, it is important that its UFID is not re-used because clients of the file service may retain obsolete UFIDs. Any attempt to access a deleted file should produce an error rather than allow access to a different file.

We should note that the UFID is not required to act as a file address. It need not contain any information concerning the address of the server it is in or the position of the file in disk storage. In Chapter 6, we consider the mapping of UFIDs to disk block addresses, using mapping tables maintained by the file service. In Chapter 8, we discuss various ways of locating the server that contains a particular file. The problem with putting locating information in UFIDs is that this is a form of early binding and constrains variability. For example we may want to migrate a file to another server, to replicate it or to place it differently on a disk.

There are a several ways to ensure that a UFID is unique and difficult to forge [Needham and Herbert 1982, Mullender 1985, Leach et al. 1983], all relying on the use of a relatively large, sparsely populated space. One way to achieve uniqueness is to construct the UFID by concatenating the host address of the server creating the file with an integer representing the position of the UFID in the chronological sequence of UFIDs created by that server. Counterfeiting can be combated by inserting an extra field containing a random number into each UFID, thereby ensuring that the distribution of *valid* UFIDs is sparse and rendering the task of a malicious user wishing to generate any valid UFID so lengthy as to be impractical. With this approach the resulting UFIDs might be represented as 112-bit records with a format such as:

48 bits	32 bits	32 bit
server identifier	file number	random number

Although this seems inconveniently large, occupying several words of memory in client and server computers, alternative schemes produce only slightly smaller representations. In the above format the *server identifier* is considered to be an Internet address, ensuring uniqueness across all registered Ethernet-based systems. In a distributed system based on a single local network a much smaller range of values, determined for example by the number of servers registered with the name server, might be used. With this approach a representation that fits within 64 bits can be defined without loss of security or uniqueness.

Access control to files is based upon the fact that a UFID constitutes a 'key' or capability to access a file. In its simplest form, access control is a matter of denying UFIDs to unauthorized clients. However, when files are shared, the owner of a file generally holds rights to perform all operations on that file, whereas others have less rights; for example they may only be allowed to read the file. A more flexible service is then required with finer degrees of access control providing selective control of access to reading, writing and the other file service operations on each file.

These more refined forms of access control can be built around an extension of the role of UFIDs in which each UFID has embedded in it a **permissions field** encoding the access rights that the UFID confers upon its possessor. For example, to control access selectively to reading and writing, a permission field of two bits would be needed in each UFID. The possession by a client of a particular UFID would then confer the right to access a file for reading only, for writing only or for both reading and writing. A five-bit permissions field would serve to control access to the file service operations that we have defined above. (There are eight file service operations but it is possible for access control purposes to combine the *Length* and *Truncate* operations with *Read* and *Write* respectively, and *Create* does not require a UFID as a parameter.)

The permissions field must be combined with the random part before giving the UFID to users. The use of an easily accessible permissions field would be insecure because the possessor of a UFID that confers restricted permissions could easily convert it to one with more permissions, for example convert a UFID for reading a file into one that confers permission to write.

We suggest two different ways a file server may hide the permissions field:

- The permissions field and the random part are encrypted with a secret key (see Section 9.3) in the UFIDs issued to clients. When clients present UFIDs for file access, the file server uses the secret key to decrypt them.
- The file server may encrypt the two fields using a one-way (see Section 9.5) function to produce the UFIDs issued to clients. When clients present UFIDs for file access, the file server applies the one-way function to its copy of the UFID and compares the result with the client's UFID.

When a new file is created, a UFID with all rights of access is returned for use by the owner, but before the owner gives the capability to other users it is necessary to restrict the capability by removing some of the rights. The way to do this is to have a function in the file server for restricting capabilities.

5.4 Access control

Any client process that has a valid UFID can use the file service to access the file that it refers to. The directory service stores mappings from users' text names for files to UFIDs. It must therefore control access to files by checking whether clients have authorization to access the files, before issuing UFIDs.

Identifying clients □ Client processes requesting UFIDs in order to perform operations on files are acting on behalf of users or services. In order to check authorization we need a way of uniquely identifying the user or service on whose behalf the client is acting. A **userID** is a numeric code that uniquely identifies a user, service or group and is usually obtained by a user after some form of authentication such as a name and password check. UserIDs are assigned when users are registered with the system. They are chosen at random from a large sparse number space to reduce the chances of counterfeiting. The authentication may be done by an **authentication service** that maintains a table of user names and service names, passwords and the corresponding userIDs. Chapter 9 contains a fuller description of an authentication service.

Owner of a file □ Each file has an **owner** and the owner's userId is recorded in the attributes by the directory service so that it may subsequently be used in identity-based access control. Initially, the owner is the creator of the file.

Access lists □ An **access list** for a file contains directly or indirectly the userIds of those users entitled to access the file with some file service operations. The following table illustrates this:

Operation	*Users with access*
Read	list of userIDs
Write	list of userIDs
Delete	list of userIDs
Length	list of userIDs
Truncate	list of userIDs

In practice the number of potential clients who require access to some files is too great to list them exhaustively. Directory services may vary widely in the flexibility of access control. Ideally, arbitrary groupings of users and services would be supported, with a separate service supporting the mapping of users to groups. The Alpine file server (developed at PARC after XDFS) [Brown et al. 1985, Mitchell 1985] uses the services of Grapevine to manage groups and to test group membership.

To provide a simpler but fully flexible protection scheme five categories of access can be defined allowing access to each of the file service operations *Read/Length, Write/Truncate, Delete, GetAttributes* and *SetAttributes*.

The access control methods used in the UNIX filing system are fairly general and can be implemented efficiently. Access control for a directory service can usefully be based upon an extension of them. We shall illustrate the notions introduced in this section by describing a simple extension of the UNIX file access control mechanisms. We have chosen for the purposes of this example to divide the universe of clients who might want to access a file into four classes:

- the file's owner,
- the directory service responsible for naming and controlling access to the file,
- a client process identified as the the *system manager* that requires special access permission in order to manage the file's contents on behalf of the owner,
- all other clients.

The following table shows a tabular representation for the access lists.

	Read	*Write*	*Delete*
Owner	×	×	×
Directory service			×
System manager	×	×	×
Everyone else	×		

In UNIX, the same file may appear in several directories. This is known as *linking* and extends the basically hierarchic file structure to a directed graph to enable users to record the names of shared files in their own directories. In order to allow a file to be recorded in several different directories, the access control lists must not be associated with a particular directory. It is therefore preferable to store access control lists in the file attributes rather than in the directory files.

5.5 The directory service

We now define a basic directory service that supports the naming of files and control of access to files. The basic directory service is designed as a generic building block for use in the construction of user directory services that specify the file naming, directory structure and access control methods. It translates text names to UFIDs in response to requests by authorized clients, and it enables clients to add and delete file names and their associated UFIDs in directories.

The directory service maintains tables containing a mapping between text names for files and their UFIDs. These mapping tables are called **directories** and are stored in files within the file service. The directory service is able to look up a name in a given directory and from that obtain a set of UFIDs, each of which grants a different form of access to the file, e.g. *Read, Write* and *Delete* for the owner, *Read* only for others or *SetAttribute, GetAttribute* and *Delete* for the directory service.

Since directories are stored as files, the directory service is a client of the file service and each directory itself has a UFID. Our definition for a directory service does not assume any particular structural relationship between directories. We define only operations on individual directories. The resulting service could be used directly by a client to operate on a single 'well-known' directory, or it could be used through another layer of software that might, for example, superimpose a recursive hierarchic naming structure similar to the UNIX file system's naming structure. Each user can have several directories and owners of files generally are able to get UFIDs giving all rights of access, whereas other users would be given UFIDs that grant less rights. For an illustration (at the end of this section), we have chosen to outline the construction of such a superimposed software layer that supports a recursive naming hierarchy.

Operations of the directory service □ Box 5.3 contains definitions for the set of directory service operations that we wish to discuss. The directory service operations are defined according to our usual notational convention and the following parameter names are used:

Dir:	UFIDs referring to directories
Name:	a textual name
AccessMode:	specifies file service operation for which UFID is required, e.g. *(Read, Write, Delete, ...)* or a combination of these
Pattern:	a regular expression
userID:	a unique identifier enabling the directory service to identify a client
NotFound:	error: name absent from directory
NoAccess:	error: caller does not have access permission
NameDuplicate:	error: attempt to add name already in directory

---

Lookup(Dir, Name, AccessMode, UserID) → (File) — REPORTS (NotFound, NoAccess)

> Locates the text name in the directory and returns the relevant UFID; reports an error if it cannot be found or if the client making the request is not authorized to access the file in the manner specified by *AccessMode.*

AddName(Dir, Name, File, UserID) — REPORTS(NameDuplicate)

> If *Name* is not in the directory: adds the *(Name, File)* pair to the directory.
>
> If *Name* is in the directory: reports an error.

UnName(Dir, Name) — REPORTS(NotFound)

> If *Name* is in the directory: the pair containing *Name* is removed from the directory.
>
> If *Name* is not in the directory: reports an error.

ReName(Dir, OldName, NewName) — REPORTS(NotFound)

> If *Name* is in the directory: the pair containing *Name* gets a new name.
>
> If *Name* is not in the directory: reports an error.

GetNames(Dir, Pattern) → NameSeq

> Returns the set of all of the text names in the directory that match regular expression given by *Pattern.*

Box 5.3   Directory service operations.

The most important operation is the *Lookup* function in which the client gives a directory to search in, the text name of a file, the sort of access required (e.g. *Read* or *Write*) and its userID. This function searches for the text name within a given directory and, if it finds it, takes the corresponding UFID and uses it to get the attributes of the file. *Lookup* checks the access list in the file attributes to discover whether the client is authorized to access the file in the manner requested in the *AccessMode* parameter. If so, a UFID allowing access to the file in the manner requested is returned to the client, otherwise an error is reported.

There are three operations for altering directories; *AddName*, *ReName* and *UnName*. *AddName* adds an entry to a directory and records the owner of the file and an access control list in the file attribute, *ReName* changes the name of a file and *UnName* removes an entry from a directory after checking that the entry has been correctly specified. *GetNames* is provided to enable clients to examine the contents of directories. It returns all or a subset of the names stored in a given directory. The names are selected by pattern matching against a regular expression† supplied by the client.

The file attributes ☐   A directory service can access and update the file attributes in order to perform access control. It will set default access permissions in the attributes of a file the first time its name is entered in a directory. However, it should provide an operation (not included in Box 5.3) to enable clients to inspect the file attributes. It may also provide operations to allow the owners of files to grant or revoke permissions for other users, or even to give up their file ownership to another user.

Access to directories ☐   A directory service is the owner of all the files containing its directories and is able to perform all the file service operations on them in order to create, write, read and delete its mappings. But there is a further question: who is allowed to perform the directory service operations *LookUp*, *AddName*, *ReName* and *UnName* and to inspect or alter the attributes? When users have separate directories (that are not shared), the UFID of the directory may be regarded as a capability and no further access control is required; but when directories are shared some form of access control is needed. One simple solution is to have directory owners and an access permission scheme similar to the one used for files.

Lost files ☐   The provision of user-level operations that combine file service and directory service operations can help to combat the problem of lost files.

Creating files
   The user level operation for creating a new file would specify a file name and a directory. This would call first the file service *Create* operation and then the directory service *AddName* operation.
Deleting files
   The user level operation for deleting a file would specify a UFID and a directory. This would call first the file service *Delete* operation and then the directory service *UnName* operation.

However, if one of the processes fails between the paired operations, it is still possible to lose files.

---

† A regular expression may be used to specify either: (1) an exact match with a literal string or (2) a match with an expression that includes literal characters, symbols denoting variable characters and symbols denoting repeated occurrences of characters or sequences of characters.

*A **tree-structured file service*** □   A tree-structured file system such as the one
UNIX provides, consists of a number of directories arranged in a tree, with links
enabling files to have several names, and can be implemented using the basic file
and directory service described above. A tree-structured set of directories is
constructed with files at the leaves and directories at the root and interior nodes of
the tree. The root of the tree is a directory and has a 'well-known' UFID.

Any leaf or node in the tree, that is, any file or directory may be named by
using a *pathname* – a multi-part name to represent a path through the tree. The
root has a distinguished name and each file or directory has its own name.

In order to construct a tree structure, we need to be able to add file names
and directory names with their corresponding UFIDs to directories and to create
new directories. The basic directory service provides the *AddName* operation and
we have described how it can be used to add file names to directories.

In a tree-structured directory service the file attributes associated with both
files and directories should include a *type attribute* that distinguishes between
files and directories. This is used when following a path name through the tree to
ensure that each part of the name, except the last, is a directory name. When a file
or directory is created, the appropriate values are put in the file attributes,
including access control lists, date of creation and so forth. Once a directory has
been created its name and UFID can be inserted in another directory using the
AddName operation.

5.6 Summary

We have discussed how the components of a conventional file system may be
distributed into separate file and directory services. A file service normally
contains a 'flat' set of files with unique identifiers. UFIDs are generated to be
unique and hard to guess and are used as capabilities for granting the use of file
operations. File data consists of simple sequences of data items, and file
operations allow users to read or write any subsequence of the file data. File
attributes are separately accessible and may contain access control lists and other
information about the file. Directory services map users' text names for files onto
their UFIDs and impose identity-based access control. The separation of file and
directory services contributes to the modular design of a distributed system but
can lead to lost files. Hierarchically structured directories can be constructed
from the basic directory service.

EXERCISES

5.1 Describe the advantages of providing a file service in a distributed system instead of a local file system in each workstation.

5.2 Describe two services that may be built as clients of a file service.

5.3 Describe the modules of a conventional file system. How could these modules be distributed between a file and directory service?

5.4 Describe how to construct file identifiers that are unique amongst the servers in a distributed system. How can UFIDs be made hard to guess? If an RPC to a file server takes about 10 msec, calculate how long it might take to forge a UFID using the scheme you describe. How can UFIDs be designed to grant different access permissions for the same file?

5.5 Define *Read* and *Write* procedures for a file service. Compare these with the UNIX *read* and *write* system calls. Explain what advantages your functions have in the design of a file service.

5.6 Describe the problems associated with servers recording state for their clients. Give an example where it might be necessary to record state information on behalf of clients.

5.7 Write client procedures that define the UNIX *read* and *write* system calls in terms of our file service operations.

5.8 What is meant by mutable and immutable files?

5.9 Describe the identity-based and capability-based approaches to the access control of shared files.

5.10 What problems other than access control are related to shared files?

5.11 Describe the role of a basic directory service.

5.12 Explain how lost files can arise when file and directory services are separated. Why does this problem not arise in conventional file systems?

5.13 The directory service could be run as a client service in each single user workstation. Describe how this would simplify the design. What are the disadvantages of this approach?

5.14 Why is it undesirable to include the address of a computer or a disk block in the UFIDs.

5.15 Discuss the problems that can arise if a file server is overloaded and clients keep repeating requests. Describe two different solutions to this problem.

5.16 Implement the UNIX operations *mkdir* and *rmdir* in terms of our basic file and directory operations.

Chapter 6
Implementation of File Services

The main objective of this chapter is to describe methods for the implementation of a basic file service such as the one defined in Chapter 5. More advanced file services providing atomic transactions and involving several server computers are discussed in Chapters 7 and 8.

We describe the implementation of a file service in terms of a **block service**. A block service provides a logical view of a disk storage system and enables a single storage system to be shared between different file services.

Stable storage is introduced as a systematic method for the reliable storage of information in potentially unreliable media. This is needed to ensure that file systems can be restored after hardware or software failures that result in the loss of any single block of storage.

The implementation methods described in this chapter are based on those used in current file servers, several of which are described in Chapter 10.

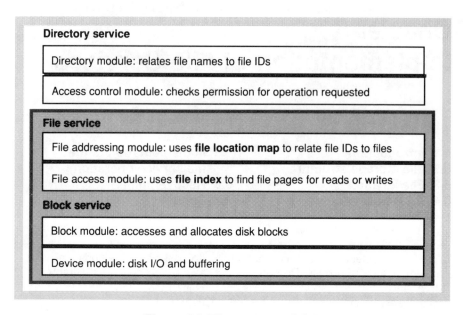

Figure 6.1 File system modules.

6.1 Introduction

The techniques used for the implementation of file services are an important part of the design of distributed systems. They must provide a service that is comparable in performance and reliability with the file systems found in conventional computer systems. Although the techniques used in the implementation of distributed file servers are often similar to those found in conventional systems, the separation of the facilities into a number of distinct services leads to a different software structure.

We have defined the interface to a directory service and outlined its construction in Chapter 5. The details of its implementation are not discussed here, since the operations and data structures used are typical of those found in simple name mapping tasks and the implementations do not differ from the approaches used in conventional filing systems [Tanenbaum 1987, pages 261 on].

The tasks of a file service can be considered under two main headings: file storage and file addressing. Figure 6.1 shows a new version of the layer diagram for a file server in which the first layer in the file server deals with file addressing by using a file location map. The file access module in the second layer deals with file storage by becoming a client of the block service and using a file index to relate parts of a file to blocks on the disk.

File storage □ A file service maintains a potentially large collection of files and provides facilities to access and update their contents, to create new files and to delete and truncate files using service operations such as those defined in Box 5.1

(Section 5.2). The content of a file as viewed by clients of the file service is simply a modifiable sequence of data items, typically 8-bit bytes. In addition to the data items, files have *attributes*, including access control data and dates and times of most recent access, which can be accessed by authorized clients.

A file server must model a file as a sequence of data items. When a file is created or extended as the result of a write operation, space must be allocated for it; and when a file is deleted or truncated, the space must be recovered. These operations require the dynamic allocation of storage to allow files to grow and shrink using non-contiguous blocks of storage.

The storage of files in contiguous blocks of disk storage is impractical – the deletion of files rapidly creates a large number of arbitrary-sized fragments of the unused disk space, and the extension of files to accommodate new data that is implied by the *Write* file service operation is impossible unless adequate space has been reserved in advance. The solution normally adopted is for the file service to store files in a non-contiguous set of blocks and record a sequence of pointers to the blocks of which each file is composed. A separate data structure is required to record the sequence of pointers to blocks (which we shall call the **file index** – not to be confused with the indexes of files used in CFS and some other file services). The file index must be organized to support both sequential and random access to the items in a file. The file attributes are not included in the file contents because they are subject to different access controls; they can conveniently be represented as a single fixed-size record that is stored with each file index.

File addressing □   One of the main tasks of a file server is to record the locations of files and their associated UFIDs in a manner that supports the efficient retrieval of the files' locations from their UFIDs. It performs this task with the aid of a stored data structure that we shall refer to as the **file location map**. Logically the mapping is equivalent to a table indexed by UFIDs, giving:

$UFID \rightarrow$ *location of file*

The mapping may be represented in a variety of ways to optimize its space or time efficiency. Some of these will be described in Section 6.3.

Storage media □   Magnetic disk storage is the dominant technology for the storage of files and is likely to remain so for some time to come. Optical disks with 'write-once' capabilities are emerging and may offer advantages for the storage of relatively permanent information. Both types of disk storage exhibit *latency*, a performance characteristic that influences the strategy for the layout and use of storage space.

When the term latency is applied to disk storage it refers to the time that must elapse after the initiation of a read or write operation before data begins to be transferred to or from a disk. The time required to access a block of data of length N can be expressed as:

$$T = t_l + t_t N$$

where t_l is the latency, i.e. the time that elapses before data from the block begins to be transferred, and t_t is the time to transfer each byte from disk storage to primary memory.

The latency for access to a particular disk block will depend upon the distance through which the disk heads must move and the arc through which the disk must rotate to position the heads over the block. Latencies for typical magnetic disk drives are in the range 10-80 msec, with average values for t_l in the region of 20 msec, whereas t_t is typically a small number of microseconds. Thus it is most effective to transfer a large number of bytes at a time.

The latency property of disk storage should be contrasted with true random-access memory in which there is no latency; for example, the semiconductor RAM used as main memory in most computers. For RAM, the time t to access any word of memory is fixed and the time to access any N words is Nt. The latency property of disk storage is the primary reason for the storage of data in blocks in file systems; a secondary reason is that the use of blocks of a single size or a small number of different sizes simplifies the management of disk space.

Block service □ In most conventional operating systems the storage of files is based upon the use of blocks of storage typically between 2 and 8 kbytes in size. Operations to allocate, read and write blocks form a software module within the file system.

In distributed systems the block operations can be implemented either as a software module embedded within the file server software or as a separate service. A set of operations for allocating and freeing disk blocks and for transferring data into and out of disk blocks is defined in Section 6.4. The file service operations can be constructed entirely in terms of these block service operations.

Some systems also provide access to a disk block service for purposes other than filing. For example, there is a Network Disk server in the the the Sun UNIX operating system that provides access to remote disk blocks for swapping and paging by diskless workstations. Simple disk servers are also used in some microcomputer networks to enable a single hard disk to be shared amongst a number of microcomputers running a simple disk operating system that is modified to use a section of the remote hard disk as a 'virtual floppy disk'. Such systems are simple to implement but offer no support for file sharing, even of read-only files.

For the implementation of a shared file service, the use of a block service as a basis offers several advantages:

- It allows differently-specified file services to coexist in a single distributed system, sharing the same disk storage devices. The description of the implementation of a simple file service in this chapter and a transaction-oriented file service in Chapter 7, both in terms of the block service, illustrates this.
- It allows the use of a variety of disks and other media.
- It separates the implementation of the file service from disk-specific optimizations and other hardware concerns.

The Amoeba system adopts this approach, providing a range of file services, including a UNIX-like file service and a sophisticated tree-structured, transaction-oriented file system based on a single block storage service. Disks can be shared between different file services, files may be distributed across different disks and types of storage devices (e.g. optical disks), and the block service can be used for applications other than file storage (e.g. program swapping and paging).

The use of a cache □   Whether or not the block layer is implemented as a separate service, the disk block access system should include a carefully-designed software caching system to reduce the cost of file access by retaining copies of recently-used blocks in local memory at the file server. Most file servers include such a caching system; Sturgis et al. [1980] report a substantial performance gain for XDFS as a result of the use of a disk block cache.

A disk cache consists of an area of main memory organized as an array of blocks that are the same size as the blocks on disk, together with the block pointer for each block. On each read operation, the block pointers in the cache are checked. If the block pointer of the required block is present, the contents of the block are taken from the cache; otherwise, the contents of the block are loaded from the disk to the cache and the associated block pointer is updated so that subsequent reads that require the same block will be able to obtain it from the cache.

To ensure that the same version of each block is used in all operations the cache must be used for writing as well as for reading. If a block referenced in a write operation is already in the cache then the new data is stored in the cached block and the block is flagged to show that it has been modified and must later be written to the disk. (This flag is often called a 'dirty bit'.) If the required block is not in the cache it must first be loaded into the cache (unless the write operation replaces the contents of an entire block or uses a block that has been newly acquired from the block service).

The area of memory used for the cache will inevitably become full when sufficient reads and writes have been executed. When a read or write request occurs one of the blocks in the cache must be released, after storing its contents on the disk if its 'dirty bit' has been set. The selection of a block for release may use one of several algorithms. A simple solution is to choose any cache block at random. One of the most effective solutions is always to release the *least recently used* block. To achieve this, cached blocks must be timestamped on every read or write operation.

We have described here a method of caching in which the results of write operations may remain in the main memory cache for as long as there is room for it. When a computer crashes the data in its cache is lost. This cannot be tolerated for write operations that are a part of atomic transactions. In Section 6.6 we describe a stable storage mechanism designed to ensure that the results of write operations are recorded reliably. For the write operations involved in stable storage operations a **write-through** operation must be used. This means that the results of write operations are stored in the cache and immediately sent to the disk before any further operations are performed.

Client caches □ It might seem to be a good idea to have a similar cache in client computers so as to avoid remote procedure calls as well as to economize on disk accesses. However, a file server generally has several clients running on separate computers, each one having a separate cache. Therefore, the various client caches would need to be kept consistent. This requires that each time any client writes new data to a block, this data must be available to any other client that subsequently reads the same block.

A partial solution can be found by making write operations on client caches always write-through – or, in other words, all data written to a client cache is immediately sent on to the file server. This ensures that changes made by a client are immediately available in the file server, but unfortunately it does not ensure that cached versions of a modified block in other clients are updated. This problem can be alleviated in one of the following ways:

1. Clients can update their caches from time to time.
2. Clients can record the time when each block in their cache was loaded. Before each subsequent read the client asks the file server whether the data in the block has changed since it was loaded. If it has changed, the cached data is renewed.

Neither solution is very satisfactory. If the first solution is adopted, the data read from the cache may sometimes be stale. If the second solution is adopted, there must be communication between client and server before each read operation.

Server caches □ File servers generally run as several concurrent processes so that they can provide a service to several clients at once. See for example the worker processes discussed in Section 4.8. If a server is constructed from ordinary processes with separate address spaces, a main memory cache cannot be shared, but if the server processes have separate caches these caches must be kept consistent, leading to difficulties similar to those described for client caches.

A server constructed from lightweight processes or threads (Section 2.4) can use shared main memory for its cache. Some synchronization is required to ensure the consistency of two simultaneous updates to the same block by different threads. This may be achieved by enclosing the operations that access cache blocks in a monitor (Section 4.8.1).

6.2 File storage structure

In this section we describe a typical storage structure for files. The sequence of data items in a file is stored in a number of blocks of a single size, say b data items per block. A file containing N data items is partitioned into a number of sub-sequences each containing b items and a final sub-sequence containing the remainder of the file. The sub-sequences are called **pages** of the file and each page has one block allocated to it; the last block is generally not completely full.

When a new file is created it has no contents and therefore no blocks are allocated to it. Each time a *Write* operation causes a file to be extended to include a new page, the file service requests a new block from the block service. When a

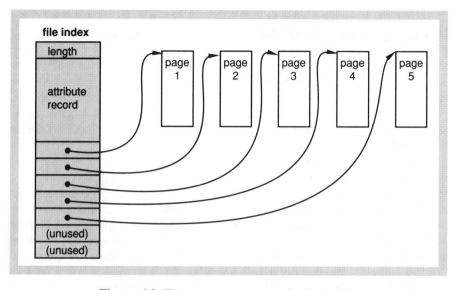

Figure 6.2 The storage structure of a single file.

file is deleted or truncated, the blocks occupied by its pages are released to the block service.

File index □   The storage structure of a file is illustrated in Figure 6.2. A structure in which the blocks in a file are chained in a sequence by pointers stored in the blocks is not used because access to a random block would be unacceptably inefficient, requiring access to all of the blocks that precede it in the file.

Instead, each file has a **file index**. A file index is a table containing a sequence of **block pointers**, one for each page in the file. The position of the beginning of any sequence of data items in a file can be converted to a page number and an offset within the page. In the implementation of the *Read* and *Write* operations (see Box 5.1) the integer argument specifying the *position* of the first data item to be transferred is converted to a page number and an offset within the page. The page number gives the offset in the index table of the corresponding block pointer.

There are some additional items of information that must be stored with each file: the file length and the attribute record (see Section 5.3) containing access control and access time information that is maintained and used by the directory service. This data should be stored with the file rather than with the name of the file in a directory because many directory systems allow files to be referenced by more than one name, but each file should always have exactly one length and attribute record.

The length of a file cannot be calculated by inspection of its index because the last page of the file may not be full. It must be stored with the file index and updated each time the length changes. The file attribute record (see Box 5.2) is stored in the same block as the index or in a block that is referenced from the index. (In UNIX, for example, the file attributes are combined with some of the block pointers in a single file definition block called an **i-node** [Thompson 1978].)

Structure of the file index □ The file index occupies one or more disk blocks; the number of blocks it occupies is determined by the size of a block pointer and the number of pages in the file. If, for example, a block pointer occupies 4 bytes and there are b bytes in each block, an index containing $b/4$ block pointers can be stored in a single block and files of up to $b^2/4$ bytes long can be represented by a one-block index. If, for example, $b = 1024$ bytes then 256 block pointers can be stored in the index and each page is 1024 bytes in length, allowing a maximum file size of 256 blocks or 256 kbytes.

Files of greater length than this are often needed. To allow longer files to be represented, the index is constructed as a tree when a file is too long for its index to be contained in a single block. In this case, the root block contains block pointers of further index blocks, each of which contains pointers to blocks of the file. This sort of index is illustrated in Figure 6.3. In our original example with a block size of 1024 bytes and 256 block pointers per block, the root page can refer to 256 lower blocks, each of which can contain 256 block pointers to file pages. The maximum file length that can be achieved with this index is 256×256 blocks or some 67 million bytes. Some file systems allow for even larger files than this, using an index tree containing three or more levels.

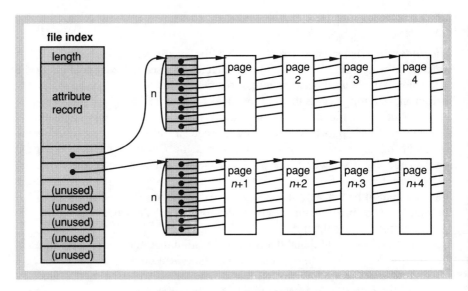

Figure 6.3 A two-level file index.

The Cambridge File Server (CFS) [Needham and Herbert 1982] uses a variant of this scheme in which the first part of each file shares a block with the file index and attributes. Thus, a small file can be stored in only one block. When the file grows, this block is used to hold block pointers and the file data occupies other blocks. This scheme is efficient in both space and time to access small files.

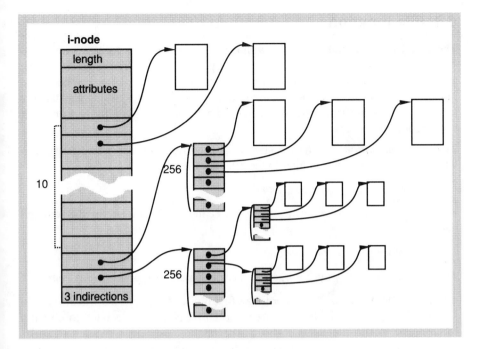

Figure 6.4 UNIX file index structure.

Most versions of UNIX use tree-structured file indexes in which the root (that is, the i-node) occupies 64 bytes (Figure 6.4). I-nodes contain 13 block pointers and the file attribute information (including the owner of the file, access permissions, number of links and dates of access). The first 10 block pointers are used to point to the blocks containing the first 10 pages of the file. In most versions of UNIX the block length is 1024 bytes. The first 10 block pointers in an i-node are therefore sufficient for files of up to 10 240 bytes. When a file is longer than 10 pages, the eleventh block pointer in the i-node is used to point to an index block that contains pointers to a further 256 blocks of the file, giving a maximum length of approximately 266 kbytes. For bigger files, the twelfth block pointer in the i-node is used to point to another index block that contains pointers to 256 other index blocks each of which contains pointers to data blocks giving a maximum file length of approximately 16 million bytes. Finally, if necessary, the thirteenth block pointer in the i-node can be used as the root of a tree of index blocks with three levels of indirection, allowing files containing up to 16 billion bytes.

6.3 File location

The UFID of a file and the offset within the file of the data to be accessed are supplied in each file service request. These parameters are translated by the file server to obtain the location of the file index and of the file pages accessed by the request. This method is used for referencing file pages to ensure that the file service requests are stateless, but because the translation is performed once for every request it must be fast.

Two-step translation □   The translation is often done as a two-step process in which the first step gets a pointer to the relevant file index:

   UFID → block pointer of file index

and the second accesses the file index to get the block pointer for the required page p in the file:

   p → block pointer for page p

There are at least two ways to organize the file system to support the first step:

1. Each UFID contains a pointer to the first block of the relevant file index. No file location map is then required; the UFID is simply decoded to obtain a pointer to the file index. This is the method used in CFS and a similar technique is used in UNIX to obtain file locations. In most versions of UNIX, file indexes are stored as fixed-size records called i-nodes and all of the i-nodes are stored together in a sequence of disk blocks. Within a single UNIX filing system i-node numbers correspond to UFIDs and the location of each file index can be calculated from its i-node number. This method is not widely used in file servers because it makes it difficult or impossible to relocate a file index (or, in CFS, the first page of a file) and because it is incompatible with systems that maintain replicated copies of files in several servers. Inability to relocate files severely constrains the management of disk space in file servers.
2. A stored table or map is maintained giving the correspondence between UFIDs and file index block pointers. This is called the **file location map** and may be represented in several ways, discussed below. The advantage of this is that the location of any file index can be changed, so disk storage can be managed more flexibly.

One-step translation □   In the XDFS system the file location map and the file indexes are combined as a single table, giving:

   UFID × p → block pointer for page p

The representation of this map requires a large data structure optimized for searching to locate specific *UFID × p* pairs.

Implementation of file location maps □   UFIDs are allocated randomly from a very large range of integers in order to ensure uniqueness and security. The translation of UFIDs to file locations therefore requires a lookup operation.

Similar data structures and lookup methods can be used for both translation methods. In the two-step method only the UFID is used as a search key. In the one-step case, the two parameters *UFID* and p – the page number in the file – are combined to form a single search key, for example by concatenating them so that the higher-order bits represent the UFID and the lower-order bits the page in the file.

In both cases a stored data structure is used to represent the table of pairs (f_i, B_i) where f_i is the search key and B_i is a block pointer. This data structure must have the following properties:

- The number of pairs can vary.
- Looking up f_i and delivering B_i is fast.

B-trees are an effective method for structuring a searchable set of data. B-trees were developed as a general-purpose data structure by Bayer and McCreight [1972] and are described fully in Knuth [1973] (on pages 473–479) and Ullman [1984]. For the translation of UFIDs to file locations B-trees were first used in XDFS and have since been used in several other file servers.

A B-tree is a balanced tree of nodes, that is, all of the leaf nodes are at the same height below the root. In order to avoid rearranging the tree too often, each node may be less than full. All nodes with the exception of the root node must be at least half full. The node size is chosen according to the number of pairs to be stored and to restrict the maximum height of the tree to some limit that can be tolerated.

To represent our mapping, the tree will require one block per node. Each leaf node contains a sequence of pairs, these are (f_i, B_i), $i = 1,2,..$ where the B_i are numbers of blocks that contain pages of files. The nodes above the leaves also contain such pairs, but, in this case, the B_i are the numbers of blocks containing lower nodes of the tree.

When a B-tree mapping is used for one-step translation (as it is in XDFS) it provides fast access from $UFID \times p$ to block pointer, the speed depending on the height of the B-tree. Having found the block pointer for one page of a file, successive pages will be found in successive entries in the same leaf of the B-tree, or in the adjacent leaf. Some implementations of B-trees maintain a link to the next leaf. On the other hand, the B-tree must contain an entry for every page in every file, so access to small files is penalized in comparison with the other methods described and the absence of file indexes in the one-step method means that file attributes must be stored with the file itself.

6.4 A block service

A **block service** manages and accesses the contents of a large collection of disk blocks. It must provide service functions that enable clients to:

- obtain new blocks,
- release blocks that are no longer required,
- transfer data into and out of blocks, using checksums to detect errors.

Block pointers are generated by the block service in response to requests for new blocks. They are constructed so that the address of the relevant disk block can be derived from a block pointer by some simple transformation. For example, if the set of blocks managed by a block server resides on a single disk drive, a block pointer could simply be the address of the block on the disk. But block servers generally manage blocks stored on several disks and the block pointers include a prefix that identifies the disk.

AllocateBlock( ) → Block
> allocates a new block and delivers its pointer.

FreeBlock(Block)
> releases *Block*.

GetBlock(Block) → Data — REPORTS(CheckSum, InvalidBlock)
> delivers the sequence of data items stored in *Block*. Error report if data doesn't agree with the checksum on the block or *Block* is not a valid block pointer.

PutBlock(Block, Data) — REPORTS(CheckSum, InvalidBlock)
> copies the sequence of items in *Data* to *Block*. Error report if data doesn't agree with the checksum on reading back or *Block* is not a valid block pointer.

Box 6.1   Block service operations.

The block service supports block read and write operations, implementing them in terms of more primitive disk operations, and manages the space on the disks, maintaining a free-block list or a map of free blocks. A possible set of block service operations is defined in Box 6.1 using our usual notation, with *Block* standing for a block pointer. We shall discuss the implementation of the file service operations in terms of these block operations in Section 6.5.

Size of block pointers □   The size chosen for block pointers determines the maximum number of blocks that can be stored by the block server. If a block pointer is represented as a 32-bit integer, then the block service can manage a storage system containing $2^{32} \approx 4 \times 10^9$ blocks. If we further assume that each block contains 1024 bytes (i.e. $b = 1024$), we get a total capacity of 4×10^{12} bytes (or 4 Gigabytes) for the storage system. This has been considered adequate for practical purposes in most of the file systems and file servers developed to date, allowing the block service to manage the space on several disk drives, but continuing developments in storage technology are likely to produce storage systems with larger capacities.

Although we shall assume 32-bit block pointers in this chapter because that size can be represented by an integer in most programming languages, there is no intrinsic difficulty in extending the size of a block pointer to say 48 bits, and it would be prudent to do so in systems designed to exploit future developments in storage technology.

Size of blocks □   The use of large blocks reduces the effect of latency and the complexity of the file index for large files, hence reducing access times, whereas the use of small blocks improves the utilization of disk storage when there are many small files in a file system. If the block size is b bytes and the block pointer requires 4 bytes, then an index tree with two levels allows a maximum file size of only $b^2/16$ blocks. If $b = 512$, this gives an upper bound of 8 Mbytes. Files larger than this require an index tree with three or more levels. To represent a file of length 2^{32} bytes with a two-level index, b must be at least 4096.

A more important reason for the use of large blocks is that the speed of sequential access to the data in a file consisting of several blocks is strongly affected by latency. We saw in Section 6.1 that the time t_l to initiate access to a disk is approximately 1000 times as long as the time t_t to transfer each byte of data. Because of this, if a program accesses all of the data in a file, the total time is approximately proportional to the number of blocks that the file is stored in. Larger block sizes reduce the contribution that latency makes to access times. On the other hand, the use of large blocks can lead to considerable wasted space because, on average, half a block is wasted at the end of each file. Measurements have demonstrated that, in most UNIX systems, there is a preponderance of small files [McKusick et al. 1984].

Some examples of block sizes used in current systems are:

File system	Block size b	Page size in bytes	
XDFS	1024	1024	
CFS	2048	2048	
UNIX Version 7	512	512	
UNIX System V	1024	1024	
UNIX BSD 4.2	4096 or 8192	512,...,4096,8192	(see below)
Amoeba	2048	variable up to 32k	(see below)

In the first four cases the page size is the same as the block size. In the Amoeba system the page size can be anything up to 32 kbytes. A large page is represented by a linked list of blocks and the file index refers to the first block in the list. This helps to keep the size and complexity of file indexes down, while avoiding the space inefficiency of large blocks.

Multiple block sizes □   We have noted that large blocks are desirable to reduce the effects of latency when accessing large files, while small blocks are useful to optimize space utilization when there are many small files in a file system. In some recently developed systems, including the 4.2 BSD version of UNIX, a number of different block sizes are used. Space management is handled by extending the scheme already describe for equal-sized blocks to include a separate list of available blocks of each size.

In BSD 4.2 UNIX, blocks are divided into 2, 4 or 8 *fragments*. A file consists of a number of blocks followed by a number of fragments. A file of length N bytes consists of $(N/b)-1$ blocks, the remainder $r = (N \ REM \ b)$ bytes is made up of fragments. The fragments are of length (b/2), (b/4) or (b/8) bytes respectively and a file will contain zero or one fragment of each of these lengths in addition to the complete blocks.

This scheme allows block sizes as large 8192 bytes to be used, with a substantial gain in the speed of file access and without significant loss of space efficiency when storing small files, because several can be stored in a single block. This and other efficiency measures that were incorporated in the BSD 4.2 file system resulted in a substantial improvement in its performance compared with the original UNIX file system. McKusick et al. [1984] report that the improved BSD 4.2 file system is able to transfer data in read and write operations at speeds in the range 30–47% of the raw disk bandwidth, whereas the performance of the original system was in the range 2–5%.

6.5　Implementation of the file service operations

We will now outline the implementation of the file service operations defined in Chapter 5, with a two-step translation of the UFID given in the requests and the page number (derived from the *Position* argument) to a block number through a file location map and a simple file index.

File index operations □　A set of operations suitable for the manipulation of file indexes is defined in Box 6.2. They are privileged operations for the manipulation of file indexes, available for use only within the file server software.

ToIndex(File, PageNo, Block)
>　records the *Block* pointer for *PageNo*, in the index of the file whose UFID is *File*.

FromIndex(File, PageNo) → Block — REPORTS(FileOverflow)
>　returns the block pointer associated with *PageNo* in the index of the file whose UFID is *File*. Error reported if *PageNo* refers to a page position beyond the end of the file.

SetLength(File, l)
>　sets the length of *File* to *l* (recording it in the file index). This operation is needed for implementing *Write* and *Truncate*.

GetLength(File)→ l
>　returns the length *l* of the file whose UFID is *File*.

CopyIndex(File1, File2)
>　replaces the index of the file with UFID *File2* with a copy of the index of the file with UFID *File1* (used in Chapter 7).

Box 6.2　File index operations.

They would be implemented as a separate layer or service accessible only to the file server software and depending only on the block service operations. File service operations can be defined in terms of the block service operations as follows:

- The *Create* operation generates a new UFID, allocates the space needed for the file index and file attributes and adds a new item to the file location mapping. It sets the file length to zero.
- The *Delete* operation removes the relevant item from the file location mapping and releases all of the blocks in the file including the blocks occupied by the file index and file attributes.
- *Truncate* alters the recorded value of the file length and frees the surplus blocks.
- *Read* is defined using *GetBlock* and *Write* is defined using *AllocateBlock* and *PutBlock*.

The Write operation □   As an illustrative example we show in Figure 6.5 an implementation for the file service *Write* operation defined in Section 5.2. The data to be written may extend across a number of pages and the first and last pages are only partially overwritten by the new data. Where the entire contents of a block is to be replaced by new data, there is no need to read the old contents of the block into the *buffer*, but for simplicity we have not optimized the program to recognize this as a special case.

If the sequence of data to be written extends the file into one or more new pages, *FromIndex* will cause an error report *FileOverflow*. In this case a new block is allocated and its block pointer is recorded in the index of the file using *ToIndex*. The data items to be written are copied to a buffer one page (or partial page) at a time using a procedure *CopyData* that we have assumed to exist, and then written to the appropriate block using the block service operation *PutBlock*.

6.6 Recoverability

File servers should ensure that the files that they hold are accessible after all kinds of system failures except the most catastrophic. In particular, the file location map and the file indexes must be recoverable if the system fails while updating them or a disk error occurs resulting in an invalid block. As mentioned in Chapter 2, the effects of failures are often more pervasive in distributed than in centralized systems because client and server computers may fail independently and there is an even greater need to design servers so that they can recover from failures without loss of permanent data.

In both conventional and distributed systems, disk hardware and driver software can be designed to ensure that if the system 'crashes' during a block write operation, or a data transfer error occurs during a block transfer, partially-written data or incorrect data are detected. To achieve this, blocks are recorded with a checksum and the following procedures are used to detect errors:

1. A checksum is computed and recorded with each block whenever the contents of the block are altered.
2. When reading a block the checksum is recomputed from the data and compared with the stored checksum. If there is a discrepancy the block is re-read. If there is still a discrepancy after a predefined number of re-tries an

```
(* assumes
        constants:          PAGESIZE              : integer;
                            FileOverflow    : ErrorType;
        procedures:    GetLength — defined in the file service interface
                            ErrorExit — server reports error to client
                            SequenceLength  — length operation for data sequences
                            CopyData — local procedure to copy blocks in memory
    *)
PROCEDURE Write(File : UFID; Position : CARDINAL; Data : Seqptr);
VAR  page, firstPage, lastPage, blockPtr, lastItem, length : CARDINAL;
        buffer: Block;
BEGIN
        length := GetLength(File);
        IF Position > length THEN
                BEGIN ErrorReport := FileOverFlow; ErrorExit END
        lastItem := Position + SequenceLength(Data) - 1;
        firstPage := (Position DIV PAGESIZE);
        lastPage := (lastItem DIV PAGESIZE);
        FOR page := firstPage TO lastPage DO
            blockPtr := FromIndex(File, page);
            IF ErrorReport = FileOverflow THEN (* we are creating a new file page *)
            blockPtr := AllocateBlock();
            ToIndex(File, page, blockPtr)
            ELSE (* we are updating an existing block *)
              GetBlock(blockPtr, buffer)
            END
            CopyData(buffer, Data, Position MOD PAGESIZE, page-firstPage);
                (* copies the next portion of the Data sequence to buffer *)
            PutBlock(blockPtr, buffer);
        END;
        IF lastItem ≥ length THEN SetLength(File, lastItem+1);
END Write;
```

Figure 6.5 Implementation of *Write*.

error condition is reported to the client. This procedure guards against transient errors while reading a block and ensures that any blocks containing partially-written data following a system crash will be detected when they are next read because the partial data in such blocks will not correspond to the stored checksum, whether or not the new checksum was successfully written before the crash.

3. After each block write operation the contents of the block is read back from the disk and compared with the value that was written. If there is a discrepancy the write operation is repeated. If the discrepancy persists after a predefined number of attempts to write the block, a pointer to the block is

recorded in a list of 'bad blocks' and an error is reported to the client. The client should then request a different block from the block service and write the data in the new block. This procedure ensures that data is correctly written unless the system fails during a write operation.

Disk driver software that operates in this manner is described as providing *careful* block transfer operations. This careful property is assumed for the *PutBlock* and *GetBlock* operations in the block server described in the previous section. *Careful* block transfers are an essential step towards the achievement of reliable file storage, ensuring that errors made when recording data in files are detected, but they do not by themselves ensure the recoverability of the file system's structure after system failures. For example, if the system fails while writing a file index block, all of the blocks referenced from the index block may become inaccessible; if a failure occurs while writing a block that is part of the file location map all of the files referenced from the block may become inaccessible.

File system integrity and recovery □   Transient errors are adequately dealt with by the *careful* transfers described above. However, inconsistency may arise even with *careful* block transfers because a system failure during a write operation may result in a partial transfer of the data – leaving a block containing detectably bad data. The data in such blocks cannot sensibly be used, so vital information such as file indexes and the file location map must be reduntantly stored, at least in duplicate, if the file system is to be recoverable. But if an error (of the sort described in (2) above) occurs while reading vital structural information or when checking the consistency of the file store after a system crash, the server must be able to use the redundant information to restore the file store to a consistent state.

There are many ways in which the structural information used in a file server can be redundantly stored. In CFS, for example, the structural information is stored in two quite different forms. *Form 1*, which is the one used for normal access, resembles the file indexes and file location mapping tables described in the preceding section. *Form 2* uses a set of *cylinder maps*. There is a cylinder map associated with each cylinder of disk storage, holding an entry for each block in the cylinder. Each entry in a cylinder map holds the allocation state of the block, and if it is in use, the UFID of the file to which block belongs and the position of the block in the file's index. The server software that updates the file structure is careful to alter the Form 2 information only when the Form 1 information is known to be consistent, and vice versa. A damaged file index block can be reconstructed by processing the cylinder map and similarly a cylinder map block can be reconstructed by processing all of the file indexes.

Stable storage □   In XDFS and some other file servers, the use of redundant storage for structural information is implemented as a separate abstraction provided by the block service, called **stable storage**. Stable storage is a generic approach designed to ensure that any essential permanent data will be recoverable after any single system failure, including system failures during a disk write operation and damage to any single disk block. Operations on stable blocks are implemented using two disk blocks to represent each stable block and holding the contents of each stable block in duplicate. As stable storage operations are more costly in disk space and in time than conventional block service operations, they are normally used by file servers only to hold vital structural information.

Lampson [1981b] developed the principles of stable storage. He defined a set of operations on **stable blocks** that mirror our block service operations. Box 6.3 gives their definitions. These additional service functions could be included in the operations provided by a block server, offering clients (i.e. file servers) *careful* and *stable* operations as appropriate. When that is done, the block pointers used to refer to stable blocks should be distinguished from those used to refer to ordinary blocks by their type, or in a typeless language, by the range of values that they may have.

AllocateStableBlock() → *StableBlock*
        allocates a new stable block and delivers its pointer.
FreeStableBlock(StableBlock)
        releases *StableBlock*.
StableGet(StableBlock) → *Data*
        delivers the sequence of data items stored in the *StableBlock*.
StablePut(StableBlock, Data)
        copies the sequence of items in *Data* to *StableBlock*.

Box 6.3 Stable block service operations.

Implementing stable storage □   A pair of disk blocks is used to represent each block of stable storage. If possible, the blocks are located in different disk drives to reduce the chances that both will be damaged in a single mechanical failure. The server ensures that the following **invariant** is maintained for each pair of blocks:

- Not more than one of the pair is bad.
- If both are good, they both have the most recent data, except during the execution of *StablePut*.

A block pointer given as an argument to the stable storage operations is translated by the block server into two conventional block pointers referring to the two blocks that represent the stable block. The translation is defined by a simple algorithm; for example, the stable block pointer may be identical to the conventional pointer for one of the pair and the second may be calculated by adding a fixed offset.

The procedure *StableGet* reads one of the pair of representative blocks using *GetBlock*. If an error condition is detected then it reads the other representative.

StablePut writes the *Data* in each of the two representative blocks sequentially using *PutBlock*, ensuring that the first *PutBlock* is successful before commencing the second. In order to exclude other processes from access to the pair of blocks during the *StablePut* operation, a monitor (see Section 4.8.1) is used to exclude other *StablePut* operations.

If a server halts or crashes during *StablePut* a recovery procedure is invoked when the server is re-started. After a server halts, the pair of blocks representing each stable block will be in one of the following states:

1. both good and the same,
2. both good and different,
3. one good, one bad.

The recovery procedure is designed to maintain the invariant. It inspects the pairs of blocks and does the following in each the above cases:

1. nothing,
2. copies one block of the pair to the other block of the pair,
3. copies the good block to the bad block.

Combating decay □   We can extend this stable storage scheme to deal with *data decay* in the representative blocks of stable storage by running the recovery process at regular intervals. If decays are known to occur with a maximum time frequency, the recovery process must be run at a similar frequency so that the likelihood of both blocks in a representative pair decaying is vanishingly small.

6.7 Summary

File systems are usually implemented by storing file data in blocks of a fixed size; the use of blocks overcomes the latency problems associated with disk access and a fixed size simplifies storage management. Each file has a *file index* recording the block pointers of disk blocks in which its pages are stored. This enables immediate access to the data in a particular page and allows files to be stored in non-contiguous blocks. File indexes are built as tree structures for efficient access to large files.

The file service is divided into two layers and these may be implemented as separate services, a block service dealing with disk block allocation and access, and a file service dealing only with the location of the pages in files, passing requests for operations on the pages to the block service.

A file server must be able to map a UFID onto the location of its file. If the UFID contains the block pointer of the disk block containing the file index, the file may be found quickly; but unfortunately this forces a fixed location on the file index, so a preferred method is to use arbitrary UFIDs and a file location map.

Stable storage provides recoverable disk blocks by writing each block of data to two separate disk blocks, guaranteeing that at least one is correct even when a computer or disk fails.

EXERCISES

6.1   Suggest three alternatives to or variations on the use of B-trees to hold the file location map; consider the advantages of each.

6.2   Define the file service *Read* operation in terms of the file index operations of Box 6.2 and block service operations of Box 6.1.

6.3   Modify the *Write* operation given in Figure 6.5 so that, if an entire block is to be written to disk, the data is not first read into the buffer.

6.4   Describe the necessary components of a data structure for implementing a cache. Describe the effect on your data structure of reading from a disk block and writing data to a disk block. Explain what happens when the cache is full.

6.5   Discuss the relative merits of building a disk block cache in the block service and in the file service.

6.6   Assume as in Figure 6.5 that disk blocks and file pages contain *PAGESIZE* bytes and that a block pointer is a *CARDINAL*. Define a data structure that is suitable for holding the length of a file and its file index, assuming that it will fit in a single disk block. Use this data structure to define procedures implementing the file index operations shown in Box 6.2 in terms of the block service operations (Box 6.1). You may assume the existence of a function *FindFileIndex* that maps a UFID onto the block pointer of the disk block containing the file index.

6.7   In your answer to question 6.6, assume that *PAGESIZE* is 2048 bytes and a block pointer 32 bits. What is the maximum length of file you could represent? What are the advantages and disadvantages of increasing *PAGESIZE*?

6.8   Describe a simple implementation of a file location map that fits into a single disk block. You should assume that the block pointer cannot be calculated from the UFID. Describe a data structure for representing the file location map and use it to define the function *FindFileIndex* that maps a UFID on to the block pointer of the disk block containing the file index. When would entries be added to the file location map? How many files can you map if you assume the same block and block pointer sizes as in question 6.7?

Chapter 7
Shared Files

An *atomic transaction* is a set of operations that is indivisible in two senses:
- A transaction is all-or-nothing in its effects.
- The partial effects must be invisible to other transactions.

There are two factors that threaten the atomicity of transactions:
- failure of processes and computers;
- concurrency.

We discuss two approaches to recovery after failures:

intentions lists
   An intentions list contains the proposed operations in a transaction.
file versions
   A file version represents the proposed changes to a file.

Concurrency control is needed to preserve atomicity in the presence of concurrent transactions. We discuss three forms of concurrency control:

locking
   the data being used by a transaction;
optimistic concurrency control
   is based on checks at the time that a transaction closes;
timestamps
   show when items of data were last read or written.

Finally, we describe the implementation of a transaction service using stable storage.

7.1 Introduction

If a basic file service such as that described in Chapter 5 is used concurrently by several client programs to read and write data in the same file, the resulting effect on the file is, in general, unpredictable. If the client programs are executed without synchronization, the sequences of read and write operations requested in the different programs may be interleaved in many ways, some of which would not leave the file in the intended state.

The provision of **atomic transactions** in a file service enables a client program to define sequences of operations on files that must be performed without interference from other clients. A file server that supports transactions must synchronize the operations sufficiently to ensure that this is so. In addition, if a server or client process halts unexpectedly due to a hardware fault or a software error before a transaction is completed, the server subsequently restores any files that were undergoing modification to their original state.

An atomic transaction is a sequence of file operations that forms a single step from the client's point of view, transforming the stored data from one consistent state to another. For example, when a sum of money has to be transferred from one bank account to another, the first account must be debited and the second credited. The transaction consists of two banking operations (debiting and crediting) and both of these operations must be carried out. The customer details and balance for each account would be stored in a file, and the banking operations would be implemented using file operations (*Reads* and *Writes*). If these operations are performed by a server on request from a client program, either of the conditions mentioned above – interference by other client programs or a client or server failure – could produce undetected errors unless steps are taken to prevent it. Interference by other clients who are also updating the same account data could produce an incorrect balance. See the description of the *lost update* problem in Section 5.3. If a client or server failure occurs during the transaction one account's balance might be debited before the failure but the other might be left unchanged.

To prevent such occurrences, systems that support atomic transactions must satisfy two requirements. First, each transaction must be **recoverable**; when a client or server halts unexpectedly, the changes to files within the transaction must either be completed or the effect must be the same as if the transaction had not been started. That is, all the *Write*, *Create*, *Delete* and *Truncate* operations within a single transaction must either be done completely or not done at all. Secondly, the concurrent execution of several atomic transactions must be **serially equivalent** in the sense that the effect of performing them concurrently is always the same as if they had been done one at a time in some arbitrary order.

In general a transaction may involve several files and may include file service operations that have any of the following effects: create new files, change the values of data items in files and add new items, inspect the values of items in files and delete or truncate files. These are just the operations that a basic file service can perform. In the following discussion of atomic transactions we shall generally refer to the unit of data which is accessed or modified by a client operation as an 'item in a file'. This term may be taken to mean whatever is appropriate in a particular application; it may for example be a bank account record or a database record and we assume that such an item is retrieved by one *Read* operation and stored by one *Write* operation.

A **transaction service** may be regarded as an extension or a variation of a file service that provides atomic actions on some or all of its files. An atomic transaction is achieved by cooperation between a client program and a transaction service; the client specifies the sequence of operations that are to comprise a transaction and the transaction service guarantees to preserve the atomic property of the whole sequence. The client specifies the operations within a transaction by requesting a sequence of operations on one or more files, prefacing the sequence with an *OpenTransaction* operation to introduce each new transaction and concluding it with a *CloseTransaction* operation to indicate its end.

Normally, the transaction service notes the start of each new transaction and performs the client's requests until it receives a *CloseTransaction* request. If the transaction has progressed normally the server then reports to the client that the transaction is **committed** – this constitutes an undertaking by the service to the client that all of the file changes requested in the transaction are permanently recorded and that any future transactions that access the same data will see the results of all of the changes made during the transaction.

Alternatively, the transaction may have to **abort** for one of several reasons related to the nature of the transaction itself, to conflicts with another transaction or to the failure of processes, computers and disks. When a transaction is aborted the transaction service must ensure that the files accessed within the transaction revert to the state that they were in before the transaction started.

A transaction is either successful or it is aborted in one of two ways – the client aborts it (using an *AbortTransaction* call to the server) or the server aborts it. Figure 7.1 shows these three alternative life histories for transactions.

Successful	*Aborted by client*	*Aborted by server*	
OpenTransaction	*OpenTransaction*		
file operation	*file operation*		*file operation*
file operation	*file operation*		*file operation*
•	•	*SERVER*	•
•	•	*ABORTS→*	•
file operation	*file operation*		
CloseTransaction	*AbortTransaction*		

Figure 7.1 Transaction life histories.

When a transaction is aborted the transaction service must ensure that files updated during the transaction are restored to the state that they were in before the transaction started. The possibility that a transaction may have to be aborted means that all of the file update operations performed during a transaction must be done in a *tentative* manner. That is, the update operations are performed in such a way that they may either be permanently recorded or undone. If and when a transaction is committed, all of the operations are made permanent in a single step during which other transactions are excluded from access to the data that is being altered.

7.1.1 The need for transactions

The following example will be used to illustrate the need for synchronization of file updates and to show how a form of serialization meets that need. Suppose that a banking system is built as a distributed system utilizing a file server to store the database of customer account records. Consider the following pair of simple actions on three bank accounts called A, B and C. Action T transfers $2 from account A to account B. Action U transfers $3 from account B to account C.

Transaction T:
Read balance (a) of account A
Read balance (b) of account B
Write new balance (a–$2) to account A
Write new balance (b+$2) to account B

Transaction U:
Read balance (c) of account C
Write new balance (c+$3) to account C
Read balance (b) of account B
Write new balance (b–$3) to account B

Figure 7.2 Two banking transactions.

Figure 7.2 contains an informal description of two programs that might be used to perform these actions. Two client processes execute the transactions T and U by communicating with a file server, using the simple *Read* and *Write* operations defined in Chapter 5. Note that the clients might issue their requests for file operations over an extended period of time. The time taken to complete the transactions would be particularly extended if the program was designed to interact with a human user, allowing the user, for example, to check that account A contained sufficient funds to complete the transaction. The net effects of executing the transactions T and U should be to:

- decrease the balance of account A by $2,
- decrease the balance of account B by $1,
- increase the balance of account C by $3.

If the transactions are executed sequentially so that one of them is completed before the other starts, this is the result obtained.

The need for serialization of transactions □ Now consider the effects of allowing the two transactions T and U to progress concurrently. Initially, let us assume that the file server makes no attempt to serialize the execution of the transactions.

Transaction T	*Transaction U*
Read (a)	
	Read (c)
	Write (c+$3)
Read (b)	
Write (a–$2)	
	Read (b)
Write (b+$2)	
	Write (b–$3)

Figure 7.3 One possible interleaving of T and U (time down the page).

Figure 7.3 shows† one possible interleaving in time of the operations in the transactions T and U. Both transactions read *b* and then alter it and, as U writes its result after T, the result is incorrect, decreasing the balance of account B by $3 instead of $1. This is another illustration of the *lost update* problem in which U overwrites T's update without seeing it.

Transaction T	*Transaction U*
Read (a)	
	Read (c)
	Write (c+$3)
Read (b)	
Write (a–$2)	
	Read (b)
	Write (b–$3)
Write (b+$2)	

Figure 7.4 A second possible interleaving of T and U.

Another possible interleaving of the two transactions is shown in Figure 7.4. U writes its value to *b* before T does and the final result is again incorrect, increasing the balance of account B by $2. Here we have another lost update – this time U's update is lost.

The results produced in Figures 7.2 and 7.3 are clearly wrong. The cause of the error is that both clients are accessing the balance of account B and then altering it in a manner that depends upon its previous value. In terms of file accesses, the balance of account B is a part of record in a file that is read and written by the two transactions. When the two transactions proceed concurrently without synchronization, we cannot predict the actual sequence of reads and writes that will occur.

---

†   In Figures 7.2 to 7.4 we show the operations that read or write the balance of an account on successive lines down the page, and the reader should assume that an operation on a particular line is executed at a later time than the one on the line above it. The operations are abbreviated so that for example 'Read (a)' means 'Read the balance *a* of account A'.

Serial equivalence □ We could get the correct balance for account B by forcing the transactions T and U to be performed serially, completing one before the second is allowed to commence, but the complete serialization of all transactions that access the same data is unnecessarily restrictive and can produce long delays in the completion of tasks.

It is possible to allow some parts of the transactions T and U to be interleaved in time and still achieve the correct effect. Figure 7.5 shows one such interleaving in which the operations that affect the shared account, B, are actually serial, for transaction T does all its operations on B before transaction U does. Another interleaving of T and U that has this property is one in which transaction U completes its operations on account B before transaction T starts.

An interleaving of transactions in which the combined effect is the same as if the transactions had been performed one at a time in some order is a **serially equivalent** interleaving.

Transaction T	Transaction U
Read (a)	
	Read (c)
Read (b)	
Write (a–$2)	
	Write (c+$3)
Write (b+$2)	
	Read (b)
	Write (b–$3)

Figure 7.5 A serially equivalent interleaving of T and U.

Serial equivalence is used as a criterion for the correctness of concurrently executing transactions. If each of several transactions is known to have the correct effect on files when it is done on its own, then we can infer that if these transactions are done one at a time in some order the combined effect will also be correct. Such transactions can be performed concurrently by interleaving their operations in time and still produce the correct results provided that the combined effect is serially equivalent.

In Section 7.3 we shall introduce methods that can be used to control the concurrent execution of transactions. There are three main approaches based on:

- *locking*: in which each file item is locked by the first transaction that accesses it so that no other transaction may access the item until the first transaction has committed or aborted.
- *optimistic concurrency control*: in which it is hoped that no conflicts of access will occur. Transactions proceed until they are ready to commit, when there is a check. If conflicts with earlier transactions have occurred, a transaction is aborted and must be restarted.
- *timestamps*: in which each transaction has a timestamp and file items are timestamped each time they are accessed. Transactions are aborted and restarted when they are too late to perform an operation on a particular item.

Such methods for concurrency control are designed to allow two or more transactions to be executed concurrently while maintaining the serial equivalence property.

The effects of failure on concurrent transactions □   The possibility that a transaction may abort has implications for concurrent transactions. Suppose that, in the executions illustrated in Figure 7.5, the transaction T aborts after writing the new value of b. Then the transaction U will have seen a value that never existed, since b will be restored to its original value. Various unpredictable effects can occur depending whether b is restored to its original value before or after U writes its new value.

Isolated values of file items □   As a client progresses through the operations of a transaction, it may make repeated use of the same item in a file. For example, it may read an item, write back an increased value of the item and subsequently read it again. On the second read operation, the client should be given the increased value rather than the original value of the item, but if other transactions that are interleaved with it read the same data items, atomicity requires that they should see the original data values until the first transaction is committed.

As a client progresses through a transaction, tentative values of file items are made on its behalf. These values are not only tentative, but also must be *isolated* in the sense that they are visible to the transaction in which they were made but are invisible to all other concurrent transactions. Later operations in a transaction use these isolated values instead of the original values in the file, but no other transaction may have access to the isolated values as they will not be valid if the first transaction is aborted. Finally, when a transaction is committed, the isolated tentative values are incorporated into the appropriate files. In the rest of this chapter we shall generally refer to such values as 'tentative', but the reader should assume that we mean to imply that the values are isolated as well as tentative.

Recovery after a process halts unexpectedly □   A transaction requires co-operation between a client and a transaction service based on one or more servers and it can only exist so long as none of them halts. When a computer halts and then restarts, its main memory will contain unpredictable values whereas the servers' disks and the main memory in the other computers still contain information about any transactions that they were involved in at the time.

A transaction service requires a recovery procedure that restores files that were undergoing modification to a consistent state. Consider the execution of transaction T defined in Figure 7.2 and suppose that either the client or the server halts unexpectedly after the balance in account A has been decreased, but before the balance of account B has been increased. If the accounts are left in this state, they will of course be wrong (although the bank might profit from it!). The transaction service that holds the files containing the account records is responsible for ensuring that, if the transaction T is unable to complete, the files are returned to the state they were in before the transaction started.

Service actions for recovery □   If a transaction service is unable to complete all of the operations of a transaction, it will be left holding the tentative values of files produced during the uncompleted atomic transaction. It must restore their values to those they had before the transaction started before any other client is given access to them. The process of restoring files to a state that is known to be consistent is called **recovery**.

When a server halts unexpectedly it must deal with outstanding transactions when it starts up again. All committed transactions must be completed and all other transactions must be aborted and the previous state of their files recovered.

When a client halts unexpectedly during a transaction, the server must be able to recognize this in order to cope with the situation. Servers can give each transaction an expiry time and abort any transaction that has not completed before its expiry time.

Client actions relating to aborted transactions □   If a server halts while a transaction is in progress the client will become aware of this when one of the operations fails to return a result. If a server halts and then restarts during the progress of a transaction, the transaction will no longer be valid and the client must be informed as a result of the next operation. In either case, the client must then formulate a plan, possibly in consultation with the human user, for the completion or abandonment of the task of which the transaction was a part.

Sometimes the client program may need to abort a transaction, for example if the user decides to abandon the current task. The client can do so by using an *AbortTransaction* call to the server.

7.1.2 The transaction service

A *transaction service* is a form of file service that supports atomic transactions on its files. It supports a construct to allow a client program to group together the file service operations that comprise an atomic transaction. Box 7.1 shows the definitions of the operations in a transaction service interface. The operations are defined according to our usual notational convention and the following new argument name is used:

    Trans: transaction identifiers or TIDs.

In addition to the usual file service operations three new operations are provided to open, close and abort transactions. When a transaction is opened, the service delivers a unique transaction identifier (TID) to the client. All of the procedures with the exception of *OpenTransaction* would report an error for an invalid TID, but these errors are not shown in Box 7.1. The client uses the transaction identifier delivered by *OpenTransaction* to indicate which of the subsequent file operations (up to the close of the transaction) are to be included in the particular transaction it identifies. All of the file service operations defined in Chapter 5 are included in the transaction service with a modified interface. In this modified interface, each procedure call requires an additional argument to specify the transaction identifier and the procedure names are modified to indicate the difference: *TRead, TWrite, TCreate, TDelete, TTruncate* and *TLength*.

Normally, when a client has performed the file operations that comprise the transaction, it terminates the transaction using *CloseTransaction* which delivers a *Commit* result, indicating that the transaction has committed and that subsequent

---

OpenTransaction → *Trans*

    starts a new transaction and delivers a unique TID *Trans*. This identifier will be used in the other operations in the transaction.

CloseTransaction(Trans) → *(Commit, Abort)*

    ends a transaction: a *Commit* returned value indicates that the transaction has committed; an *Abort* returned value indicates that it has aborted.

AbortTransaction(Trans)

    aborts the transaction.

TWrite(Trans, File, i, Data) — *REPORTS(BadPosition)*

    has the same effect as *Write(File, i, data)* but records the new data in a tentative form pending the completion of the transaction *Trans*.

TRead(Trans, File, i, n) → *Data* — *REPORTS(BadPosition)*

    delivers the tentative data resulting from the transaction *Trans* if any has been recorded, otherwise has the same effect as *Read(File, i, n)* .

TCreate(Trans, filetype) → *File*

    records a tentative *Create* pending the completion of the transaction *Trans*.

TDelete(Trans, File)

    records a tentative *Delete* pending the completion of the transaction *Trans*.

TTruncate(Trans, File)

    records a tentative *Truncate* pending the completion of the transaction *Trans*.

TLength(Trans, File) → *Length*

    delivers the tentative new length resulting from the transaction *Trans* if any has been recorded, otherwise has the same effect as *Length*.

Box 7.1 Transaction service operations.

---

transactions by other clients will see the results of all of the changes to files made within the transaction. If the transaction has been aborted an *Abort* result is delivered from *CloseTransaction*. Figure 7.6 shows how the modules of a transaction service may be built from a block service and a stable block service.

7.2 Recovery

Recovery cannot be achieved by just restoring the altered file items to the state they were in before the transaction started, for other concurrent transactions may meanwhile have made changes to some of these items. Nor is the notion of 'reversible' changes to data items useful, because the changes to permanently stored data items must be invisible to other transactions until the transaction is closed, in case the transaction in question is aborted.

    Two approaches to recovery are commonly used. In one, the transaction service makes an **intentions list** for each transaction, listing the file changes to be done, but does not actually perform the operations until the transaction is

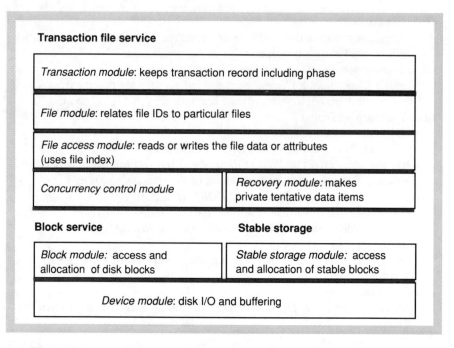

Figure 7.6 A transaction service, block service and stable block service.

committed. This approach is applicable to mutable files (see Section 5.3) – that is, files whose values can change and are updated in place. In the second approach, the server makes new **versions** of the files containing the changes and if the transaction fails the new versions are discarded.

In both approaches, the server regards a transaction as having two phases with three associated states: *tentative*, *committed* and *aborted*. A transaction is in the *tentative* state throughout the **first phase**, which commences when the server receives an *OpenTransaction* request from the client and ends when a *CloseTransaction* request is received. The **second phase** then commences and the *committed* state is entered if possible. If the *committed* state cannot be entered, the *aborted* state is entered and the client is informed that the transaction has failed.

Figure 7.7 shows the phases in relation to the operations requested by the client in a successful transaction. A transaction is in the *tentative* state throughout the **first phase** while the client is issuing requests to the server for operations on files. In the **second phase** the server makes the tentative values of the changed items permanent by inserting them into the appropriate files. This phase must be atomic; that is, once started it must eventually make all of the tentative values permanent. If the server halts during the second phase it must be repeated. For this to be possible: (1) the record of the tentative values of the files must be available when the server restarts and (2) repeating all or part of the second phase a number of times must have the same effect as doing it once.

Client operations	Phase	Server actions

OpenTransaction
  and file access
  requests
	first phase	make tentative copies of changed
		  file items

CloseTransaction	*COMMIT*	
	second phase	incorporate tentative copies into files

Figure 7.7 The two phases of a transaction.

A transaction can only be aborted while it is in the first phase. None of the clients files will have been permanently affected by its operations, so all that needs to be done by the server to deal with an aborted transaction is to dispose of the tentative copies of the changed items in the files.

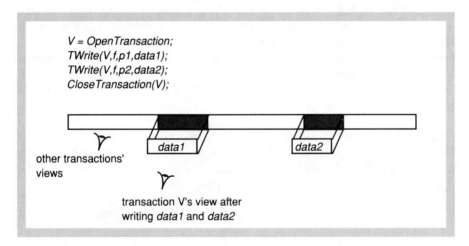

Figure 7.8 Representation of a file during phase 1 of a transaction.

Figure 7.8 illustrates the representation of the file f when the transaction V has been executed up to just before the *CloseTransaction* request. The initial state of file f is represented by the upper rectangle. Tentative values produced by *TWrite* operations are shown as rectangles labeled *data1* and *data2*. The shadows show the positions where the tentative values are to be incorporated into the file if the transaction commits. Within the transaction the client sees the file as consisting of the sequence of data items given by the white rectangles. Any other client accessing the file sees the data in the upper rectangle until the transaction is completed. When the transaction is committed, the tentative values move into the file at the positions indicated by the shadows. The operations used to move them are to be *repeatable* (see Section 5.3), so that they may be repeated if the server fails while committing the transaction. If the transaction is aborted, the tentative values are discarded.

There are two distinct approaches to the implementation of a two-phase transaction mechanism. One is the use of an **intentions list** [Gray 1978, Lampson 1981b] and the other is the use of **file versions** [Reed 1983, Mullender 1985]. In both approaches, the information needed to restore consistency after a server has halted must be stored in such a manner that it will be available when the server restarts. We propose that stable storage (see Section 6.6) be used for this purpose. We shall introduce these two approaches here by describing the effect of the *TRead* and *TWrite* operations in each method.

7.2.1 The intentions list approach

A server makes a list of all the actions that it intends to carry out if a transaction commits. The **intentions list** may be regarded as a log of the operations of a transaction. The tentative copies of file items are recorded in the form of an intentions list together with a **commit flag** for each transaction. The commit flag is a record of the state of the transaction (*tentative*, *committed* or *aborted*).

An intentions list contains a record for each of the *TWrite* operations and the other operations that will make changes to files. The intentions list is kept in stable storage, separate from the files involved in the transaction. As each *TWrite* operation in a transaction is executed, its intention is recorded in the intentions list instead of writing the data to the file involved. The description of the intention of an operation must contain sufficient information to make it possible to carry it out at a later time.

Thus the intention of a *TWrite* operation is to put some new values at a particular position in a particular file. The information added to the intentions list for each *TWrite* operation is the data to be written and the intended destination, that is, the UFID for the file to be changed and the position in the file. Figure 7.9 shows the intentions list for the transaction V in Figure 7.7.

Client operations	Phase	State	Intentions records
OpenTransaction $\rbrace$			
TWrite(f, p1, data1) $\rbrace$	first phase	tentative	{"write", f, p1, data1}
TWrite(f, p2, data2) $\rbrace$			{"write", f, p2, data2}
CloseTransaction	COMMIT		
	second phase	committed	intentions → files

Figure 7.9 Intentions list construction.

If data items requested in a *TRead* operation have already been changed by a *TWrite* operation in the same transaction, the *TRead* takes the data from the intentions list, otherwise it takes the data from the file. The commit flag associated with the intentions list is *tentative* during the first phase and is set to *committed* or *aborted* when *CloseTransaction* is received. The change from *tentative* to *committed* or *aborted* must be performed as an atomic action. When the commit flag has been set to *committed*, the server must complete the transaction. The transaction is completed by carrying out the operations in the intentions list and then removing the intentions list and the commit flag.

Even if the server halts during a transaction, the server must discover the intentions list and process it whenever it restarts. When a server is restarted after halting, it inspects all of its intentions lists before commencing any new transactions. If an intentions list is in the *committed* state, it carries out the intentions listed therein. If the intentions list is in the *tentative* or the *aborted* state, the server removes it.

The server may halt again while it is processing the intentions list and subsequently be restarted. This may happen any number of times and each time the server will attempt to do the operations in the intentions list. Therefore, the operations used to incorporate the tentative values into the files must be *repeatable* – able to be performed any number of times and still have the correct effect.

In addition, the intentions lists and commit flags must be recorded on the server's disk in such a way that they will remain intact after a server has crashed or halted. Stable storage, described in Section 6.5, provides the necessary guarantees against the incorrect recording of data and provides a high degree of protection against the subsequent decay of the recorded data.

When transactions are aborted by clients or by the server their intentions lists are marked (in their commit flags) as *aborted*. Aborted intentions lists must be purged from the server from time to time.

7.2.2 The file versions approach

In this approach to recoverability a file is regarded as having a chronological history consisting of a sequence of versions, each of which is written once only. The current version of a file is the most recently committed version and other committed versions represent past states of the file. Tentative versions represent possible future states of the file.

When an operation in a transaction modifies a file, the server creates a tentative version. This is based on the current version of the file, behaving like a copy of the current version containing the changes made by the *TWrite* operations in the transaction. If a transaction modifies more than one file, there is a tentative version for each file. When the server commits a transaction the tentative version of each file modified in the transaction becomes the current version of the file and the previous current version is added to the sequence of old versions.

Two kinds of conflict may arise when two or more concurrent transactions have accessed the same file:

1. A **version conflict** is one in which concurrent transactions have accessed the same file, but none of the data items modified in any of the transactions have been accessed or modified by any other transaction. Version conflicts can be resolved by a merging action, described below.
2. Under optimistic concurrency control, **serializability conflicts** are not resolved until a transaction closes. These conflicts occur when two or more concurrent transactions are allowed to access the same data items in a file, and one or more of the accesses is a *TWrite* operation (or some other

operation that modifies the value of the data item). Such conflicts are prevented by locking and are resolved when they occur in timestamping.

The server maintains a **transaction record** for each transaction, including a **commit flag** whose value may be *tentative, committed* or *aborted*. During the first phase, the transaction record also contains the UFID of the tentative version of each file modified in the transaction so that the UFIDs in client *TRead* and *TWrite* operations can be mapped onto the tentative versions of files. This information must survive if the server halts or even if its disks suffer decay, for it is vital to the task of maintaining consistency. Stable storage can be used to ensure that this is so.

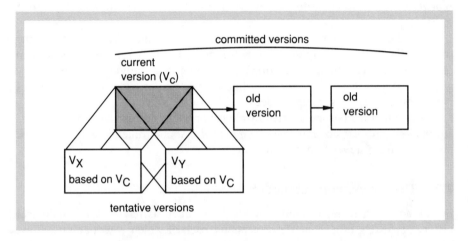

Figure 7.10 Representation of a file affected by two transactions X and Y.

Version conflict resolution □ In general a file is represented as a sequence of versions headed by the current version together with some tentative versions based on the current version. Since a file may be involved in several concurrent transactions, there may be several tentative versions existing at the same time, e.g. V_X and V_Y made by transactions X and Y in Figure 7.10. When the first transaction closes the server discovers that its tentative version is based on the current version of the file, so it can commit the transaction. It does so by altering the transaction's commit flag to *committed*. (This is an atomic action because there is only one commit flag per transaction.) The tentative version associated with the committed transaction then becomes the current version. The remaining tentative versions are no longer based on the current version, since they are now derived from a version that is no longer the current one.

The other concurrent transactions are handled as follows. If there are no serializability conflicts, then each tentative version is merged with the current version when its transaction closes, creating a new current version that includes the changes made by all of the transactions that have already committed. If there are serializability conflicts, then all of the transactions that are involved except the first to commit are aborted.

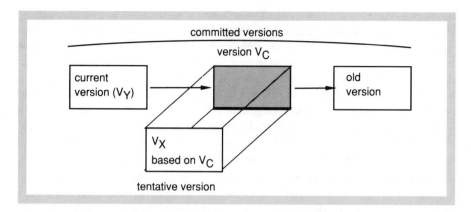

Figure 7.11 Y has committed and X is about to commit.

In the example illustrated by Figure 7.11 suppose that Y closes before X. The server commits the transaction, making V_Y the current version. V_C becomes an old version. So when X closes, its tentative version V_X is based on an old version. In our example, when X commits (after Y), its tentative version is merged with the new current version created when Y closed, incorporating the changes in both V_X and V_Y.

7.2.3 Implementation of file versions

Mechanisms for implementing versions have been described by Reed [1983] and by Mullender and Tanenbaum [1985]. Our description is based on their work. The tentative versions of files behave like copies of the file version from which they are derived, but fortunately it is not necessary to make a full copy of a file to create a new tentative version.

First, we note that the tentative, current and old versions of a file can all be assigned unique **version numbers,** since the server that holds a file is responsible for creating all of its versions and can number them as they are created. Now consider the representation of files using a file index as described in Section 6.2, in which the file index of a file contains pointers to the disk blocks containing the pages of data in that file. We can expand the index entries to associate a **version number** with each page. The version number is updated when the page is created and each time it is modified. The version numbers show the 'vintage' of the pages in a file – they associate the contents of each page with a particular version of the file.

The **shadow pages** technique may be used to make new versions of files. Initially the new version of a file can be constructed just by copying the file index of the current version. Each index entry contains a pointer to the block containing a page in the file and a version number. Unmodified pages are shared between versions. The first time a *TWrite* operation affects a page, the server gets a new disk block and writes the new tentative value in it. The tentative version of the page is called a shadow page. (Some authors refer to the original version of the page as the shadow page.) The block pointer of the shadow page and the version number are recorded in the file index. In effect the new page is inserted into the tentative version associated with that transaction. Subsequent writes to the same file page make use of the same shadow page. Thus, each version of a file consists of a file index with pointers to some blocks containing changes made by the transaction that created it, together with pointers to the blocks containing the unchanged pages of the file it was based on. When the transaction is closed, if there are no version or serializability conflicts, each tentative version of a file created by the transaction becomes a current version.

Merging conflicting versions □   When a transaction closes with a tentative version of a file that is not based on the current version and there are serializability conflicts, then, as we have already explained, the transaction must be aborted. In this case, the new tentative version is discarded.

If there are no serializability conflicts, a new current version is created by merging the index of the tentative version with the index of the current version, choosing the pages with the latest version numbers from each. Thus the new current version will contain all the modifications made by the newly committed transaction, and all of the modifications made by other transactions since the tentative version was created.

Summary of server actions with file versions □   We can summarize the actions taken by a server that supports file versions for each of the possible operations in a transaction:

- *OpenTransaction*: The server makes a new transaction record and commit flag with value *tentative* and delivers a transaction identifier to the client.
- *TWrite*: The first time that a transaction alters a particular file, the server makes a new tentative version by copying the file index for the current version of the file. The new tentative version has associated with it a new version number and a reference to the commit flag for the transaction. Each *TWrite* operation is then performed by substituting references to shadow pages in the file index.
- *TRead*: The server selects the appropriate file version to access as follows: if the transaction has already made a tentative version of the requested file it reads from that, otherwise it reads from the current version of the file. This ensures that the client has access to the intermediate values made by its own transaction, but not to those made by other clients.
- *CloseTransaction*: The transaction record contains references to the tentative versions belonging to the transaction. If there are tentative versions that are not based on the current version, the actions needed to resolve version conflicts are performed. (We will discuss serializability conflicts in Section 7.3.2.) The commit flag is set to *committed*. Each tentative version of a file becomes the new current version. The transaction record is then deleted.
- *AbortTransaction*: An *AbortTransaction* action may arise either by explicit action on the part of the client or due to a processor halting. The server records an aborted transaction by setting the value of the commit flag to

aborted. When a server restarts, the only work to be done is to find all commit flags whose values are *tentative* and change these values to *aborted*. The server must have a scheme for discarding aborted transactions and their file versions. This will involve inspecting the transaction records in the server from time to time.

- *Create*: The files resulting from *Create* operations are tentative until the transaction is committed.

- *Delete*: The deletion of a file involves the removal of all of its versions. The operation must be recoverable in case the transaction aborts, so all *Delete* operations are recorded in the transaction record and performed when the transaction commits.

- *Truncate*: The *Truncate* operation alters the length of the file (see Box 6.1).

Retention of previous versions of files □   Optimistic concurrency control depends upon the retention of several previous versions of each file as long as there are any tentative versions in existence. The recently-committed versions are used to detect serializability conflicts. Non-current versions of a file may also be retained as an archive for use when a client needs to revert to an earlier state. When file versions are needed only for this purpose, the information about the transactions that made them can be deleted from the server, just leaving an indication in the version to show that it is committed.

7.3 Concurrency control

When transactions run concurrently, there are many different possible interleavings of their read and write operations and, if they access the same file items, their effects are unpredictable. The examples in Section 7.1.1 show some possible interleavings of the reads and writes in two transactions.

Transactions must be run so that their effect on shared data is serially equivalent. One way to achieve this is to run them one at a time, but a total elimination of concurrency is neither acceptable nor necessary. A transaction file service contains a large number of items and files and a typical transaction accesses only a few of them and is unlikely to clash with other transactions that are current. A server can achieve serial equivalence of transactions by serializing access to the items of data. However, if an item of data is subject only to *TRead* operations by a pair of transactions, there is no need to serialize their access to that item.

A simple solution is to run transactions concurrently if they are using different file items and in series if they are using the same file items. This solution is not altogether satisfactory for, (1) it is usually not possible to predict which items will be used by a transaction, and (2) a pair of transactions may use the same item for only a small fraction of their time. Figure 7.5 shows an example of how serial equivalence can be achieved with some degree of concurrency in which one transaction completes its access to account B before the other transaction starts accessing it.

The server must serialize access to shared data items, and the shared portion to which access must be serialized should be the smallest possible part of the file, that is just the items involved in the *TRead* and *TWrite* operations. If a larger part, for example the entire file, is the unit for serial access by processes, concurrency is reduced unnecessarily.

Three alternative solutions are commonly used; these are **locking**, **optimistic concurrency control** and **timestamps**. When locking is used, the server sets a lock, labelled with the transaction identifier, on each data item just before it is accessed and removes those locks when the transaction has completed. While an item is locked, only the transaction that it is locked for can access that item; other transactions must *wait* until the item is unlocked.

In optimistic concurrency control, a transaction proceeds to the end of the first phase, and before it is committed a check is carried out to discover whether it has used the same data items as an earlier transaction, in which case it must be aborted and will *restart*.

In timestamping a server records the most recent time of reading and writing on each data item and each transaction compares its own timestamp with that of the data item to determine whether the current operation can be done or not. Basically, concurrency control can be achieved either by clients waiting for one another or by clients restarting after conflicts. We will discuss the use of locks in Section 7.3.1, optimistic concurrency control in Section 7.3.2 and timestamps in Section 7.3.3. In all of these methods, we assume that each transaction has its own isolated record of the changes it is making and that each transaction is unable to observe the other transactions' tentative values.

7.3.1 Locks

A server places locks on data items to ensure that only one client at a time may access each one. (We will discuss shared locks in a later section.) When a client requests access to a data item, another client's transaction may already be using the data item and the client that makes the request must wait. When a client's request is granted, the server locks the data item so that the client may use it. When the client has finished with the item, it is released, the server removes the lock and it may then be used by other clients' transactions. By using locks and waiting the server forces serial equivalence on clients and transactions by partially ordering them according to the time sequence in which they first access each item of data. The use of locks can lead to **deadlock** with client programs waiting for each other to release locks; as, for example, when a pair of clients each has an item of data locked that the other needs to access. We shall return to the deadlock problem and some remedies for it later in this section.

An item of data accessed by two clients' transactions may be regarded as a shared resource from which they must be mutually excluded. A condition variable (see Section 4.8.1) is a useful component from which to construct locks; the client that needs to access a locked item *waits* on the condition variable and when the server unlocks the item it *signals* on the condition variable. Note that, when several clients *wait* on the same locked item, the semantics of *wait* ensure that each client gets its turn. A lock can be defined by a record composed of three variables:

- a two-state variable that indicates whether it is locked or not,
- a condition variable on which processes may *wait* or *signal*,
- a variable containing the identifier of the transaction that set the lock.

The *granularity* with which locks can be applied to files is an important issue since the scope for concurrent access to a single file will be severely limited if locks can only be applied to whole files or to relatively large parts of files. In our banking example, if many customer accounts are stored in a single file, and locks are applied to entire files, only one bank clerk could perform an on-line banking transaction at any time – hardly an acceptable constraint! On the other hand, in some multi-user environments there are few shared databases and locking of entire files is acceptable.

The description of locking schemes given below does not assume any particular granularity, and we use the term *data item* to refer to units of data that are lockable. However, for general use, locking at the level of logical data records is likely to be required. Where this is done, the management and allocation of storage for locks must be considered in the server implementation and the lock records are likely to be stored separately from the data records with each lock record containing a UFID and the logical record in the file to which it refers.

Transaction T		Transaction U	
Operations	*Locks*	*Operations*	*Locks*
OpenTransaction			
TRead (a)	locks *a*		
		OpenTransaction	
		TRead (c)	locks *c*
		TWrite (c+$3)	
TRead (b)	locks *b*		
TWrite (a–$2)			
		TRead (b)	waits on T's
TWrite (b+$2)		.	lock on *b*
CloseTransaction	unlocks	.	
	a and *b*	.	*TRead(b)* succeeds,
			locking *b*
		TWrite (b–$3)	
		CloseTransaction	unlocks
			b and *c*

Figure 7.12 Transactions T and U with locks.

In the simplest forms of locking scheme the file server attempts to lock any item that is about to be read or written by a client's transaction and unlocks all the items used by the transaction when the transaction has been committed or aborted. If a client attempts to access an item that is already locked due to another client's transaction, the first client must wait until the item is unlocked. We illustrate the use of locks in Figure 7.12, which is like Figure 7.2, but has an extra column for each transaction showing the locking, waiting on locks and unlocking. In this example, it is assumed that, when transactions T and U start, the records *a*, *b* and *c*, containing the balances, are not yet locked.

When the client with transaction T is about to read the account *b*, it is not locked and the server locks it for T. Subsequently, when the client with transaction U is about to read *b*, it is still locked for T, and the client waits. When transaction T is committed, *b* is unlocked whereupon the client with transaction U is resumed. The use of the lock on *b* effectively serializes the access to *b*. This example illustrates one further point about locks, that if a server has already locked an item for a client its transaction is free to use the item without locking it again.

All of the locks belonging to a transaction are released by the server when that transaction is committed or aborted.

Two-phase locking □   The first phase of each transaction is a 'growing phase' during which new locks are acquired. In the second phase of a transaction locks are released (a shrinking phase). This is called **two-phase locking**. During the first phase, a transaction has its own isolated tentative record of its changes which is invisible to other transactions. However, until a transaction commits or aborts, it cannot be decided whether other concurrent transactions should use the values of affected data items as they were before the transaction started or as they will be after the transaction has committed. Therefore locks cannot be released until after a transaction has committed and the data items have been permanently updated. See Eswaran et al. [1976] for a fuller discussion of the reasons why a transaction must not release a lock.

---

1. When a client operation accesses an item within a transaction:

   (a)   If the item is not already locked, the server locks it and proceeds to access the data for the client.

   (b)   If the item is already locked for another transaction, the client must wait until it is unlocked.

   (c)   If the server has already locked the item in the same transaction, it can proceed to access the item.

2. When a transaction is committed or aborted, the server unlocks all items it locked for the transaction.

Box 7.2   Use of locks.

The rules for the use of locks are summarized in Box 7.2. To ensure that these rules are adhered to, locking is performed by the transaction service as a side-effect of *TRead* and *TWrite* operations and the client has no access to operations for locking or unlocking items of data.

Read and write locks □   Some transactions read items but do not alter them and this does not conflict with other transactions that only read the same items. Therefore, a simple lock that is used for both read and write operations reduces concurrency more than is necessary. These considerations have led to the adoption of locking schemes that control the access to each data item so that there can be several concurrent transactions reading an item, or a single transaction writing an item, but not both. Such locking schemes are commonly referred to as 'many reader/single writer' schemes.

We cannot abandon the locking of items to be read, for there are many situations where it would be wrong for one transaction to be reading an item and another to be altering it. One such case is where the first transaction subsequently alters the item. Another arises when a transaction that reads several items expects them to be a consistent set; the set would not remain consistent if another transaction were to alter one of them.

In order to provide more concurrency than that provided by simple locks, read locks and write locks are used. A write lock is used on any item affected by a *TWrite* operation in a transaction. A read lock is set on any other items accessed during the transaction. An item locked with a write lock cannot be accessed (read or written) by another transaction. An item locked with a read lock cannot have its value changed by another transaction, but more than one transaction may *share* a read lock on the same data item. The *TRead* operation causes read locking and the *TWrite* operation causes write locking for the transaction it belongs to.

Lock already set	*Lock to be set*	
	Read	*Write*
none	ok	ok
read	ok	wait
write	wait	wait

Figure 7.13 Lock compatibility.

The table in Figure 7.13 shows the compatibility of read locks and write locks and can be regarded as an extension to rule 1(b) in Box 7.2. The first column of the table shows the locking already done by other transactions. The second and third columns show the effect of trying to read lock or write lock the same item. In addition, the rules for use of locks in Box 7.2 is extended to include rule 1(d) as defined in Box 7.3.

1(d) If the transaction is attempting to write an item on which it has previously placed a read lock, the read lock is converted to a write lock.

Box 7.3 Use of read-write locks.

The use of read and write locks increases concurrency in comparison with the use of simple locks, but it can still lead to deadlock. Consider the use of read locks and write locks shown in Figure 7.14. The locks column now shows when

Transaction T		Transaction U	
Operations	Locks	Operations	Locks
TRead (a)	read locks a		
		TRead (c)	read locks c
		TWrite (c+$3)	write locks c
TRead (b)	read locks b		
TWrite (a–$2)	write locks a		
		TRead (b)	shares read lock on b
TWrite (b+$2)	waits on U's		
...	read lock on b	TWrite (b–$3)	waits on T's
...		...	read lock on b

Figure 7.14 Deadlock with read and write locks.

the server locks an item and when the client must wait. This differs from the simple locks of Figure 7.5 in that both transactions can now read the balance *b* and share the read lock, but when T wants to write to *b* it must wait until the other transaction unlocks it. Similarly when U wants to write to *b*, it must wait until T unlocks the item. This is a **deadlock** situation – two transactions are waiting and each is dependent on the other to release a lock so it can resume.

This is a particularly common situation when clients are involved in an interactive program, for a transaction in an interactive program may last for a long period of time, resulting in many data items being locked and remaining so, thus preventing other programs from using them. An interesting example of such a program is the Violet system described by Gifford [1979b] and Lampson [1981c]. The Violet system illustrated in Figure 7.15 provides a calendar or diary database that can be viewed and updated interactively by a number of users. It allows users to view unions of pages from other people's diaries before arranging meetings. A user who wants to make an appointment with someone views that person's diary and then writes in an appointment. Another user may have the same idea at the same time and also view a copy of the diary and subsequently attempt to add an appointment on the same day. We can regard one day in a diary as an item of data and viewing it will result in a read lock on it. Adding an entry will require altering the read lock to a write lock. It is permissible for two users to view the same object at the same time and this is implemented by sharing the read lock on the item. However, neither user will be able to write an appointment, as it is not permissible for either client to convert the read lock to a write lock in the presence of the other transaction's shared read lock on the same item.

Deadlock resolution □ Deadlock is a state in which each member of a group of transactions is waiting for some other member to release a lock.

One solution is to *prevent* deadlock. An apparently simple, but not very good way to overcome deadlock is to lock all of the files to be included in a transaction when it starts. Such a transaction cannot run into deadlock with other

View: {Smith.qmc,Jones.qmc}

January 1988

25 Monday	26 Tuesday	27 Wednesday	28 Thursday	29 Friday
9:00–10:00 Jones unavailable	10:00–12:00 Jones unavailable	9:00–10:00 Jones unavailable	9:00–12:00 Jones Smith unavailable	
13:00–14:00 Jones Smith unavailable	11:00–12:00 Jones unavailable	14:00–15:00 Jones Smith unavailable		

View: Meetings.qmc

January 1988

25 Monday	26 Tuesday	27 Wednesday	28 Thursday	29 Friday
	10:00–12:00 hardware research		9:00–12:00 Equipment planning	
13:00–14:00 Dept. meeting		14:00–15:00 Dr. Visitor Interesting Facts		

Figure 7.15 An illustration of Violet showing the union of some diaries.

transactions, but locking groups of entire files is not a good solution, for it unnecessarily restricts access to shared resources. If this were applied to the Violet system, the diary database would only be accessible to a single user at a time. Deadlock can also be prevented by requesting locks on data items in a predefined order, but this would result in locking too soon and a reduction in concurrency.

Deadlock detection is based on a *wait-for graph* containing transactions and locks in the nodes. See Figure 7.16 which illustrates the wait-for graph corresponding to the deadlock situation illustrated in Figure 7.14. When a transaction, T, gets a lock on an item i, an arrow is drawn from i to T, but if T has to wait for i then the arrow is drawn the other way. Deadlocks are indicated by cycles in the graph. Having detected a deadlock, the server must select a transaction to abort. See Ceri and Pelagatti [1985] for a discussion of detecting deadlocks in distributed databases.

Timeouts □ Lock timeouts are a method for resolution of deadlocks that is commonly used in file servers. Each lock is given a limited period in which it is invulnerable. After this time, a lock becomes vulnerable. Provided that no other

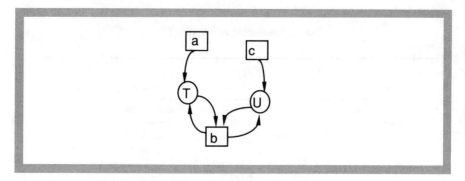

Figure 7.16 The wait-for graph for Figure 7.14.

process is competing for the item that is locked, an item with a vulnerable lock remains locked. However, if any other clients are waiting to access the item protected by a vulnerable lock, the lock is broken (i.e. the item is unlocked) and the waiting process resumes. The transaction whose lock has been broken is normally aborted.

Transaction T		Transaction U	
Operations	*Locks*	*Operations*	*Locks*
TRead (a)	read locks a		
		TRead (c)	read locks c
		TWrite (c+$3)	write locks c
TRead (b)	read locks b		
TWrite (a–$2)	write locks a		
		TRead (b)	shares read lock on b
TWrite (b+$2)	waits on U's read lock on b		
...			
		TWrite (b–$3)	waits on T's read lock on b
...		...	
...	(timeout elapses) T's lock on b becomes vulnerable, unlock B, abort T	...	
		TWrite (b–$3)	write locks b
		CloseTransaction	unlock b, c

Figure 7.17 Resolution of the deadlock in Figure 7.14.

There are two main problems with timeouts: in an overloaded system, the number of transactions timing out will increase; and transactions taking a long time can be penalized. Timeouts also have the disadvantage that it is hard to decide on the length of a timeout, whereas servers can make a choice when deadlock detection is used.

Using lock timeouts, we can resolve the deadlock in Figure 7.13 as shown in Figure 7.17 in which the read lock for T on b becomes vulnerable after its timeout period. Transaction U is waiting to alter it to a write lock. Therefore T is aborted and it releases its share of the read lock on b allowing U to resume, convert its read lock to a write lock and complete the transaction.

The question arises: why maintain vulnerable locks in place; why not remove a lock and abort the transaction when the timeout period has elapsed? This would be wasteful of resources if there are no other transactions competing to access the locked item; a vulnerable lock allows the original transaction to proceed to completion unless a competing transaction attempts to access the item. A vulnerable lock acts as an indicator that the transaction that placed the lock still has an interest in the data item and should be notified as soon as the lock is broken. If the relevant data item is not accessed by any other transaction the original transaction may proceed to completion, eventually committing and removing the lock when the transaction is complete. If another transaction does access the data item, the client owning the original transaction must at least be notified and in most cases the transaction should be aborted, since the value of the data item may have changed since the transaction started.

It is possible that the correctness of the transaction does not depend on the value of the item and, in that case, it may not be necessary to abort the transaction. In the XDFS file server [Israel et al. 1978, Mitchell 1982], the client is notified when a read lock is broken and may voluntarily unlock the item it protects, in which case the transaction may continue and commit successfully. If the client has not unlocked the item after the lock is broken, a commit would fail.

Intention-to-write locks □   We have seen that the use of separate read and write locks is preferable to the use of simple locks of a single type, for it does allow several concurrent transactions to read the same item. However, the existence of a read lock prevents any other transaction from writing the locked data item. This reduces concurrency more than is necessary; a transaction that only reads an item should allow another transaction that writes the item to proceed with its tentative writes until it is ready to commit. The value of the item will not actually change until the writing transaction commits, so, if it is suspended at that point, the item remains unchanged until the reading transaction releases its lock.

Lock already set	Lock to be set		
	Read	I-write	Commit
none	ok	ok	ok
read	ok	ok	wait
I-write	ok	wait	wait
commit	wait	wait	wait

Figure 7.18 Lock compatibility (read, *I-write* and commit locks).

The solution proposed by Gifford for Violet and implemented in the XDFS file server is to use an 'intention-to-write lock' (*I-write*) and a *commit lock*, instead of a write lock. As each *TWrite* operation is done, an *I-write* lock is used to lock the item. The *I-write* lock is compatible with read locks (this is because the effects of write are not permanent until a transaction commits), although not with other *I-write* locks.

When the transaction is committed, the *I-write* lock is converted to a commit lock. The latter is incompatible with both reading and writing. If there are outstanding read locks, the transaction must wait until it is possible to set the commit lock. The compatibility of these locks is shown in Figure 7.18.

If there are also timeouts on locks, the rules for converting an *I-write* lock to a commit lock are:

- If another process has a vulnerable read lock, the server breaks the vulnerable read lock and converts the *I-write* lock to a commit lock.
- If the *I-write* lock is vulnerable and another process has a read lock that is not vulnerable, the server aborts the transaction owning the *I-write* lock.
- If neither the *I-write* lock nor the read lock of another process is vulnerable, the server waits until one of these is the case; or the read transaction may close and release its lock.

Transaction T		Transaction U	
Operations	Locks	Operations	Locks
TRead (a)	read lock a		
		TRead (c)	read lock c
		TWrite (c+$3)	I-write lock c
TRead (b)	read lock b		
TWrite (a–$2)	I-write lock a		
		TRead (b)	shares read lock on b
TWrite (b+$2)	I-write lock b		
. . .			
		TWrite (b–$3)	waits on T's I-write
. . .		. . .	lock on b
CloseTransaction	wait on U's read lock on b		
			read lock on b now vulnerable
	commit locks b		aborts U

Figure 7.19 Read, *I-write* and commit locks in T and U.

Returning to our example of the interleaved transactions T and U we see the rules for commit locks illustrated in Figure 7.19, where transactions T and U share read locks and subsequently T converts its read lock to an *I-write* lock. When U wants to write it waits; meanwhile T has written its item and is ready to commit. At first neither lock is vulnerable, but eventually the read lock in U becomes vulnerable and T is allowed to convert the *I-write* lock to a commit lock. This results in U being aborted.

Returning to the discussion of Violet: the use of *I-write* locks allows the first of two clients accessing the same day of the diary to write in a new appointment, for an *I-write* lock is compatible with a read lock. However, the second client's transaction will not able to write in the appointment, for it cannot set a second *I-write* lock on the same item, so the client will wait. Eventually the first client will close its transaction and it will start waiting to make a commit lock. Since the second client has a read lock on the item, the first must now wait until the read lock becomes vulnerable; it will eventually do so, allowing the first client's transaction to complete.

7.3.2 Optimistic concurrency control

Kung and Robinson [1981] have identified a number of inherent disadvantages of locking and proposed an alternative *optimistic* approach to the serialization of transactions that avoids these drawbacks. We can summarize the drawbacks:

- Lock maintenance represents an overhead that is not present in systems that do not support concurrent access to shared data. Even read-only transactions (queries), which cannot possibly affect the integrity of the data, must, in general, use locking in order to guarantee that the data being read is not modified by other transactions at the same time. But *locking may be necessary only in the worst case*.

   For example, consider two client processes that are concurrently incrementing the values of n data items. If the client programs start at the same time, and run for about the same amount of time, accessing the data items in two unrelated sequences and using a separate transaction to access and increment each item, the chances that the two programs will attempt to access the same data item at the same time are just 1 in n on average, so locking is really *needed* only once in every n transactions.

- The use of locks can result in deadlock. Deadlock prevention reduces concurrency severely and therefore deadlock situations must be resolved either by the use of timeouts or by deadlock detection. Neither of these is wholly satisfactory for use in interactive programs.

- So that a transaction may be aborted, locks cannot be released until the end of the transaction. This may significantly reduce the potential for concurrency.

The alternative approach proposed by Kung and Robinson is 'optimistic' because it is based on the observation that, in most applications, the likelihood of two clients' transactions accessing the same data is low. Transactions are allowed to proceed as though there were no possibility of conflict with other transactions until the client completes its task and issues a *CloseTransaction* request. During this first phase of a transaction, read requests are performed immediately, and write requests are recorded in a tentative form that is invisible to other transactions. In addition two records are kept of the data items accessed within a transaction: a *read set* listing the data items read by the transaction and a *write set* listing the items written, created or deleted by the transaction.

When the *CloseTransaction* request is received, the transaction enters the second phase. In the second phase the transaction is *validated* to establish whether or not the write operations should be performed in a permanent fashion. If the validation is successful, the write operations are recorded in the relevant files and the transaction completes successfully (i.e. *CloseTransaction* delivers *Commit*). If the validation fails, the transaction is aborted and *CloseTransaction* delivers *Abort*. The validation is based on the notion of serial equivalence (Section 7.1.1). A transaction is valid if it can be shown to be equivalent to a transaction performed in the absence any other concurrent transactions.

In the validation process, the read set and the write set of the transaction to be validated are compared with the write sets of all of the concurrent transactions that reached the end of their first phase before it. If any member of the write sets of these 'preceding concurrent transactions' refers to the same data item as a member of the read set or the write set of the transaction to be validated, the validation fails.

Optimistic concurrency control requires that old versions of files corresponding to recently committed transactions are kept in the server. This is not necessary with either locking or timestamping.

Our description of the validation process captures the essentials of the method, but it does not define very precisely the term 'preceding concurrent transactions', nor does it suggest any very effective way in which to perform the necessary checks. We shall therefore now describe Kung and Robinson's algorithm in greater detail.

To assist in performing validation, each transaction is assigned a *transaction number* when it completes the first phase (i.e. when the client issues a *CloseTransaction*). If the transaction is validated and completes successfully it retains this number; if it fails the validation checks and is aborted, the number is released for re-assignment. Transaction numbers are integers assigned in ascending sequence; the number of a transaction therefore defines its position in time. A transaction with the number T_i always *precedes* a transaction with the number T_j if $i < j$. Furthermore, at any instant, the current transaction number, tn, can be used as a pseudo-clock that ticks whenever a transaction completes. This fact is used to record the time *start_tn* at which each transaction starts its first phase and the time *finish_tn* when it finishes the first phase by recording the current transaction number at that time.

Whenever a transaction is successfully validated, its transaction number, *start_tn, finish_tn* and write set are recorded in a *preceding transactions list* that is maintained by the transaction service. Note that this list is ordered by transaction number. Entries in this list are retained until there are no unvalidated transactions with which they might conflict, that is, a transaction T_{old} can be deleted when there is no unvalidated transaction T_j such that $T_j.start\_tn \leq T_{old}.finish\_tn$.

As we have already stated, if a transaction T_j is to pass the validation check it must be serially equivalent with respect to all preceding transactions. To ensure that this is so, the validation process must check that T_j does not conflict with any of the previously validated transactions in the preceding transactions list. Figure

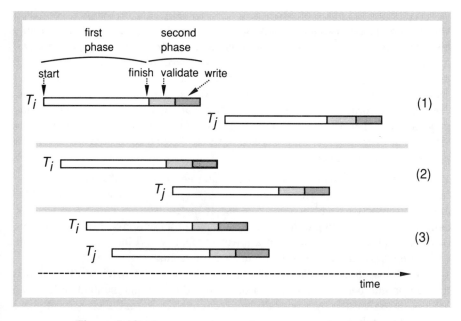

Figure 7.20 Three ways transactions may overlap in time.

7.20 shows the three ways in which a transaction T_j may overlap in time with an earlier transaction T_i, with time increasing from left to right. In (1) there is no overlap in time, but (2) and (3) do overlap.

1. shows a transaction that had completed before T_j started.
2. shows an overlapping transaction that committed before T_j finished the first phase. (The second phases do not overlap.)
3. shows an overlapping transaction that finishes the first phase before T_j does. (The second phases do overlap.)

The validation test proceeds as follows:

1. It compares $T_j.start\_tn$ with $T_i.finish\_tn$ for each transaction T_i in the list, passing over all transactions that were completed before T_j started.
2. It next considers all the transactions in the list that committed between $T_j.start\_tn$ and $T_j.finish\_tn$. The current transaction T_j only passes the test if the writes of T_i did not affect any of the same data items as the reads of T_j.
3. Lastly it considers transactions whose second phase was partially concurrent with the second phase of the current transaction. These transactions should not have updated any of the items that T_j read or updated.

Each of these three tests requires more computational resources than the last. If a test is positive for a given T_i no further tests are needed for conflict with that transaction. If T_j, the transaction to be validated, fails all three tests for any T_i, then T_j cannot be validated and it must be aborted.

As the second phase of a transaction is generally short in duration compared with the first phase, a simplification may be achieved by making the rule that only one transaction may be in the second phase at one time. When no two transactions may overlap in the second phase, the third test is unnecessary. To prevent overlapping, the entire second phase can be implemented as a critical section or an entry procedure in a monitor so that only one client at a time can execute it. In order to increase concurrency, part of the validation and writing may be implemented outside the critical section, but it is essential that the assignment of transaction numbers and entry in the preceding transactions list is performed strictly sequentially.

When to assign transaction numbers □   The transaction number is assigned just before the validation phase so that a transaction always finishes its first phase after all transactions with lower numbers. If the transaction number were to be assigned at the beginning of the first phase, then a transaction that reached the end of the first phase before one with a lower number would have to wait until the earlier one had completed before it could be validated.

If a transaction contains no writes, it will not need a permanently-assigned transaction number, although it must be validated to see that the items it has read have not been written by any of the transactions that finished their second phase during its first phase.

Starvation □   When a transaction is aborted, it will normally be restarted by the client program. But in this scheme there is no guarantee that a transaction will ever pass the validation checks, for it may come into conflict with other transactions for the use of data items each time it is restarted. The deprivation of a transaction from ever being able to commit is called **starvation**.

Occurrences of starvation are likely to be rare, but a server that uses optimistic concurrency control must ensure that a client does not repeatedly have its transaction aborted. Kung and Robinson suggest that this could be done if the server detects a transaction that has been aborted several times. They suggest that when the server detects such a transaction it should be given exclusive access by the use of a critical section protected by a semaphore.

An application of optimistic concurrency control □   In the design for the Amoeba distributed system, Tanenbaum and Mullender [1985] have adopted a scheme that combines optimistic concurrency control with locking. A file service contains all sorts of files, some of which are shared by many clients, some are read only and others are accessed only by one client, usually the owner. They suggest that locking should be used in transactions in which several files are changed and where the chance of two clients using the same item is high; and optimistic concurrency control for transactions using one file and in which the likelihood of two clients accessing the same item is low.

7.3.3 Timestamps

In concurrency control schemes based on timestamping, each operation in a transaction is validated when it is carried out and if the operation cannot be validated the transaction is aborted immediately and it can then be restarted. Each transaction is assigned a unique timestamp value that defines its position in the time sequence of transactions. The basic timestamping rule is very simple:

> A transaction's request to write a data item is valid only if that data item was last read and written by older transactions. A transaction's request to read a data item is valid only if that data item was last written by an older transaction.

A refinement to the rule is needed to make allowances for the tentative values of data items belonging to other transactions in progress at the same time. This refinement ensures that the tentative values of each data item are committed in the order determined by the timestamps of the transactions that made them. This is achieved by transactions waiting, when necessary, for earlier transactions to complete their writes. The write operations may be performed after the *CloseTransaction* operation has returned, without making the client wait. But the client must wait when read operations need to wait for earlier transactions to finish. This cannot lead to deadlock since transactions only wait for earlier ones (and no cycle could occur in the wait-for graph).

A server may use its clock to assign timestamps or, as in the last section, it may use a 'pseudo-time' based on a counter that is incremented whenever a timestamp value is issued. We defer until Section 8.1 the problem of generating timestamps when the transaction service is distributed and several servers are involved in a transaction.

We will now describe a form of timestamp-based concurrency control following the methods adopted in the SDD-1 system [Bernstein et al. 1980] and described by Ceri and Pelagatti [1985]. A similar scheme using timeouts is described by Reed [1983]. Another scheme described by Thomas [1979] uses the timestamping of data items, both for an optimistic form of concurrency control and for the replication of data files in several servers. These methods are discussed in Sections 8.3.2 and 8.4.

Every data item has a *read timestamp* and a *write timestamp* associated with it. The server updates the read timestamp or the write timestamp of a data item whenever a read or write operation is performed, using the timestamp of the transaction requesting the operation. As usual, transactions have two phases and write operations are recorded tentatively and are invisible to other transactions until a *CloseTransaction* request is issued and the transaction is committed. When a transaction is in progress there will be a number of data items with tentative new values and write timestamps. When a transaction is committed, the tentative values and timestamps become permanent.

The server checks read and write operations for serializability with other transactions by inspecting the timestamps on the relevant data items, including tentative values of data items belonging to incomplete transactions. If the timestamp on a data item is the same as that of the transaction requesting an operation on the item, it must have been set by the current transaction (since transactions are always assigned unique timestamps) and the operation may proceed.

T's operation	U's operation	
	read	write
read	ok	no
write	no	no

Figure 7.21 Transaction conflicts.

The possible conflicts between two transactions T and U are shown in Figure 7.21. We see that write operations conflict with both read and write operations of other transactions.

When the timestamps differ, the following rules are used. For a **write operation** there are two cases:

w1 The timestamp of the current transaction is more recent than the read and (committed) write timestamps of the data item. A tentative write operation is performed.

w2 The timestamp of the transaction requesting the write is older than the timestamp of the last read or committed write of the data item. This implies that the write is arriving too late – another transaction has accessed the item since the current transaction started – and the current transaction is aborted.

The tentative values of a data item can be kept in a list ordered by their transaction timestamps. The effect of a tentative write is to insert the tentative value in the appropriate place in that list. In the case of a **read operation** only the time of writing data need be considered and there are three cases, illustrated in Figure 7.22:

r1 The timestamp of the current transaction is more recent than the write timestamps of all committed and tentative values; the read operation can be done, but:
   (a) if there are no tentative items the read can be done immediately;
   (b) if tentative values exist, the current read operation waits for their transactions to complete.

r2 The timestamp of the current transaction is older than the timestamp of the most recent (committed) write to the data item; the transaction is aborted.

r3 The timestamp of the transaction is older than that of a tentative value of the data item made by another transaction, although it is more recent than the timestamp of the permanent data item. The transaction proceeds.†

When a client closes a transaction the server has to make the tentative values resulting from write operations permanent. A transaction can only reach this point if its operations have been consistent with those of earlier transactions. Therefore it can always be committed although it may have to wait for earlier transactions that have tentative copies to commit.

---

† If the transaction reads the data again after the tentative value has been committed it falls under case r2 and will be aborted.

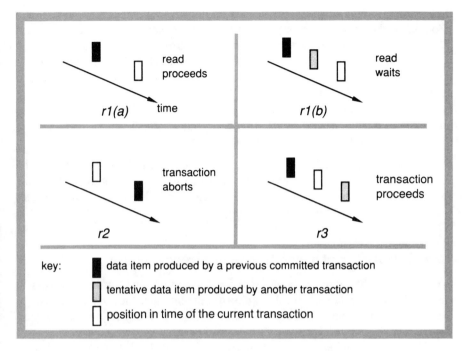

Figure 7.22 Read operations and timestamps.

		Timestamps					
		t_a		t_b		t_c	
T	*U*	*read*	*write*	*read*	*write*	*read*	*write*
TRead (a)		t_T					
	TRead (c)					t_U	
	TWrite (c+$3)						t_U
TRead (b)				t_T			
TWrite (a–$2)			t_T				
	TRead (b)			t_U			
TWrite (b+$2)							
Aborts							
	TWrite (b–$3)				t_U		

Figure 7.23 Timestamps in transactions T and U.

We return to our illustration concerning the two concurrent banking transactions T and U introduced in Figure 7.2. Figure 7.23 shows transaction T reading *a* and *b* and then writing both whereas transaction U reads and writes *c* and then reads and writes *b*; t_T and t_U are the timestamps assigned to the two transactions T and U. We assume that initially the timestamps on the account records are the same for reading and writing and initially are, of course, older than t_T and t_U. We also assume that t_T is earlier than t_U. The right-hand column in our table shows the timestamps that are set on the data items a, b and c as each step is carried out. The example shows that when transaction T is ready to write b it will be aborted because the timestamp set by transaction U is more recent. In this example, the outcome is the same as for read and write locks with timeouts to avoid deadlock as shown in Figure 7.9.

The basic timestamp method just described does avoid deadlock, but is quite prone to restarts. A modification known as 'ignore obsolete write' rule is an improvement. This is a modification to the rule $w2$:

If a write is too late, then if it had arrived in time its effects would have been overwritten anyway. Therefore it can just be ignored instead of aborting the transaction. However, if the earlier transaction had read the item, the later one will fail due to the read timestamp on the data.

7.3.4 Comparison of methods for concurrency control

We have described three separate methods for controlling concurrent access to shared data files: data locking, the optimistic method and time stamping. All of the methods carry some overheads in the time and space they require and they all limit to some extent the potential for concurrent operation.

The time stamping method is similar to locking in that the server detects conflicts between transactions as each data item is accessed, but the additional information contained in the timestamps enables some transactions to proceed that would be prevented from doing so with locks. When optimistic concurrency control is used all transactions are allowed to proceed, but some are aborted when they close. This results in relatively efficient operation when there are few conflicts, but a substantial amount of work may have to be repeated when a transaction is aborted.

In simple timestamping schemes, if a transaction accesses an item with a later date it is aborted, whereas a lock would cause a client to wait. Immediate abortion in timestamping can be contrasted with locking and waiting and subsequently either committing or aborting to avoid deadlock. The wait that occurs in the timestamping method when a read operation encounters a more recent tentative value is equivalent to waiting on a write lock. The ordering of two transactions is determined by first access to a common item if locking is used and by the transactions' time of starting if timestamps are used.

There is still a lot of current research into methods for concurrency control and more experience is needed with implementations in interactive environments before it is possible to determine which approach is the most suitable. Locking has been in use for several years in database systems and file servers, but timestamping has been used in the SDD-1 database system and some file servers.

7.3.5 Some practical issues

There are some applications for which the automatic recovery of files to their initial state after a client or server failure is inappropriate. For example an editor log file is a record of the user's commands during an editing session, intended to be used to repeat the editing operations automatically on restart after an editor process halts unexpectedly.

To serve its purpose the log file must include all of the user's commands recorded until the client or server halted. If a log file is written using a single transaction and the client process fails, causing the transaction to abort, the recovery mechanism would cause a log file to revert to its state before the transaction and the logging information would be lost.

Thus the use of log files and similar techniques requires a facility for excluding certain files from the recovery mechanisms included in transaction servers. It is therefore useful for servers to have **excluded** files whose write operations are not atomic as well as transaction files. When a file is created it would be defined as being either excluded or a transaction file. Both the Cambridge file server and Alpine allow for excluded files.

In a general-purpose transaction file server, there are many files that are almost 'read only', for example, executable software files. Once these files are put in place they are used by many different clients but are not altered by them; such files do not require either a recovery mechanism or concurrency control. Other files such as a user's private documents and temporary or scratch files used within client programs are not shared and there is little need for such files to be subject to concurrency control. When such files predominate in a server, it is important that concurrency control mechanisms should be chosen so as to have a very low overhead for read operations.

7.4 Implementation of a transaction service

We shall discuss the implementation of the transaction service operations defined in Box 7.1, using the *TWrite* procedure to illustrate points of detail. We have already outlined how to implement file versions in Section 7.2.3; we now turn to a discussion of intentions lists and locks.

In Chapter 6, we described an implementation of a basic file service and in Section 6.5 gave the details of the *Write* operation. To summarize those parts of Chapter 6: a file is constructed as a sequence of pages and each page is stored in a block; so the *Read* and *Write* operations are implemented in terms of the block service operations *PutBlock* and *GetBlock* and the sequence of pages in a file is recorded as a sequence of block pointers in the file's index. The implementation of a transaction service may use a similar file representation but it must maintain some further data structures to deal with recovery and concurrency control.

The technique of **shadow pages** may be used to implement atomic actions. In the shadow page technique, any page that is altered by a *TWrite* is written to a new block, leaving the original page unchanged. We refer to these new tentative pages as shadow pages. If the transaction is committed, the file index is updated by entering the block pointers of the shadow pages in its file index.

The use of shadow pages is appropriate when most *TWrite* operations result in changes to a page or more of data. This is frequently so in the case of general-purpose file servers and for that reason the shadow pages technique has often been used in the implementation of file servers. In database applications where the write operations frequently refer to records that occupy less than a file page the intentions lists should be based on a different representation for the tentative updates to achieve a more efficient use of disk storage.

7.4.1 Implementation of intentions lists

In this section we will consider the implementation of recovery based on intentions lists as described in Section 7.2.1. The implementation of locks for concurrency control in combination with intentions lists is discussed in the next section, and the actions required when a transaction commits in the presence of locks and an intentions list are described in Section 7.4.3.

In the general case, an entry must be made in the intentions list for any operation that will change the value of a file. The operations that can do this are *TWrite*, *TCreate*, *TTruncate* and *TDelete*. Each entry in the intentions list consists of a record of the information required to perform a *TWrite*, *TCreate*, *TTruncate* or *TDelete* operation. In the case of a *TWrite* the entry consists of block pointers to shadow pages containing the data to be written, the UFID of the file and the position in the file where the data is to be written.

GetIntention(OpType, Trans, File, PageNo) → IntentionPtr
        — REPORTS(NoIntention)

    If the intentions list for the transaction with TID *Trans* contains an intention to perform an operation *OpType* on *PageNo* of *File*, delivers a pointer the intention record. Otherwise reports an error.

SetIntention(OpType, Trans, File, PageNo, ShadowPtr)

    Records an entry in the intentions list for *Trans*.

RemoveIntentionsList(Trans)

    Removes the intentions list for the transaction with TID *Trans*. (Used in the second phase of transactions.)

GetIntentionsList(Trans)→ IntentionsRecordPtr

    Delivers a pointer to the list of intentions records for the given transaction.

Box 7.4 Operations on intentions records.

The data may affect one or more pages in the file and a shadow page will be made for each of these pages. The form of entries in the intentions list can be simplified by recording each *TWrite* that affects more than one page as several entries, one for each page affected.

The transaction service maintains an intentions list for each transaction in the form of a list of *intentions records* in stable storage. The intentions record must record the type of the operation that has generated it (*TWrite*, *TCreate*, *TTruncate* or *TDelete*), the transaction identifier, the file and page to which the intention refers and a pointer to the block that holds the shadow page. Since the length of a file may increase (as a result of a *TWrite*) or decrease (as a result of a *TTruncate*), we will provide for both by a single operation called *SetLength*. Thus a possible declaration for intentions records would be:

```
TYPE IntentionRecord = RECORD
    OpType: (Write, Create, SetLength, Delete);
    Trans, File, PageNo, ShadowPtr, ShadowLength:INTEGER;
    Next: ˆIntentionRecord;
END;
```

Box 7.4 defines some privileged operations that may be used only within the server for storing and accessing intentions records.

```
PROCEDURE TWrite(Trans : TID; File : UFID; Position : CARDINAL;
    Data : Seqptr);
VAR    page, firstPage, shadowptr, last, length : CARDINAL;
    buffer: Block;
    I : ˆIntentionRecord;
BEGIN
    length = TLength(File);
    IF Position > length THEN ErrorExit END;
    last := Position + SequenceLength(Data) - 1;
    firstPage = Position DIV PAGESIZE;
    FOR page := firstPageTO (last DIV PAGESIZE) DO
        I := GetIntention(Write, Trans, File, page);
        IF ErrorReport = NoIntention THEN
            shadowptr := AllocateBlock();
        ELSE
            shadowptr := Iˆ.ShadowPtr
        END
        GetBlock(shadowptr, buffer);
        CopyData(buffer, Data, Position MOD PAGESIZE, page-firstPage);
        PutBlock(shadowptr, buffer);
        SetIntention(Write, Trans, File, page, shadowptr);
    END
    IF last ≥ length THEN
        SetIntention(SetLength, Trans, File, 0, last+1)
    END
END TWrite;
```

Figure 7.24 *TWrite* with intentions lists.

We are now in a position to give in Figure 7.24 a version of the *TWrite* procedure that implements transactions based on intentions lists. This version will support recovery from aborted transactions, but does not yet exclude concurrent updates.

When a transaction is committed, the block pointers of the shadow pages are copied into the file index, replacing the block pointers of the original blocks. In order to make this an atomic operation, a copy of the file index is made, the block pointers of the shadow pages are added to it and then the original index is replaced by the copy. If the index occupies only one page, it may be written in place with one *PutBlock* operation. If a file index occupies more than one block, it has several levels. The lower levels can be updated in shadow pages.

The use of shadow pages to implement intentions lists has the advantage that there is no need to copy blocks in the second phase of the transaction. It has two main drawbacks. (1) It involves entire pages of the file in each intention, instead of the exact range of items specified in a *TWrite* operation. (2) Intentions lists must be stored in stable storage even during the first phase of a transaction, so that the server will be able to reclaim the blocks containing the shadow pages when it recovers after a crash.

7.4.2 Implementation of intentions lists with locks

We outline here an implementation of the transaction service operations using intentions lists for recovery and read-write locks for concurrency control. The version of *TWrite* presented in the previous section is extended to support read-write locks, using lock operations that we define in this section. The actions that must be performed on *CloseTransaction* are described in the Section 7.4.3.

Although our file and transaction service operations are defined to allow read and write operations that access data items of arbitrary size, for simplicity we shall assume that locks are applied at the level of file pages. This does not imply any loss of generality, since client operations that access more than a single page will result in locks on each of the pages affected, but it does result in some loss of concurrency when clients access small portions of pages, since two concurrent transactions cannot access different data items in the same page.

In environments where this loss of concurrency is significant, an implementation based on record or byte-level locking should be used (see, for example, Lindsay et al. [1983]). Such methods are not compatible with the use of shadow pages, since the shadow pages are accessible only to the transaction that has created them. Two transactions may not share a shadow page, even when they are accessing different data items within the page. An alternative approach to the representation of intentions lists, based on data items rather than pages, is therefore necessary when locks are applied to items smaller than pages.

The server maintains a set of locks for each page of a file. There may be several read locks, one write lock or no locks associated with each page. Box 7.5 defines the operations required on locks. The lock operations are used in the implementation of *TRead*, *TWrite* and other transaction service operations. To avoid conflicts between different transactions modifying the locks concurrently the operations should be protected by a monitor so that only one transaction at a time can execute *TWrite*, *TRead* or *UnLock*. This constraint appears to restrict

---

LockWait(Trans, File, Page, LockType)
    If there is a lock set on the *Page* of the *File* that conflicts with *LockType* (i.e. the lock is for a different *Trans* and *LockType* is Read and a Write lock is already set or *LockType* is Write and a Read or Write lock is set), *LockWait* waits on the lock condition variable, *LockFree*. Otherwise *LockWait* returns immediately.
SetLock(Trans, File, Page, LockType)
    Adds a new lock of type *LockType* to the set of locks on *Page* of *File*.
UnLock(Trans, File, Page, LockType)
    If there is a lock of type *LockType* on *Page* of *File* on behalf of the transaction *Trans*, *UnLock* removes the lock and *signals* on the associated *LockFree* condition variable, thus allowing any transactions waiting in a *LockWait* for this page to proceed.

Box 7.5 Lock access functions.

---

the scope for concurrency within the server quite severely, but since locks are associated with particular pages of files, two transactions can conflict only when they are accessing locks on the same page. In practice, a number of monitors could therefore be instantiated, each of which may be executing a *TRead* or a *TWrite* concurrently on a different file or a different page of the same file. The number of monitors used would be determined by the degree of concurrency desired in the server. The set of locks associated with each file page may be represented by a list of locks and a condition variable (and defined inside the monitor that includes *TRead*, *TWrite* and *Complete* as entry procedures).

```
TYPE
  LockSet = RECORD
    File: UFID;
    Page: CARDINAL;
    lockSet: ^LockRecord;
    LockFree: SIGNAL        (* a condition variable *)
  END;
  LockRecord = RECORD
    trans: TID;
    LockType: (Read, Write);
    next: ^LockRecord
  END;
```

The version of the *TWrite* procedure shown in Figure 7.25 uses *LockWait* and *SetLock* to establish the appropriate locks or wait on the condition variable if there are conflicting locks. The locks are removed when the transaction commits or aborts. This version differs from the version of *TWrite* presented in the last section only by the insertion of the lock testing and setting operations. We have chosen to give the two versions of *TWrite* for clarity of presentation, but of course only one version, implementing both locks and intentions lists, need be included in a transaction service.

```
PROCEDURE TWrite(Trans : TID; File : UFID; Position : CARDINAL;
    Data : Seqptr);
VAR    page, firstPage, shadowptr, last, length : CARDINAL;
    buffer: Block;
    I : ^IntentionRecord;
BEGIN
    length = TLength(File);
    IF Position > length THEN ErrorExit END;
    last := Position + SequenceLength(Data) - 1;
    firstPage := Position DIV PAGESIZE;
    FOR page := firstPage TO (last DIV PAGESIZE) DO
        I := GetIntention(Write, Trans, File, page);
        LockWait(Trans, File, page, Write);          (* check lock *)
        IF ErrorReport = NoIntention THEN
            shadowptr := AllocateBlock();
        ELSE
            shadowptr := I^.ShadowPtr
        END
        GetBlock(shadowptr, buffer);
        CopyData(buffer, Data, Position MOD PAGESIZE, page-firstPage);
        PutBlock(shadowptr, buffer);
        SetIntention(Write, Trans, File, page, shadowptr);
        SetLock(Trans, File, Page, Write);
    END
    IF last ≥ length THEN
        SetIntention(SetLength, Trans, File, 0, last+1)
    END
END TWrite;
```

Figure 7.25 *TWrite* with locks and intentions lists.

7.4.3 The commit phase

In the second phase of a transaction the server must transfer the data in the shadow pages into the appropriate files, release the locks and recover the storage used to represent the transaction record and intentions list. It must guarantee to perform these tasks completely, even in the face of crashes in the server or the client.

The server maintains a transaction record for each active transaction (see Box 7.6 for operations on the transaction record). The transaction record contains two items, the transaction identifier and the commit flag recording the current phase of the transaction (*tentative*, *committed* or *aborted*). *OpenTransaction* calls *AddTrans* to generate a new transaction record with commit flag value *tentative*.

AddTrans→Trans
   Makes a new transaction record in stable storage in the server and returns
   a TID.
GetPhase(Trans)→Phase — NonExistent
   Returns the phase of a transaction.
SetPhase(Trans, Phase)— NonExistent
   Sets phase of a transaction.
DeleteTrans(Trans)— NonExistent
   Deletes a transaction record.
ListAllTrans()→ TIDList
   Returns a list of the TIDs of all recent transactions in the server.

Box 7.6   Transaction record functions.

PROCEDURE Complete(Trans: TID; phase: Phase);
VAR
   I   : IntentionRecord;
   Ilist: ^IntentionRecord;
BEGIN
   SetPhase(Trans, phase);
   Ilist := GetIntentionsList(Trans);
         (should copy index of each file *)*
   IF phase = committed THEN
      FOR I := <each member I of the intentions list> *Ilist DO*
         ToIndex(I.File, I.PageNo, I.ShadowPtr);
      END
   END
   RemoveIntentionsList(Trans);
   FOR I := <each member I of the intentions list> *Ilist DO*
      unLock(Trans, I.File, I.PageNo, I.OpType);
                  (also signals waiting processes *)*
   END
END

Figure 7.26 Completing: commit or abort.

The procedure called *Complete* defined in Figure 7.26 is an internal
procedure designed for use by the server whenever a transaction aborts or a
CloseTransaction request occurs. This procedure should copy the file index of
each file affected by the transaction before updating it and then replace all of the
indexes. We have omitted these details. When a transaction is to be aborted
Complete sets the commit flag to *aborted* and clears the locks and the intentions
list belonging to the transaction. Otherwise *Complete* initiates the second phase

of the transaction by setting the commit flag to *committed*, carries out the intentions recorded in the intentions list and clears the locks and the intentions list.

The procedure *Complete* is intended to be used for recovery. When the server restarts, it starts its recovery procedures that inspect the transaction records of all the recent transactions. The phase of each associated transaction may be found by using *getPhase* and then each intention list is treated according to its phase. If the phase is tentative or aborted, *Complete* is called with *phase = aborted*. If the phase is committed, *Complete* is called with *phase = committed*. The recovery procedure can be repeated any number of times.

7.5 Summary

We have shown how a basic file service may be extended to provide atomic transactions. The provision of a transaction service enables clients to specify sequences of operations that are to be performed as an atomic unit. The service cooperates with the client in order to carry out transactions atomically. There are two factors that threaten the atomicity of transactions. The first is the failure of processes and computers and is handled by recovery. The second is the concurrent execution of transactions and is handled by concurrency control based on notions of serial equivalence. All transactions complete in one of three ways: (1) they are committed, (2) they are aborted by the server, (3) they are aborted by the client.

Transactions are carried out in two phases. During the first phase, tentative changes of file items are recorded in intentions lists or as file versions. This has two important effects – if the transaction is committed, the tentative changes may be made permanent and if it aborts they may be discarded and the tentative changes are invisible to other transactions.

Concurrency control may be achieved by the use of locks, timestamps or optimistic concurrency control. When locks are used, clients must wait for other clients' transactions to release their locks and the use of locks can lead to problems of deadlock. These problems may be alleviated by the use of timeouts or deadlock detection, but in either solution clients transactions are aborted and must be restarted.

Optimistic concurrency control is based on comparing changes made by the current transaction with those made by recent preceding transactions and is advantageous to read-only transactions; but transactions that fail validation tests are restarted. In a busy server with many conflicting requests, the use of optimistic concurrency control can lead to starvation.

The use of timestamps orders the operations on data items according to the transactions' timestamps. It can result in transactions waiting for earlier transactions to complete their operations, but this does not cause deadlock. It also leads to transactions aborting and restarting when they are too late to alter data items already accessed by transactions with later timestamps. The problem of concurrency control is not yet completely solved and most of the new ideas in this area are concerned with the increasing of concurrency.

A transaction service may be implemented on top of the block service and stable storage described in Chapter 6. We described this using locks and intentions lists based on shadow pages. The file service operations are modified to include calls to functions that add intentions and set locks for each page of a file.

EXERCISES

7.1 Describe the meaning of the term *atomic transaction*.

7.2 What are the two main factors that threaten the atomicity of transactions?

7.3 Describe how a transaction is carried out in two phases and how this ensures atomicity, both when it commits and when it aborts.

7.4 Describe the technique of *shadow pages*. How may this technique be used to make a new version of a file.

7.5 The tentative versions of data items made during the first phase of a transaction have two different purposes. What are these?

7.6 Explain why the client operations for transactions do not include operations to set locks.

7.7 The transactions T, U and V are defined as follows:

T	U	V
OpenTransaction	*OpenTransaction*	*OpenTransaction*
Read(a)	*Read(b)*	*Read(c)*
Write(a+1)	*Read(c)*	*Write(c+4)*
Read(b)	*Write(b+3)*	*Read(a)*
Write(b–1)	*Write(c–3)*	*Write(a–4)*
CloseTransaction	*CloseTransaction*	*CloseTransaction*

Describe the use of locks, timestamps and optimistic concurrency control to control these three transactions.

7.8 Define the term *serial equivalence*.

7.9 Describe the use of two-phase locking. Give the lock compatibility tables for intention-to-write locks and ordinary read-write locks. Discuss the advantages of intention-to-write locks when compared to ordinary read-write locks.

7.10 Discuss the importance of granularity of locks.

7.11 Give an example to illustrate how deadlock can arise when exclusive locks are used and when read-write locks are used.

7.12 State the rules for validating transactions in optimistic concurrency control.

7.13 Describe the basic timestamping mechanism. What is the main difficulty in implementing timestamping in a service with several servers?

7.14 The transactions T, U and V are defined as follows:

T	U	V
OpenTransaction	OpenTransaction	OpenTransaction
Read(a)	Read(a)	Read(a)
Write(a+1)	Read(a+3)	Write(a+4)
CloseTransaction	CloseTransaction	CloseTransaction

If these transactions are allowed to run concurrently, and the value of a is initially 10, list the different final values of a that could occur.

Chapter 8
Collaborating Servers and File Replication

In this chapter we consider the design of a file service that manages a set of files distributed over several collaborating servers. We discuss collaboration between servers under three main headings:

1. The distribution of a basic file service, supporting the file service operations described in Chapter 5 but with the files located in several servers. Two new issues arise in designing a basic distributed file service:

   * the placement of files,
   * locating a file, given its UFID.

2. The provision of a distributed transaction service, supporting atomic transactions that may include files in several servers.

3. The provision of replicated file service, in which each file may be represented by one or more copies located in separate servers.

8.1 Introduction

This chapter is about the design of an integrated file service that combines several server computers in a single local area network or in linked local networks. From the client's point of view, the file service should present the same service operations regardless of the number of servers, their geographic locations and the location of the files in these servers. That is, the file service should be transparent to location, distribution and replication of files.

When a file service is designed to use varying numbers of servers with different capabilities it can be configured to suit the needs of a particular application and can be extended when more resources are required; when a single integrated service covers widely dispersed locations, servers may be placed at each separate location with files that are needed in several locations replicated at each.

The basic file service described in Chapter 5 is location-independent; clients need not be aware of the location of the server holding the files that they use and no particular policy for the location of files is implied. The file service functions defined in Box 5.1 provide access to a set of files referenced by UFIDs that are unique throughout the system; the file service can be implemented by a single server or by a number of servers, each holding a subset or **partition** of the total set of files.

In Chapter 6 we have discussed the implementation of a basic file service that manages a set of files in a single server. Such a server could be used to hold all of the files in a distributed system or to hold a partition of the total set of files. Additional problems to be solved when the set of files is partitioned between several servers include the **placement** problem – the need to choose a server to hold each file when it is created – and the **location** problem – the need to discover which server holds a file whenever a client wishes to refer to it. Other issues that may arise are the need to allow for files to be relocated after they have been created and the need to replicate files in several servers for performance and reliability reasons.

If the files involved in an atomic transaction are located on different servers, there must be an additional level of coordination to ensure that all of the servers complete the updates when the transaction commits. The service functions for the transaction-based service defined in Chapter 7 require a unique transaction identifier. Several files may be accessed and updated within a single transaction and each transaction must be coordinated to ensure that it is atomic.

File replication can be used to overcome performance limitations when a file is shared between several clients, allowing several copies of the same file to be placed in different computers. When several clients located in different local networks, linked by an internet, need to access the contents of a single file their speed of access to the file can be improved by placing a replicated copy of the file in a server on each local network. But this gain in speed of access for reading the contents of replicated files is balanced by a loss in performance for updating operations. Replicated file systems should be transparent; clients should see a file service interface similar to the one provided by a non-replicated file service but with improved performance and reliability. The main problem to be solved in the design of a replicated file system is maintenance of consistency between the copies when a replicated file is updated. A timestamp or a version number must be associated with each replicated copy of a file and the access and update algorithms must ensure that up-to-date versions are used.

Time and timestamps □   In transaction and file replication services that rely on timestamps to record the order of the actions in a set of concurrent transactions there is an additional problem when several servers are involved: the clocks used to generate the timestamps in different servers participating in a transaction must be adequately synchronized.

A key observation is that synchronized clocks or event counts are only required when processes in disjoint computers are actually cooperating. Since cooperation always involves message passing as the only means of communication between distributed processes, synchronization can safely be associated with message passing operations. There are two requirements for timestamp generation in a distributed system:

1. There must be a method for generating timestamps that are unique throughout the distributed system.
2. The ordering of two events in the same computer should be reflected in their timestamps. If a timestamp A is sent through the network in a message, and the receiving computer compares its current timestamp on receipt, B, then $A < B$.

Lamport [1978] has shown that this can be achieved without reference to a 'global clock', but only with a precision equivalent to the time taken to transfer a message between two computers in the distributed system. Lamport describes a mechanism for the synchronization of clocks in a distributed system based on the inclusion in each message of the time according to the clock at the sending location, enabling the receiving process to adjust its real-time clock. The two requirements given above may be satisfied as follows:

1. Each server has a method for generating local timestamps and can generate system-wide unique timestamps by concatenating its local timestamps with its own server identifier. Servers generally keep their timestamps adjusted approximately to real time and the server identifier is made the least significant part in a timestamp so that timestamps are ordered by time rather than by server identifier.
2. Servers may generate timestamps and allot them to events in such a way that the ordering of events at a single site is reflected in their timestamps. Synchronization between sites is achieved by including the local timestamp at the time of sending messages. If the receiving server's current time is 'slow', it resets it by adding an interval less than the average message transmission time to the time in the received timestamp.

Readers are referred to Lamport [1978] or Ceri and Pelagatti [1985] for a more detailed discussion of this topic.

8.2 A basic distributed file service

A distributed file service consists of a set of files managed cooperatively by a number of file servers to provide a service in which the distribution of files is transparent to clients. As servers can only execute file service operations referring to files that they manage, file service requests must be sent to the appropriate server. We recall from Section 5.3.2 that UFIDs are constructed to include the identifier of the server creating them (sometimes called the file's **birthplace**). If files are never relocated then the location of a file can be determined from the birthplace information embedded in its UFID, but if the file service supports file relocation then the server identifier part of a UFID may not identify the server that currently holds the file. In that case the birthplace must be regarded as merely a 'hint' to the file's location and further information about the location of files that have been relocated must be used.

Once a UFID is assigned to a file it must remain the same for the duration of the file's existence because clients that hold UFIDs may store them in private storage or files independently of the 'official' directory service. If UFIDs could change during the lifetimes of files there would be no way to propagate their changed values to these private copies.

The role of the user package □   The user package is conceptually a part of the file service, running in the client machines. In a simple file service based on a single server the user package performs the standard role for user packages described in Chapter 4, establishing communication with a file server by presenting the text name for the service required to the RPC system, which obtains the relevant server identifier (internet address) from the system binder or name service. In a file service that is based on several file servers the binder returns the server identifiers for all of the file servers and the user package must perform the additional role of *locating files*, choosing the appropriate server based on hints encoded in UFIDs or held by clients or servers.

Note that with this scheme a server of the distributed file service can run in any computer in the network, including workstations, provided that it registers its interface with the binder.

Placement of files □   When a client creates a new file, the user package selects one particular server to hold the file. The server selected generates a new UFID containing its own server-id and subsequently manages the file. The selection of a location for a new file may be done automatically or the client may be allowed to indicate a preference for a particular server when creating a file. An automatic placement algorithm might have the aim of minimizing the communication delays from client to server or of balancing the workload or the storage utilization across all of the servers.

Some file location algorithms □   In systems that allow files to move between servers an algorithm is needed in the user package to locate files that have been moved. Since the majority of files remain where they were created, the algorithm is needed only for a minority of file accesses. When the user package has located a file for a particular client, it retains the information for future reference during the lifetime of that client (or until the file is moved again).

We now give a brief description of the location algorithms in some systems that provide for location independence.

The **Apollo Domain** operating system [Leach et al. 1983] is described fully in Section 10.9. Its *object storage system* holds data objects with unique identifiers. Apollo objects may be regarded as analogous to files. Object identifiers are made unique by concatenating the ID of the server that creates them and a timestamp from the server's clock. This birthplace information embedded in the UFIDs is to be regarded only as a hint to the current location of an object. A separate file locating service is responsible for obtaining the locations of files given their UFIDs.

The algorithm used by the locating service uses hints about object location. The first source of hints is the birthplace and the second source of hints is a *hint file* held in each client computer. Any software component may add information to the hint file. A third source of hints is the directory service; it guesses that objects are stored in the same server as the directory they are in. The authors of the paper referenced suggest allowing user input to the hint file to improve the effectiveness of the search, but they conclude that objects seldom move from their original server and that this provision does not seem to be necessary.

The **Locus** distributed operating system [Popek and Walker 1985] distributes its files among a number of servers and assigns each file to a *synchronization site* – a server that records a mapping from the UFID of a file to the server that currently stores the file. The address of their synchronization sites is incorporated into the UFIDs of files so this remains constant whereas the file itself can be transferred from one server to another and each time it moves the information at the synchronization site must be brought up to date.

At Cambridge University a prototype for a new distributed file service called the **Mayflower file server** [Bacon and Hamilton 1988] has been designed to use a hint-based algorithm exploiting three sources of information for locating files: the file's birthplace as recorded in the UFID, a record maintained in client computers of the server at which the file was 'last seen' and a list held by each file server of the destinations of files that have been moved to other servers (forming a chain of server identifiers that leads to the file) [J. Bacon 1988, private communication].

8.3 A distributed transaction service

The transaction service whose operations are defined in Box 7.1 can be extended to support transactions involving files in more than one server in such a way that the distribution of the files participating in a transaction is transparent to clients. Servers that execute file operations as part of such a joint transaction need to communicate with one another to coordinate their actions when the transaction commits in order to achieve recoverability and concurrency control over the entire set of file operations in the transaction, but clients' requests to access and update the files involved in a transaction are sent to the server that holds the relevant file to avoid the additional communication that would arise if client requests all had to pass through a single server.

We shall first describe the client interface and the implementation approach for distributed transactions with a coordinating server described by Israel et al. [1978] and implemented in the XDFS file service. The implementation approach is based on the two-phase commit algorithm first described by Gray [1978] and detailed further in Ceri and Pelagatti [1985] and Date [1983].

AddServer(Trans, server-id of coordinator)
Informs a server that it is involved in the transaction *Trans*.
Box 8.1   Extra transaction service operation.

A client may open a transaction by sending an *OpenTransaction* call to any server. The server that is contacted executes the *OpenTransaction*, and returns the resulting transaction identifier to the client. The first server in a transaction becomes the **coordinator** for the transaction and is responsible for aborting it or committing it and for adding other servers, described as **workers**. The distributed transaction service includes one new service function: *AddServer* (defined in Box 8.1). It must be used by a client before any operations are requested in a server that has not yet joined the transaction. It enables the coordinator and the workers to collect the extra information that will be needed at commit time.

The user package makes the distribution of files in a transaction transparent to the user-level programs in the client by recording the identifier of the server that opens the transaction and issuing an *AddServer* call when a new server joins the transaction with the identifier of the coordinator as an argument. When the transaction ends the user package calls the procedure *CloseTransaction* or *AbortTransaction* in the coordinator.

Commitment of distributed transactions □   At some point, a distributed transaction will come to an end and must be committed or aborted. At this point the servers in the transaction must communicate with one another to reach a joint decision as to whether the transaction is to be committed or aborted by all of them. After this, each server in the transaction must complete the transaction according to the joint decision, using the usual procedures to carry out all of the writes in the intentions lists or none of them. The transaction records contain information to enable a distributed transaction to be committed or aborted and each server records whether it is a *coordinator* or a *worker*. The coordinator stores a list of all the other servers that join the transaction, whereas each of the workers records the identifier of the coordinator.

The effect of a server receiving an *AddServer* request from a client is that it applies to the coordinator to join the transaction by calling the *NewServer* procedure in the coordinator, makes a new transaction record containing the TID and the server-id of the coordinator, and initializes a new intentions list to record the updates to local files from the transaction. The intentions list at each server records only the operations that apply to it, so the complete intentions list for a transaction may be divided between a number of servers.

NewServer(Trans,server-id, capability)→ok

    Call from a new server (in *AddServer*) to the coordinator. Caller supplies its server-id and a *capability*; the coordinator records *server-id* and *capability* in its worker list.

CanCommit?→ yes / no

    Call from coordinator to worker to check whether it can commit.

    Worker replies with *yes/no*.

DoCommit(Trans,capability)

    Call from coordinator to worker to tell worker to commit its transaction.

HaveCommitted(Trans,server-id)

    Call from worker to coordinator to confirm that it has committed transaction.

        Box 8.2 Internal operations of distributed transaction service.

NewServer is one of several internal server-to-server operations used in distributed transactions and summarized in Box 8.2. When the coordinator executes *NewServer* the identifier of the new worker is added to its list of workers.

The other functions in Box 8.2 are discussed in detail in a later section, but they may be summarized as follows. When a transaction is due to enter the second phase, the coordinator calls the procedure *CanCommit?* in each worker in its list to discover whether the latter is able to commit the transaction. If all of the servers can commit the transaction, the coordinator calls the procedure *DoCommit* in each worker; the latter call *HaveCommitted* in the coordinator when they have finished.

Security of a service based on communicating servers □ In Box 8.2 we show a function *NewServer* that enables its caller to pass a capability that is used to protect the integrity of a distributed transaction. The *DoCommit* procedure is used by a coordinator to instruct the workers in a transaction to commit their parts of the transaction. However we do not want any processes other than the coordinator to call *DoCommit*, for they cannot be trusted to do so at the right time. Neither the TID nor the server-id of the coordinator can be used as a capability for the purpose of committing a transaction, as the client knows the former and the user package knows the latter. In our scheme, a worker issues a capability when it calls *NewServer* and only obeys the *DoCommit* call if its argument contains the capability it issued.

The security of the *DoCommit* procedure call is an example of a more general problem related to the security of a distributed service, where the correct completion of a joint task is based on communication between collaborating servers. Such tasks may be done by procedures that should be executed only if the call comes from trusted processes and potential recipients can ensure the authenticity of other processes by issuing them with capabilities to be passed back in subsequent calls.

8.3.1 Multi-server commit

We will describe the two-phase commit algorithm given by Gray and used to commit transactions involving several servers in the XDFS system. In Israel et al. [1978] the method is described in terms of messages passed between the collaborating servers, but we describe it here in terms of the remote procedure calls outlined in Box 8.2.

We have already noted that in multi-server transactions there is one server that acts as the coordinator for the transaction, but that the client may issue file service requests direct to any of the servers in the transaction. Each server maintains its own transaction record, giving the transaction identifier and the identifier of the coordinating server, and its own intentions list. When the client calls *CloseTransaction* the coordinator and the workers in the transaction have tentative intentions lists describing the operations that affect their own files. The coordinator is responsible for deciding whether the transaction should be aborted or committed, for if one of the servers is unable to commit, then the whole transaction must be aborted. If the client or one of the workers calls *AbortTransaction* in the coordinator, the latter will have a value of *aborted* in its commit flag and the decision is already made.

The *CloseTransaction* is executed by the coordinator in two phases – preparing to commit and the commitment itself:

Phase 1:
1. The coordinator has a list of the server-ids of the workers, and its commit flag is *tentative*; it issues a *CanCommit?* call to each of the workers in the transaction, with a timeout.
2. When the workers receive the *CanCommit?* call, each one does as follows:
   - If the value of its commit flag is *tentative* and the worker is able to commit (i.e. it has not previously aborted its part of the transaction), it returns *yes* to inform the coordinator it is ready.
   - Otherwise the worker's commit flag is set to *abort* and it returns *no* as the result.

Phase 2:
3. At this point either the coordinator has received *ok* or *no* from each worker, or the *CanCommit?* call has timed-out.
   - If the coordinator has had an *ok* return value from all of the workers in the transaction, it sets the value of its commit flag to *committed*, and makes the *DoCommit* call to all the workers. At this point, the transaction is effectively completed, since the coordinator and the workers are now committed to perform the updates in their intentions lists, so the coordinator can report success to the client.
   - If any of the replies was *no* or any worker has been timed-out, the coordinator sets its commit flag to *abort* and calls *AbortTransaction* in each of the workers, reporting failure to the client.
4. When a worker receives the *DoCommit* call it sets the value of its flag to *committed* and sends a *HaveCommitted* call to the coordinator. It eventually carries out its intentions list and erases it.

5. The coordinator carries out its own intentions list and erases it. When the coordinator has received *HaveCommitted* calls from all the other servers it erases its list of servers.

Locks are handled exactly as in single-server transactions; each server sets locks for the files that it manages and when it completes its part of the transaction it removes them.

Recovery procedure □   We now consider the conditions that may arise when a server is started up after a failure. As we noted in Chapter 7, when a server is restarted all of its intentions lists are inspected; any committed transactions are completed and uncommitted transactions are aborted. For multi-server transactions there are four different cases to consider; an intentions list may be in a coordinator or in a worker and they may show that the transaction has already committed, or not committed (aborted or tentative).

1. *List in coordinator, transaction not committed:* The server instructs the other servers to erase their intentions lists by using *AbortTransaction* and, when this has been done, it erases its own coordinator's intentions list.
2. *List in coordinator, committed transaction:* The server carries out its own intentions list, sends a *DoCommit* to all of the workers (in case it had not done so before it failed) and resumes the commit sequence at step (4) above.
3. *List in worker, transaction not committed:* The worker does nothing. It must wait for the coordinator to instruct it either to commit or to abort the transaction.
4. *List in worker, committed transaction:* The worker sends *HaveCommitted* to the coordinator and carries out its part of the transaction. (Even if this has been partially done before the failure, it can be repeated without inconsistency, because the file service operations are repeatable.)

8.3.2 Implementation using timestamps

Reed [1983] describes an implementation of distributed transactions in which the treatment of recovery and synchronization is combined, using timestamps. The method was tested in the Swallow experimental file server [Svoboda 1984], but no practical applications have yet been reported. Reed describes the algorithm in terms of operations on arbitrary-size data objects, rather than file pages, but we will describe it here in terms of *TWrite* and *TRead* operations applied to file pages.

There is a single transaction record for each transaction containing a *commit flag* giving the current status of the transaction (*tentative, committed* or *aborted*) and an expiry time that can be used to abort any transaction that is not completed expeditiously and obstructs other transactions. The transaction record is created and stored in the server that initiates the transaction. Each client involved in a transaction is given a reference to the transaction record and this must be given as a parameter in all file service calls.

Each file page is represented by a history consisting of a sequence of versions ordered in time. A *TWrite* operation makes a new tentative version carrying a timestamp and a reference (consisting of the server identifier of the initiating server and the TID of the transaction) to the transaction record and inserts it into the sequence of versions at the appropriate position. Because each page contains a reference the transaction record it is possible to say for each page whether it is in the *committed, tentative* or *aborted* state. Aborted versions are eventually removed from page histories. Each page has another timestamp that holds the timestamp of the most recent transaction that has read the page.

Reading a page □ Servers can discover whether pages belong to the same transaction as a *TWrite* or *TRead* operation by comparing the transaction record reference in the page with the transaction record reference associated with the operation. (Note that this does not require access to the transaction record itself, which might be stored in a different server).

To do a *TRead* operation, the server looks for the most recent version of the page that was written with a timestamp that earlier than, or the same as, the current transaction's timestamp. If the page is committed, or if it is a tentative version made by the same transaction the contents are read and returned immediately. If the page is tentative and belongs to another transaction, the client that invoked the *TRead* must wait for one of the following events:

1. the other transaction is committed; whereupon the server returns the new committed version;
2. the other transaction is aborted, because it passes its expiry time or for some other reason; the server deletes the aborted version and does the read on the previous version. (A transaction that has passed its expiry time is only aborted when another transaction requests a page that it has written.)

When a *TRead* operation returns a result, the time stamp of the operation is stored with the most recent version of the page as the most recent time of reading.

Coordinating reads and writes □ There is no guarantee that operations arrive at a server in the order of their timestamps (e.g. because of differing network transmission delays). If a *TWrite* operation arrives after a *TRead* operation with a later timestamp, the *TWrite* is aborted. In all other cases the server does the *TWrite*, inserting the new tentative version of the page with its timestamp at the correct position in the history.

Commit algorithm □ When a transaction is committed, the commit flag in the transaction record is changed to *committed*. This is an atomic operation and the transaction is logically complete when this has been done. Any transaction that subsequently accesses one of the pages altered by the transaction will see the page as committed; the server that holds the page will see the committed status when it accesses the transaction record that the page points to to check the page's status.

The use of a single transaction record has two drawbacks that must be addressed to achieve a practical implementation:

1. The performance of the file service is diminished because every access to a page requires access to the transaction record for the transaction that created it in order to check its status.

2. If the transaction record may be located in a server that is remote from the server holding the page the need to access the transaction record diminishes the performance still more, and reduces the system's reliability in the face of server or communication failure.

(1) is addressed (a) by updating each page to hold a null value in place of the transaction record reference on the first access to the page after the commit; or (b) by storing a back-pointer in the transaction record to each of the pages affected by the transaction and storing a null value in the page immediately after the commit.

(2) can be addressed by the distribution of replicated copies of the transaction record, but note that it should only be required in case (a) of the previous paragraph, since (b) obviates the need to access the transaction record.

Pseudo-time for timestamps □   Reed uses *pseudo-time* instead of real-time ordering. Timestamps are associated roughly with real time. The method depends on servers having approximately synchronized real-time clocks (see Section 8.1).

Pseudo-time generators produce timestamps with the property that the time interval for one transaction does not overlap the time interval of any other transaction. The operations within a transaction have increasing timestamps within the time interval allotted to the transaction.

When a transaction is opened, a new *pseudo-time generator* is spawned. This is a process that lives for the duration of the transaction. The operations in a transaction apply to its generator for timestamps. When the generator starts up it constructs a creation timestamp by concatenating the time on its clock with its server-id. The generator must ensure that no two clock readings on its own timestamps are the same.

On request for a timestamp, a pseudo-time generator makes a complete timestamp by concatenating its creation timestamp with the time on its clock. In comparing two timestamps, the higher-order part contains the creation timestamp – keeping time intervals of transactions disjoint – the lower-order part contains the time on the generator's clock and orders timestamps within a transaction.

An example illustrating Reed's method □   We use our example transaction T from Section 7.1 (in which \$2 is transferred from account A to account B) to illustrate Reed's distributed transactions. This time we assume that the accounts A and B are stored in separate servers S_1 and S_2 and that, when the transaction starts, a *tentative* transaction record is made at $\hat{S}_1$, the first server contacted. A pseudo-time generator is started and this will be used to give timestamps for each of the operations in the transaction as shown in the following table.

Steps in transaction T		
Step	*Operation*	*Timestamp*
1	*Read(a)*	*t1*
2	*Read(b)*	*t2*
3	*Write(a–$2)*	*t3*
4	*Write(b+$2)*	*t4*

The timestamps are ordered so that $t1 < t2 < t3 < t4$ and all pseudotimes used by other transactions are either less than $t1$ or greater than $t4$. At (1) and (2) the timestamps of the transaction are $t1$ and $t2$ and it will read versions of A and B and the following steps (3) and (4) will create new tentative versions of A and B.

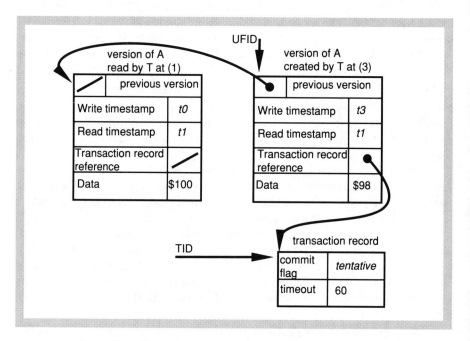

Figure 8.1 History of account A at step (3) in transaction T.

Figure 8.1 shows the previous and new tentative version of account A at step (3) in transaction T, assuming that the timestamp on A was $t0$ and the balance of the account was $100 before the transaction started. When the transaction closes, the state of the commit record is set to *committed*. If another transaction with a pseudo-time later than $t3$ reads account A, after the tentative version has been made, it will wait until T has committed or aborted.

Note that if another later transaction were to have read one of the accounts before T had made its new versions, it would have succeeded in changing the read timestamp and then T would be too late and would be aborted.

8.4 Replication

A replicated file is represented by a number of copies located in separate servers. We refer to each of the set of copies that comprises a replicated file as a **representative** of the replicated file. The provision of replicated files can:

- reduce communication traffic in a distributed system and improve response time by providing clients with local representatives;
- increase system availability by making it possible to access the same file on more than one server, thereby reducing the effect of server and communication failures;
- enable several clients' requests for access to the same file to be serviced in parallel by different servers, with a resulting improvement in system throughput.

Two approaches to file replication have been pursued in practice.

The first is the **master/slave strategy**. With this approach there is one primary server and several secondary servers for each replicated file. The primary server holds a maser copy of the file and services all the update requests. The other representatives of files – the slave representatives – are updated by receiving notification of changes from the primary server or by taking copies from the master copy. Clients can read data from both the master and the slave representatives. This strategy is only suitable for applications, such as the maintenance of system software files, in which files are changed infrequently and changes can be accepted at a central point.

The second strategy is to provide **distributed update control** for replicated files. There are several algorithms for the maintenance of a consistent set of representatives without a distinguished master copy. We shall describe two of them in Sections 8.4.3 and 8.4.4.

8.4.1 A master/slave system

The Sun Yellow Pages (YP) service [Sun 1987a] is an example of the master/slave strategy. The YP service provides replicated read-only files (called *maps*) containing sets of (*key, value*) pairs, in which clients may look up entries with single keys or enumerate all the pairs in a set. Updates are always performed first on the master copy and then propagated to the slave copies. The YP service interface does not include a method for updating the master files because they can be regarded as conventional UNIX files and updated using conventional UNIX file operations.

The YP protocol is designed for applications in which the frequency of updates to files is of the order of tens per day. It is used, for example, in UNIX systems for distributed password files and network host address tables. Each YP file is held by a primary server and some secondary servers.

YP service operations are supported by a user package that runs in a client machine using a YP binder to locate any YP server, primary or secondary, to which the client may address its access requests. Domains provide a second level of naming and protection for sets of files enabling organizations to subdivide their distributed information into chunks for security purposes.

Maps contain internal timestamps that are set when they are created and updated each time they are are modified. Slave servers are intended to try to keep their maps up to date by getting copies from the master, whenever they discover an entry with an old timestamp. If the primary server is unavailable, secondary servers may communicate with one another to establish the current versions of maps. The YP protocol includes server-to-server operations that are used to propagate map updates amongst the servers:

- an operation that enables the primary server to tell a secondary server to get a new version of a map;
- an operation to enable a server to enquire of another server about the timestamp of its map and which server is the primary for a given file.

Two further administrative operations are available: to make a primary server tell slave servers about new versions of maps; and to tell secondary servers to get new versions of maps.

There is no locking during the propagation of updates and maps are certain to be inconsistent some of the time, although they should converge to a consistent steady state. There is no guarantee that the results of an enumeration of all the pairs in a mapping will all come from the same version of a map.

The YP protocol does not specify how changes are to be propagated but there are a number of ways that it can be done, for example, manually after altering the master copy; or more likely by a YP server starting a process that is designed to copy maps. Servers may use the client operations for matching keys and enumerating maps in other servers in order to get the information needed to update their maps.

The use of a master server with centralized control makes it relatively easy to resolve conflicts between requests and to maintain consistency. The main disadvantage of the master/slave strategy is that replicated files cannot be updated during any period of time in which the server with their master representative is unavailable. Unavailability can occur for various reasons such as server failure or network failure.

8.4.2 Systems with distributed control of updates

Some files, for example those that are used to represent databases and electronic bulletin boards, are updated frequently by clients at different locations. To satisfy the needs of these and other such applications, a distributed update control mechanism is needed in which updates can continue even when some of the servers containing representatives are unavailable. Any server that holds a representative of a file should be able to accept changes to that file and to issue those changes to the other representatives in such a way that clients making enquiries or updates have a consistent view of the data. This requires a distributed update control mechanism that can resolve conflicting updates and ensure consistency of the replicated file.

File suites □   We use the term **file suite** to refer to the set of representatives that comprise a replicated file. A file suite is defined by a list of representatives containing at least the UFIDs and the server identifiers of the representative files. In order to support a strategy for replication in which updates can be accepted by any server with a representative, the definitions of file suites are stored at each server mentioned in the suite.

If perfect consistency were achievable, all the representatives in a file suite would have the same initial values and after each change all the representatives would be instantly updated in the same way and would remain identical throughout time. However there are reasons why the representatives are not always kept identical:

- A server containing one of the representatives may be unavailable at the time of an update operation.
- It may not be desirable to update all representatives immediately for reasons of performance.

An alternative looser form of consistency can be adopted, in which all representatives will eventually be updated, so that the representatives converge to the same value at some time interval after updates have stopped. It is to be expected that only some of the representatives of a replicated file are up to date at any given time and the file service must ensure:

- that the result of a *Read* operation is based on data from one of the up-to-date representatives (the server contacted will if possible use its own local representative);
- that *Write* operations are applied only to current representatives;
- that out-of-date representatives are made current by replacing them with copies of current representatives when a server becomes available or when there are insufficient representatives;

The set of representatives affected by a *Write* operation may be extended by continuing the operation in the background after the client's call for the operation has returned.

Replication transparency □   Replication of files should be designed to be transparent to the client, so that the user of a replicated file has the view that only a single file exists. Therefore the *Read*, *Write* and other file operations should have the same client interface whether they apply to a single file or to a replicated file.

Perhaps the choice of servers for placement of representatives of replicated files may be regarded as a client task, for the selection of a number of servers would normally be determined by clients' requirements. The placement of copies of a replicated file identifier in directories local to the servers with representatives is also regarded as a client responsibility.

Version numbers □   Not all of the representatives of a replicated file need be altered immediately after an update operation and therefore servers must be able to determine from version numbers or timestamps whether representatives are up to date before reading from them.

We may regard the current state of a file as the most recent version in a series of versions with version numbers. The initial state of a file is the first version and after each change to a file we have a new version of that file. In a replicated file each representative has a version number; but only the representatives that are up to date have the current version number, whereas out-of-date representatives have earlier version numbers.

A *Read* operation should be given data from a representative with the current version number and a *Write* operation should be applied only to representatives with the current version number. A server that receives a *Read* or *Write* request on a replicated file could determine which of the representatives are current if it could obtain their version numbers. We therefore propose that, after each *Write* operation, servers record the current version number with representatives they have updated; and in addition to this, servers respond to queries from other servers about the version numbers of their own representatives of replicated files.

Determining the up-to-date representatives □   A server that receives a call for a *Read* or *Write* operation on a replicated file can request version numbers from the other servers listed in the file suite and the result of such a request is a set of version numbers in which the largest number belongs to the current version.

How many representatives should be written? □   Although the performance of a *Write* operation can be increased by reducing the number of representatives that are updated immediately, the consistency of the file suite must also be taken into account when deciding on the minimum number of representatives to be updated immediately

Provided that a version number enquiry is sent to all the servers in a file suite, the current version number can be assessed correctly, even when only a small proportion of the representatives are current. However it may not be possible, for reasons of availability, or desirable, for reasons of performance, to make version number enquiries to all of the servers in a file suite.

If a majority of the representatives are updated as a result of each *Write* and a majority are included in each version number enquiry, then, since any two majorities must contain at least one common member, the current version number could always be assessed correctly.

When a server receives a version number request, it responds by returning the version number of its own representative of a replicated file. The server that made the version number request may regard the results as 'votes' as to the current version number.

Use of voting□ The use of voting is applicable (1) to replication, since any two majorities must contain at least one identical member – the majority ensures that the most recent version is always available; and (2) to concurrency control with replication, since a single *veto* can be used to reject an update that is based on a non-current version of the file.

8.4.3 Majority consensus

Thomas [1979] describes a **majority consensus** algorithm in which servers holding the representatives of a replicated file vote on the acceptability of each update request. For a request to be accepted and applied to all the representatives, only a majority of servers need approve it. Each file item is timestamped to show the time of the most recent update.

Clients read data items by requesting their values and timestamps, from any server holding a representative, but if they wish to ensure up-to-date versions, they may read several (or a majority). Clients request updates by submitting the old values of a set of data items, their timestamps and the proposed new values to one of the servers. Each request is evaluated by the servers using a voting rule that enables a decision to be reached by a majority of the servers holding representatives of the files concerned. When an update request is accepted, each server subsequently does the update. The client is informed of the result and, if the update request was rejected, it may re-try.

Communication □   Thomas describes three different patterns of communication that a set of servers may use to assess a majority consensus.

1. The server that receives a client request may *broadcast* the request to the other servers that return their votes to the original server.
2. Each server that receives a request forwards the request, its own vote and the votes collected to another server. This is referred to as *daisy chaining*. It is the method we describe here.
3. In a variant of daisy chaining a timeout enables a server to forward the request to an alternative server if the first one does not respond.

The procedure for getting a majority consensus terminates as soon as the request can be resolved. Figure 8.2 shows the patterns of communication in the first two cases. The daisy chaining method of communication allows any server to decide on the outcome of the vote when it sees a majority.

Voting rules □   Each server considers the request, comparing the timestamps with those it holds, allowing it to decide whether its data items have been altered since the client read them. If the client's timestamps are older, it vetoes the request, voting *reject*. If they are the same or later, it accepts, voting *ok*. After voting, each server checks whether its vote has resolved the request for consensus. As soon as a majority of *ok*s has been collected, the request is *accepted*, and all of the servers are instructed (by the server that collected the votes) to apply the update. The important property of a majority consensus is that, for any two majority decisions, at least one server has voted *ok* for both.

Between the time a server votes *ok* and the request is resolved, the request is *pending* at that server. Therefore the server that made the request must notify servers when a request is resolved, even when the result is a rejection. The voting rule is made a little more complicated to allow a server to consider requests that conflict with pending ones: if the pending request has a more recent timestamp, it votes *pass*, otherwise it defers voting until the pending request is resolved.

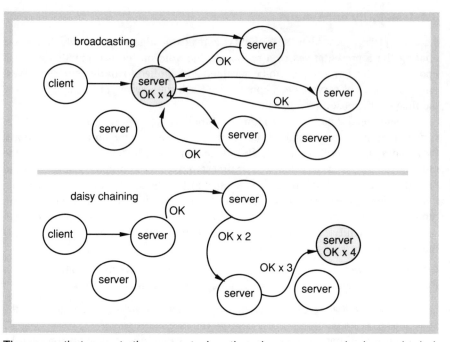

The server that accepts the request when there is a consensus is shown shaded.

Figure 8.2 Alternative patterns of communication for obtaining a consensus.

Thomas's algorithm ensures serialization of updates as well as consistent replication, since timestamps are used to order updates in a manner similar to that described in Section 7.3.3. The algorithm has the properties we want for a flexible replication scheme, it enables files to be updated when only a majority of the servers holding its representatives are available; and the control of the algorithm is distributed – the members of the majority are determined dynamically and the votes are tallied by each server, until a majority or a veto is reached. Timestamps are applied on a fine-grain (to data items), although they could be applied on a course-grain (to entire files or to pages of files).

Replicated update request: R	
Operation	*Timestamp*
Read(a)	*t1*
Write(a-$2)	*t1*

An example illustrating majority consensus □ Suppose that there are three representatives of a replicated file, A, in servers S_1, S_2 and S_3 and that a client performs a transaction R containing the steps shown in the table above. Then the sequence of actions for a successful update starting at server S_1 is shown in Figure 8.3, in which the first column shows the requests made and the three columns headed S_1, S_2 and S_3 show when a server has voted OK and when the

Step	Request	S_1	S_2	S_3
1	Client→S_1: Read(a)			
2	Client→S_1: Write(a–$2)	OK		
3	S_1→S_2: Request consensus	OK		
4	S_2 votes OK	OK	OK	
5	S_2 accepts update	OK	DONE	
6	S_2→ S_1 do update	DONE	DONE	
7	S_2→ S_3 do update	DONE	DONE	DONE

Figure 8.3 Action sequence for R.

update has been done. The update request contains the new and old values of the data and the transaction timestamp. The request for consensus also contains the votes collected so far. At (1) and (2) the client *Reads* the value of A and makes an update request to server S_1 which votes OK. At (3), server S_1 votes OK and requests a vote from server S_2, enclosing the vote, and the request, and at (4) and (5) S_2 decides there is a consensus and accepts the update. At (6) and (7) S_2 does the update and tells S_1 and S_3 to do their updates.

8.4.4 Majority consensus with weighted voting

Gifford [1979a] has developed a file replication scheme in which a number of votes are assigned to each representative in a file suite. A vote can be regarded as a weighting related to the desirability of using a particular representative. The number of votes allotted to each representative is recorded in the file suite definitions.

Each *Read* operation must first obtain a read quorum of r votes before it can proceed to read from any up-to-date representative and each *Write* operation must obtain a write quorum of w votes before it can proceed to update the file suite. r and w are set for each file suite such that w is more than half of the votes and $r+w$ is more than the total of votes assigned to the file. This ensures that any pair, consisting of a read quorum and a write quorum or two write quora, must contain common representatives.

To perform a *Write* operation a write quorum is collected by making sufficient version number enquiries to find a set of current representatives, the sum of whose votes is not less than w. The updates specified in the *Write* operation are then applied to each representative in the write quorum, the version number of each is incremented and completion of the *Write* is reported. The remaining representatives of the file suite (i.e. those not included in the write quorum) are then updated as a background task. Any non-current representatives encountered are updated by replacing their entire contents with the contents of one of the current representatives.

To perform a *Read* operation a read quorum is collected by making version number enquiries until set of representatives has been identified, the sum of whose votes is not less than r. Not all of the representatives need be current. Since each read quorum has members in common with every write quorum, every read quorum is certain to include at least one current representative; the representatives with the highest version number will be current representatives.

The actual read operation may be performed using any current representative in the read quorum; since their version numbers are the same, their contents must be identical.

In a *Write* operation, if less than w current representatives can be found, some of the non-current representatives must be replaced with copies of current representatives before the operation can go ahead.

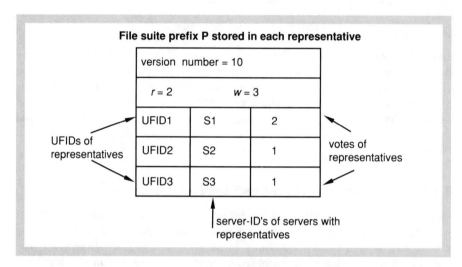

Figure 8.4 File suite prefix for Gifford's algorithm.

Implementation □ In order to implement Gifford's algorithm a file suite prefix (shown in Figure 8.4) is stored in each server that contains a representative of a replicated file. The prefix contains the version number of the representative in that server, the values of r and w, and a list of each of the representatives in the suite together with their votes. Before using a replicated file, the client reads the file suite from one of the representatives.

We consider what happens when a client wants to write data to a replicated file with representatives in three servers S1, S2 and S3, shown in Figure 8.5. The client tries to collect a write quorum by requesting version numbers from S1 and S2. These two servers return their version numbers, which in this case are both up to date. If one of them was not current, the client would make a version number enquiry at S3 in order to attempt to complete a write quorum. The client must then direct the write operations to the same quorum.

Transactions □ Gifford uses transactions to provide recovery and concurrency control, using locks; but the replication algorithm is completely separate from issues of consistency.

The distributed transaction mechanism (described in Section 8.3) can be used with replicated files; when a server receives a *Write* request it selects the representatives to be updated, and their servers can join the transaction. The

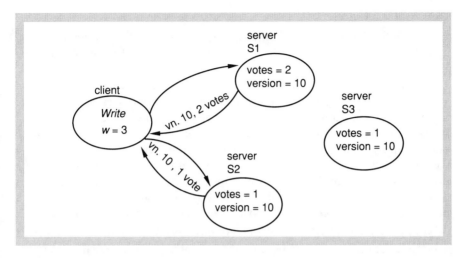

Figure 8.5 Collecting a write quorum Gifford's algorithm.

request for version numbers from the servers in a file suite need occur only once during the first phase of a transaction; the atomicity provided by the transaction mechanism prevents other clients' transactions from making conflicting changes to the files in the transaction.

When a transaction is committed and its writes are completed, a new version number is calculated by increasing the current version number by one and this version number is recorded by each server whose representative was updated. Even if two transactions simultaneously update separate items in the same replicated file with the same current version number, and both transactions are able to commit, they will record the same new version number on their representatives.

Locks □   A client's *Read* or *Write* operation to a replicated file results in an appropriate lock being set by the servers on the data items in the representatives involved and locks are removed when a transaction closes. Gifford discusses the use of various sorts of locks and chooses *I-write* locks (see Section 7.3.1), in which data is only unavailable during the commitment of transactions.

A *Write* operation causes locks to be set on the representatives in the write quorum, whereas a *Read* operation causes only one item to be locked. Although we would expect read locks to be needed on the representatives in the read quorum, this does not matter when *I-write* locks are used. Since a write quorum always includes a majority of the votes assigned to the representatives of a file, any two concurrent transactions will always lock intersecting sets of representatives.

The use of locks can result in data having less availability than it does in the algorithm devised by Thomas. However, in Thomas's algorithm, conflicting updates can lead to waiting, and rejected updates must be resubmitted. The possibility of needing to resubmit a request could lead to 'starvation', for, as in optimistic concurrency control, there is no guarantee that a particular update request will ever succeed.

Configurability of file suites □   An important property of the weighted voting algorithm is that it enables users to synthesize file suites with properties suitable for various applications.

Gifford designed his algorithm to exploit private local disk storage in workstations as well as shared file servers. File representatives held in private disk storage are called *weak representatives* and are always allocated zero votes; this ensures that they are never included in a read or write quorum, but, since *Read* operations may be performed using any up-to-date representative once a read quorum has been obtained, weak representatives can be used to speed up read operations. Once the general reliability and performance of a file suite is established by its voting configuration, the reliability and performance of writes may be increased by decreasing w and similarly for reads by decreasing r.

An example from Gifford □   Gifford gives three examples showing the range of properties that can be created by allocating weights to the representative in file suites and setting r and w appropriately.

We now reproduce Gifford's examples, which are based on the following table:

		Example 1	*Example 2*	*Example 3*
Latency	Rep. 1	75	75	75
(msec)	Rep. 2	65	100	750
	Rep. 3	65	750	750
Voting	Rep. 1	1	2	1
configuration	Rep. 2	0	1	1
	Rep. 3	0	1	1
Quorum	r	1	2	1
sizes	w	1	3	3
Derived performance of file suite:				
Read	Latency	65	75	75
	Blocking probability	0.01	0.0002	0.000001
Write	Latency	75	100	750
	Blocking probability	0.01	0.03	0.03

The *blocking probabilities* give an indication of the probability that a quorum cannot be obtained when a *Read* or *Write* request is made. They are calculated assuming that there is a 0.01 probability that any single server will be unavailable at the time of a request.

Example 1 is configured for a file with a high read-to-write ratio in an application with several private representatives and a single server. Replication is used to enhance the performance of the system, not the reliability. There is one server on the local network that can be accessed in 75 msec. Two clients have chosen to make weak representatives on their local disks which they can access in 65 msec, resulting in lower latency and less network traffic.

Example 2 is configured for a file with a moderate read-to-write ratio which is primarily accessed from one local network. The server on the local network is assigned two votes, and the servers on two remote networks are assigned one vote apiece. Reads can be satisfied from the local server and writes must access the local server and one remote server. The file will remain available in read-only mode if the local server fails. Clients could create local weak representatives for lower read latency.

Example 3 is configured for a file with a very high read-to-write ratio, such as a system directory, in a three-server environment. Clients can read from any server and the probability that the file will be unavailable is small. Updates must be applied to all copies. Once again, clients could create weak representatives on their local machines for lower read latency.

8.5 Implementation of a replicated file service

This section describes an extension to our file service as defined in Chapter 5, giving the extra information that must be obtained and stored by servers and the procedures needed for inter-server communication in a simple replicated file service built as a layer above the simple file service of Chapter 5. Our replicated file service uses file suites composed of the simple files of Chapter 5 and presents an interface to clients that is very similar to the simple file service interface of Chapter 5, but with a different set of unique identifiers, *RUFIDs*, as parameters that refer to file suites.

We assume here that file version numbers are used to determine whether files are current, that version number enquiries are made and that simple majorities are used to determine current version numbers and when updates are made.

A file suite consists of a set of files managed by separate servers and may be described by a list:

fileSuiteDef = { *(UFID1, server-id1), (UFID2, server-id2), ... }*

giving the UFID and server-id of each representative in the suite.

We propose that such lists should be stored in servers as a component of a **replicated file map** that relates RUFIDs to file suite descriptions. The replicated file map can contain additional information related to the replication strategy, such as Gifford's *r* and *w* values, votes or perhaps a measure of the accessibility of a representative.

A client's file operations are intended to refer to the UFID of an ordinary file or the RUFID of a replicated file and, in the latter case, eventually the operation must apply to some or all of the representatives in the file suite. A server that receives a client request for a replicated file operation uses the UFIDs in the file suite definition to enable it to perform operations on its own files and to request the operations at other servers in the list.

A file service needs to be able to distinguish between RUFIDs and ordinary UFIDs so that it can act appropriately when a client calls one of its operations.

For an ordinary UFID the server uses the file location map to get the blocks of a file. In the case of a RUFID, it must first locate the definition of the file suite, make version number enquiries, and then in the case of a *Read* operation select a server that contains one of the files in the suite to read from, or, in the case of a *Write* operation, the server selects a number of servers containing files to write to. Therefore a server that supports replicated files has some new tasks. It must:

- distinguish replicated files from ordinary files by inspecting the file identifier; *RUFIDs* could be constructed as ordinary *UFIDs* in which one bit is reserved to indicate that a file is replicated;
- use the RUFID and the replicated file map to find the file suite;
- make version number enquiries and respond to such enquiries, using a new internal operation *AskNumber*, described in Box 8.3, which enables servers to make enquiries at other servers in the suite;
- see that *Read* and *Write* operations are done in the appropriate servers; the choice of servers is made according to the chosen algorithm for replication, for example, using majorities or using Gifford's algorithm;
- calculate and record the current version number after a representative is updated;
- prevent clients from reading and writing directly from copies of a replicated file; this is done by issuing only RUFIDs to clients.

The last point is important, for if clients had access to the ordinary UFIDs of representatives they could alter representatives of a replicated file, thus destroying its consistency.

Each server provides a new procedure *AskNumber* which is intended to be used by other servers that are making version number enquiries. This is not part of the service interface provided for clients, but, unlike the server-to-server calls for distributed transactions described in Box 8.2, no special security measures are used to prevent clients from calling it, for such calls would be harmless.

AskNumber(RUFID)→ VnNumber
> The server contacted returns the version number on its representative of the replicated file.

Box 8.3   Internal version number enquiries.

Building a file suite □   When a client needs a new replicated file it selects some servers to hold the files in the suite. The file service creates a replicated file by (1) creating a new file at each server requested by the client; (2) defining a file suite containing a list of (*UFID, server-id*) pairs; (3) generating a RUFID and making an entry in the replicated file map at each server; (4) returning the RUFID to the client.

We propose client operations to build a replicated file incrementally, rather than by listing all the servers that are to contain representatives at once. In Box 8.4, we define two new service functions *InitReplicatedFile* and *AddRepresentative*; the former makes a replicated file containing one representative in the server called, the latter adds a new representative in a different server.

InitReplicatedFile() → RUFID
> The server that receives the call creates a new file and a RUFID, makes a file suite containing the UFID of the file, makes an entry in the replicated file map relating the RUFID to file suite, and returns the RUFID.

AddRepresentative(RUFID, id of new server)
> This is a call to a server that already contains the replicated file to make a new representative in a new server.

Box 8.4   Operations to build a file suite.

When a client calls *AddRepresentative*, the server contacted calls *Create* in the new server and receives a UFID as a result. The original server updates its file suite and calls *UpdateFileSuite* described in Box 8.5 to send the updated file suite to the other servers in the suite, including the new server.

The server that executes *UpdateFileSuite* checks whether it has an entry with the given RUFID in its file map. If there is no such entry, it makes a new entry, only provided that the file suite contains its own identifier with the UFID of one of its own files. If there is already an entry, it checks the file suite given as argument against the one in its replicated file map.

UpdateFileSuite(RUFID, file suite)
> The server contacted makes a new entry or updates the existing entry in the replicated file map.

Box 8.5   Server-to-server operations for building a file suite.

Clients may store *RUFID*s in directories local to servers that manage representatives of the replicated file. When files are replicated, the severity of the problem of locating the server containing a particular file is reduced, for it is likely that any server that the client contacts will contain a representative.

8.6 Summary

The capacity of a single file server cannot be expected to meet the needs of all user environments. A distributed file service is one in which files are located in more than one computer, but are seen by clients as part of a single integrated file service. This is an important aspect of *scaling transparency* – the ability to expand a system without change to the system structure or application algorithms. UFIDs should be location-independent, although they may contain the file's *birthplace*, which is a strong hint as to the file's location. Other hints may be maintained by the servers or the clients.

The placement of files is an optimization problem; the solution is simple for files that are used primarily by a single client – place the file near the client – but there is no well-defined solution for files that are accessed by many clients. File replication is used to overcome the performance limitations of shared files, allowing several copies of the same file to be placed in different computers.

Concurrency control based on the two-phase commit procedure has been used in most distributed file services developed to date, but more optimistic timestamp-based methods are emerging which may offer a more flexible and efficient solution.

EXERCISES

8.1 Describe what will happen in the multi-server commit procedure described in Section 8.3.1 if one of the 'other' servers has halted (a) at step (2), (b) at step (4).

8.2 The files X and Y are stored in separate servers S_1 and S_2 and a client does transaction T:

Transaction T
OpenTransaction
Read(X)
Read(Y)
Write(X+1)
Write(Y+2)
$\leftarrow$ *here*
CloseTransaction

Describe the two-phase commit on transaction T if S_1 is the coordinator and S_2 the worker. Describe the result of the recovery procedures if S_2 halts at the point marked 'here' but restarts quickly. Describe the recovery procedures if S_1 halts at 'here' but S_2 does not.

8.3 Can clients obtain UFIDs of replicated files by using any of the calls described in Boxes 8.4 and 8.5 and thereby break the consistency of a file suite?

8.4 Describe a check that may be made in *UpdateFileSuite* to ensure that the call is genuine.

8.5 Describe examples of applications with replicated data in which
(a) it is not critical that the data being read is not the most current,
(b) it is critical that always the most current data should be read.
If an algorithm like Thomas's is in use, suggest how a client could locate the most recent version of data.

8.6 X and Y are replicated files, each with three copies stored in servers S_1, S_2 and S_3, and Thomas's algorithm with pure daisy chaining communication is used. Describe in detail the sequence of actions that occurs at S_1, S_2 and S_3 as the result of the two following situations, mentioning the operations to read the data, the update request, the voting to resolve the request, the acceptance of the result, the update itself and the reply to the client.

(a) A client operation reads from X and then writes back a new value to X when there are no conflicting update requests and all three servers are available.

(b) Two separate transactions T and U both access the files X and Y and T has an earlier timestamp than U.

8.7 Repeat the previous exercise assuming that Gifford's algorithm is used and that the servers' votes are all equal to 1, with $r = 2$ and $w = 2$.

8.8 Use the answers to the two previous exercises to compare Thomas's and Gifford's algorithms in situations where (a) there are likely to be few conflicting updates and (b) there are likely to be many.

8.9 X ,Y and Z are files, stored in servers S_1, S_2 and S_3. T and U are transactions with timestamps 11-20 and 21-30 that use these files.

T	U
OpenTransaction	
	OpenTransaction
Read(X)	
	Read(X)
Read(Y)	
	Write(X+3)
Write(X+1)	
	Read(Z)
Write(Y+2)	
	Write(Z)
	CloseTransaction
CloseTransaction	

Initially the timestamps on X, Y and Z are 1, 2 and 3 respectively. Describe the tentative and committed versions made, showing their timestamps, and explain the outcome of the two transactions (assuming that Reed's method is used).

8.10 In a banking application, a bank may keep all of the records relevant to local accounts in a computer at each branch. Transactions involving local accounts would not require any coordination branches, but operations such as a transfer from an account at one branch to an account at another would. Consider how atomic transactions and data replication could be applied in this application.

Chapter 9
Protection and Security

The users of distributed systems must be confident that the system affords protection against unauthorized and erroneous access to data and against interference with the operation of the system. The communication channels must be protected as well as the storage and processing resources of the system. The protection must be compatible with facilities for users to share data and to access both local and remote system resources and services.

These requirements provide the motivation for the protection mechanisms discussed in this chapter. These include techniques for controlling access to files and other objects, user authentication, data encryption to protect data from unauthorized access and the construction of digital signatures to authenticate the origins of electronic documents.

Just as the provision of a lock on a door does not ensure security unless there is a policy for its use, protection mechanisms do not in themselves ensure the security of a system; a security policy is necessary, specifying how and where the protection mechanisms are to be applied. We do not attempt to define security policies since they must depend on the social and organizational context in which a computer system is used, but we illustrate the special security problems of open systems with some simple examples.

9.1 Introduction

The security policies used within a group of users of a distributed system should be determined by the needs of the users and the organization operating the system. To implement security, protection mechanisms are required providing facilities for authenticating users (for example by a password check), for controlling access to files, communication channels and other objects, and for encrypting data before transmitting it through exposed communication channels.

Protection mechanisms must be designed and implemented as an integral part of a system if they are to provide guarantees that the security of the system is maintained. They should be designed to support as wide a range of security policies as possible, to meet the needs of different user environments. Most computer systems apply a significant degree of protection by default, but the default level of protection represents a compromise between the needs of users for access to shared data and resources and the need to protect the integrity of the system and the privacy of the users' data, and it is generally the responsibility of the system administrator and the users of a system to apply the protection mechanisms so as to implement a security policy that matches these needs more precisely [Needham 1985].

The distinction between security mechanisms and policies is evident in many contexts outside the computer domain. For example, the need in government departments to protect sensitive information has led to a range of security classifications that are applied to documents (such as: unclassified, commercially confidential, secret, most secret) and another range of classifications that can be applied to individuals to specify their 'clearance level'. These classifications can be considered as mechanisms for the application of security to government information, but their application may vary depending upon the government of the day, the social and political context (changing for example in time of war). The point here is that the mechanisms (classifications for documents and clearance levels for individuals) are applicable over a wide range of security policies.

Forms of attack □   We shall refer to both accidental and intentional attempts to avoid or disable a system's protection or security as *attacks*. Software errors and bugs are the most frequent source of accidental attacks on system integrity. Hardware failures are another, less frequent source of accidental attacks.

The perpetrators of deliberate attacks include professional spies, fraudsters and tricksters, and the less harmful amateur variety, often referred to as 'hackers'. Methods available to spies, fraudsters, tricksters and hackers include not only the electronic analogues of conventional eavesdropping and code-breaking, but also the bombardment of systems with large numbers of random messages to discover holes in their armour and the infiltration into systems of 'Trojan horse' programs to acquire privileged information or interfere with the operation of the system. Some of their activities have been well-publicized, but the extent to which the integrity and security of systems is compromised continues to surprise the owners of systems and the general public. While there is clearly a substantial distinction between accidental and deliberate attacks from the point of view of the owners of computer systems and in their consequences for the perpetrators if they are detected, the effects of accidental and deliberate attacks on the integrity of systems are often similar for the system itself – they are likely to lead to its failure.

The security of a computer system is intricately tied up with that system's environment, use and implementation. It therefore comes as no surprise that the security concerns of distributed systems differ from those of non-distributed systems simply from the circumstances of distribution. Some of these circumstances tend to ease security problems, but most tend to add to the already difficult problems of securing a centralized computer system. Saltzer and Schroeder [1975] and Jones [1978] have given excellent surveys of these problems.

The two characteristics of distributed computer systems which are the principal reasons for their special security concerns are:

- multiple points of execution,
- exposed communication channels.

Multiple points of execution □ Distributed systems offer many potential points of execution for a process. This simplifies some security concerns while introducing others. The simplifications arise from the potential to disperse both computation and data. The new problems are associated with the circumstance that not all parts of a distributed system need reside within the same administrative framework or even under the control of the same social, political or economic entity.

The security advantages of a distributed architecture were recognized as a part of the work by Baran [1964] that led to the development of the ARPA wide-area computer network. The dispersal of information resources may be used to avoid presenting a high-value target to a potential attacker. This is analogous to a principle widely employed by military planners. For example, imagine a system which contains the list of a Our Company's customers and prospects (of great interest to our arch rival, CompetiCorp). We will also suppose that CompetiCorp is willing to spend 1000 shekels to acquire our list. If we store the list in a single node then CompetiCorp has no trouble in identifying the target and will concentrate their 1000 shekels on breaching that single node's security. In contrast, imagine that Our Company has a distributed system implementation in which the customer list is dispersed over many, say 10 out of 30, nodes. Many security benefits result, as follows. CompetiCorp no longer has a clearly defined target. Instead they have a puzzle – which 10 of our 30 nodes contain the data? Solving this puzzle will absorb some, possibly all, of CompetiCorp's attack budget. For example purposes let's say that solving the puzzle costs all but 300 shekels. CompetiCorp must now launch attacks against 10 nodes. The average amount which CompetiCorp can spend per attack is only 30 shekels. Also, CompetiCorp risks ten chances of being caught in the act.

The potential in distributed systems for multiple points of execution is not always beneficial for security, however. Some nodes may be installed in places which are outside of the social, political or economic control of the system's owners. For example, a manufacturer might install nodes of his planning system in the plants of its principal customers in order to improve the quality of interaction between the customers and itself [Estrin 1985]. Especially good security provisions would then be required to prevent either accidental or deliberate access by a node in a customer's plant to much of the information in the system. For example, other customers' orders, plans for unannounced products, manufacturing costs, and pricing strategy.

Exposed communication channels □   A second aspect of distributed systems which has far-reaching security implications is that communication channels connecting nodes may be exposed to attackers who may try to breach the security of the system by observing, modifying or disrupting the communications.

Centralized computer systems often include exposed channels between their terminals and the central processor, and many types of attack have been successfully developed and launched against such channels with potentially devastating effects to the security of the application [Kahn 1980, Selfridge and Schwartz 1980]. The difference that arises in the case of distributed systems is that the channels that interconnect nodes carry system-level messages in addition to application-level messages.

We have seen many examples of such system-level messages in earlier chapters. Remote procedure calls from clients to servers may contain data that is private to the client; attackers tapping the network can breach the privacy at the user level by reading the RPC messages and other client–server communications. In addition, unauthorized clients might disable a server by sending deliberately or accidentally disruptive messages to damage stored information (for example, by deleting or writing to system files) or pre-empt limited resources (for example, by hogging the server's processing capacity or filling a disk with useless files).

Distributed systems are even more vulnerable where system-level components such as servers communicate with each other through the network; in centralized computer systems each system component is designed on the assumption that its communication with the other system components is private, and that other system components can be trusted not to request it to perform operations that would damage the system's integrity. In distributed systems, system components are located in more than one computer, and they share a communication network with user-level software. They must protect themselves against accidental or intentional requests from user-level software that appear as a requests from another system component. The communication that takes place between file servers involved in a distributed atomic transaction described in Section 8.3 provides a good example of communication at the system level that is vulnerable to such attacks.

Attacks against the communication channels in distributed systems therefore have the potential of doing devastating damage to the security of the distributed system as a whole. It is as though the system's innermost connections were exposed to the world. The solutions to these problems lie in the concealment of private data (by encryption) and in the deployment of effective authentication and access control techniques by system services.

Naming and security □   There exist societies that believe that knowledge of an individual's name gives the knower certain powers over that individual [Frazer 1922]. These include the North American Indians, Australian Aborigines and various other tribes from the Atlantic to the Pacific. Steps are therefore taken to protect names. Babies are named in secret; only a few close family members ever know one's real name. They never speak it aloud, and even think it with great caution and respect. Life is carried on using one or more pseudonyms.

In computer systems, the control of access to stored information is often achieved by controlling the distribution of the names or references to the information. This method of access control depends upon the distinction between the external names used by the human users of a computer system to refer to the objects in the system, and the internal names, or identifiers, used within the system. The text names of files and many other objects may be widely known to users and client programs, but internal names must be used to access or alter the objects; these are supplied by directory services, but only to programs that are running on behalf of users with the appropriate access rights.

In the context of this book UFIDs are the internal names used to refer to files; *host identifiers, port capabilities, transaction identifiers* and *user identifiers* are all used in distributed systems to refer to other classes of object. Control of their distribution and protection against counterfeiting is an important part of the system's security.

It is important to note that the requirement for the sharing of files and other objects in computer systems is independent of their external names or their position in the file system. In some early operating systems the control of access to files was achieved by the exclusion of users from access to all files not located in their own directories. While this is effective in the protection of users' files from access by other users, it wholly precludes the possibility of files that are shared between users, except for those files that are located in system directories designated for the purpose and managed by a single administrator.

9.2 Security loopholes

Openness in system architectures brings many security hazards. System administrators prefer systems that can be closed to external interference; they may wish to apply protection mechanisms rigorously to prevent programs installed by one user from entering the domains occupied by objects that belong to other users. However, a degree of openness is almost inevitable in all network-based computer systems. For example, electronic mail may be used to transmit programs or simple command files into the mailbox of a user who then installs the program or executes the command file.

We have defined *open systems* in Section 2.4.1; in open systems, services may be defined and installed by users, whereas in a closed system the services are a part of a fixed set of system software (the operating system) which can be extended only by the system's administrator. Open systems are a particularly natural and effective approach to the construction of a general-purpose distributed computing environment; just as the users of distributed systems are able to extend the networked hardware configuration, they should also be able to add to the system software.

Of course, not every user wishes or is able to construct or install major system software components such as file servers, but the acquisition and installation of application programs by users is a common requirement and the examples described below illustrate that, in the absence of adequate security measures, systems can be compromised by the installation and shared use of application programs or even the distribution of files of system commands ('shell scripts' in UNIX terminology).

The consequences of openness have been exploited to attack the security of systems, in some cases with far-reaching consequences. Such attacks often take the form of **virus** or **Trojan horse** programs. Viruses are programs that multiply themselves throughout the network and then consume the systems' resources or violate some loophole in the protection scheme. Trojan horses are programs that appear to be benign or even useful, and are therefore accepted by users into a part of the system where they can obtain access rights that should not be available to them. We shall give two examples, the first based on a report in the Guardian newspaper [Boddington 1988] and the second based on the personal experience of one of the authors.

The Christmas tree virus □   In December 1987 a user of EARN, a European academic computer network, composed a virus program in REXX, a command language available in the CMS operating system on IBM computers. When executed, the program displayed a view of a Christmas tree with a Christmas greeting. The programmer then sent the program in an electronic mail message to several friends with instructions to extract the program from the message and execute it to see a Christmas greeting. When they did so, the program displayed a Christmas tree as promised, but it also accessed certain files in the file space of each recipient containing mailing lists for electronic mail distribution and the log of messages recently received or sent that is maintained by the mail handling program. The program proceeded to send an automatic message to every user in each recipient's mailing list and to all of the users whose mail addresses were recorded in the logs of recent mail activity. The message that it sent was a replica of the original message, including, of course, the program itself. The program then deleted itself.

The effect was quite devastating. Each new recipient of the message innocently obeyed the injunction to extract the Christmas tree program and to execute it. As a result, the message quickly permeated virtually all of the computers in the EARN network, replicating itself wherever it was received in a computer that could interpret programs in the REXX language. Since the mailing lists and the mail logs held by different users generally overlap and cross-reference each other, some users received many copies of the message, filling their file storage and tying up much of the network's bandwidth. But the damage did not stop there.

The EARN network is connected to BitNet, a network that links many universities and research establishments in several countries including the United

States, Canada, Europe and Japan. Some of the EARN users who received the virus message had in their mailing lists addresses for users on computers in BitNet and within a few hours the virus had spread to many of the computers in BitNet. In a similar way the virus also quickly spread from BitNet to IBM's private network, called VNET. The majority of the computers in VNET run the CMS system, and most of their users maintain extensive mailing lists. The virus quickly became rampant, swamping the communication channels of VNET and filling large quantities of file storage in the host computers. The VNET network had to be shut down for 72 hours in order to remove the virus, interrupting all use of the network for that period; the costs to IBM must have been substantial.

The methods used for the removal of the virus message from the EARN network and from BitNet are particularly interesting. They included the construction of another, 'benign' virus program that traced the course taken by the Christmas tree message using the same log files used by the original message, deleting each of the messages at its destination before the recipient could be duped by it.

The Christmas tree program was a virus that also had some of the characteristics of a Trojan horse attack, using a misleading external appearance to dupe the recipients of the message into executing what they believed to be a benign program. The security surrounding mail and mailing lists is so weak in most computer systems that the program did not need to use very much subterfuge to achieve its goal. The ultimate consequences of this prank were certainly well beyond the intentions of its perpetrator.

What are the more general lessons to be learned? The importing of programs into any system environment needs special attention in formulation of security policies. By default in many systems, when a program is executed by a user it automatically assumes the protection status of the user, regardless of the program's origin. The program then has access to all of the user's private files and other objects in the protection domains to which the user has access.

An alternative policy may be more appropriate for open distributed systems; programs should be executed with the protection status of their originators unless another user chooses to 'adopt' a program, conferring his or her access rights upon it. Such a policy could prevent attacks such as the Christmas tree virus, but only if it is applied to programs in all languages, at all levels of interpretation.

The Trojan horse coursework □   One of the authors of the present book was the victim of an ingenious Trojan horse attack by students on one of the UNIX systems used to teach computer science at Queen Mary College, London. The students were asked to submit as coursework a completed program, leaving the program as a binary file in one of their directories with a specific name. The teacher would then test each program by executing the program and observing the results.

Some of the students were able to construct a program that, when executed by the teacher, not only fulfilled the coursework requirements, but also created a security loophole, leaving an executable command file in the student's file space that had the protection status of the teacher. The students could then edit the command file to contain any system commands that they wished to perform; they could use it, for example, to access or alter any of the private files of the teacher (including the grades awarded), log on to other networked machines and perform privileged operations available to staff members but not to students.

In UNIX, programs assume, by default, the protection status of the user on whose behalf they are running. This includes the right to create new programs or command files with the user as owner. It is also possible (using the UNIX *set user id* facility) to create programs and command files that do not follow the default, but execute with the status of the user who created them, regardless of the identity of the user running them. It was this property that the students exploited to arrange for their coursework program to create the privileged command file.

This is another example of a Trojan horse style of attack; the program was presented as coursework for the teacher to test. To test it, she had to execute it. Again, the lesson for system designers is that programs should not so easily assume the status of users other than their originator. If the coursework programs had retained the protection status of their originators, even when executed by the teacher, the attack would not have been possible. It is arguable that the UNIX default behaviour is inappropriate in an open environment.

Worm programs □   In spite of the negative effects of viruses, there are some good uses to be made of programs that can replicate themselves in a controlled way amongst the computers in a network. Such programs can be deployed to make use of idle computers, for example at night, but lie dormant when there is no spare capacity. Shoch and Hupp [1982] conducted a series of experiments with **worm** programs that consist of several segments, each running in a different computer. Each segment knows how many segments are required for a complete worm. The segments communicate with one another and, if one segment fails, the others attempt to find a free machine and start a new segment of the worm in it. As segments of the worm join and leave the distributed program, the worm seems to move about the network. Shoch and Hupp constructed a worm of this type at Xerox PARC to make use of idle computers. The cooperation of the workstation software and the confidence of users was required to enable the successful running of their worm program which distributed its segments into the idle workstations on the Ethernet.

They used the basic worm mechanism to support loosely-coupled distributed computations. One of these was an application of computer graphics to generate frames in an animation sequence. Each segment of the worm constituted a 'graphics machine', with a program that could generate raster images from descriptions of the objects included in a three-dimensional scene. This task is well known as one demanding substantial computation resources, consuming many hours of processing time on large mainframe computers.

The work was done using up to 100 Alto workstations to construct animations overnight. The individual graphics machines or 'workers' were fed with descriptions of the different frames by the head segment, which subsequently received a message containing the corresponding raster image from each worker, and inserted it in the sequence of frames, until a full animation sequence was obtained.

9.3 Capabilities

A capability is an identifier for a stored data object or a system resource that also grants rights to perform certain operations on the object or resource. The rights that a capability grants must be either protected or hidden so that user processes cannot alter them to grant themselves better rights. The UFIDs referred to throughout this book are capabilities, and their construction and use is discussed in Section 5.3.2. Capabilities are typically represented by a bit sequence consisting of three parts:

- a unique identifier for the object or resource that the capability refers to;
- a specification of access rights to the object (perhaps containing one bit for each class of operation applicable to the object);
- a random part to make the capability hard to guess.

The rights part is typically scrambled with the random part to prevent clients from reconstructing the rights. Capabilities are frequently used in distributed systems to identify objects such as files, directories and ports that are shared between processes and therefore need to be accessed by processes holding a variety of access rights (some possible classes of access rights to files were defined in Chapter 5 including: read, write, alter attributes). Capabilities for objects are constructed by the service that manages them and must also be made available with the appropriate rights to clients.

When a new object is created for a client, the server constructs a capability with a full set of rights and returns it to the client. If the new object is for the sole use of that client, there is no need either to modify the rights or to give it to another client. Example of objects used by a single client are personal files and directories, but many objects are shared and users need different rights of access. For example a mailbox may be read only by its owner's processes but can be written to by other processes. This leads to a requirement to modify the rights of capabilities and to make them available for use by processes other than those of the owner.

The modification of access rights may be made a part of any service that grants capabilities for objects, allowing a client to present a capability together with a specification of the rights required and in return to be given a new capability with those rights. But, to be secure, the service should only reduce the rights of capabilities presented to it by clients, otherwise clients with few rights could apply for more. When a new object is created, a capability with a full set of rights is returned to the client which may subsequently request restricted versions of the capability for use by other clients.

A client with the right to do so may request that a server withdraw access to an object, by revoking the capability. Copies of the capability may have been distributed to a variety of client processes and neither the client nor the server necessarily knows the whereabouts of all them. However, the server may revoke the capability by altering the random part and returning the new capability to the client.

Storing capabilities □   Objects such as files and directories generally last longer than the lifetime of the client processes that receive their capabilities. The users of such objects therefore need some way to store capabilities for subsequent retrieval. We discussed the storing of file capabilities (i.e. UFIDs) by a directory service in Section 5.5. The requirements for storing the capabilities of other objects are similar. First the capability is associated with a textual name suitable for use by humans when retrieving it. Secondly the association must be made completely secure – that is, it must be accessible only to authorized processes. This may be achieved by storing the associations in secure directories from which only processes acting on behalf of authorized users may retrieve the capabilities.

Any service providing a mapping from textual names to capabilities needs to be sure that a process really is acting on behalf of the user it claims to be representing. In a later section we describe a user authentication service which may be called by clients and servers. **Authentication** means verifying the identity of the user or other agent on whose behalf a process is acting.

Protection of capabilities □   If capabilities are to be useful as a protection mechanism, they must themselves be protected. In particular, capabilities must be protected against forgery and against modification. Without protection against forgery a client process could fabricate a capability from scratch, thereby by-passing the system's protection mechanism. Without protection against modification a client process could alter a capability either to name a different object or to increase the set of privileges. Either modification, or a combination of both, would result in unauthorized access.

Capabilities have been used in a number of centralized computer systems as the main protection and access control mechanism. The requirements in such systems are that capabilities should provide a quick and efficient means for programs to access data objects, while maintaining the security of the system. Hardware-supported data type tags or protected data segments have been used in centralized systems to ensure that capabilities cannot be forged or tampered with. Examples of tagged capability architectures are the Burroughs descriptor-based machines [Siewiorek et al. 1981] and the experimental Basic Language Machine [Iliffe 1968]. Examples of segmented capability machines are the Cambridge CAP machine [Wilkes and Needham 1979] and Plessey PP250 [Cosserat 1974]. In a distributed system capabilities are given to clients and processes and cannot be restricted to the operating system or even to a single computer. The use of hardware protection is impractical in such systems.

9.4 Access control

A model of protection that is independent of the object naming structure (Figure 9.1) is needed in order to provide for the controlled sharing of data and system resources. For example, when it is applied to the protection of files, the model must provide an orthogonal view of the objects in a hierarchic file system, allowing protection to be applied to each file as required.

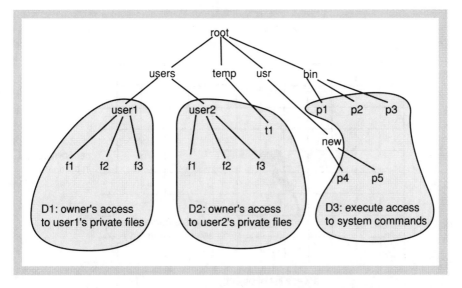

Figure 9.1 Protection domains are independent of naming.

A general model has been developed for the control of access to objects in computer systems based on **protection domains** within which processes are created and run [Lampson 1969, Graham and Denning 1972]. Each domain contains access rights that allow the processes within the domain to perform certain operations on some of the objects in the system. No other operations are allowed. Each process is located within one or more domains and its access rights are defined by those domains.

Protection domains do not imply any particular naming structure for files and other objects or any internal representation for object names; a domain is simply an abstract definition of a set of access rights. For example, a domain might contain a right to access a particular file F for reading, but not for writing. A process running within that domain would be able to read the file F, but not to write it (unless the process was also in another domain that contained an access right to write file F).

We can view a set of domains as a table or matrix (called the **access matrix**, Figure 9.2) relating objects to domains. Elements of the matrix define the access rights to particular objects from particular domains. The access matrix is too large to be represented directly (it would need as many columns as there are distinct objects in the system that require protection), but the information that it contains must be represented in the system in some form.

Since many of the files and other objects in distributed systems are private to a single user, and others are shared between all users, the access matrix is generally very sparse and can be represented by a set of lists containing only the non-empty elements. There are two commonly-used implementations for the domain model, corresponding to the representation of the access matrix by columns and by rows.

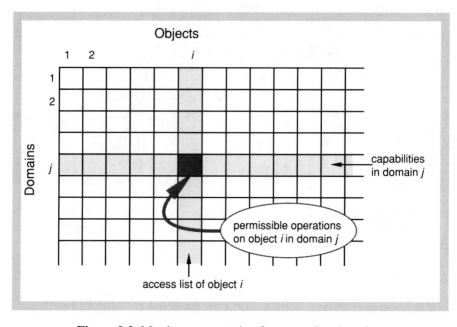

Figure 9.2 Matrix representation for protection domains.

- *Access lists:* a list is associated with each object, giving the domains that have access to the object and the operations permitted in each domain.
- *Capability sets:* a set of capabilities is held by each process according to the domains in which it is located.

In both cases, the access matrix is not identifiable as a single data structure because its rows or columns are dispersed. In the first case the columns are stored with each protected object and in the second the rows are replicated and stored with each of the processes that occupy a domain. These representations are discussed further below.

Processes are generally assigned to domains according to the identity of the user on whose behalf they are executed. The processes that run on behalf of each user are in a protection domain containing access rights to all of the files and other objects that are private to that user and also in some domains that provide access rights to shared objects. Access rights for shared objects may be located in a domain that is associated with a specific group of users or with the universal group, consisting of all users. Domains may also be used to provide access rights to processes that are given particular privileges, not associated with any particular individuals.

UNIX as a domain-based system □   In UNIX, domain-based protection is applied to files. It is structured around a fixed set of domains to simplify the implementation. There is a domain associated with each *user* and another domain called the *superuser*. The superuser in UNIX systems is not a person, but a name for a domain within which the most privileged processes, needing access to all of the objects in the system, may run. Each file has a designated user as its *owner* (usually the user who created the file) and the access rights in each user's domain include the owners access rights for all of the files that the user owns. Another domain is associated with *all users* and this contains rights to read or execute (for binary files) many shared system files including all of the programs for all of the system commands. Groups of users can be defined with access rights to files that are shared between users within the group, but the groups are strictly disjoint (no user can be in more than one group) and this severely restricts their usefulness.

When a user executes a program it runs as a process in exactly three domains; the domain associated with the user, the domain associated with the user's group, and the domain of *all users*. The only exception is for programs that are run with superuser privileges; these are in a special domain that has unrestricted access rights.

The implementation of the domain model in UNIX is based upon the storage with each file of a standardized access control list in a compressed form (9 bits) giving access rights for the file's owner, for the owner's group and for all users. This corresponds to a representation of the access matrix by columns in the context of the above discussion and Figure 9.2. The rights of a process to access a file are checked when the file is opened. No further checks are made when the open file is accessed.

Capabilities versus access lists □   The objects in a distributed system are managed by servers that take responsibility for their protection. Servers receive messages containing requests to perform actions on the objects they manage. These messages may have come from any user and any computer in the network. They may also have been altered in transit, but we will defer the discussion of ways of detecting altered messages to a later section.

Each server computer must therefore be able to protect its own objects and cannot rely on protection being carried out by the senders of request messages. There are two contrasting approaches to protection in servers:

- Service requests include a capability giving the server proof that the client is authorized to access the object the capability refers to with the operations specified by the capability.
- The server authenticates the client and checks the access list of the object at each request for service. Authentication is generally achieved by setting up a conversation between the client, the server and an authentication server.

Capability-based implementations of the domain model are commonly used in file servers as it would not be practical to check an access list and authenticate the identity of the user on whose behalf the client is acting on every request for access to a file. The pure capability approach helps to minimize the state information that servers must hold on behalf of clients.

Another approach in file servers uses a hybrid implementation method in which the client is authenticated when a transaction is opened. The server makes a new transaction identifier and returns it to the client, keeping a record of the client's identity together with each current transaction identifier. The transaction identifier is a form of capability and is presented with each request. The access rights of a client are checked on the first access to each file and a temporary capability is issued to the client for use with a limited timespan. The server records state with the temporary capability representing the rights to access a particular file in a particular transaction.

We saw in Section 9.3 that, at some point, capabilities are generally mapped onto textual names for permanent storage. For example, a directory service maps the textual names of files onto capabilities for files. It is quite common for a directory service to require authentication from clients and to check the access lists of files before issuing file capabilities to clients. In the purest capability approach, authentication takes place only each time the user logs in and the process acting on behalf of the user is given an initial set of capabilities granting access for example to the user's private directory and some other shared objects. In this approach, each directory contains capabilities for further files and directories and no further authentication is required.

9.5 Authentication

We have seen in Section 9.4 that users' processes run in protection domains that define the operations on objects that are available to them. The set of domains in which each process runs is derived from the identity of the user on whose behalf the process runs. The identities of users must therefore be authenticated so that the access rights to their private files or privileges are not available to other users. This requirement exists in both centralized and distributed systems; its implementation in distributed systems raises problems concerning the uniqueness of user identifiers and the security of the authentication mechanism.

Authentication in centralized systems □   In a centralized computer system, a password file is normally used to associate user names and encrypted passwords with user identifiers and group identifiers. When users log in, they type their name and password and the login program checks the validity of the password to authenticate their identity and determines the internal identifiers for the protection domains available to processes running on their behalf. The kernel makes a private record of the domains accessible to each process and uses it to allow processes the appropriate access rights. This information cannot be altered except by processes with special privileges. The file system software checks that the access rights required by each file operation are available within the domains a process is executing in.

Authentication in integrated distributed systems □   We described in Section 2.2.3 the integrated model for a distributed system, in which a set of autonomous computers runs a single distributed operating system. The Locus system and Sun's NFS system are examples of UNIX-like integrated distributed systems (both of which are described more fully in Chapter 10). An integrated system requires that each user's login name, user identifier and group identifier are unique throughout the entire distributed system. Popek and Walker's book on Locus [1985] discusses the problems that arise when merging two previously separate Locus sites into a single Locus system. They require system administrators to decide in case of conflict which user's name should be altered and what it will become. All of the file systems in both Locus sites then require processing to take the changes into account.

The Locus password file contains a globally unique user name, user identifier and group identifier for each user – the file itself is replicated in each computer. When a user logs in, the kernel in the local computer checks the name and password to determine the protection domains available to processes running on his or her behalf. Files in Locus are accessed by the kernel in the computer on which they are stored, but they may be used by clients in other computers. We describe Locus file access in more detail in Section 10.2, but the relevant point here is that, when a file is opened, the file i-node is copied into a structure available to the kernel in the user's computer. The i-node contains the relevant information to enable the kernel local to the user to grant access appropriate to the domains available to the process. Note that in an integrated system, as in a centralized system, the security and validity of the user's identity is ensured because a system kernel performs both of the roles related to validating a user's rights to access files:

- It performs the password check and determines the domains available to the user's processes.
- It uses its knowledge of the domains available to user processes to perform access control to files.

Authentication in open client–server systems □   The requirement for globally unique user names and user identifiers holds for an open distributed system as it does for an integrated one, but in an open distributed system other factors must be considered:

- Users log in at workstations. There is no reason why any server or other computer in the distributed system should rely on the authenticity or correctness of the software in the user's workstation.
- Client operations on resources such as files and directories, which are subject to access control, are requested from workstations but are performed by servers in separate computers.

In client–server distributed systems, each type of object is managed by a service that performs all operations on objects of that type. Each service manages a collection of objects with an associated set of protection domains. For each service the protection model is based on an access matrix like the one shown in Figure 9.2; the columns corresponding to the objects managed by that service. The access matrix for a complete distributed system of this type can be thought of as composed of the access matrices of its services arranged side by side. Each service must ensure that access rights exist for all the operations it performs on behalf of client processes in the domains available to those processes.

Clients in distributed systems generally use various name mapping services to obtain capabilities granting access rights to the objects managed by other services. For example, directory services are used to map file names onto file identifiers. In Section 5.4 we described a very simple scheme in which the directory service requires the identity of the user to check the file access list before issuing a UFID with the appropriate access rights. This is equivalent to asking the client to give its protection domains as arguments of the request. However, the request comes from another computer and we did not discuss how the directory service can ensure that the domains being presented are valid. Authentication is concerned with making it possible for servers to grant operations on the objects they manage according to the rights associated with the domains in which client processes are running.

Some examples □   In XDFS clients log on to file servers by supplying the user's name and password (retained by the client process since the user logged in from the workstation that the client is running on) when opening a transaction, enabling the file server to authenticate the user and to record the user's identity against the transaction identifier. Clients supply the transaction identifier each time a new file is opened, enabling the server to use the identity of the user in checking the file access lists. The password enables the file server to authenticate the user at the start of a transaction. The transaction identifier is temporary and hard to forge.

In Accent [Rashid 1985], the Sesame file system provides a tree-structured directory, mapping text names onto file identifiers. An authentication service checks a user's login name and password. If these are valid it creates a temporary port that acts as a capability; processes operating on behalf of the user may use the port capability subsequently as a proof of identity. When the user logs out, the temporary port is closed, invalidating the capability. The authentication server keeps a record of this port together with a list of the access groups that the user belongs to. When a process acting on behalf of the user makes a request for access to an object managed by another service, it sends the temporary port capability to the server as a token of authentication together with the requests. The server in question contacts the authentication server through the temporary port and is given in return the list of that user's access groups.

A user authentication service □   We now describe a scheme for an authentication service based on the one described by Needham and Herbert [1982] for the Cambridge Distributed Computing System in which authentication is based on two separate services. An authentication service is used when the user first logs in and a separate *active name service* issues tokens of authentication and keeps a table of all the current tokens issued to users. Other services may then check with the active name service to see whether an authentication token is valid. Tokens are large integers containing a random part that makes them hard to forge and they last only for the duration of the user's session. They are a form of temporary capability granting the use of the rights associated with the domains that the user has access to. Authentication tokens may be presented when access requests are made to other services such as the directory service.

When users start work, their client process must give their name and password to an authentication server. If the password is correct, the authentication server gets a token of authentication from the active name service and returns it to the client process.

Each user is given a permanent user identifier which is unique throughout the system, but need not be secret. The active name service provides a service to servers to enable them to rely on the tokens of authentication that they receive from clients. It validates the tokens of authentication issued by the user authentication service and tokens of authentication that may be issued by other system components. The active name service is a general facility for managing authentication tokens and the entries may refer to entities other than users.

The active name service maintains a table containing all the current authentication tokens issued to users, arranged in four columns containing:

1. the user's permanent identifier,
2. a token of authentication,
3. the identifier of the authority that created the token of authentication for the user,
4. a control token.

The *authority* (3) is needed because there may be more than one way for a user to be issued with a token of authentication – for example the user might be required to produce some physical evidence of identity (a credit card or a smart card) or some personal characteristics (voice printing is one promising technology for the secure user identification) rather than just a password. Servers that require the extra security that such schemes can provide (for example for the secure storage of secret data) can reject tokens that do not carry the authority of an authentication server using such a method.

The control token is another unforgeable token that must be quoted by any client of the active name service wishing to add or modify entries in the active name server's table.

When clients use services, they present both their user identifier and a token of authentication in service requests. The server may then enquire with the active name service to discover whether the token of authentication has been given to that user.

The main operations provided by the active name service are described in Box 9.1. A further privileged operation is available for use by a trusted initialization service at a known address. This operation makes it possible to add entries to the table without possessing a token of authentication. This is needed to initialize the service by adding an entry providing a token for use by an authentication service, containing the name of the authentication service as an authority.

An authentication service uses the token recorded against its authority in calls to the *GetToken* function. The effect is that the active name service makes new authentication and control tokens and puts a new entry in the table containing the two new tokens, the user identifier and the given authority (the authentication service in question).

Services can check tokens of authentication by using the *Verify* function that tells them whether the user identifier and token have been issued by a particular authority.

GetToken(UserId, authority, oldToken) → newToken, controlToken
> The caller supplies a token of authentication, an authority and a user identifier. A new token of authentication and a control token are returned.

Verify(token, UserId, authority)→ boolean
> If there is a token corresponding to the user identifier and authority, return *true*, else return *false*.

Box 9.1   Active name service operations.

9.6 Protection of ports

Clients in distributed systems generally communicate with servers by means of remote procedure calls. Remote procedure calls are built on top of a message passing layer that uses ports as message destinations (see Section 4.5). The RPC software in the client obtains the service ports from a binder (see Section 4.4). Remote procedure calls are made by sending *Request* messages to service ports. *Request* messages include the identifier of the client's port to enable the service to send *Reply* messages. In contrast to other objects on which all operations are performed by the service that manages them, ports have operations performed on them by various processes distributed throughout the network.

The hazards associated with exposed communication channels may affect RPC messages in the same way as any other messages. These include both the passive reading of information and actively damaging or interfering with it. Encryption may be used to prevent illicit reading of messages in transit. Damaged messages can be detected by the use of checksums. An interfering agent might attempt to disrupt the operation of the system by repeating messages or altering their sequence; the checksums will still be correct but the RPC message protocols usually include sequence numbers to enable the detection of duplicates and incorrect sequences.

We now consider the protection required by ports. For a communication to take place, one process sends a message to a port and another process receives it from the same port. The simplest form of control is based on the use of a capability for each port, the possession of which would confer the right to send and receive on that port. However, it is generally the case that the processes that possess the right to send to a particular port should be different from the processes allowed to receive on that port. For example, a server should have the right to receive on its service port and many clients should be able to have the right to send messages to service ports. When a remote procedure call is made, the client generally includes an identifier or capability for its own port in the message to the server so that the latter may send a *Reply*. In a client–server situation, the right to receive on the server port should be restricted to the server process and the right to receive on a client port should be restricted to the client it belongs to. To enforce such rights, port capabilities need to have sending and receiving rights associated with them. This is similar to the association of access rights with capabilities for files in UFIDs.

We can see that there must be a mechanism for granting rights to communicate through ports and that processes must be prevented from using rights that they do not possess.

The Mach solution □　In Mach [Sansom et al. 1986], all communication between computers is performed by a network service with a network server process in each computer. Only one network server at a time may have receive rights on a port and the capability for a port is constructed from four parts:

- a public unique identifier – this is a large number containing the address of the computer that made it and a timestamp to make it unique and hard to guess;
- a secret identifier consisting of a large random number that represents send rights, so that any process with the port capability automatically has send rights;
- the address of the computer with the receive rights;
- the address of the computer that owns the port.

The network server creating a port is the owner and initially has the receive rights. In order to participate in a communication, it will pass the capability granting send rights, in messages to processes in other computers, together with a token of authenticity. The token may be used later to authenticate a different server that claims to be a receiver for the port. For example, servers will make capabilities with send rights available to clients who retain the token of authenticity for future use. Processes that possess port capabilities may pass them on to processes in other computers. As port capabilities contain the address of the receiver, processes that have been given capabilities with send rights automatically know the destination for their messages.

The network server that possesses the receive rights for a port may give them away to another network server, together with the token of authenticity. After giving away receive rights, the network server must not receive any messages on the original port, but will respond to enquiries about the address of the new receiver. When the receiver has changed, processes with send rights will need to locate the new receiver. Normally this is done by asking the old receiver. If it is not possible to contact the old receiver, they broadcast a request asking if any process knows the receiver. When a potential receiver has been found, it can be authenticated by asking it to send its token of authenticity for comparison with the one the sender has previously been given by the original receiver. This scheme prevents computers from masquerading as servers.

The Amoeba solution □　In Amoeba, servers and clients are given a secure network interface [Mullender and Tanenbaum 1986]. This is based on having separate capabilities for sending a message to a port and receiving a message on a port. A port consists of a pair of capabilities (*put-port, get-port*), to be used for sending and receiving. A message sent to a *put-port* is received by a process using the associated *get-port*. The owner of a port makes its *put-port* capability known to other processes, but the *get-port* capability is a secret known only by the process it belongs to. Servers can register their *put-port* capabilities with a binder to make them available to clients.

The *put-port* capability is a large random number but does not include the address of the computer with the corresponding *get-port*. When a process sends a message to a *put-port*, the underlying message passing software must find the computer with the (*put-port, get-port*) pair. When the location is unknown, an enquiry is broadcast asking the owner of the *put-port* to reply. Normally the correct process will reply by supplying its host address; and messages can then be sent to that destination. Once a port has been located, the information may be cached for future use.

When messages are sent addressed to *put-ports*, they must be given to processes receiving on the corresponding *get-ports*. In order to make the correct association, there must be a mapping between corresponding *get-port* and *put-port* capabilities, for example:

$$put\text{-}port = F(get\text{-}port)$$

When there is a broadcast request for a server with a given *put-port*, a process could attempt to impersonate a server by replying with its own address. The difference between the owner and the imposter is that the first has a genuine *put-port, get-port* pair, but the second does not. However, the imposter might try to calculate the *get-port* from the *put-port* it knows by applying the inverse of the mapping function *F*. If *get-ports* are to remain secret, it must not be possible to derive them from the corresponding *put-ports*. Therefore, the function *F* should be chosen so that it is very hard to find its inverse.

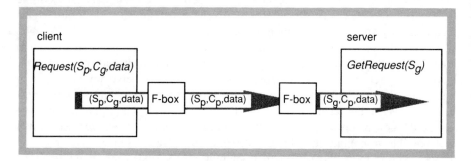

Figure 9.3 Amoeba F-boxes protect ports.

In Amoeba, a **function box** is put between each computer and the network, illustrated in Figure 9.3, in which it is designated as F-box. The function box may be implemented in hardware or in software that is in a secure part of the system. The function box contains incorruptible hardware or software that applies a **one-way function** to port capabilities. By a one-way function we mean one that either does not have an inverse or for which obtaining the inverse is very difficult. Such functions are also used in public-key encryption methods and are discussed further in Section 9.7. The one-way function is applied to *get-port* capabilities, but not to *put-port* capabilities.

In order to make a remote procedure call, a client sends a *Request* message to the server's *put-port*, S_p, and the server attempts to receive the message on its *get-port*, S_g. The message includes the client's *get-port*, C_g, which is translated to the corresponding *put-port*, C_p, when it passes through the client's function box. The server's function box translates the *get-port*, S_g, to the corresponding *put-port*, S_p, and the message is passed.

9.7 Encryption

Information is **encrypted** by being transformed in such a way that it cannot be understood by anyone except the intended recipient who possesses a secret method that makes it possible to decrypt the message. We have advocated the use of encryption to prevent the information in messages from being understood by line-tapping or impostor processes that attempt to read it.

Cryptography provides practical and useful tools for enhancing the security of information in distributed computer systems. In this section we will introduce the basic terms associated with cryptography and discuss the integration of cryptographic techniques into distributed systems. The reader interested in a more general and rigorous discussion of cryptography, or in cryptanalysis, is encouraged to read Kahn [1967] or the first 200 pages of Denning's book [1982].

Transformations and keys □ We describe encryption here as if it were being applied to text composed of letters, but messages on a network may contain capabilities and other non-textual information. The same methods are applicable, but the transformations are applied to bytes instead of to letters. A message is encrypted by the sender applying some rule to transform it from *plain text* to *cipher text*. The recipient must know the inverse rule in order to transform the cipher text received into the original plain text. Other people are unable to decipher the message unless they know the deciphering rule. Such transformations are based on substituting letters and transposing letters from one position to another. However, if this method is used, a new rule must be invented each time that other people find out the rule in use.

In order to make it unnecessary to keep on generating new rules, the transformation is based on two parts, a *function* and a *key*. In this case, transformations are based on substituting letters in the plain text with letters produced by combining them with a key, together with transpositions. Encryption of a message is achieved by applying the function and a secret key to the plain text. The corresponding decryption consists of applying the inverse function and the same key to the cipher text and producing the original plain text. The encryption and decryption functions need not be kept secret.

In order for this to work, both sender and recipient must have two parts, the *function* (or inverse) and the same secret *key*. This is illustrated in Figure 9.4, in which encryption consists of transforming plain text, p, into cipher text, c, by a function f and a key K. The decryption is done by the inverse function, f^{-1}. The function part remains constant, but the key is changed as often as necessary.

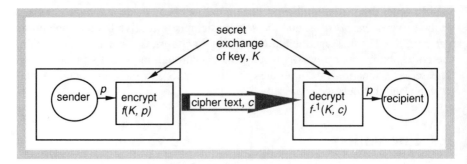

Figure 9.4 Single key encryption.

If a portion of plain text is to be encrypted with a key, but without transpositions, it is divided into blocks of the same length as the encryption key. The characters in the text and the key are converted to integers (for example, ASCII values) and the cipher text is produced by applying the function f to the corresponding characters in the key and the plain text.

Code breakers base their campaign of attack on obtaining matching pieces of plain text and cipher text and, from these, attempting to discover the key. The aim of cryptographers is to make the algorithm that defines the rules of substitution and transposition so complicated that even if the code breaker is equipped with powerful computers and plenty of corresponding samples of plain text and cipher text, the likelihood of discovering the key is very small.

In order to make encryption reliable, long keys are used and algorithms have been developed to make the encrypted text a non-linear function of the plain text. The encryption algorithm must be secure against systematic attempts to break it. When computers are used to apply the function to a key, it is feasible to use complicated algorithms and lengthy keys. Unfortunately, the power of key breakers using computers increases proportionally with the power of computer-aided encryption methods.

The Data Encryption Standard (DES) [National Bureau of Standards 1977] was developed by IBM and subsequently adopted as a US national standard for government and business applications. In this standard, the encryption function maps a 64-bit plain text input into a 64-bit encrypted output. The DES is described in Chapter 9 of Tanenbaum [1981a]. The algorithm has 19 stages and uses a 56-bit key. The algorithm would be time consuming to perform on a general-purpose computer, but it has been implemented in fast VLSI hardware as a single chip.

Despite this, the DES has been criticized on the grounds that a computer-aided attack might crack the code because the size of the key (56 bits) is small enough to yield to a brute-force attempt to find the key given an encrypted message whose contents are known – using a program that enumerates all possible key values and tries each to decrypt the encrypted text until the correct contents are produced.

Key distribution □ When the same key is used for encryption and decryption then both sender and recipient must know the same secret key. In a distributed system, the supplying of secret keys to communicating pairs can be a severe problem, for it is not convenient to communicate them without making use of the network. The solution suggested by Needham and Schroeder [1978] is to make use of a **key distribution server** that supplies secret keys to clients. To do this securely, it must communicate with its clients using encrypted messages. Typically, a client process on behalf of user A wishing to initiate secret communication with a process acting on behalf of user B needs to obtain a new key in two forms, one that it can use itself and one that it can transmit in an encrypted form to B (so that the key is not compromised during transmission). Furthermore, the processes acting on behalf of A and B and the key distribution server must all be confident of the identities of each other.

For communication with its clients the server keeps a table containing a *private key* for each user in the system, known only to the processes acting for the user. The private key is used to authenticate client processes and to encrypt the messages sent between a client and the server.

- A process acting on behalf of a user may request authentication from the key distribution server by sending the user name and a message encrypted with the user's private key. The key distribution server attempts to decrypt the message with that user's private key. If the decryption is successful, the user is authenticated, for no process acting on behalf of another user knows his or her private key.
- Conversely, the key distribution server can prove its identity to any process acting on behalf of a user by sending a message encrypted with the user's private key. When the message arrives, the private key is used to decrypt it. If the result is successful, the message must have been sent by the key distribution server, for no other clients or servers know the private key.

The key distribution service not only provides authentication, but also generates, on request by a client, a new secret key to be used to communicate with another client. When a client wants to establish communication with another client, the server sends it a message containing a new key together with an encrypted message for the second client also containing the new key. The first client sends the encrypted message to the second client. The protocol is illustrated in Figure 9.4 in which the notation $f(k, i)$ denotes the information i encrypted by using the key k.

Suppose that a process acting on behalf of user A needs a shared secret key, K, for communicating with another process acting on behalf of user B. The key distribution server has A and B's private keys KA and KB in its table.

The first step is for A's process to send a request for a new key to the key distribution server. The request includes arguments giving A, B and a temporary token, $T1$ used to pair replies with requests, so as to mask out duplicates. The key distribution server creates a new secret key, K, which will be used by A and B and composes a reply containing two parts:

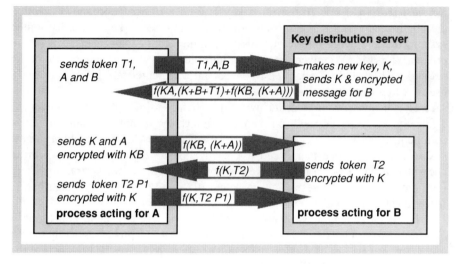

Figure 9.5 Key distribution server.

1. K, A and $T1$;
2. (K, A) encrypted with B's private key KB;

and encrypts both of these parts with A's private key KA. When A's process receives the reply, it decrypts the information, obtaining the same two parts. The first part: $(K, B$ and $T1)$ provides the secret key for communicating with B and the token sent with the request.

In the second step, A's process sends the secret key to B's process, by using the second part of the reply from the key distribution service – (K, A) encrypted with B's private key KB. When B's process receives this, it uses its private key to decrypt it and is now in possession of the secret key. However, B's process needs to be sure that the key really came directly from A, rather than being a repeat of an old message from A. B's process makes a check by using the new key to encrypt a temporary token $T2$ and send it to A. A's process decrypts it, using the secret key, subtracts one from the temporary token, encrypts it and returns it to B. When B's process has decrypted it, it may be sure that A is using the same key.

Digital signatures □   Important documents such as legal agreements and cheques are signed in handwriting to authenticate them and to make them binding. A signature can be used by the recipient of a document to authenticate it – that is, to judge whether or not the document and the signature are really made by a particular person. A handwritten signature also has a binding property in that the person that signed a document cannot subsequently repudiate it. In automated offices, documents are constructed in word processors and are transmitted electronically from one person to another. It would therefore be useful to provide a facility for a **digital signature** that has the same authentication and binding properties as a handwritten signature.

The digital signature will be attached to a document and transmitted in a message to a recipient who must be able to authenticate it. In the non-electronic world it is fairly easy to tell the difference between handwritten signatures and photocopies, but intruders could replay messages containing digital signatures and their contents would be indistinguishable from the originals. However, duplicate detection is fairly straightforward and is a component of most message passing software and it is almost as easy to detect replayed messages as to recognize photocopies. The recipient must be able to authenticate a digital signature in the sense of being sure that it was made by the supposed originator and the signatory must not be able to repudiate it.

Needham and Schroeder also describe how a key distribution server may be enhanced to provide a service for digital signatures. The fact that there is a mutual trust based on authentication between the key distribution server and each of its clients enables it to act as an intermediary in making a document with a digital signature. Users' signatures correspond to their private keys and the key distribution server has a signature based on a secret key of its own.

The digital signature service is based on a procedure that makes a recipient confident of the identity of the originator of a message and makes it impossible for the originator to repudiate it. We describe the steps in the procedure in which a user A sends a document with a digital signature to another user B:

1. The process acting on behalf of user A that wishes to attach a digital signature to a document encrypts the plain text of the document with the user's private key and sends the resulting cipher text to the key distribution server. The server receives the message and verifies the signature by decrypting the message with A's private key, obtaining the document. The server makes a signed and dated certification of A's signature on the document. It does this by making a composite text containing A's name, the document and a timestamp and encrypts it with its secret key. It sends the resulting certificate back to A.

2. User A's process sends the certificate in a message to user B who saves a copy and then sends it in a message to the key distribution server for decrypting. The server receives the certificate and uses its secret key to decrypt it. It uses B's private key to encrypt the resulting plain text and sends the result in a message to user B.

3. When the process acting for user B receives the message it uses B's private key to decrypt it. By this stage, B has two things – the plain text containing the name of A, the document and a timestamp – and the saved copy of the certificate.

The key distribution server verifies user A's signature at step 1. User B trusts the key distribution server and has a message from the server stating that user A's signature has been verified. User B can therefore accept the validity of A's signature on the document. It would now be difficult for A to claim that the signature was forged, for user B has a copy of a certificate which can be checked with the key distribution server. User A could not claim that B had forged the certificate, for B does not know the server's secret key.

Public key encryption □   An alternative encryption scheme uses two different keys, one of which is known to the sender and the other to the recipient. Each potential recipient of a message makes a pair of keys (K_e and K_d for encryption and decryption) and keeps the receive key K_d a secret. The send key K_e can be made known publicly for use by anyone who wants to communicate. The method is based on the use of a one-way function to define the relation between the two keys, so that it is very hard to determine the recipient's key from knowledge of the sender's key.

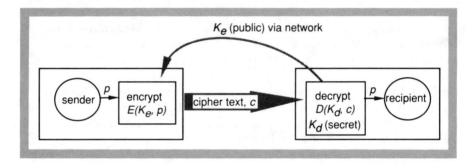

Figure 9.6 Public key encryption.

This is called public key encryption and avoids the need for communicating secret keys between users. It is based on using two separate public functions, E and D for encryption and decryption, together with two separate keys K_e and K_d for encryption and decryption. The idea is illustrated by Figure 9.6. For example, if a user A requests some secret information from another user B, then A generates of a pair of keys, K_e and K_d. A keeps K_d a secret and sends K_e to B. The latter uses $E(p, K_e)$ to encrypt the message before sending it to A. Only A knows K_d and can apply $D(c, K_d)$ to decrypt the message. Many algorithms have been suggested for public key encryption. We describe one here.

The Rivest, Shamir and Adelman (RSA) design for a public key cipher [Rivest et al. 1978] is based on the difficulty of finding factors of large numbers. The outline of the method is as follows. The receiver chooses two large prime numbers, *p1* and *p2*, and forms their product, *m*, but keeps the prime factors a secret. The encryption function taking plain text, *p*, to encrypted text, *c*, is:

$c = p^{K_e}$ *(modulo m)*

The decryption function is:

$p = c^{K_d}$ *(modulo m)*

The receiver calculates the two keys from the two prime numbers by first choosing a value for K_e that has no common factor with $(p1-1) \times (p2-1)$, for example, a prime number greater than *p1* and *p2*. Then it calculates K_d from:

$K_e \times K_d = 1$ *modulo* $((p1-1) \times (p2-1))$

This public-key method and others are described in Tanenbaum [1981a].

To encrypt text using the RSA method, the plain text is divided into equal blocks of length k bits where $2^K < m$. For each block, a block of cipher text is evaluated using the formula $p^{Ke}(modulo\ m)$.

Although public key encryption does not rely on the key used to encrypt messages being kept secret, there is still a need for a key distribution server. The sender of a message needs a means of finding out the current public key of the intended recipient. The sender also wants to be sure that the given key really belongs to the intended recipient and not to some impostor. A key distribution server may used with a slightly different protocol to record current public keys and to authenticate the parties involved in a communication.

Level at which encryption is applied □ We have seen in Section 3.2 that network software is structured in layers. The information to be sent by one process and received by another may be encrypted at one or more levels, from the application down to the link level of the ISO reference model. An analysis of the advantages of applying encryption at various levels is given in Davies [1981]. We mentioned in Section 3.2.3 that encryption is one of the functions that may be performed by the presentation layer.

The Mach system uses a secret key encryption scheme similar to the DES in which pairs of network servers share secret keys. The keys are distributed by a trusted key distribution server, using a variation of the Needham and Schroeder key distribution protocol described above. Messages are encrypted before transmission over the network, but Sansom et al. [1986] note that the main added cost of security in Mach comes from having to encrypt message data. Birrell and Nelson [1984] include facilities for providing optional encryption of RPC request and reply messages, using the DES. Keys are distributed using the Grapevine registration service (see Chapter 11).

At the highest level, applications may encrypt the information that they exchange. As an example, in electronic mail, users may be given the option of sending either plain text or encrypted messages. This has the advantage that a message can be in cipher form from its origin to its destination and cannot be read by unauthorized users, for example whilst waiting in a queue for delivery. There is also the advantage that the operation of the underlying software is completely unaffected by the presence of encoded messages, provided of course that it has been designed to accept any sequences of bits in any context, as opposed to just sequences of characters. However, encryption at a high level means that the headers and trailers added by the various protocols are not themselves encrypted, making unauthorized traffic analysis possible – one of the methods frequently used in military intelligence.

The facilities provided by the key distribution server require both client and server to have access to keys and to store encrypted messages. This requires encryption to be applied at the application level.

At the other extreme encryption and decryption may be applied at the data link level, thus disguising the addresses attached at the higher level and preventing the possibility of analysing the source and destination of messages. Another advantage is that the number of keys is small, keys being associated with communication channels.

Encryption may even be applied to the data entering and leaving the physical layer of the network. A disadvantage of applying encryption at such a low level is that information is in plain text at all levels above the level chosen for encryption, leaving it vulnerable to attack by Trojan horse and other hackers' techniques.

9.8 Summary

The security of a distributed computer system is based on mechanisms designed to protect programs, information and other resources for its users by controlling the activities of the processes that run on their behalf, providing them with a range of rights of access and modification from completely private objects to objects shared by all users.

Protection is concerned not only with the control of programs running on behalf of ordinary users doing their *bona fide* tasks, but also with defending their activities and information from attacks by programs run by users attempting to gain unauthorized access. The use of a network for the communication of information including system messages makes a distributed system particularly vulnerable to eavesdropping and interference, necessitating the encryption of messages wherever security of information or protection of the system against outside interference is required. Active interference on a communication channel can be detected by the use of checksums and sequence numbers in messages.

Another form of unauthorized access is achieved by persuading authorized users to run Trojan horse programs – programs that appear to the user to be harmless but do not belong to the user running them. When they are run they wrongly assume the rights of that user and exploit them to perform actions for which the user has access rights. Other programs are designed to replicate themselves in the computers in a network. Worm programs are replicated in a controlled manner, and can be used to perform useful tasks. Virus programs are malignant and divert resources to the detriment of users.

The processes acting on behalf of legitimate users are authorized to run within domains that define the permitted operations on sets of objects (for example, read-write for a file). The relation between domains and objects (with operations) may be represented abstractly as an access matrix in which element (i,j) represents the right of a process running in the domain i to access the object j (with the permitted operations recorded in the element), but the access matrix is too large and too sparse for direct implementation. It is therefore represented either by associating an access control list with each object or by providing each process with a set of capabilities. A capability is an unforgeable token identifying an object, granting to its possessor certain rights of access to the object and proving that such access has been authorized.

In open distributed systems users may run programs in workstations free from any form of centralized control. An authentication service is used by other services to verify the identity of users on whose behalf client processes make requests.

A port identifier is a capability granting either send or receive rights. In open systems capabilities with send rights for server ports are publicly known so that clients may send request messages to them. In order to prevent unauthorized processes from masquerading as servers, the right to receive on service ports can be restricted to the server processes.

EXERCISES

9.1 Describe the main security problems arising from the use of network communication in a distributed system. Suggest solutions to these problems.

9.2 What are the main security problems arising from the separation of system software into a collection of services running in separate computers? What particular problems are faced by services based on several server computers?

9.3 Describe the two approaches to implementing the domain model.

9.4 What is meant by the term *authentication*? Describe the problems associated with authentication in an open distributed system as compared with an integrated system such as Sun NFS or Locus.

9.5 Explain why servers using access lists for protection need to authenticate clients before each request is carried out.

9.6 What are the advantages and disadvantages of using capabilities rather than access lists for all file operations?

9.7 Explain how an authentication server is used by clients and servers to verify the identity of the user on whose behalf a client is acting.

9.8 Describe how a key distribution server may be used to establish a secret key to be used in communication between two clients.

9.9 Suggest a scheme allowing worm programs to be run but preventing virus programs from replicating in an uncontrolled manner.

Chapter 10
Case Studies in Distributed System Design

This chapter aims to consolidate the reader's understanding of the design models introduced in preceding chapters by describing their use in eight distributed systems that have been developed to exploit them:

- *Locus*: a distributed version of UNIX;
- *Sun NFS*: a networked UNIX file system;
- *Argus*: a distributed language system;
- *XDFS* and
- *CFS*: two file servers designed for use in client–server systems;
- *Amoeba* and
- *Mach*: two distributed operating systems with lightweight kernels;
- *Apollo Domain*: a distributed operating system with an integrated architecture.

We outline the design goals of each and discuss their system architectures, including the question of *open* versus *closed* architectures, file naming and distribution, support for atomic transactions and file replication, and the approaches taken to the implementation of each of these.

10.1 Introduction

In Chapters 5 to 8 we have developed a design model for a file service and described some commonly-used implementation approaches. In this chapter we survey a number of existing distributed systems, focusing mainly on the design and implementation of the file services. We shall consider each system design in relation to the issues discussed in the earlier chapters, showing how they relate to the methods described in the book.

The emphasis on file services in this and the preceding chapters reflects the importance of shared information in most applications of computers. In centralized computer systems, users can share information by running programs that access the same files. The use of files in this way can be viewed as a form of interprocess communication with arbitrary delays between transmission (by writing data in a file with an agreed name) and receipt (by reading data from the same file). With this viewpoint we can see that the file service defines an important part of the programming environment in both distributed and centralized systems, providing facilities for time-delayed communication to application programs.

We can classify the systems surveyed in this chapter under three headings.

Distributed implementations of conventional operating systems □   Some systems are designed to imitate conventional operating systems and file systems such as UNIX. This approach has the advantage that the existing large body of UNIX software may be used. We shall describe Locus and the Sun Network File System (NFS) as examples. In both, the aim is to provide an environment in which programs originally written to run in a non-distributed UNIX environment can be run in a distributed environment with access to remote files. The access to remote files is transparent, and the file abstraction supported is necessarily exactly the same as that provided by conventional UNIX.

With this approach, all of the communication required to support remote file access and other extensions to deal with the distributed environment are added to the operating system kernel. This approach to operating system design results in a *closed* system with a very large kernel (see Section 2.4) containing, amongst other things, the file and directory system, network software and process management. The client–server communication for accessing files is based on remote procedure calling between operating system kernels.

The local operating system in each computer on the network provides a filing system on its own disks as in a conventional version of the operating system. In addition to this, it must play two other roles:

1. It acts as a server providing access to its local files for remote processes.
2. It provides access to remote files for local programs, acting as a client to the remote computers.

Although both Locus and NFS are examples of the integrated model (see Section 2.2.3), it is possible to dedicate particular computers to play the role of file server. Locus is a distributed implementation of UNIX, undertaken as a research project to investigate the problems of security, reliability and resource management in distributed systems. NFS is not a distributed operating system but an extension to the filing systems in UNIX and similar operating systems that allows remote directories and files to be mapped into the local file name space on each computer and supports the UNIX file operations on remote files.

In both Locus and NFS the UFID concept presented in this book is mirrored by a network-wide extension to UNIX i-node numbers, but these are retained in the operating system kernel space, whereas, in the other systems we describe, UFIDs are available for use by application programs.

The provision of user-level remote procedure calling facilities such as the Admiral RPC described in Section 4.6 allows for the building of user-level distributed services outside the kernel.

An approach based on extending an existing operating system will to some extent be limited by the semantics of the original system. This, together with the need for open systems with lightweight kernels has led to the development of a large number of research projects into distributed systems.

Distributed language systems □   There is much research in progress concerned with the design of distributed systems as programming environments. A distributed program consists of a number of program modules performing related tasks in several computers. It is best built using a programming language that is designed for the purpose, including support for concurrency, data abstraction, remote procedure calling and the handling of permanent data in the same way as temporary data structures. Ideally, for all of the types of data structure that can be declared or constructed in a conventional programming language there should be equivalent permanent data structures that can be used not only for all of the purposes for which files are used, but also for the exchange of data between program modules while maintaining the rules constraining the types of parameters and results that apply to such data structures; i.e. permanent arrays, records and user defined abstract types. We shall describe the Argus programming language developed by Liskov and her colleagues at MIT, which supports all of these constructs and provides atomic transactions on all types of data.

Distributed operating systems □   The design goal for systems in this category is to provide distribution transparency with a programming model that is similar to that provided in centralized computers and a file system model that meets the needs for concurrency control and recovery from system failure. Distribution is based primarily on the use of file servers designed to be used by client programs running in workstations and other client computers.

The file systems run as user-level processes separate from the operating systems used in the individual computers and can communicate directly with user-level programs. In some, represented in this chapter by the XDFS and CFS servers developed in the laboratories of the Xerox Corporation and Cambridge University respectively, the operating systems used in the client computers may be heterogeneous.

There are a substantial number of projects in which lightweight kernels have been developed and used as a basis for building distributed systems. We have

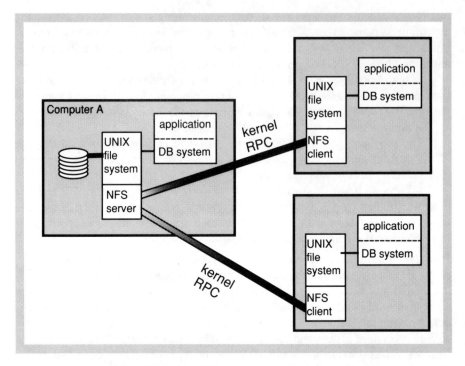

Figure 10.1 The DB system in a closed system.

discussed some of these in Section 2.4. In most of them, the kernel includes both ordinary processes and threads with shared memory, together with facilities for interprocess communication. These are *open*, extensible systems with the file system, directory system, process management and network communication built as services outside the kernel.

Many of these systems provide UNIX emulation to enable existing UNIX software to be used. The Amoeba system developed at the Vrije University, Amsterdam and the Mach system developed at Carnegie Mellon University fall into this class. There are many other projects involved in the design of distributed systems kernels; for example, we described Chorus, SOS and the V-kernel briefly in Section 2.4.

There are also two contrasting models for networked data access – the remote data access model of XDFS, CFS, Mach and Amoeba and the network-transparent data access model of Apollo Domain. The former is based on the familiar client–server model, in which client programs access services to provide the facilities they need from amongst the services available. The resulting architecture is generally a hybrid (see Section 2.2) in which the distributed operating system is composed of a collection of services available to client programs, including one or more file services, each with its own file system model. The latter aims to provide a network-wide single-level data store for use by all programs, resulting in an architecture conforming to the integrated model in which each computer runs a complete set of system software. Application programs run in user machines, getting transparent access to local or remote data.

10.1.1 The DB system: an illustrative example

To illustrate the architectural differences between the three classes of system discussed in this chapter, we use a simple example. Consider a simple non-replicated database system designed to hold a number of records with unique identifiers (*ids*) and with just two access functions:

GetRecord(id) → *RecordValue*
PutRecord(id, RecordValue)

This very simple programming interface could be used by a number of different applications and we will refer to it as the 'DB system'. For simplicity, we will assume that all of the DB records are stored in a single file on a file server and that the DB system is responsible for mapping the *ids* to records and for accessing the file (via the file server). Figures 10.1 and 10.2 show two possible software structures in outline. Figure 10.1 shows a closed system in which the file system is part of the kernel and the code of the DB system is present in each application.

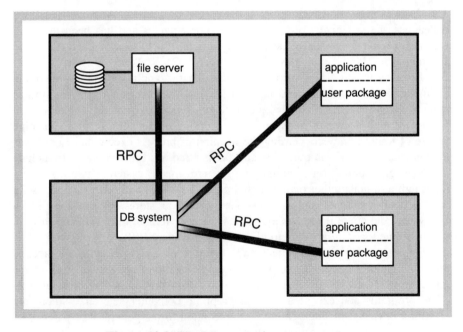

Figure 10.2 The DB system in an open system.

In Figure 10.2 the DB system is represented as a server running in a separate computer (but it could also be a server process running in the same computer as the file service). The structure shown in Figure 10.2 is simpler and potentially faster, but it cannot be achieved with a distributed implementation of a conventional filing system such as Locus or NFS, because user-level programs (i.e. applications) cannot make service requests to a remote file server.

In a more open operating system environment, with file servers designed to handle direct file service requests such as the Xerox and Cambridge file servers, direct service calls can be made from application programs to the file servers and the DB system can be implemented as a service running in a single computer servicing calls from applications running on any computer in the network. We shall consider the DB example in greater detail in relation to each of the systems discussed in this chapter as we come to them. The support provided for concurrency control by each of the systems that we shall describe is a topic of particular interest, since the DB system clearly requires some synchronization of concurrent accesses and updates to the database and application programs may also require concurrency control at a higher-level to ensure the semantic consistency of the data in the database. The simplicity and effectiveness of the solutions available varies widely for the different file services discussed in this chapter.

10.2 Locus

The Locus distributed operating system was developed by Popek and his colleagues at the University of California, Los Angeles and has been in use at UCLA for several years. It is described in a book [Popek and Walker 1985] and several papers [Popek et al. 1981, Mueller et al. 1983, Walker et al. 1983].

Locus is a UNIX-like distributed system. That is, application programs run in a simulated UNIX environment but with system-wide file naming, a file storage system with replication, and the ability to run processes remotely. The system provides a high degree of transparency concerning the location of files and some degree of transparency concerning the location of process execution. Locus was implemented on Vax computers on an Ethernet and has been extended to include a number of computer types running as a heterogeneous system. Its users access it through terminals rather than workstations. The Vaxes and other computers act both as client machines and as file servers; each Vax stores some of the files in the system and client programs may access local or remote files. To sum this up, the distributed system appears to clients like one giant UNIX system, with all of the computers playing both client and server roles and with UNIX file access, process creation (*fork*) and interprocess communication (*pipe*, *signal*) primitives implemented transparently across the network. New processes may be created by client programs and executed in an appropriate computer selected without the client's knowledge or intervention. An exception to the general transparency of the distributed implementation is that it is possible to choose the machine type and power (memory and speed) on which a process is to run.

The relationship between user processes and kernel system calls is similar to that found in UNIX, but when a client program makes a system call the local kernel may route it on to another kernel to execute it by using a kernel-to-kernel remote procedure call.

File operations □   Operations on files can involve up to three different sites. The *using site* is in the client machine that issues the access request and receives the results; the *storage site* is the place where a file is stored. Each file belongs to a *filegroup* and for every filegroup there is a *current synchronization site*. The current synchronization site records the locations where the files in its group, including replicas, are stored and is responsible for the synchronization of concurrent accesses to them. The current synchronization site for a filegroup also selects potential servers for storing new files in the group. For non-replicated files the storage and synchronization sites are usually the same, but when files are replicated at several sites each site that holds a replica can be a storage site .

The file service operations are just like those in UNIX, with an *Open* call that is used to get a file descriptor before reading or writing a file. We shall describe the actions that Locus takes when opening a file. The client program invokes the *Open* call, supplying the path name of a file and the Locus kernel at the using site searches in the relevant file directories for the path given. If the file exists this will result in a UFID for the file, possibly at a remote site. The UFID is passed to the Locus kernel at the current synchronization site with a request to return the address of a storage site for the file.

The Locus kernel at the using site then acquires, from the storage site via the synchronization site, the file index (giving the network address of the disk containing the file and the file block numbers) and all of the information such as file size, owner and access permissions. Fortunately the three sites associated with a file are quite often all the same and in that case the operation is much simpler. Searching a path name through a number of directories involves opening a directory for each step in the path using the procedure described above. Caching of file indexes and other attributes and the buffering of reads and writes adds to the efficiency of the operations described.

Once a file has been opened, the client kernel accesses its contents by issuing the normal UNIX read and write requests and these are passed to the server software running at the file's storage site.

Transactions □   Locus provides nested transactions [Moss 1981] in which all changes to a given file are atomic. To implement transactions, both the original and the changed data are kept at the storage site for the file in question, until a transaction is complete. Locus uses the shadow page technique (see Sections 7.2.3 and 7.4) for making tentative copies of files during transactions. In the first phase of a transaction, the tentative copy of a file is represented by an in-core file index. Initially the in-core file index is copied from the file index on disk, but as changes take place shadow pages are constructed by writing the data to new disk blocks and recording their block pointers in the in-core file index. The atomic commit operation is done by replacing the file index on the disk by the in-core file index. When a file is large and its file index occupies more than a single disk block, the commit operation may be made atomic as follows: the lower pages are first written to new disk blocks and then the root page on disk is replaced by the in-core root page as a single operation. If a transaction is aborted, the in-core copy of the index is discarded.

The synchronization of concurrent access to files is done at the synchronization site. The policy about shared access to a file is stored at its synchronization site which also keeps a record of whether the file is currently in use and whether it is open for reading, writing or both.

Replication □ Locus provides replication of files at the granularity of whole directories on the grounds that, if some node in a tree is inaccessible, then all of the files below that node are also inaccessible. A second reason is that replication works better for objects that are mainly read than for those that are frequently changed. Directories are read more often than written.

Replication is based on assigning physical containers to logical file groups. Each file belongs to a group and replicas of it may be stored in any subset of the group's containers. Each representative has a version number stored with it and this is used to ensure that up-to-date versions are accessed. The various representatives of a replicated file have the same UFID and this consists of the logical group number concatenated to a number unique within the group (an i-node number).

The synchronization site knows the location of all the files in a group and which representatives of replicated files are current and can select an efficient representative to access it. It also sees that representatives are updated in the background so as to keep file suites up to date. A recovery procedure reconciles file versions. This is done by read calls from the storage site that needs a copy to the site that has an up-to-date version. The copying mechanism uses the atomic commit described earlier.

10.3 The Sun Network File System

Sun's NFS is an extension of the UNIX operating system that provides a distributed file service based on networked UNIX systems. It is included in the software supplied with Sun workstations and has been widely adopted by other manufacturers supplying networked workstations and server machines. NFS has also been installed in MS-DOS on IBM PCs and some other non-UNIX operating systems.

NFS provides remote access to conventional UNIX file stores. In a computer on which NFS is installed it is possible to mount remote file directories that have been *exported* by other computers as a part of the file name space in the local file store. On each server computer there is a file with a well-known name (*/etc/exports*) containing the names of directories that are available for remote mounting. Client computers can request to mount a remote directory using the UNIX *mount* command, giving host name and path name of the remote directory, the local name with which it is to be mounted and the network name of the remote computer. Normally, such requests are performed as a part of the UNIX */etc/rc* command file. Since */etc/rc* is executed automatically whenever a UNIX system is initialized, users need not be concerned with the details of the filestores that are remotely mounted, but if an individual user wants to change the standard configuration this can be done by using *mount* explicitly. The remote-mounted

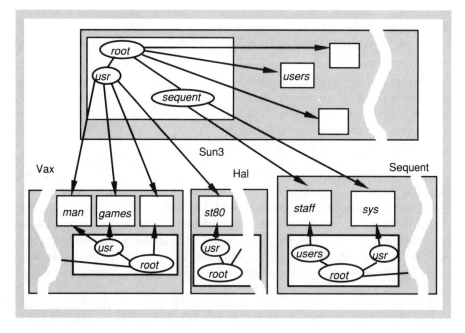

Figure 10.3 Local and remote filestores accessible from a workstation.

directories are located on other NFS-equipped computers in the same local network. The remote directory name that is given as a parameter to the *mount* command may be the root of an entire remote file system or it may be a sub-tree of a remote file system.

Once the appropriate remote filestores have been mounted users and client programs need not be aware that the files that they are using are distributed. Programs in a client can access remote-mounted files and directories via the usual UNIX primitives, so programs written to operate on local files can be used with remote files without modification.

Thus NFS provides a useful form of distributed file sharing where the file system model is precisely the same as that provided by conventional UNIX systems. It is widely used in network environments based on BSD 4.3 UNIX and Ethernet. In Figure 1.6 we showed a diagram of a network in use at Queen Mary College, London. All of the UNIX computers on that network run with NFS. Figure 10.3 shows the remote mountings on one of the Suns of Figure 1.6. White boxes represent file stores in local and remote machines. Names of directories are shown in italic; directory entries are shown by lines, mounts by arrows.

The NFS service is implemented in terms of remote procedure calls between kernels. Any computer running NFS software can become a server machine by making some of its file system available for remote clients to mount. When application programs use the UNIX file access primitives to access a local file the local kernel behaves as it would in a conventional UNIX system. If the file is in a remote directory the local kernel makes a service call to the appropriate remote kernel. Any computer running NFS can be both a client and a server of files and directories.

Integration of NFS and UNIX □   The NFS software consists of a set of extensions to the UNIX kernel and a set of commands and library procedures to enable user-level programs to mount remote file systems and to export local file systems. The kernel extensions enable a UNIX kernel to act as a client to other kernels when accessing remote files and to act as a server of local files when receiving access requests from other kernels.

As we saw in Chapters 5 and 6, most distributed file systems assign unique internal identifiers – UFIDs – to files; these are used by the directory service and by client programs to access the files. Application programs often use the UFIDs indirectly, relying on library procedures to access the directory service and the file service to 'open' files and retain their UFIDs.

In Section 6.2 we saw that the pages of files are accessed in conventional UNIX systems via a tree-structured indirection table known as an *i-node*. Each i-node is referred to by a number that is unique amongst the files in a file store. There may be several filestores in a single computer, but when an i-node number is combined with a file store number it is unique within the computer and plays a role within the local UNIX system similar to that of the UFIDs in distributed systems. The main difference between UNIX's i-node numbers and our UFIDs is that the i-numbers are used only within the UNIX kernel; this is feasible in UNIX systems because the directory system is built in to the operating system.

NFS uses an extension of i-node numbers, called *v-node numbers*. The v-node numbers consist of a triple:

(computer-id, file store number, i-node number)

and are unique amongst the files accessed locally or remotely from a single kernel. Because NFS appears like a conventional UNIX filing system to application programs, the v-node numbers are not visible to user-level programs; they are used only within the operating systems of the client and server computers.

The NFS file system is designed so that no computer acting as a server retains any state information on behalf of its clients. In a conventional UNIX system, the kernel maintains a table of open files for each program, holding the i-node number and current position of the read-write pointer for each file. In NFS, the local kernel holds this information for remote files, with the i-node number replaced by a v-node number. Kernels acting as servers perform file operations on files identified by their v-node number when requested to do so by client kernels. They retain no information about their clients between requests.

A client crash therefore has no effect on the servers it is using, but when a server crashes clients can no longer get the service they require. In spite of the use of stateless servers, users can experience difficulties when a local directory is mounted on the filestore of a remote computer that halts and the users' programs subsequently try to access the files in that directory. In such cases, the kernels local to the users make remote procedure calls to the computer that has halted and, each time a call fails, they re-try over and over again, with the result that the users of an application program sit watching an unending sequence of 'NFS not responding' messages.

There are some remedies for this problem based on the use of timeouts on the kernel's attempts to make remote procedure calls, but when users have realized that a remote server has crashed, they must unmount the remote directory manually or else desist from accessing it.

For example, it is quite common to hold one copy of the UNIX manual pages on-line in a server on a local network with several UNIX systems in it. */usr/man* – the directory that is the root of the sub-tree containing the manual pages – is then exported by the computer that holds it and other computers in the network can mount it with a pathname */usr/man* or any name that is convenient to them, but if the server holding */usr/man* crashes, users attempting to reading manual pages may have the frustrating experience just described.

Caching □   In conventional UNIX systems file pages that have been read from the disk are retained in a *buffer cache* until the space that they occupy is required for other pages. If a program then issues a read or write request for a page that is already in the cache, it can be satisfied without another disk access. If a page has been altered (by a write request), its new contents are written to disk only when the buffer page is required for another page. To guard against loss of data in a system crash, the contents of buffer pages that have been altered are also written to disk every 30 seconds. In a conventional UNIX system there is a single buffer cache, and read or write requests by all of the programs running in the system are processed with reference to it, so they all see the latest version of blocks that have been recently altered.

The NFS system uses caching in both client and server computers. Clients cache the results of read operations from remote files and write operations destined for remote files in an attempt to reduce the number of requests transmitted to servers. Servers cache the pages of files that they access just as they would for local files.

The effect of the client caches can produce surprising results when files are concurrently accessed by more than one client. Suppose, for example, that a client process reads from a remote file and that the data is taken from the client's cache, which was previously loaded with data from the remote file. If the same file has meanwhile been updated by a second client in a different computer, the first client may be given out-of-date or inconsistent data.

NFS attempts to rectify this situation using the modify dates that record the date and time (in seconds) of the last modification to each UNIX file. When remote files are opened, their modify dates are recorded by the client kernel together with the local time of making the recording. The modify dates are checked by making an enquiry to the remote kernel whenever a read is done more than 3 seconds after they were recorded (or 10 seconds in the case of a directory).

This is a costly procedure and does not guarantee the same consistency of files that is provided in conventional UNIX where all the cache buffers are shared in a single kernel. It is unfortunate that the modify date enquiries must be made whether files are shared or not. The times between checks on modify dates are configurable, but decreasing them could reduce performance. Recent updates are not always visible to clients sharing the file; there are two sources of time lag, the delay before the updated data leaves the cache in the updating client's kernel and the time to complete the modify date enquiry in the reading client's kernel.

As a further measure to overcome these problems, there is a facility to give individual files that are open in a client a 'write-through' property. For such files, the results of a write operation are transmitted to the server and written to the disk before the write operation returns control to the user program. However, in practice, most UNIX applications do not depend critically upon the synchronization of file updates and most installations using NFS have few difficulties from this source.

10.3.1 The DB system in Locus and NFS

Returning to our DB system of Section 10.1, we know that both Locus and NFS can support transparent access to remote data, but the DB software that is needed in order to identify and access the records in the database must be present in the application programs on each client computer, and the operating system in each computer must be involved in every file access request.

This is because Locus and NFS provide access to remote files only via the kernel of the operating system in each computer. We outline below an implementation of a DB application based on NFS as shown in Figure 10.1.

- The DB records are stored in a file on one of the computers (labelled *Computer A* in the figure), for example the file might be named */remoteDB/DBData* in the directory */remoteDB* (which must be the root directory in a separate UNIX filestore). Other files in the same directory might be used to hold the mapping tables that map DB *id*s to records.
- A library of procedures is provided that implements the two functions of the DB system, *GetRecord* and *PutRecord*, in terms of UNIX file system operations on the files in a directory called */usr/lib/DB*. Each application process that is to access the database contains a copy of the library.
- Computer A exports the filestore */remoteDB* and each of the remote computers running applications that use the DB system uses the command:

      /etc/mount A:/remoteDB /usr/lib/DB

   to mount the remote directory *A:/remoteDB* as a local directory with the name */usr/lib/DB*.
- The application programs that include the DB library can then proceed normally; the library procedures use the normal UNIX system calls to access the files with local pathnames such as */usr/lib/DB/DBData*.
- NFS offers no support for concurrency control. In some versions of UNIX there is provision for locking entire files, but even that is not a standard feature of all versions of UNIX. In Locus there is provision for file locking.

   For the DB system, file locking is a poor solution. It could be used by an application process to ensure the consistency of the DB data while it performs a transaction that might involve several updates, but only at the expense of totally excluding all other application processes from access to any part of the database for the entire duration of the transaction. But it is difficult to envisage a more satisfactory solution in the context of a conventional filing system without any support for transactions.

10.4 Argus

Argus is an integrated programming language and system for implementing distributed programs. The Argus language includes facilities for the declaration and use of permanent abstract data objects, enabling concurrency control to be applied at the level of the objects created and manipulated by application programs. The continued existence of permanent abstract objects in the face of hardware and software crashes is guaranteed by the Argus system and the serialization of updates to permanent objects is ensured by the Argus language.

Argus has been developed by Liskov and other members of the Argus research group at MIT and is described by Liskov and Scheifler [1982]. The basic primitives are detailed in Liskov [1979] and the methods for implementing atomic data types in Weihl and Liskov [1985]. An experimental implementation of Argus on a single computer had been completed and a distributed implementation was under development at the time of the last paper.

The Argus language has been designed to enable programmers to build distributed programs with modules running in several computers in a network, to support applications such as distributed database systems and office information systems that must maintain permanent shared and distributed data. In such systems, the data is long-lasting and the programs that provide access to it must support atomic updating and recovery after system crashes. By embedding these mechanisms in the language, the designers of Argus hope to ensure that they are used by all applications, avoiding the duplication of effort and possibility of error that arise if each application or each operating system includes such mechanisms.

The Argus language enables programmers to define abstract data types from which permanent atomic objects fitting the needs of the application can be created. An abstract data type consists of a set of objects and some operations for manipulating those objects. The requirement for atomicity of objects implies that such operations are indivisible. The basic data types in the language are similar to those in other procedural programming languages, including arrays, records and variant record types as well as integers, characters and strings. However, the objects that are declared with these types may be *stable* (i.e. permanent) or *volatile*. When objects are declared as *stable*, the Argus system ensures that they are updated atomically, and that they persist until the process within which they are declared deliberately terminates. User-defined atomic types can also be built using the basic atomic types as building blocks. If a process that is responsible for some atomic objects crashes, the system restarts it, aborts any incomplete transactions (called *top-level actions* in Argus) and restores the stable objects to their state before the crash.

In other programming languages that support the use of abstract data types, stack or heap objects may be generated in volatile memory, but the former live only for the duration of the execution of the procedure and the latter for the duration of execution of the process creating them. The data in such programs that is intended to be permanent has to be converted into a form suitable for filing in order to make it live longer than the process that creates it. When future processes make use of such data, they take copies of the filed versions and convert them back to the form used within the code that implements the abstract data type. Some languages, such as Smalltalk or Lisp, allow for saving an image of the current state of execution and resuming execution from the image at a later date. However, an image represents the volatile state of a single program and does not provide for sharing of objects with other programs; neither does it make objects resilient in the face of system crashes. In Argus, processes that create atomic objects are permanent and there is no difference of structure or access methods between objects currently being used as data by a process and objects that are not in use.

An application program consists of a number of *actions* that make use of modules called *guardians*. An action in Argus is roughly equivalent to a transaction. A guardian consists of some data objects and some processes to manipulate them. Guardians in Argus are analogous to servers. Each guardian has an exported interface consisting of *handlers* that are analogous to the procedures in a service interface.

The language □   The Argus language is based on CLU [Liskov et al. 1981], an object-oriented language† developed earlier at MIT. The language CLU allows programmers to define abstract data types in a manner similar to Modula-2. The main difference is that in CLU, as in other object-oriented languages, for example Smalltalk, abstract objects in the form of instances of abstract data types are created dynamically on a heap during the running of the program. (Recall that the abstract objects are composed of some data values and some procedures that are used to operate on the data values.) Objects once created may continue to exist for as long as the creating program survives and the thread of execution can enter and leave the operations (i.e. the procedures) within the objects. When programs execute operations within objects, those operations access and update the data of the object.

The main extension in Argus relative to CLU is the provision of long-lived objects with atomic properties based on stable storage (see Chapter 6). As in CLU, the compiler type-checks programs. Each Argus program manipulates a collection of objects, of which some are in stable storage and others are in volatile store. Volatile objects are used for redundant information such as indexes, buffers and so forth.

---

†   The description 'object-oriented' is used here in a weak sense; it simply describes a language in which new classes of data object can be defined and instances of them can be created and manipulated without restrictions. Other attributes of object-oriented languages, such as a class inheritance structure and dynamic binding of procedure names, are not present in CLU or Argus.

Actions □   An *action* in Argus is an atomic activity that terminates by either committing or aborting. If it commits, any changes to atomic objects that it has made become permanent. As an action performs its operations, new temporary versions of the objects are constructed in volatile storage. The operations in an action access and update the temporary versions whereas actions in other programs access the old permanent versions. This separation of objects into temporary and permanent versions ensures that clients do not see the temporary effects of actions belonging to other clients. If an action is committed, the temporary versions are copied to stable storage. If an action is aborted or if the computer or program crashes, the volatile copies are lost and the objects remain in their original state.

Read and write locks are used to restrict access to the objects used in an action. Locks are set before an action accesses an object and last until the action commits or aborts. Locks are recorded in volatile memory so that they are automatically lost if the system crashes. The loss of locks corresponds to the loss of the temporary versions they are protecting, for both are recorded in the same computer. Quite complex modes of locking may be used to match the requirements of a particular abstract data type. For example, an entire array need not be locked, just the elements in use. Again, a queue that has items added at the end and removed from the front need not be locked against either of these operations unless it is empty.

Nested actions □   An atomic action can be constructed from a number of other atomic sub-actions that may be executed in sequence or concurrently, but to an outside observer the main action appears to be indivisible in the same sense as an atomic transaction. The sub-actions are each atomic in that they do not observe one another's partial state and that they either do all or none of their actions. Sub-actions can commit and abort independently and aborting does not necessarily force the main action to abort, but the commitment of the sub-actions is conditional on the commitment of the enclosing atomic action. It is only when the main action commits that the versions made by sub-actions are converted to permanent versions.

Guardians □   A guardian is a persistent process or group of processes in a single computer that maintains and imposes control of access to a collection of objects of the same abstract data type.

Guardians have a global state consisting of stable objects and volatile objects. The objects in guardians are made resilient by the use of stable storage that is guaranteed to survive crashes. After a crash, the system restarts the guardian and it will be able to use the most recent permanent versions of its objects, whereas the temporary versions will all have been lost. Before the re-started guardian can do anything useful, the recovery procedure designed for it by the programmer is run and any volatile objects, for example buffers, are re-created. After this, the guardian is ready to accept handler calls. The recovery procedures can use information in stable storage to reconstruct volatile storage consistent with the information in stable storage.

Actions are executed within guardians. A guardian is an environment within which one or more actions can be executed either concurrently or serially.

RPC □   The communication between guardians is based on RPC calls to handlers, with at-most-once semantics (see Section 4.2.4). Although several guardians can share a computer, they must still communicate with one another by means of handler calls. The arguments in handler calls are always passed by value, so no handler can do anything to alter the data in another guardian. This ensures that each guardian retains complete control over its own objects.

Guardian definitions □   The definition of a guardian is written as an Argus program module consisting of sections specifying:

- the name of the guardian and some parameters that must be given when a new guardian instance is created together with a list of handler names (rather like an export list in Modula-2);
- declarations of stable and volatile variables to be used respectively to contain stable objects and volatile objects – stable objects are always atomic;
- declarations of initialization procedures to be performed whenever an instance of the guardian is created or restored after a crash;
- a recovery section that is run after crashes and restores the volatile state, for example re-making indexes and buffers;
- a background section that can do processing that is independent of calls to the handlers;
- definition of the handler interfaces;
- definitions of other procedures local to the guardian.

Instances of guardians are created dynamically, whereupon the initialization procedures are run and any background processes are started. After this, the guardian waits for handler calls from other guardians.

Handlers □   Handlers are analogous to the procedures in service interfaces. They are called by programs in other guardians by using handler calls (RPC). The calling program is typically part of an action in another guardian. The calling action suspends until the result is returned by the handler. When a handler call arrives at a guardian, a new process is created to do the work of executing the handler program. Therefore, at any particular time, guardians may be running some background processes and a number of concurrent processes servicing handler calls from remote clients. The representations of objects in guardians can be defined as requiring mutual exclusion of processes. We discuss this in the next subsection.

The operations performed by handlers generally correspond to sub-actions of larger enclosing actions; therefore the execution of any particular handler call can correspond to a part of an atomic action. When a number of concurrent actions make handler calls to the same guardian the operations on objects made on their behalf can become interleaved. Guardians therefore must synchronize concurrent access to their data objects.

During its execution, the handler process locks the atomic data objects with built-in types that it uses in order to prevent other actions using handlers in the guardian from making inconsistent changes. It also makes new temporary versions of all of the objects with built-in types that it changes.

Handlers can terminate normally or can signal an exception and may return results in either case. When the handler terminates, the process executing it terminates too; but the new versions of the objects are still temporary and the locks it has set remain in existence.

Handler calls are regarded as sub-actions of the calling action (or in some cases they may be a single main action). The sub-action may abort for a number of reasons, either because the execution of the handler program results in signalling an exception or for a number of other reasons including message failures and the guardian computer crashing.

Typical application programs make calls to handlers in a number of guardians and the result must be that all or none of these are committed. During the progress of an action, the system keeps a record of the guardians visited. A two-phase commit protocol (see Chapter 8) is used to commit actions. In the first phase, the system checks if all the objects are still locked and, if so, copies their temporary versions to stable storage. If the first phase succeeds, the second phase is entered and the locks are released and the new stable copies become the new versions of the objects. If the first phase fails, the action is aborted, and the objects revert to their previous values, and all temporary and stable copies are discarded.

User defined atomic types □   User defined atomic types are built from a combination of atomic and non-atomic types. Programmers must design the synchronization and recovery of their own user-defined types. In order to do this, they must be able to design their programs to detect whether actions have committed or aborted. The language provides constructs to enable programs to determine whether previous actions on built-in atomic types have committed or aborted.

There are provisions for synchronizing concurrent processes accessing the same data, for example producers and consumers sharing buffers. This is based on a *mutex* data type that may be used as a container for any other objects. Only one process at a time may access a mutex object. The *seize* statement is used to obtain exclusive use of a mutex object and, if no other process is currently using it, the caller gets it immediately and then executes its program. When execution finishes the process relinquishes its possession and another process may seize it. If another process is already using a mutex object at the time of the seize, the calling process waits until the using process relinquishes it. Processes may also relinquish possession of an object temporarily by using the *pause* instruction, for example if they are waiting for a sub-action to commit or abort. The effects produced by the use of mutex objects with seize and pause instructions is similar to the use of monitors, in that processes are mutually excluded from access to the protected object. In a monitor, signalling processes specify condition variables and the processes waiting on the condition variables resume. In Argus, it is different; a pause is just a delay and no particular conditions can be assumed by resumed processes.

10.4.1 The DB system in Argus

Figure 10.4 shows the DB application example configured using Argus.

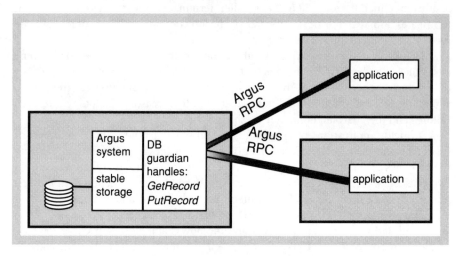

Figure 10.4 The DB system with Argus.

- The DB system is a guardian. The *GetRecord* and *PutRecord* operations are provided to applications as a handler interface exported by the DB guardian. Within the DB guardian the database records could be declared and initialized as stable data structures (arrays or records). There would be no need to explicitly transfer the database records to disk storage, since stable data objects are maintained by the Argus system for as long as the program retains them, using a stable storage system that copies the permanent data to a non-volatile storage medium behind the scenes.
- The application programs are conventional Argus programs (although they probably would not need to use the stable storage features of Argus). Each application would import the DB handler and access the database records through the handler procedures.
- The accesses and updates to individual records could be synchronized by using atomic actions within the DB guardian. Applications requiring synchronization at a higher level, involving several records, could achieve it by defining guardians that provide atomic actions on higher-level data abstractions.

10.5 The Xerox Distributed File System

This distributed file system was developed at Xerox PARC in 1977. XDFS was the third in a pioneering series of file server designs built at Xerox PARC and running on the Alto minicomputer (see Section 1.3.1). The first two, IFS and WFS [Swinehart et al. 1979] were programmed in BCPL. XDFS was designed by Israel, Mitchell and Sturgis and implemented in the Mesa language [Lampson 1981c, Sturgis et al. 1980, Mitchell and Dion 1982, Mitchell 1985, Israel et al. 1978].

XDFS is a file service running on several servers accessed by clients in the Xerox Internet. The number of server computers and their disk capacity can be chosen to suit the needs of a particular site. It supports atomic transactions including any number of files on several cooperating servers and provides concurrency control using locking on portions of data within files. Amongst many applications, it was used to build a distributed diary/calendar known as Violet (see Section 7.3.1).

Each file has a unique identifier that is effectively a large integer, generated when a new file is created. XDFS does not include directory facilities, but a separate directory service was provided as a client of XDFS. Application programs and other clients generally store the UFIDs of new files in directories and retrieve them by giving a text name in a request to the directory service, but in some cases, e.g. temporary files used as working space within a single program, there is little need to record the file in a directory. It is the client's responsibility to record files in the directories and to delete files that are no longer required. If a client process exits without recording the UFID of a file that it has created in a directory or in some private file, the file becomes permanently inaccessible. There is no provision in XDFS for recovering the disk space occupied by such inaccessible files. This is an example of the pitfall that we describe in Section 5.2.

The separation of the directory service from the file service and the fact that clients are free to record UFIDs in private files means that XDFS cannot undertake garbage collection to recover inaccessible files because it does not have access to all of the stored UFIDS. But in practice a user package can be designed to ensure that UFIDs are recorded in a directory service as soon as files are created, preventing inaccessible files. Mitchell and Dion report that the loss of disk space arising from inaccessible files is not significant.

File service operations □   Every file operation must be part of a transaction. Several files may be involved in a transaction and the files may be in different XDFS servers. The service functions are described fully in Mitchell [1985]. They are similar to the service functions for a transaction service described in this book in Chapter 7, Box 7.1.

Before accessing XDFS, clients must open a transaction using the *Login* function, giving a name and password, which is used to check their identity. *Login* delivers a *transaction handle* as result. Transaction handles are similar to the transaction identifiers (TIDs) of Chapter 7; they identify a transaction and the coordinating server for the transaction and define the access rights of the user who has initiated the transaction. Identity-based access control is performed by the file service (not the directory service) in XDFS.

To include another *worker* server in a transaction, the *AddServer* operation is called (see Section 8.3). The arguments are the *transaction handle*, the coordinator, the user name and password. A new transaction handle is returned and this must be used in all operations involving the added server.

To access a file, the client must first open it using the *OpenFile* request, quoting the transaction handle, the UFID of the file it wishes to access and the mode of access required (read, write, execute) and obtain a *FileHandle*:

OpenFile(TransHandle, UFID, accessMode) → FileHandle

The server checks that the client with that transaction handle has sufficient access rights to the file to satisfy the *accessMode* requested. The server then returns a single *FileHandle* that refers to a file, a transaction and server. The *FileHandle* is given as argument in file operations that allow clients to *Read* and *Write* sequences of bytes at specified positions in files.

Mitchell and Dion report that the inclusion of all file operations in transactions results in difficulties when programming some applications. The two main problems are: (1) every file operation carries the overheads required for transactions, and (2) application programs whose state is maintained in volatile storage cannot easily maintain a log of the sequence of inputs and use it to recover the state after a system crash (as discussed in Section 7.3.5).

Directory service □   Creating a new file and recording its name and UFID in a directory should be performed within a single transaction. Two clients would be involved in such a transaction: the original client and the Directory Service. These two clients should have different access rights: the original client may access the new file, but cannot access the files containing directories directly, whereas the directory service can access and alter the contents of directory files.

This difficulty is resolved by allowing several clients to participate in a transaction, each using a different *TransHandle*. In our example, the original client uses the *Login* operation to open a transaction and the directory service uses the resulting transaction handle in an *AddServer* call. This results in the creation of a separate 'worker' process and a new transaction handle with different rights is given to the directory service.

Communication between clients and servers □   In addition to the normal request and reply messages communicated between clients and servers, XDFS file servers may also send unsolicited messages to clients, for example, when locks have been broken.

Because of the unsolicited messages, communication between clients and XDFS servers is by asynchronous message passing. Results are not guaranteed to arrive in any particular order and clients use request IDs to match results to requests as described in Section 4.5. Clients request file server operations by sending a request message containing the operation requested, the arguments and a request ID. When an XDFS server receives a request message, it carries out the request and sends a reply message containing the request ID supplied by the client. The client must acknowledge the server's reply message – an example of the *RRA* protocol described in Section 4.5.2.

File location maps and file indexes □   XDFS combines the file location map and file index in a single mapping:

   UFID × page → block pointer

This mapping is stored in the form of a B-tree, as described in Section 6.3. Each disk contains a single B-tree that records the location of the pages of all the files stored on it. It also contains a record of whether each block is allocated or free in the form of a bit map.

Stable storage □   The B-tree index and the free store bit map are recorded in stable storage so that the information in them is guaranteed to survive crashes that cause the information in one disk block to be recorded incorrectly. We have described stable storage in Section 6.6, but the reader is referred to the paper by Israel et al. [1978] describing its use in XDFS. Stable storage is used because it is a method for storing information redundantly that does not depend on the interpretation of the information. It therefore has the advantage that it may be used for any number of differently-structured classes of information.

Transaction implementation □   When *Write* operations are performed, the new versions of the altered pages are recorded as shadow pages in separate blocks from the original versions. If a transaction fails, the shadow pages are freed and the file reverts to its original form. If a transaction succeeds, the new pages are placed in the file instead of the original ones.

   When a transaction is in the first phase, the list of shadow pages is recorded as an intentions list, containing for each shadow page:

   UFID, page, block pointer of shadow page

when the transaction is committed, this list is written to stable storage.

   The second phase consists of updating the B-tree map and freeing the old pages. The B-tree is updated from the bottom up – shadow pages are made as the B-tree is copied and, finally, the root page is replaced – an atomic action.

   The two-phase commit protocol for multiple servers that we describe in Section 8.3.1 was first used in XDFS; this is carried out by means of messages passed between the coordinator and the participating servers, rather than by remote procedure calls as in our description. The protocol is described fully in Israel et al. [1978].

   When a server is started up, recovery procedures are carried out. The recovery procedure inspects the intentions lists and tries to commit the transactions recorded in them. Some transactions in progress when the server halted may have had no intentions lists recorded. In such cases, their shadow pages must be freed. The server detects such shadow pages by tracing all pages in use in the B-tree map and the intentions lists.

Concurrency control □   Locks are set on the sequences of bytes affected by *Read* and *Write* operations as a side-effect of these operations. The XDFS locking scheme was designed to maximize concurrency by reducing the granularity of locking to protect only the precise sequence of data that is in use and by inventing soft write locks (*I-write*) as described in Section 7.3. Locks become vulnerable and may be broken by other transactions after a timeout period has elapsed. Clients are notified when their locks are broken. If an *I-write* lock is broken the transaction is automatically aborted. Clients with broken read locks may either abort their transactions or clear the broken read lock and continue, taking care not to rely on the data that was covered by the broken lock.

The Alpine file server – successor to XDFS □   After XDFS, the Alpine file server was developed at Xerox PARC [Brown et al. 1985, Mitchell 1985]. Alpine was written in the Cedar language and environment (see Section 2.4.2) running on the Dorado computer, making use of the Cedar remote procedure call facilities developed by Birrell and Nelson and described in Chapter 4. It was designed to be used for databases and supports atomic transactions with multiple servers. Alpine provides both normal and transaction files but, in other respects, its client interface is similar to that of XDFS. Brown et al. give a comparison of the performance of the two file servers, showing that Alpine is faster for several reasons including the use of a faster computer and different algorithms to implement transactions.

10.6 The Cambridge File Server

The Cambridge File Server is part of the Cambridge Distributed Computing System (CDCS) developed in the Computer Laboratory at Cambridge University and described in Needham and Herbert [1982].

In the CDCS, several computers are reserved for use as servers for filing and printing and a name server is used to map the names of services onto their locations. Servers are also used for a number of other tasks such as authentication and access control. The CDCS uses the processor pool approach to the problem of providing personal computing resources to users with differing requirements, on the grounds that the provision of personal workstations is not the best solution. If small workstations are provided, users may have to use other computers for their more complex tasks. On the other hand, powerful workstations are not needed to cope with the majority of users' tasks such as editing files and compiling simple programs. The CDCS solution is to provide users with terminals or very simple personal computers that can only perform a few tasks locally but can be connected to pool processors, as described in Section 2.2.2. The pool processors can be used in the same way as personal computers – that is, users get sole use of them while they are connected and can run whatever software they choose. The main difference is that the pool processor is available for use by other users as soon as a user disconnects from it.

The CDCS runs over the Cambridge Ring (discussed in Section 3.3.2). The pool processors are diskless and therefore access users' files from a number of file servers. The file service is designed as a 'universal file service' [Birrell and Needham 1980], on top of which a number of different filing systems may be built. This is generally known as the Cambridge File Service (or CFS) and is described and compared with XDFS in Mitchell and Dion [1982].

CFS is designed to enable the diskless pool processors to be loaded quickly and to provide page-swapping facilities as well as general-purpose filing facilities. In addition the CDCS contains a number of computers with their own operating systems which are able to use CFS for their filing; for example, CFS is used as the file store for an experimental computer system (the CAP machine [Wilkes and Needham 1979]) and for the TRIPOS operating system [Richards et al. 1979].

CFS was programmed in the BCPL language and originally ran on a Computer Automation LSI4/30 minicomputer with 64K 16-bit words of main memory and 80 Mbyte disks.

The CFS file server □   CFS provides both **files** and **indexes**. A CFS **index** is a structure designed to hold the UFIDs of files. UFIDs are chosen from a sparse space and are regarded as capabilities for access to the file. No distinction is made between capabilities for reading and writing.

Each index contains a sequence of UFIDs referring to files or indexes. Indexes are provided as a building block for the construction of directory services; they are distinguished from other files so that the UFIDs that are stored in them can be discovered by the CFS garbage collection algorithm (discussed below). Directory services are not included in CFS; they are provided by the operating systems used in the CDCS, acting as clients to CFS. The index facilities are sufficiently flexible to support the file naming schemes used in most operating systems. A directory service holds the text names of files in whatever form is required by the host operating system and maps each text name to a position in a CFS index.

The set of client operations on indexes includes the following:

- create a new index and store its UFID in another index,
- read a UFID at a given position in a given index,
- replace or erase a UFID at a given position in a given index,
- delete a given index.

A CFS index is illustrated in Figure 10.5. The indexes in CFS do not describe the internal structure of files and should not be confused with the *file indexes* described in Section 6.2.

The *Read* and *Write* operations are similar to those described in Chapter 5, Box 5.1. Another operation sets the length of a file, intended to be used as a limit check when reading and writing files, but the blocks used for storing file pages are allocated only as a result of a *Write* operation. When files are created a pattern is specified by the client and this should be returned when data is read from pages that have not yet been written. Files may have a number of other attributes, some of which are used by the file service and others are stored for use by clients.

The index structure □   The creation of a file and the recording of its UFID in an index is done as a single operation before returning the UFID to the client. Clients delete files by removing their UFIDs from indexes.

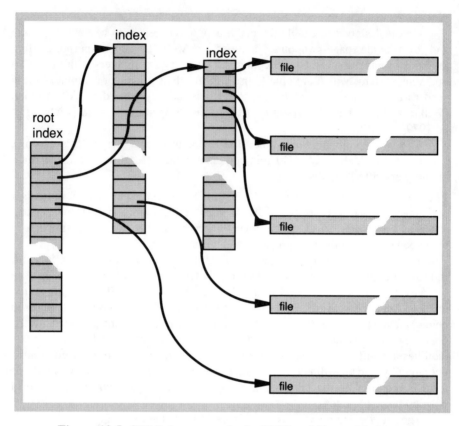

Figure 10.5 CFS indexes contain the UFIDs of files and indexes.

The UFID of any file or index may be stored in an index known to the client. There is one distinguished root index and indexes may be constructed in directed graph structures descending from the root index. The UFID of the root index is a capability for accessing all the other indexes and is not supplied to clients. Several separate filing systems may coexist within CFS with the roots of their file stores in the root index. Each of these, for example the Tripos operating system, knows the UFID of the index that is the root of its own filing system.

The UFID of a file or index may be recorded in more than one index, for example, by clients sharing files. Each file or index remains in existence provided that its UFID is accessible by one or more paths from the root index. CFS includes a garbage collector that runs periodically to detect inaccessible files and reclaim the disk blocks they occupy.

File structure □ The file store layout is designed to provide fast access to small files and to make the best use of disk space. This is achieved by the use of two different disk block sizes – small blocks of 512 bytes and large blocks of 2048 bytes. The small blocks are used to store file headers and the first part of the data in files and indexes. The large blocks are used to store data. Each file or index has a header block (directly accessible from the UFID as shown in Figure 10.6)

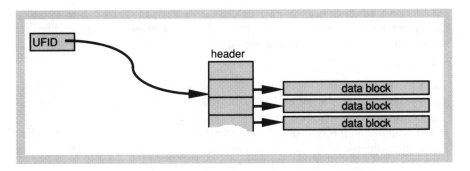

Figure 10.6 CFS header block and file index.

containing its size and other information together with part or all of the file index.
If a file is small enough its data is stored in the header block. Otherwise, the
block addresses of large blocks containing the data are listed in the file index.
File indexes for larger files have two levels, the top level referring to a number of
small blocks that contain the addresses of large blocks containing data. When a
file is created it initially occupies only the single small header block. As it grows
in size, the data is stored in large blocks and an index is formed in the header
block.

Each UFID contains the address of the header block for the file that it refers
to. This design obviates the need for a *file location map*, but inhibits the re-
organization of disk storage, since the root blocks of files cannot be moved.
Mitchell and Dion [1982] report that this restriction has not proved a drawback in
practice. Should a header block become unwriteable, an indirection can be
inserted in the cylinder map (see below).

Transactions and locking □ A simple form of atomic transaction is provided,
allowing only a single file in each transaction. When a file is created, the client
specifies whether it is to be a *transaction file* or a *normal file* (i.e. one that is
excluded from transaction processing). Clients supply the UFID of a file to open
a transaction and are given a temporary UFID in return. Since a transaction can
apply only to operations on a single file, temporary UFIDs are regarded as
transaction identifiers when supplied as arguments to the *Read* and *Write* and
other file or index operations. The temporary UFIDs serialize access to files,
using the many reader/single writer locking scheme described in Section 7.3.1.

The operations between *Open* and *Close* on a transaction file are
implemented as an atomic transaction on that file and the *Close* operation may
specify either committing or aborting the transaction. Deadlock is avoided by
using a timeout of 15 minutes on temporary UFIDs.

A single *Read* or *Write* operation on a transaction file may be made using an
ordinary UFID as argument and the server will open a transaction, get a
temporary UFID and then close the transaction. This is an optimization to reduce
communication between clients and servers. Operations on normal (or non-
transaction) files may be serialized by using *Open* and *Close* operations and
temporary UFIDs.

Disk space management □   CFS records a cylinder map on each disk cylinder. The cylinder map contains an entry for each disk block on the cylinder, but the information in the entries has three distinct uses:

1. It shows which blocks are free and which are allocated.
2. It is used to record intentions lists for transactions, holding pointers to the shadow pages for tentative writes against the file pages involved in transactions.
3. It records the position of each allocated disk block in a file or index. This enables the recovery algorithms described in Section 6.6 to be applied when an index block or a file index is damaged.

Garbage collection □   The CFS garbage collection process is designed to run concurrently with file server operations. It runs in a separate computer and is initiated from time to time by the file server. The algorithm used is described fully in Needham and Herbert [1982]. The procedure is designed to be repeatable, so that the effect of a garbage collection is atomic. It is carried out in three phases:

1. finding 'probably unwanted blocks';
2. marking 'unwanted blocks' in a tentative manner;
3. committing the intention to remove 'unwanted blocks' and removing them.

In the first phase, the garbage collector is given the address of the root index and walks all the indexes accessible from it, making a list of all the accessible blocks – these are 'wanted blocks'. Blocks not on its list may be 'unwanted', but because garbage collection is concurrent with file operations, some blocks not included in the 'wanted' list could have become 'wanted' during the first phase.

In the second phase, the garbage collector calls the file service to mark all the 'unwanted blocks' as an intention. During the first and second phases of garbage collection, the file server sends a message informing the garbage collector each time it stores a UFID in an index, so that the garbage collector can keep the list of unwanted blocks up to date. When all of the messages have arrived, the 'wanted blocks' list can be updated to include all of the blocks referenced from the newly-recorded UFIDs. When this has been done, the garbage collector enters the third phase, telling the file server to suspend operations on the objects containing unwanted blocks and commit the intention.

The garbage collector then works through its list instructing the file server to return the 'definitely unwanted blocks' to the free list.

Performance comparisons □   Mitchell and Dion [1982] compare the performance of CFS and XDFS, showing that XDFS has large overheads for opening and closing transactions in comparison with CFS, attributed to the recording of intentions lists separately in stable storage. Again, in writing large amounts of data to normal files, CFS is faster, for it avoids transaction overheads, and the page size is larger. In other respects, when machine performance is taken into account, the two are similar, reading 256 bytes taking 41msec and 76 msec for CFS and XDFS respectively; writing 256 bytes to a transaction file taking 73 msec and 142 msec. Note that 256 bytes was chosen as a unit that did not match the page size of either server.

10.7 Amoeba

Amoeba is a research project on distributed systems at the Vrije (Free) University and CWI, Amsterdam. It has been described in a number of papers [Mullender and Tanenbaum 1985, 1986, Mullender 1985, Tanenbaum and van Renesse 1985]. An experimental Amoeba distributed system has been developed at the Vrije University.

We have outlined the architecture of Amoeba in Section 2.2.2, where we described it as a *hybrid* because it contains both single-user workstations and a pool of processors that can be allocated to servers or client programs. There are many different servers described in the Amoeba papers, for example, a block server, several different file servers, a directory server, a boot server, a loader server and database server. In addition a library has been written to allow UNIX programs to run on Amoeba.

The Amoeba kernel was designed to be a basis for an *open* system (see Section 2.4.1) with many of the components of a conventional operating system, such as the file service, outside the kernel; all of the computers in the Amoeba system run this kernel. The kernel includes facilities for creating processes as clusters of threads as described in Section 2.4.1; and interprocess communication based on a triple of message passing primitives designed to support RPC messages as discussed in Section 3.4.1; *Request*, for use by clients to make remote calls; *GetRequest* and *PutReply* for servers to receive and respond to service calls.

Users are intended to view Amoeba as a collection of processes and information objects maintained by servers. The objects and servers are identified by sparse capabilities (see Section 5.3.2). A capability is like a UFID; it allows its possessor to perform certain operations on the object it names. Initially, a client program is given capabilities to access a small number of essential services. Clients obtain other capabilities by requesting them from the services, which issue them after checking the clients' authorizations. Security of capabilities is based on their being hard to guess and F-boxes that protect server ports as described in Section 9.5. Capabilities that refer to files fulfil the role of UFIDs.

Several different file systems have been built in Amoeba, including a UNIX file system with UNIX system calls, a flat file service and an advanced transaction-based file service called the Free University Storage System (FUSS).

Capabilities in Amoeba □   Capabilities for all kinds of objects in Amoeba have a single format. They contain four fields, as shown in the table below:

48 bits	24 bits	8bits	48bits
service port	object number	rights	random part

The service port field is a sparse address that identifies and provides access to the service that manages the object and objects stay with their creating servers. The object number field identifies a particular object and is unique amongst the objects managed by its server. The rights part specifies which of the service operations are permitted to the possessor of the capability. The rights and random part of capabilities are encrypted before they are delivered to clients to protect the servers against forgery of capabilities by modifying the access rights part of an existing capability.

FUSS □   The Free University Storage System is built in layers with a block service at the bottom. The block service manages virtual disk blocks of three kinds: (1) volatile blocks, (2) stable storage blocks, (3) replicated blocks with atomic write on all copies simultaneously. The block service provides clients with functions for allocating, reading, writing and freeing blocks similar to those described in Section 6.4. Blocks can be locked on behalf of clients' transactions. Stable storage blocks are implemented with the two copies of each page on separate disks managed by different servers.

The layer above the block service provides the file service with *file versions* and a combination of locking and optimistic concurrency control. Locks are used for large transactions and optimistic concurrency control for small ones. Database services and directory services are built on top of the file service.

The file system is implemented as a tree of pages in which sub-trees are files. Files can be grouped into super-files that are like ordinary files but also contain references to other files and other super-files in their root pages. The root pages of all the files are in stable storage on disks provided by the block server, but the design is such that the lower pages may be stored either on disk or on write-once media such as optical disks.

File representation □   A file is a set of versions ordered in time. When a new version is created, it shares its page tree with the current version and only modified pages are duplicated. The root of the page tree for each file version is called the *version page* and contains a *commit reference*, two locks, and capabilities referring to the file and the version. The commit references in the committed versions of a file point to the next committed version, providing a sequence of committed versions with the current version at the end of the sequence. There is no commit reference in the version page of the current version of a file nor in tentative versions.

The page layout is shown in Figure 10.7. Pages contain a *header area* containing a reference to the page in the previous version that the page is based on (i.e. copied from), a *client data area* and an array of references to pages lower in the file tree. A page reference consists of a block number and some information recording when a page was last copied (C), read (R), written (W) or searched (S) and when the page references in it were last modified (M). The access information recorded in the page references is used in concurrency control.

Clients read or write a page at a time. Pages can vary in length up to 32 kbytes and writing a page is atomic, even for very large pages. Pages that occupy more than a single storage block are written back-to-front as a linked list of blocks, with the head written last. Contiguous blocks of store are used wherever possible.

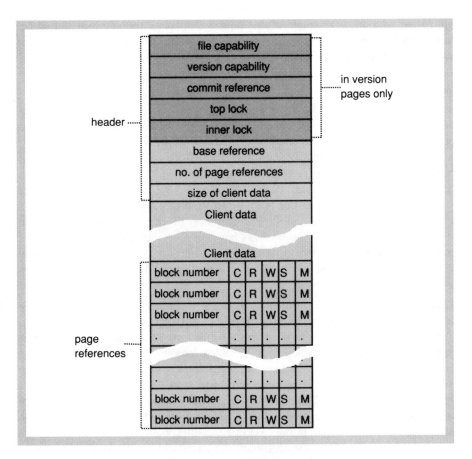

Figure 10.7 Amoeba FUSS page layout.

Page indexes and sharing between versions □   Each page in a file may be reached via its parent page and the array of page references that it contains. An arbitrary page can be accessed from the root page of the file by indexing into the arrays of references in several pages, starting from the root. Using this method, pages have pathnames consisting of strings of integers.

When a new version of a file is created, there is a new version page, containing a copy of the page reference table from the previous version and initially the new version shares all of the pages of the previous version.

A 'copy-on-write' mechanism is used – this means that pages in a new version are shared with the old version until they are written. When the data in a page of a new version is written, new blocks are allocated, the header and reference tables are copied from the previous version of the page and the new data is written. The page reference in the parent page must be updated to hold the block number of the first block in the newly-written page and the W field must be updated. But this alteration to the parent page must not be in the original shared copy of the parent page, so if this is the first change in the new version a copy of the parent page must be made at this point. Similarly, the parent of the parent must also be copied if it is shared with the previous version, and so on, all the way up the file tree to the version page.

Versions and optimistic concurrency control □ When several transactions make new versions concurrently, the server must validate that the changes can be serialized. This is done using the optimistic concurrency control algorithms described in Section 7.3.2. It must also build a new version combining the pages of the concurrent versions as described in Section 7.2.2.

The concurrency test uses the information stored in the page trees with the page references to determine whether pages have been read, written, searched, copied or references modified. Parts of the tree that were not copied need not be tested and when a page has not been copied, the pages below it have not been copied either. Similarly, finding the presence of pages that have not been searched implies that their descendants have not been searched either. The tree comprising the file version is traversed once to do the concurrency tests and to prepare the new version by combining the updates made by the concurrent transactions.

Locking □ Although the optimistic concurrency control algorithm could handle all conflicts, it would not be very efficient to rely on it in situations where the likelihood of conflicts is significant, because the cost of aborting a transaction is quite high. Updates to super-files in FUSS use locking as they consist of a large number of pages and are more likely to incur conflicting accesses. Two sorts of locks are applied to pages, top locks and inner locks. The top lock is set in the version block and inner locks on all other pages of super-files. When a new version of a file is created, the top lock is set (unless the file is already locked, in which case a wait occurs). In the case of super-files, both top and inner locks are checked whereas, in ordinary files, only the inner lock is checked. This means that operations on ordinary files may proceed concurrently, for the inner locks are checked and the top locks set, whereas operations on super-files wait for one another as they check both. Also, when the pages of a super-file are visited, the inner locks are set and this prevents interference from operations on single files.

The directory service □ The directory service enables users to map text names to UFIDs. Capabilities for directories enable their possessors to perform directory operations, for example, to search a directory or to change or add an entry. The capabilities for directories can be stored in other directories, thus making a hierarchic directory structure with searching by pathname as in UNIX. The default directory service also associates users with home directories when they log in. The home directory contains capabilities enabling users to access standard services. As Amoeba is an open system, there could be other directory services with different structures.

As the directory server holds capabilities, it is made secure against two forms of illicit access: firstly users may log in as other users, secondly users may try to decode the files that contain directories. The first issue is tackled by the authentication service, the second by encryption of the UFIDs of the files stored in the directories. When a new directory is created, the directory service creates a key that it uses to encrypt the UFIDs stored in it. This key is embedded in the capability and given to the client. The directory service does not store the key, but instead stores the result of applying a 'one-way function' to it. It can check capabilities given to it by clients by applying the same function to them and comparing them with the value it has stored, but it can only make use of directories when clients give it capabilities to access them.

10.8 Mach

The Mach distributed system kernel has been developed at Carnegie Mellon University, Pittsburg [Rashid 1986, Acetta et al. 1986, Mason 1987, Young et al. 1987]. The work on Mach follows earlier work on the Accent kernel [Rashid and Robertson 1981, Rashid 1985, Fitzgerald and Rashid 1986] and many of Mach's features are derived from Accent. The approach in both Accent and Mach has been to design and build a kernel that is suitable for distributed systems and is also able to emulate UNIX. The UNIX emulation enables Mach to provide an environment in which users may continue to use programs that use the UNIX system call interface. This is essential for practical reasons because so many UNIX application programs exist. This is quite different from the Locus approach where UNIX was extended to work in a distributed manner – with the resulting system having some of the same limitations as UNIX. Mach has been designed to take advantage of multiprocessor architectures (see Section 1.1.2) and has been implemented for Vax, MicroVax, IBM PC/RT, Perq, Encore, Sequent and Sun machines.

Mach includes the Matchmaker remote procedure call interface language [Jones and Rashid 1986] that enables distributed programs to be built in several existing programming languages including C, Pascal, Ada and Lisp. This can be contrasted with the Argus system in which distributed programs are built using a purpose-built programming language.

Mach is an open system based on a lightweight kernel running in each computer with services such as the file system, network service and process management outside the kernel. These services replace the system calls found in conventional operating systems such as UNIX and their relationship to the kernel is shown in Figure 10.8. The model provided by Mach is a service model in which objects are managed by servers, and clients make requests for operations on objects by using remote procedure calls. Remote procedure calling in Matchmaker is supported by efficient and flexible interprocess communication facilities in the kernel.

The Mach kernel □   The main functions of the Mach kernel are:

- *Clusters and threads*: There are two sorts of processes – clusters (called *tasks* in Mach) and threads. A cluster is an execution environment within which threads may run. The cluster runs in a paged virtual address space with protected access to resources such as virtual memory and capabilities for ports. A thread is the smallest independent unit of execution running

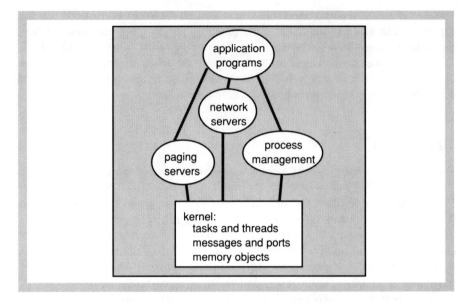

Figure 10.8 The Mach kernel and services.

within a cluster and shares the memory and other resources in the cluster. Threads are an example of the sort of lightweight processes that we have described in Section 2.4.1. When a program is running in a tightly coupled multiprocessor, the kernel allows threads to execute in parallel.

- *Ports*: In Mach, messages are sent to ports which are communication channels. In order to send a message, the sending cluster must possess a capability for the port to which it is to be sent. The alternative (used, for example, in the V System) is to send messages to processes.
- *Message passing* Messages may be of any size and can contain port capabilities and references; but the latter are typed.
- *Memory objects* A memory object is a secondary storage object, or unit of virtual memory, that may be mapped into the virtual address space of a cluster. The memory object is used as a basis for building file systems using disk storage outside the kernel.

Program execution is based on clusters and threads. Clusters may be created, terminated, suspended and resumed by other clusters. Cluster creation in this way results in sets of clusters related in tree structures. When a new cluster is created, it is given capabilities for ports by its parent cluster. A cluster may inherit regions of virtual memory from its parent for use as read-write or copy-on-write. Threads may be created within clusters and may also be terminated, suspended and resumed. Clusters send messages to ports and receive messages from ports.

Virtual memory □   A cluster's address space consists of an ordered collection of memory regions and clusters may allocate regions within the virtual address space on page boundaries. When a new cluster is created, the parent cluster may specify that the new child cluster can share (read-write) or copy any portion of its address space. This enables separate clusters in the same inheritance tree and by implication in the same computer to make use of shared memory. The memory shared between clusters is intended to be used only for fine grain communication, but message passing is the more normal method of communication. **Copy-on-write** sharing is used to make virtual memory copying and message passing efficient. A copy-on-write page is shared between two clusters until one of them writes to it; at that time, a new page is placed in the address space of the writing process in place of the shared page.

Mach allows clusters outside the kernel to handle virtual memory management functions for 'paging in' – providing pages of memory objects to be copied into main memory – and 'paging out' – taking charge of pages that are removed from main memory. When virtual memory is allocated, an *external pager* may be specified to handle paging requests – if no external pager is specified, a default one is used. An external pager is a cluster that has access to a memory object generally stored on a disk. For a memory-mapped file (described below), a file system is chosen for the pager. When a new page is required, the kernel requests data from the file system and when an altered page is to be 'paged out', the kernel gives it to the file system. The use of a file system for a default pager removes the need for separate paging and filing.

Message passing □   A cluster sends a message by using the *Send* operation and another cluster receives it by using the *Receive* operation on the same port. Messages have a small header of a fixed length and in addition a collection of other data including port capabilities and references. Port capabilities and references must be typed so that they can be recognized for what they are. It is essential for security that port capabilities are not confused with other data items.

Both blocking and non-blocking communication may be used. In the case of blocking communication, the message is transferred directly to the recipient cluster at the time when it invokes the *Receive* operation. For non-blocking communication, the message is passed in two stages, by copying from sender to kernel and from kernel to recipient. In both blocking and non-blocking communication, large messages, for example a few megabytes, may be transferred efficiently using the copy-on-write mechanism. In non-blocking communication, the message will reside temporarily in the kernel address space without being written and then will eventually be transferred to the recipient's address space.

A third primitive *rpc_message* is designed for making remote procedure calls. It allows the invoking thread to send a call message and then to receive a reply. It includes a specification for timeouts on sending and receiving. The use of a special RPC protocol at the message level in this way simplifies the RPC protocols described in Section 4.5.1. The request message contains a *RequestId* enabling the transport layer in the server to return the reply to the caller.

Ports □   A port is a queue to which messages may be appended by *Send* operations and from which they may be taken by *Receive* operations. Clusters may create ports for their own use and initially all rights of access belong to the creator. In order to establish communication, clusters may send port capabilities in messages to other clusters. A cluster can use the send and receive operations on a port only if it holds a capability for it. Capabilities grant one of the following access rights:

- *Receive*: only one cluster at a time may have receive rights to a port, allowing it to take messages from the queue.
- *Owner*: only one cluster at a time may own a port; it will inherit receive rights from a terminating cluster; conversely the receiver may inherit ownership. Usually receiver and owner are the same cluster.
- *Send*: many clusters at a time may have send rights to a port and may queue messages there. When there is no cluster left with send or receive rights, a port is removed.

A cluster can only get access to a port created by another cluster by receiving a capability in a message sent by another cluster. Any of the above rights may be conferred by the capability.

Ports and messages are secure in that only the cluster with receive rights can obtain messages sent to a port, only clusters with send rights can send to it, and messages are revealed only to recipient clusters. Ports' capabilities contain random parts and cannot easily be forged or otherwise obtained fraudulently.

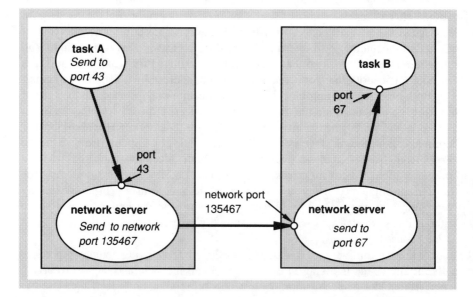

Figure 10.9 Sending a message across the network.

Network communication □ The Mach facilities for communication over a network are provided by *network servers* outside the kernel that support message passing using port capabilities, so that communicating clusters cannot tell whether they are in the same computer or linked by a network.

A network server acts as a local representative for clusters on remote sites. Messages destined for ports with receivers in remote computers are sent to the local network server and clients cannot tell whether a port is local or remote. Figure 10.9 shows the steps involved in sending a message from a cluster in one computer via a pair of network servers to a cluster in another computer.

Network servers communicate with one another via *network ports*. A network port is accessible to network servers in several computers and is addressed by a **network port identifier**. Network servers store mappings from ports used by clusters on the local computer and the corresponding network port identifiers. For example, to send a message from a client to a server:

- The client sends a message to a local port (known to be the server port) and it is received by the network server.
- The network server uses its mappings to translate the local port to the network port identifier of the network server on the server computer. It then sends the message to that network port.
- The destination network server uses its mappings to obtain the local port of the server and sends on the message.

Network servers transmit messages from one to another using datagrams containing an identifier and a timestamp. This allows the recipient to assemble them in order and to detect duplicates and lost messages. Messages in transit are protected by encryption using secret keys known to pairs of network servers.

Network port identifiers are capabilities containing:

64 bits	64 bits	address	address
public unique ID	secret ID	receiver	owner

The public unique identifier is used to locate the destination computer; the secret identifier is a random number and to know the number grants send rights. The receiver address may not be up to date as rights may be transferred. Senders have to locate receivers by various methods, such as asking the previous receiver. For further details of the security measures in Mach see Sansom et al. [1986].

Memory-mapped files □   Mach provides **memory-mapped files** which are files that can be mapped into the virtual address space of a cluster, in a manner similar to the storage system originally adopted for a centralized system in the Multics operating system [Organick 1972] and the IBM System/38 [French et al. 1978]. Users of memory-mapped files can treat file data in the same way as normal memory. This provides a single-level storage system similar to the one described in the section on Apollo Domain; but in Mach the single-level store is available to clusters outside the kernel. In the Mach UNIX implementation, program loading is achieved by memory-mapped files. Mach also provides conventional files and the standard input/output library has been implemented twice – using memory-mapped files and using normal files – with a useful performance gain for memory-mapped files. In the standard input/output library, when a file is opened, the whole file is mapped into the caller's address space, although the semantics of the library remain the same, although the data in write operations are saved in the main memory and are not written to the file until the file is flushed or closed.

We mentioned earlier that, when virtual memory is allocated, an external pager may be chosen and for a memory-mapped file the choice is a file system. The requests from a kernel to an external pager to provide pages for paging in and to receive pages that are paged out are remote procedure calls and are addressed to a port (as usual). Therefore the external pager may be used by any number of kernels that are either local or remote. This enables memory-mapped files to be shared by clusters running in computers distributed throughout a network. Mach provides functions to enable a kernel and an external pager to cooperate in the use of shared files. The data manager can request the kernel to accept new copies of pages or to give it the latest versions of pages and to lock pages. In addition to requesting pages of a memory object and writing them back, the kernel can create memory objects, initialize them and ask for them to be unlocked.

Matchmaker □ Matchmaker was originally developed in the Accent project and is now available with Mach. It is built on top of objects represented by ports and operations invoked by RPC messages, but Matchmaker hides these from the programmer, allowing services to be defined by procedural interfaces. The interface language is similar to those described in Chapter 4, but it allows clients and servers in several different languages to communicate.

The environment provided by Mach and Matchmaker has enabled several interesting applications to be developed. The Flamingo window manager [Smith and Anderson 1986] uses a port to represent a window on a screen and clients perform operations on the window by sending messages to that port. The TABS prototype [Spector et al. 1985] provides operating systems support for distributed transactions on shared abstract data types. It was implemented with a modified version of the Accent kernel with recoverable memory objects.

The Sesame distributed file system was originally implemented for Accent [Rashid 1985]. It provides a uniform distributed name space for all data and services, transparent access to files and authentication of users. Sesame includes a tree-structured directory system mapping hierarchic names either to file identifiers or to port capabilities. The tree-structured directory is partitioned amongst a number of Sesame servers and each directory can be updated at one server at a time. It includes mapping names to port capabilities to enable clients to locate service ports if they satisfy authentication checks.

Performance □ Rashid [1986] reports that the performance is a little better than 4.3BSD UNIX. Operations such as *fork* that are typically expensive in UNIX have been made faster. Mach's *Send* and *Receive* perform better than UNIX pipe reads and writes.

The same paper reports that the UNIX support functions such as the file system and process management are currently being run as kernel tasks, but that they will eventually be achieved through user tasks.

10.9 Apollo Domain

The Apollo Domain system [Leach et al. 1983] was developed by Apollo Computer Incorporated in 1979. It runs in workstations on a token ring network and provides a transparent data access model: local files and remote files stored in other workstations or servers are referenced and accessed by client programs in exactly the same way. Any client program with the appropriate access rights can access any of the files and other data objects in the system because UFIDs are used for naming and accessing both local and remote objects. Apollo Domain also implements a single-level storage model, mapping open files into the virtual address space of client processes, but all access to the single-level store is through the kernel – in contrast to Mach where it is available to user-level programs.

In the server model of XDFS, CFS and Amoeba, remote data is accessed by servers, for example, tasks such as file accesses and directory searches are performed only by servers. Client programs use message passing or RPC to request an action by a server running on a server computer. The Apollo Domain system conforms to the integrated model in which each computer runs system software that includes a file service, a directory service and other data management services supporting transparent access to data. Underlying these services is a data access system based on a paging service that obtains the data required by the services at each workstation from the site where it is stored and, if the client modifies the page, sends the modified page back to its storage site.

Amongst the other systems described in this chapter, the Apollo Domain model is closest to the Sun NFS and Locus systems in that access to remote files is handled entirely within the client machine's operating system, but there are substantial differences; in Sun NFS, access to remote files is only possible if the appropriate remote file store has been pre-mounted, and in both Locus and Sun NFS the data access model is based on the UNIX file access operations, which do not map files into the client's virtual address space. Although Domain is an integrated distributed system, some computers may be allocated server tasks, for example, a computer with large disks may be used to store shared files accessed by clients in many other computers, as is the case with Locus and NFS.

Object storage system □   Here we shall describe the object storage system separately from the single-level storage model, assuming that clients perform explicit read and write operations. The single-level storage system can be thought of as a separate software layer that allows clients to directly address pages in the files that have been mapped into their virtual address spaces, removing the need for explicit reads and writes.

Clients store all permanent data as *objects*. Object identifiers (corresponding to our UFIDs) are unique throughout the network and are constructed by concatenating the ID of the computer on which the object is created with a timestamp from the local clock. Note that, although this ensures that UFIDs are unique, it does not imply a requirement that the object should remain in the computer on which it was created; the UFID is simply an internal name for the object and remains valid throughout the life of the object – it is also used as a hint to the location of the object.

Each object is made up of a sequence of pages, all of which are stored on the disk of the object's *home* computer. Client programs can read from and write to objects a page at a time using a main memory cache in the local computer that holds object pages that have been accessed recently.

When a client program makes a request to read an object page, the page is returned immediately if it is already in the local cache. If the requested page is not in the cache, the page service is invoked to bring it to the local cache. If the object containing the required page is stored locally the page will be transferred from the local disk to the cache. If the object's home computer is remote, then the page is obtained by the local page server making a remote request to the page server on the object's home computer. This request is handled at the object's home computer in the same way as for a local page request, returning the page from the main memory cache if it is there and, failing that, transferring the page from disk to its cache before delivering it to the client machine. This is illustrated in Figure 10.10.

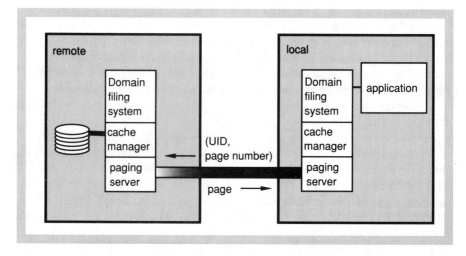

Figure 10.10 Accessing a remote page in Apollo Domain.

When a client program makes a request to write an object page it will be cached in the local computer and if this is the object's home computer it will eventually be written to disk. If the object's home computer is different from the client's local computer, the page is sent to the home computer where it is again stored on disk via the cache in the home computer.

The cache on each computer can contain object pages from three separate sources:

1 pages requested by local client programs and stored on its own disk,
2. pages requested by local client programs and stored on a remote disk,
3. pages requested by remote client programs and stored on its local disk.

If several clients in different hosts are accessing the same object page it may be stored in several caches and the system must ensure that client programs are given the most up to date versions of pages and that old pages are purged from the caches. We shall discuss in a later subsection how the Domain system synchronizes these caches.

The locating service □   We have already described in Section 8.2 how the locating service identifies an object's home computer. We summarize this briefly now. The locating service uses the object's UFID as a hint in finding the home computer. The computer ID in the UFID is the first place to look, but, failing this, a hint file is used. When any program finds the location of an object it can add the information to its hint file. In practice, objects are usually near to their directories and their locations can be determined from the name server. Clients access data via local caches that are filled by the paging server.

Operations on objects □   Objects are implemented as sequences of pages of bytes and also have a number of attributes containing, for example, access control lists, type descriptor, length and a timestamp giving the time of the most recent update. Attributes are stored for use by modules at higher levels. The storage structure is similar to that used to implement the file servers we have described in Chapter 6. Operations include creating, deleting, extending, truncating objects; reading and writing pages; getting and setting attributes.

Client programs requesting to read or write the pages of objects specify the UFID and the page number. If the page in question is not in the local cache, it must be transferred from local or remote disk to the local cache. We discuss here the storage structure that enables the system to locate the pages of objects stored on its local disk.

Each disk contains a file location map with an entry for each object it is currently storing. This map associates the UFIDs of objects with the pages containing their file indexes and their attributes. The file index of an object associates the numbers of its pages with the disk blocks containing the data in the pages. Each page contains, in addition to the data, the UFID and page number of the object page it holds. This redundant information is sufficient to rebuild the file location map and file indexes. Each page also has a timestamp, recording the time that it was most recently updated.

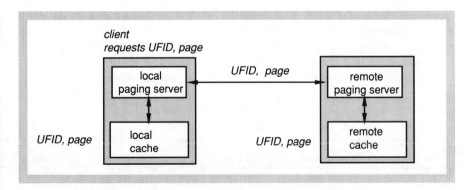

Figure 10.11 The Apollo Domain paging service.

Remote objects □   Each Domain computer runs a *locating service* and a *paging service* that handle remote clients' requests to read or write the pages of objects. If the object's home computer is remote, the locating service must be used to discover the home computer and then the paging service transfers the pages requested to the client computer.

If a client makes a read request for a page of a remote object, the system local to the client makes a request to the paging service in the remote computer, giving as arguments the UFID of the object and the number of the page. This is illustrated in Figure 10.11.

Interprocess communication □   Messages are sent to sockets in the form of unreliable datagrams addressed to (*computer ID, socket ID*) pairs. Each of the basic services, such as the network paging service, has a well-known socket ID that is the same in every computer in the network. Service requests to such services are sent to well-known sockets. Computers offering services listen on reply sockets that can be dynamically allocated and deallocated. Request messages contain the socket ID of the sender, so that servers may use them to address reply messages. The socket mechanism does not provide reliability such as guaranteed delivery of messages and removal of duplicates. Reliability can be built in at a higher level where necessary, using, for example, idempotent operations and stateless servers.

A higher-level facility for IPC is provided in the form of *mailboxes*. A mailbox is an object that is intended to contain a queue of messages. It has a UFID like any other object and messages may be sent to mailboxes for storing and subsequently read from mailboxes.

Mailboxes are intended to be used by servers to receive request messages. A server offering a new service creates a mailbox and registers a name for it together with its UFID in a name server. Clients that know the name can obtain the UFID from the name server and send messages to the mailbox.

Consistency of the object store □   The object storage system gives client programs fast access to distributed data by caching it in the main memory of computers in the network. This is substantially different from replicating data by keeping copies on the disks in a number of servers, but the issue of synchronizing updates of multiple copies is quite similar. As each object page may be cached in several different computers, and may be updated at a number of separate locations, synchronization is required to guarantee consistent updating, and to give programs a consistent view of the current versions of objects.

The object storage system does not itself guarantee consistency or the use of the current version but it detects inconsistencies and provides operations that enable mechanisms at higher levels to build consistency.

Timestamps are the basis upon which the storage system determines when consistency has been violated. Objects have timestamps recording their most recent times of modification. When the paging service in the home computer of an object accepts a request to read or write object pages, it returns the timestamp of the object to the caller. Computers also record object timestamps for the pages in their caches.

A write operation originating at the home computer of an object results in a new version of the page with a new timestamp being written through the local cache. Soon after this, the timestamp of the object containing the page is updated.

When write operations originate from remote computers, the proposed new versions of object pages are sent to the home computers, together with the local idea of the object timestamps. Home computers only accept write requests when they are based on up to date versions of pages. When new versions of pages are accepted by their home computers, they write them to disk through the cache, then return their new timestamps to the originators.

Read operations involving pages of objects whose home computers are remote can result in pages being read from remote computers, in which case the timestamps of objects are returned with their pages. The recipient compares the object timestamps with any others it already holds, enabling it to detect if it has any out-of-date pages in its cache.

To enable consistency in the form of transactions to be built at a higher level, there is an operation to clear out-of-date pages of an object from the cache, and another operation that sends modified pages of an object to its home computer.

Use of locking □   If clients require a stronger form of concurrency control, they may use locks applied to entire objects. The locking mechanism is independent of the single-level storage mechanism. Each computer has a lock database recording all the objects it has locked, whether they be local or remote. It also records all of its local objects that have been locked by other computers. There are several sorts of lock requests available, such as many readers/single writer or intention-to-write locks. Requests to lock and unlock objects are sent to the databases concerned. There is no waiting for locks for they are either accepted or rejected immediately.

When a remote object is locked, the request goes to the database at its home computer and its timestamp is returned and its out-of-date pages are cleared from the local cache. Before a remote object is unlocked, the modified pages are sent back to its home computer.

Naming □   Objects can have textual names that are valid throughout the network. The names of objects are built into hierarchical trees containing files and directories. A naming server translates the text name of an object into its UFID. Leach et al. [1983] report that implementing the naming server directly on top of the single-level object store is less efficient than the usual method for layering services using RPCs.

The DB system in Domain □   Figure 10.12 illustrates our database example under Apollo Domain.

- In the Domain architecture, the DB software is installed in every computer where clients access the database.
- When a client first accesses a database, the DB software submits the UFID of the object holding the database to the Domain filing system. The filing system locates the object and maps it into the address space of the client

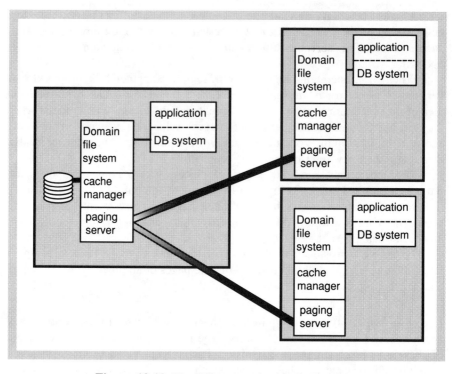

Figure 10.12 The DB system in Apollo Domain.

process, but no pages are transferred to the local cache at this stage.

- When a client makes a request for a record in a page that is not in the local cache, the page is transferred by the paging service to the local cache and then mapped into the client's address space.

- When a client makes a request for a record in a page that is already in the local cache, if the page is already mapped into the client's virtual address space the computation proceeds without any further action. If it is not already mapped, the paging system just has to modify the client's page map to include the cached page.

Servers versus the single-level store □   The authors of the Domain paper compare the use of a single-level store with the use of servers. One important point is that, when data must be protected for security reasons, trusted software must be used at the computer holding the data. In this case, for example when authentication is needed, a server is required to do the task, for if single-level storage is used the program and its data will need to be present in every computer using it.

The Domain team implemented a *registry* consisting of a database of users and access control information, using the object storage system. The internal structure of the registry database is quite complicated and is managed by software running in each computer. The software with the knowledge of the internal structure of the database runs at every node and it is hard to make changes to the structure since new software must be installed at every computer after each change. In the client–server model, this problem would not be so severe.

However there are many applications where the data is simple, for example text files, and where concurrency control is not important. In such cases the single-level storage model has some advantages in terms of simple access to data, caching and local processing of data.

The Apollo Domain system is now being used in over 20 000 workstations [Levine 1987]. The largest Domain network contains over 1800 computers in nine buildings in two states in the USA.

10.10 Summary

The systems described in this chapter have been chosen to illustrate the design principles presented in earlier chapters and to introduce the reader to some recent developments in distributed systems. Most of the systems are experimental – that is, they were built to evaluate the usefulness of a set of system design concepts.

Three of the distributed systems described here have been developed as products or converted into products – Locus, Sun NFS and Apollo Domain. All three are integrated systems in the sense that they aim to provide a single, unified application programming interface that is similar to that of a conventional operating system, but with access to remote files and other resources as well as local ones. A closed system architecture has been used in all three cases, although there is no reason in principle why the same result could not have been achieved with a more open architecture.

Open architectures are based on a system kernel in each computer that supports a minimum set of process management and communication primitives. Other facilities are constructed as services running at the client level, with a well-defined interface to each service. Applications and other client programs import only the interfaces to the services that they need. Services may be added at will, since their addition does not affect the kernel or existing applications. Open architectures are illustrated at the level of system kernels by Mach, Amoeba and Argus and at the level of services by XDFS and CFS. Grapevine, discussed in Chapter 11, is an example of a more specialized service provided in an open system for user authentication and mail delivery.

Two kinds of support for building distributed application programs were illustrated in this chapter. Argus provides a purpose-built language with support for interprocess communication and atomic transactions embedded in the language, while RPC interface languages such as Matchmaker enable distributed programs to be constructed from software components in more than one language, but support for the higher-level operations on data objects needed in distributed applications must be provided in each component.

Some distributed file servers have provided transaction-based operations on individual files and sets of files, but the problems associated with shared distributed objects cannot be considered as fully solved. The Argus system illustrates a promising approach in which the semantics of operations on objects may be used to improve concurrency.

EXERCISES

10.1 Propose an alternative structure to the one in Figure 10.1 for the DB system, assuming that a user-level RPC facility is available in a Locus or NFS-like system. Does your structure eliminate all of the unnecessary inter-process communication that is present in Figure 10.1?

10.2 The goal of distribution transparency requires that users should not be able to tell which computer their program is running on and where their files are stored. To what extent is this goal achieved in existing systems?

10.3 'In the workstation/server model, each computer may be dedicated to a particular task.' Is this the case in practice?

10.4 'Distributed systems are extensible and transparent to the effects of scale.' Discuss this claim with reference to an example of an integrated system and one other example.

10.5 'High reliability and availability can be achieved by replicating data.' Has this been achieved in practice?

10.6 In the integrated model, each computer has a high degree of autonomy. Discuss the advantages and disadvantages resulting from autonomy.

10.7 Discuss with reference to Mach and Amoeba the components that should be included in a lightweight kernel suitable for use as a basis for construction of workstation and server software.

10.8 Discuss with examples the use of capabilities in user space for naming and protection of all objects in a distributed system.

10.9 Consider the effect of the read locks and *I-write* locks used in XDFS when two users are using an interactive program to examine and edit the same database record. Under what conditions can an alteration by one user be committed while the other user is examining the same record? How should the interactive program used by the other user behave? Does XDFS provide sufficient information to enable the program to do so?

10.10 'The provision of servers of persistent objects with their own operations is a solution to the problems of reliability and synchronization of shared data in a distributed system.' Discuss this with reference to Argus, giving examples to illustrate the discussion.

Chapter 11
Grapevine: A Case Study

This chapter is a commentary on the original paper describing the Grapevine system which is reprinted in Appendix 2. The system has been chosen as a case study because it implements many of the design goals discussed in this book in a simple and effective way, in a specific application context. Grapevine provides facilities for electronic mail delivery, name interpretation and user authentication. It is an early example of a distributed service with decentralized control, exhibiting many of the forms of transparency defined and advocated throughout this book.

Because the services that it provides are tailored for a particular set of applications, it was possible to set design goals that simplified the implementation in some areas. For example, a looser consistency criterion for replicated data than that adopted in Chapter 8 was used, enabling the distributed and replicated databases that Grapevine supports to be implemented with only relatively simple support for replication and without atomic transactions.

11.1 Introduction

Appendix 2 is a reprint of a paper that has had a considerable influence in demonstrating the benefits of decentralized data and control in distributed systems. The paper describes the Grapevine distributed mail delivery, object naming and user authentication service developed by Birrell, Levin, Needham and Schroeder at Xerox PARC in1978–80 [Birrell et al. 1982]. The paper gives a very good insight into the detailed design and implementation of a non-trivial distributed system designed to address many of the issues of transparency identified in Chapter 1 (Section 1.3) of this book.

Because the paper goes into some detail in describing the algorithms and structures used in the Grapevine system, the overall structure and behaviour of the system are sometimes difficult to grasp. This chapter is intended to serve as an introduction and a commentary on the paper, outlining Grapevine's main features. The parenthesized section numbers, e.g. (A2.3.5), link the commentary to sections in Appendix 2.

Grapevine was designed for use in the Xerox research computing environment, comprising several hundred single-user workstations and server computers on many local networks. The local networks are Ethernets, linked by gateways and long-distance data links to form an inter-network known as the Xerox Internet (A2.1.1). The gateways and long-distance links that connect the local networks are slow compared with the Ethernet (by a factor of 10^3 for long-distance links) and we shall see that this has an important effect on the need for replicated data. Figure 11.1 shows the Grapevine servers based on a stylized topological diagram of the Xerox Internet given in Schroeder et al. [1984]. The number of servers is related to the size of the user population at the site. Thus the *pa* registry has five servers and two Ethernets linked by a 56 kbaud line. The *wbat* registry has no servers, so clients at that site must obtain their service from a server at another site. Clearinghouse [Oppen and Dalal 1983], a Xerox product that evolved from Grapevine's registration service, is in operation in 200 internetworks, distributed across Japan, North America and Western Europe with about 350 Clearinghouse services in operation [Gealy 1987].

Grapevine provides the message transport and user identification services needed by the computer mail systems operating on the Xerox Internet to deliver messages to their intended recipients. In addition Grapevine's facilities for identifying, authenticating and locating users and other network entities are used in several other network applications in the Internet (A2.1.2).

To provide a computer mail service a *mail interface program* is required in addition to Grapevine. The mail interface program provides interactive facilities for users to compose, send and receive computer mail. The mail interface program is separate from the Grapevine system because it was envisaged that a variety of mail interfaces would be needed to match different user requirements and workstation environments.

Several mail interface programs have been implemented for use with Grapevine (A2.9). The facilities of Grapevine enable a simple mail interface to be constructed very easily. A simple interface would consist of two programs,

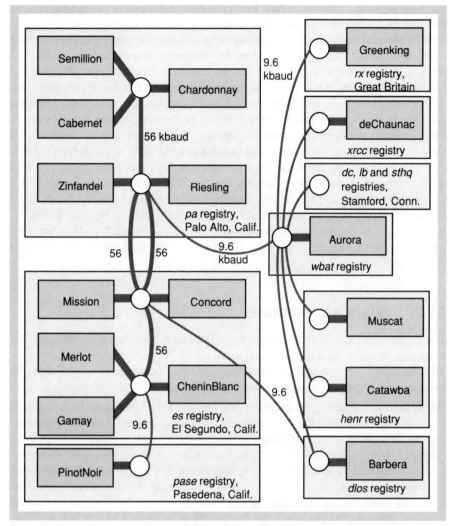

Servers are shown in small grey boxes; circles represent Ethernets. User populations and registries are associated with groups of Ethernets at a single geographical site as shown by the large boxes.

Figure 11.1 The location of Grapevine servers in the Internet.

one for sending mail and the other for receiving it. The mail sending program provides facilities for users to compose the text of a message (e.g. using a conventional text editor) and to list the names of the intended recipients (A2.1.2). When this has been done the sending program uses the Grapevine service function *accept message* (A2.3.2) to request the delivery of the message. The receiving program checks on behalf of users whether there are any messages pending for them (using the *message polling* service function). If there are pending messages, the receiving program uses the *retrieve messages* service function (A2.3.2) to obtain them and display on the workstation screen.

In practice computer mail systems offer a variety of other facilities such as mail distribution lists, confirmation of delivery, automatic forwarding of messages, filing and searching of messages already received, etc. All of these facilities can be provided in a mail interface program, but not all of them will utilize Grapevine facilities. Grapevine provides support for everything concerned with the buffering of messages in mailboxes before receipt and the delivery of messages, but not for the permanent storage of messages already received. A mail interface program may also need to use a general-purpose file server.

For example, to construct an interface program that provides users with shared access to a database of messages (as in a computer-based bulletin board), Grapevine could be used to deliver messages to the bulletin board system, but a file server would be needed to hold the contents of the bulletin boards. Similarly, if users wish to file the computer mail they receive, the interface program they use for receiving mail must use local storage in the workstation or a file server to store them.

11.2 System architecture

The implementation of the services that Grapevine provides is based upon the existence of some specific databases in a set of cooperating server computers. The databases are partitioned according to the locations of users, and the partitions are replicated as appropriate to achieve adequate performance.

Partitioned databases □ A database may be divided or partitioned according to some attribute of the data that it contains. Each partition may then be replicated – that is, it may have representatives stored in several separate servers. An everyday analogy for this can be found in the (book form) telephone directory. Logically, there is a national directory containing entries for all telephone users, partitioned for efficiency into local directories, using the user's address as the basis for partitioning. Replicas of the directories for local areas are made available in each user's home.

Grapevine services □ The distribution and replication of data in Grapevine enable the server computers to share the service workload and are the basis for a guarantee that the failure of any single server computer will not result in the unavailability of the Grapevine services to any client (A2.2 and A2.4.4). The main database used in Grapevine is partitioned to assist its replication. Each partition is replicated only at network locations where it is likely to be used, or where extra copies are essential to ensure reliable operation of the service.

The services that Grapevine provides depend on two databases maintained by the Grapevine system:

1.   a *registration database* containing information about human users, Grapevine servers and their network addresses and services available on the network;

2.   a set of *inboxes*, each of which contains messages awaiting delivery to a
     particular recipient.

Each partition of the registration database is replicated in at least two Grapevine
computers. Inboxes are not replicated, but users (and other recipients of
messages) normally have at least two inboxes and messages can be delivered to
users through any of their inboxes.

The replication of the registration database does not result in an
unacceptable degree of redundancy because the database is partitioned into
geographically-relevant parts called *registries* (an analogy with the name often
used for the record-keeping office in academic and other institutions) and several
copies of each registry are maintained. The allocation of users to registries in
Grapevine is not required to follow any particular rules, but if the allocation is
based on the organizational or geographical structure in which users are located,
the management and updating of the registration database and the handling of
distribution lists is likely to be more efficient.

Each server holds copies of several registries; the copies of a registry are
generally located at the servers on which they are likely to be most frequently
accessed, although network reliability may also be taken into account, is choosing
the locations for copies of a registry. This strategy minimizes communication
delays in a fully-operational system while ensuring that all of the database
partitions are accessible to any client even if the most conveniently-located server
is down (A2.3.4).

Because Grapevine was developed early in the history of distributed
systems, it was designed to stand alone; Grapevine's designers were compelled to
address many issues that might have been handled by other services in a general-
purpose distributed system. With the exception of a simple name server, it
includes within it all of the storage and communication functions that it uses, but
because Grapevine is not a general-purpose distributed system they were able to
take advantage of the characteristics of the intended application domain to
achieve reliability, recoverability and consistency of the distributed data without
incurring all of the overheads associated with general-purpose transaction
mechanisms as described in Sections 7.2–7.3.

11.3 RNames

Names of users, groups of users, servers and other entities in Grapevine are
known as *RNames*. There are several Grapevine service functions that require
one or more RNames to be quoted, as for example in the list of recipients that
accompanies each message submitted for delivery.

For each RName there is an entry in the registration database, containing the
information needed by Grapevine when processing service requests that quote
RNames. The entries are of two types: *individual* and *group*. Individual entries
are used to identify individual users, servers and network hosts. Group entries are
used to identify groups of users and groups of servers.

RNames have two parts, the first part names an individual or group and the second part names a registry. Thus *E.R* is the name of individual *E* in registry *R* (A2.3.3).

In computer mail systems, users must be uniquely identified, so some stylized form of naming is inevitable. RNames are not a user-friendly notion; the two-part name that identifies each user often bears little resemblance to their natural name, and the second part of the name carries an organizational or geographical implication. (In this sense they are reminiscent of the early English custom of naming people by their trade, role in society or the location of their home, from which many of the most common English surnames derive, e.g. Baker, Smith, Mariner, Ford and many others.) To overcome the inconvenience of RNames a directory service should be provided; this was not available in the Xerox environment, but is a part of the proposed CCITT X400 standards for Computer-based Messaging Systems [CCITT 1984]. One of the functions of a directory service is to maintain a database giving the correspondence between users' mail names and their real names and organizational affiliations. When a directory service is available, the mail interface program to Grapevine would use it translate between a user's RName and their full name and affiliation.

In the Grapevine registration database there is a record for each individual containing an *authenticator* (a password), a *connect site* and a list of *inbox sites*. The connect site entry is used only for those database entries that refer to Grapevine servers rather than to users, as described below. The inbox sites are addresses used to contact the message servers assigned to hold pending messages for the individual concerned. The need for multiple inboxes for each individual derives from the reliability requirements that we have already mentioned. The method of using the inbox list when delivering messages is described in Section A2.4.2.

For group entries the registration database records a list of the names of the members of group (which may be individuals or other groups) and two other lists of names concerned with the access permission, defining those individuals who may change the group's membership and those who may join the group (A2.6.1 and A2.6.5). With each of these lists a set of timestamps is stored that are used to ensure that updates are propagated consistently to all of the replicated copies of the registry, as described in Sections A2.6.1 to A2.6.4.

11.4 Software structure

There are three software components in Grapevine: a procedure library called GrapevineUser, a registration server program and message server program. Each is written in the Mesa programming language.

The GrapevineUser package is a library of procedures for use in mail interface programs and other client programs that use the services provided by Grapevine. The procedures in GrapevineUser therefore run in the workstations, a copy is bound in to each client program that uses them, providing a convenient programming interface to Grapevine at a level above that supported by the raw server programs. The use of GrapevineUser by client programs cannot be enforced, since the Internet protocols can be used by client programs to make service requests directly to the Grapevine servers, but this package is the intended programming interface to Grapevine and is very much to be preferred for ease of applications programming to the raw interfaces supported by the servers. GrapevineUser makes the entire set of Grapevine servers look like a single service. A client using the GrapevineUser package need never mention the name or the network address of a particular Grapevine server (A2.3.4). The service functions listed in Section A2.3.2 are those provided at the GrapevineUser level. The provision of a separate user agent that interacts with the message transfer system has been adopted in the CCITT X400 recommendations for message handling [CCITT 1984].

For readers familiar with the programming interfaces provided for input/output in UNIX systems there is a useful analogy; the distinction between the interface supported by the GrapevineUser package and the interface supported directly by the registration and message servers is similar to the distinction between the interface supported by the UNIX Standard Input/Output (STDIO) Library and the UNIX system call interface. In both cases, the purpose of the additional layer of library software is to integrate and simplify the programming interface provided by the primitive functions that constitute the system's lowest-level external interface. The GrapevineUser package provides client programs with an integrated *location transparent* service interface, giving a purely logical view of the services offered and the data stored within the servers.

There are a several Grapevine computers on the Internet. Each Grapevine computer contains a message server process and a registration server process. The two server processes in a server computer operate independently, communicating with each other and with the server processes in other Grapevine computers using Internet protocols. Server computers are located in the Internet according to the work loads at the different sites, but there is a second criterion for the location of servers; they are also located so that the failure of a single link in the Internet will not result in an interruption in the Grapevine service [Schroeder et al. 1984].

11.5 Registration database

We have noted that the registration database is divided into several partitions called registries. Registries are simply convenient groupings of the data that is held in the registration database. We can identify two kinds of registry; *user registries* hold information about users and *system registries* hold information that is needed for the running of the Grapevine system.

User registries are given names that relate to the organizational or geographical affiliations of groups of users. Two-letter registry names are used, derived from place names (i.e. sites of Xerox offices) in the Xerox research environment. These are the names shown in ellipses in Figure 11.2. The use of names longer than two letters would not result in any change to the system structure. Registries contain just two types of entries: *individual entries* and *group entries*. Individual entries record the information about individuals that is required by the Grapevine servers. A group entry consists of a set of RNames and is used to specify the membership of a group. Thus the RNames in a group entry may be the RNames of individual or other groups. The membership for a group is defined to be the individual RNames in the group entry together with the members of the groups referenced by group RNames in the entry.

There are two system registries, called GV (GrapeVine) and MS (Message Server). GV is used solely to hold the names and location details of all registration servers and is replicated everywhere. MS is used solely to hold the names and location details of message servers.

The GV registry contains an individual entry for each registration server in the Internet and a group entry for each registry, and the MS registry contains an individual entry for each message server. Thus *Cabernet.gv* is the registration server process running on the *Cabernet* computer and *Cabernet.ms* is the message server process running on the same machine (A2.3.5). There are also group entries in the GV registry. These are used to define the group of servers at which each registry is replicated. Thus if there are eight replicas of the *pa* registry, located in the servers called Semillon, Cabernet, Zinfandel, Chardonnay, Riesling, Mission, Concorde and Aurora (Figure 11.1), then the RName *pa.gv* refers to a group entry in the GV registry holding those names. Figure 11.2 shows a part of the contents of the GV registry corresponding to the Grapevine configuration of Figure 11.1. The diagram is considerably simplified, omitting many of the data items actually recorded. For full details see Section A2.6 and Figure 3 of Appendix 2.

The *connect site* field of the individual entry for a server process gives its Internet address. The Internet address of a server defines the port address on which it receives service requests. The GrapevineUser package locates the service interface to any server from the registration database by obtaining its connect site address.

Since GV is itself a registry, it must include a group entry named *gv.gv*, giving the names of those servers that contain replicas of the GV registry. Because the GV registry is replicated in every server, the group named *gv.gv* contains the names of all of the Grapevine registration servers in the Xerox Internet.

Registries may be replicated; Grapevine maintains several identical copies of a registry in different servers. The number and locations of replicas of a registry are determined by the system administrator responsible for the registry. When the contents of a registry are modified, the modifications are automatically distributed to all of the replicas, using the mail service. Access requests can be satisfied by reading any copy and updates may be applied to any copy, with the eventual result that all of the copies will be updated. When a registry is updated, the Registration Server takes responsibility for distributing the update to all of the replicated copies. This takes some time. In the meantime, there will be a difference between the replicated copies of a registry, but this is preferable to locking all of the databases until they have been updated. Applications of

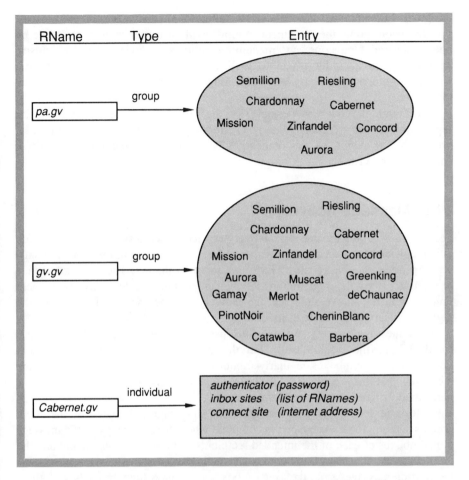

RName	Type	Entry

Figure 11.2 Part of the contents of the GV Registry (simplified).

Grapevine are expected to tolerate the use of out-of-date versions of the registration database during this update process. In the case of interpersonal messaging the timescale on which users expect the changes to take effect is long compared with the typical time to distribute updates.

How are the replicas of registries placed? System registries are replicated in each server computer. The GV registry holds the information required to locate the registration servers and registries; it must be replicated in every server because it serves as the map that enables client programs to locate other registries. The MS registry holds the information required to locate the message servers and is normally treated similarly, although its universal replication is not essential because the GV registry contains the locations of the MS replicas.

Each user registry is replicated in more than one registration server but not in all of the servers. In general, no registration server has replicas of all of the user registries. This distribution of replicas of user registries is required by the design goal of continued service after the failure of any single server.

Decisions about the placement of replicas of each user registry are made by one of several Grapevine system administrators who update the GV registry accordingly. In deciding where to replicate a registry, system administrators would be guided by the efficiency and reliability criteria that we have already mentioned.

Although it would be possible for the Grapevine system to initiate the replication implied by a change to the GV registry automatically, synchronization problems may result, so the replication is triggered manually by the system administrator (A2.8.1).

11.6 Message delivery

Section A2.4 details the message delivery service. The message delivery service is implemented by a set message server processes. In general, there is a message server process running on each Grapevine server computer. The message service is separate from the registration service and communicates only as a client process with it. As we shall see, the delivery service uses the facilities of the registration service to locate users' inboxes.

The message delivery service is also used to deliver housekeeping messages for the Grapevine system itself. For this purpose, each server has an inbox. Servers poll their inboxes regularly (about every 30 seconds) and act upon the messages that they contain. All communication between server processes is performed using the server's inboxes.

Message delivery is in two stages. The first stage is initiated by the client process sending the message and is complete when there is a copy of the message in the inboxes of each of the intended recipients. The second stage is initiated by the recipients when they activate a mail reading program. The program obtains the waiting messages from the user's inbox and displays them or deals with them in whatever manner the user commands.

A client process submitting a message for delivery uses the *accept message* function to pass the message and a list of intended recipients to the Grapevine delivery service. The *accept message* request can be addressed to any message server process. Messages may be sent to more than one recipient and the recipients' inboxes may well be at several different sites, so there would be little to be gained by routing the *accept message* request to any particular server.

The message server receiving the *accept message* request takes responsibility for locating all of the recipients' inboxes and delivering a copy of the message to each. To deliver a message to a recipient's inbox, the message server first obtains the address of the message server holding the recipient's inbox from the registration server. If the inbox is in the same message server the message is appended to it. If the inbox is in a remote message server the message is transmitted to the remote message server's inbox with a *steering list* indicating how it should be handled.

There are two special points to note about inboxes. First, the entries in an inbox are just references to local copies of the messages themselves. One copy of each message sent to a message server is stored on the server's disk. If there are two recipients whose inboxes are on the same server computer, each inbox will contain a reference to the message, but only one copy of the message is stored on the server's disk.

The second point is that the paper states that users may have several inboxes in different server computers (A2.3.4). This is necessary so that the delivery of messages to the user will not be interrupted if the network is severed or a server computer fails, but it causes some difficulty in the presentation. The presentation becomes clearer if we note that the multiple inboxes belonging to an individual normally appear as a unified *virtual mailbox* to client processes of the message service. Thus the *receive messages* function polls all of the user's inboxes and concatenates their contents before delivering them to the user and the *accept message* function chooses one of the inboxes of each recipient and transmits a copy of the message to that inbox only.

A user's inboxes are listed in priority order in the user's registration database entry. The *accept message* function delivers messages to the first (or *primary*) inbox unless it is prevented from doing so by a network or server failure. In the case of such a failure, it uses the next inbox in the list that is accessible to it. A user's inboxes can be located so that one or other of them is accessible to every message server after most network breakages. The sole purpose of multiple inboxes is to provide this backup facility, so that the *accept message* function can be executed in case of system failures, and users continue to receive those messages that have been delivered to the inboxes that are accessible.

Registration server updating □   Updates are not atomic across all of the replicas of a registry (A2.6). Updates are applied initially to a single copy of a registry. Each data value in a registry is timestamped with the date, time and host identifier of the server at which the most recent update was initiated. The server that receives the update uses mail delivery to send a change message to propagate the update to the replicas in other servers. The timestamp functions as a version number and servers use it to merge the updates arriving in change messages with their own copy of the information.

11.7 Summary

Grapevine provides a service that spans an internetwork of naming domains, enabling clients to name and locate objects throughout the internetwork. It has been used for various applications, for example:

- The Alpine file server [Brown et al. 1985] tests membership in access control lists by calling Grapevine to perform membership tests for RNames that name groups.
- Birrell and Nelson [1984] use the Grapevine database for RPC binding. The RPC package maintains two entries in the Grapevine database for each

interface name, a group entry giving a member list and an individual entry giving a connect site. The group entry uses an RName for each interface and the members are the RNames of the server computers that have exported instances of that interface. Each individual entry records the RName of a server computer and its connect site – its internet address.

- Various mail system interface programs were developed, including Laurel [Brotz 1981].

Schroeder et al. [1984] describe their experience of Grapevine in use by a user community whose size was increasing. The increase in size was handled by adding more registries rather than by putting more information in existing registries. There are two problems associated with the increase in scale. Distribution lists are based on users interests rather than on organizational status and, in some cases, the expansion of all of the group entries in a mail distribution list could take 10 minutes for a single mail item. A second problem of scale relates to the increasing size of the internet. Grapevine delivers mail messages by direct connection from the accepting message server to the preferred inbox site. The path taken by a mail message can include up to 11 steps.

Schroeder et al. made suggestions for improvements that were taken as a basis for the Clearinghouse system. Clearinghouse uses a three-level naming hierarchy $L{:}D{:}O$ giving local name, domain name and organization name, enabling a larger user community to be served. Each server holds a selection of $D{:}O$ partitions. Clearinghouse allows an expandable set of named attribute values to be associated with names in the database. It has been used for a range of applications to store arbitrary information about named objects in which the interpretations of attribute names and values are defined by the clients.

EXERCISES

11.1 Discuss the approach taken by Grapevine to each of the modes of transparency in distributed systems identified in Section 1.3.

11.2 Discuss the security of the Grapevine system in the light of the distribution of responsibilities between the GrapevineUser package and the two servers.

11.3 Give a general description of the intended uses of the Grapevine system and its two server components.

11.4 Describe the contents of the registration database and describe how it is partitioned and replicated.

11.5 Outline the progress of a mail message through the stages of message delivery.

Appendix 1
RPC Implementation

In this appendix, we use a program in Modula-2 to explain the details of the implementation of remote procedure calls using processes with shared variables protected by a monitor. The implementation uses *send* and *receive* operations to pass messages between processes in different computers.

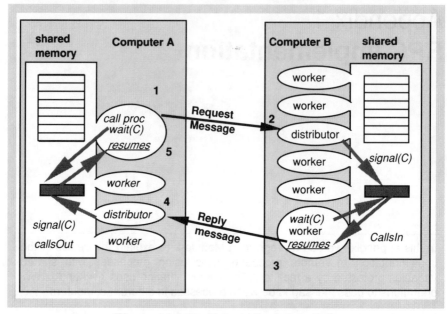

Figure A1.1 The Remote Procedure Call.

In Section 4.8 we described how to implement remote procedure calls in a system with lightweight processes. To summarize: each computer has a single process devoted to receiving and distributing incoming *Request* and *Reply* messages together with a number of worker processes that execute remote procedure calls.

Figure A.1 shows the sequence of events that occurs when a remote procedure call is executed by a server on behalf of a client. The numbers in the diagram correspond to those in the list below:

1. The *client* process (in Computer A) makes an RPC by *send*ing a *Request* message containing the procedure name and arguments to Computer B. It leaves a copy of the message and a condition variable in the *callsOut* set in shared memory and *waits* on the condition variable.
2. The *distributor* process (in Computer B) *receives* this message; puts a copy in the *CallsIn* set in the the memory shared with worker processes; and *signals* to a worker.
3. A *worker* process (in Computer B) resumes execution; picks up a message from the shared memory; interprets the procedure name and arguments; executes the procedure, puts the result and message identifier in a *Reply* message; and *sends* the message to Computer A.
4. The *distributor* process (in Computer A) *receives* the *Reply* message; finds a message with same identifier in the *callsOut* set in shared memory; copies the result to the message in the *callsOut* set; and *signals* on the corresponding condition variable, causing the calling client to resume.

5. *Client* process (in Computer A) resumes and gets the result from the *callsOut* set in shared memory.

Although the figure shows Computer A as client and Computer B as server, both computers could perform either role.

RPC Implementation □   We assume the existence of *send* and *receive* operations for message passing between computers.

The main procedures of this program are:

- *DoCall* and *DoReturn* in the *RemoteCall* monitor that protects the *callsOut* set (shown in Computer A) in Figure A1.1;
- *StartCall* and *EndCall* in the *CallServer* monitor that protects the *callsIn* set (shown in Computer B) in Figure A1.1.

The definition of the *CallServer* and *RemoteCall* monitors is derived from a program given by Lampson in the Mesa programming language at the end of Chapter 14 of Lampson [1981b]. The server checks for duplicate calls by comparing the *messageId* in the *Request* message with the *messageId* of those currently waiting to be executed, but the server does not retain reply messages after sending them to the client, so this is not strictly at-most-once call semantics.

The program consists of the following five modules:

- *message module*: Definition of a record type suitable for a message value, see Section 4.5.1 and Figure 4.10 for an explanation. The *CallOut* record type is also defined in this module. It is designed to be used for the *callsOut* set in the *Remote Call* module and the *callsIn* set in the *CallServer*. A member contains a copy of the message sent and in the *callsOut* set the condition variable that the client is waiting on.
- *distributor module*: Definition of the program of the distributor process that executes a procedure that receives all incoming messages and deals with them. For a *Request* message, makes a remote procedure call, by calling *StartCall* in the *CallServer* monitor. For a result returning in a *Reply* message, it calls *DoReturn* in the *RemoteCall* monitor.
- *set operations*: The two monitors make use of some operations on sets that are defined in the *callset* module, but the implementation is not included here. As Modula-2 does not provide sets of records, they can be represented in terms of other data structures.
- *remote call module*: Definition of the *RemoteCall* monitor that protects the shared variables in the set *CallsOut* in the computer that makes the remote procedure call (Computer A in the figure). This set is used by the client when it calls the procedure *DoCall* and the distributor when it calls *DoReturn*.
- *call server module*: Definition of the *CallServer* monitor that protects the shared variables in the set named *CallsIn*. The distributor adds RPC messages to the set by calling the *StartCall* procedure. The worker processes remove them by calling the *getMessage* procedure.
- *worker module*: Definition of the worker process that takes calls, executes them and sends *Reply* messages.

The sequence of events in Figure A1.1 may now be described in terms of the procedures in the two monitors, once again, the numbers correspond to those in the figure:

1. Execute *DoCall* in client's process in Computer A:

    result := DoCall(destination, procId, arguments):result;

    the action of *DoCall* is:
    (a)   make a new message and fill in the fields;
    (b)   *send* the message to destination (Computer B);
    (c)   add member to *callsOut* set containing a copy of the message and condition variable;
    (d)   *wait* until *signal* is generated by a corresponding *DoReturn*.
2. The message from *DoCall* is *received* by the distributor process in Computer B. The distributor process:
    (a)   recognizes that it is a *Request* message;
    (b)   executes *StartCall(m:Message)*
        • places message in the shared set, *CallsIn* for the worker process;
        • signals to cause a worker process to resume.
3. Worker (in Computer B):
    (a)   calls *getMessage* to get message from *CallsIn*;
    (b)   performs the procedure specified in the message, makes a result message, *m*, setting the message type to *Reply*;
    (c)   does an *EndCall(m)*
        • sends message to Processor 1,
        • if *callsIn* is empty, *wait*; else to (3).
4. Distributor (in Computer A):
    (a)   receives *Reply* message;
    (b)   finds corresponding *Request* message in *CallsOut*, replaces it by result message;
    (c)   *signals* to corresponding original client.
5. Client (waiting in *DoCall*) resumes execution and removes result from *CallsOut*.

(* Modula-2 version of Butler Lampson's Mesa program *)

(* message module *)

```
DEFINITION MODULE Message;
FROM Processes IMPORT SIGNAL;
EXPORT QUALIFIED Message, State, Port,
  FlattenedList, Status, CallOut, send, receive;
CONST MAXWORD = 20;
  MAXARGS = 20;
TYPE
  Port = (p1, p2, p3);
  messageType = (Request, Reply);
  Alpha = ARRAY[1..MAXWORD] OF CHAR;
  FlattenedList =ARRAY[1..MAXARGS] OF
Alpha;
  Message = RECORD
    state: messageType;
    sourceAddress: Port;
    messageId, requestId: CARDINAL;
    procedureId: CARDINAL;
    args: flattenedList;
  END;
  Status = (good, bad);
  CallOut = RECORD
    m:Message;
    received :SIGNAL
  END;

PROCEDURE send(p:Port; m:Message);
PROCEDURE receive( VAR s:Status;
  VAR m:Message);
END Message.
```

(* set operations *)

```
DEFINITION MODULE callset;
FROM Message IMPORT Message, CallOut;
FROM Processes IMPORT SIGNAL;
EXPORT QUALIFIED initset, addset,
  remset, getmember, isempty, Callset;
TYPE
  Callset = (*SET OF*) CallOut;

PROCEDURE initset(VAR s:Callset);
  (* makes argument s = {} *)

PROCEDURE addset(VAR s: Callset;
  m:CallOut);
  (* adds member m to set s *)

PROCEDURE remset(VAR s:Callset;
  m:CallOut;VAR mrem:CallOut);
  (* removes member whose id component
  matches c.m.id, delivers removed member by
  mrem argument *)

PROCEDURE getmember(VAR s:Callset;
  VAR mgot:CallOut);
  (* removes a member  and delivers it*)

PROCEDURE isempty(s:Callset): BOOLEAN;
  (*delivers T if set empty,  F otherwise*)
END callset.
```

(* distributor module *)

```
DEFINITION MODULE Distributor;
FROM Message IMPORT Message, Status,
  messageType, receive;
FROM CallServer IMPORT StartCall;
FROM RemoteCall IMPORT DoReturn;
EXPORT QUALIFIED distribute;
PROCEDURE distribute;
END Distributor.


MODULE Distributor;
PROCEDURE distribute;
VAR m:Message; s:Status;
BEGIN
  WHILE TRUE DO
    receive (s, m);
    IF s = good THEN
      IF m.state = Request THEN
    StartCall(m)
      ELSE DoReturn(m);
      END;
    END;
  END;
END Distribute;

BEGIN
END Distributor.
```

(initialize shared variables
    start workers *)*

```
MODULE initialize;
FROM Distributor IMPORT distribute;
FROM worker IMPORT initProcesses;
FROM CallServer IMPORT CSinit;
FROM RemoteCall IMPORT RCinit;
FROM Processes IMPORT StartProcess;
CONST WSIZE = 1000;

BEGIN
  CSinit;
  RCinit;
  initProcesses;
  StartProcess(distribute, WSIZE);
END initialize.
```

(* RemoteCall monitor: client calls DoCall to make RPC,
distributor calls DoReturn *)

```
DEFINITION MODULE RemoteCall;
FROM Message IMPORT Message, Status,
    Port, flattenedList, CallOut;
FROM Processes IMPORT SIGNAL, WAIT, I
    nit;
FROM callset IMPORT initset, addset,
    remset, Callset;
EXPORT QUALIFIED DoCall, DoReturn,
    RCinit;

PROCEDURE DoCall(destination:Port;
    procedureId:CARDINAL; arguments: F
    lattenedList);

PROCEDURE DoReturn(m:Message);

PROCEDURE RCinit;
END RemoteCall.


MODULE RemoteCall;
VAR callsOut: Callset; (* set of CallOut *)

PROCEDURE ThisMachine():Port;
BEGIN
    (* delivers Port ID for this machine*)
END ThisMachine;

PROCEDURE UniqueId():CARDINAL;
BEGIN
    (* delivers a unique ID *)
END UniqueId;
```

```
PROCEDURE DoCall(destination:Port;
    procedureId:INTEGER;
    arguments:flattenedList):
    flattenedList;
VAR m :Message;
    call, callReturn: CallOut
BEGIN
    m.source := ThisMachine();
    m.requestId := UniqueId();
    m.dest := destination;
    m.procedureId := procedureId;
    m.arguments := arguments;
    m.messageType := Request;
    call.m := m;
    Init(call.received);
    REPEAT
        call.m.messageId:= UniqueId();
        addset(callsOut, call);
        send(destination, m);
        WAIT(call.received);
        remset(callsOut, call, callReturn);
    UNTIL  CallReturn.m.state = Reply;
    remset (call, m, callReturn);
    RETURN callReturn.m;
END DoCall;

PROCEDURE DoReturn(m:Message);
VAR call:Callset;
BEGIN
    remset(callsOut, m, call);
    call.m := m;
    addset(callsOut, call);
    SEND(call.received);
END DoReturn;

PROCEDURE RCinit;
BEGIN
    initset(callsOut);
END RCinit;

BEGIN
END RemoteCall.
```

(* CallServer monitor – (protects callsIn)
distributor process calls StartCall, worker process calls EndCall *)

```
DEFINITION MODULE CallServer;
FROM Message IMPORT Message, CallOut;
FROM Processes IMPORT SIGNAL, SEND,
  WAIT, Init, StartProcess;
FROM callset IMPORT initset, addset,
  remset, getmember, Callset;
FROM RemoteCall IMPORT DoReturn;
EXPORT QUALIFIED StartCall, EndCall,
  getMessage, CSinit;
VAR haveWork :SIGNAL;
PROCEDURE StartCall(m:Message);
PROCEDURE EndCall(m:Message);
PROCEDURE getMessage(VAR m:Message);
PROCEDURE CSinit;
END CallServer.


MODULE CallServer ;
VAR callsIn: Callset;


PROCEDURE StartCall(m:Message);
VAR call, callrem:CallOut;
BEGIN
  call.m := m;
  remset(callsIn, call, callrem);
  IF(callrem.m.requestId = call.m.requestId) THEN
    callrem.m.messageId := m.messageId;
    addset(callsIn, callrem);
  ELSE
    addset(callsIn, m);
    SEND(haveWork);
  END
END StartCall;
```

```
PROCEDURE EndCall(m:Message);
BEGIN
  IF m.messageId # 0 THEN
    send(m.source, m) END;
  IF isempty(callsIn) THEN
    WAIT(haveWork) END;
END EndCall;


PROCEDURE getMessage(VAR m:Message);
VAR call:CallOut;
BEGIN
  getmember(callsIn, call);
  m := call.m;
END getMessage;


PROCEDURE CSinit;
BEGIN
  initset(callsIn);
  Init(haveWork);
END CSinit;
END CallServer.
```

(* worker module *)

```
DEFINITION MODULE worker;
FROM Message IMPORT Message,
  messageType;
FROM CallServer IMPORT getMessage,
EndCall;
FROM Processes IMPORT StartProcess,Init,
  WAIT;
EXPORT QUALIFIED initProcesses;
PROCEDURE initProcesses;
END worker;


MODULE worker;
CONST MAXWORKER = 30;
  (*no. of worker processes *)
  WSIZE = 1000;


PROCEDURE initProcesses;
VAR i:INTEGER;
  m:Message;
BEGIN
  FOR i:= 1 TO MAXWORKER DO
    StartProcess(doWork, WSIZE);
(*concurrent*)
  END
END initProcesses
```

```
PROCEDURE doWork;
VAR i:INTEGER;
  m:Message;
BEGIN
  m.messageId := 0; (*null message*)
  EndCall(m);
  WHILE TRUE DO
    getMessage(m);
    (* args := m.procedureId(args); *)
    m.messageType:= Reply;
    EndCall(m);
  END
END doWork;


BEGIN
  initProcesses;
END worker.
```

Appendix 2
Grapevine: An Exercise in Distributed Computing

Andrew D. Birrell, Roy Levin, Roger M. Needham
and Michael D. Schroeder

Xerox Palo Alto Research Center

Grapevine is a multicomputer system on the Xerox research internet. It provides facilities for the delivery of digital messages such as computer mail; for naming people, machines, and services; for authenticating people and machines; and for locating services on the internet. This paper has two goals: to describe the system itself and to serve as a case study of a real application of distributed computing. Part I describes the set of services provided by Grapevine and how its data and function are divided among computers on the internet. Part II presents in more detail selected aspects of Grapevine that illustrate novel facilities or implementation techniques, or that provide insight into the structure of a distributed system. Part III summarizes the current state of the system and the lessons learned from it so far.

Reprinted from:
Communications of the ACM, Volume 25, Number 1, April 1982,
with the permission of the Association for Computing Machinery.

Part I Description of Grapevine

A2.1 Introduction

Grapevine is a system that provides message delivery, resource location, authentication, and access control services in a computer internet. The implementation of Grapevine is distributed and replicated. By *distributed* we mean that some of the services provided by Grapevine involve the use of multiple computers communicating through an internet; by *replicated* we mean that some of the services are provided equally well by any of several distinct computers. The primary use of Grapevine is delivering computer mail, but Grapevine is used in many other ways as well. The Grapevine project was motivated by our desire to do research into the structure of distributed systems and to provide our community with better computer mail service.

Plans for the system were presented in an earlier paper [Levin and Schroeder 1979]. This paper describes the completed system. The mechanisms discussed below are in service supporting more than 1500 users. Designing and building Grapevine took about three years by a team that averaged two to three persons.

A2.1.1 Environment for Grapevine

Figure A2.1 illustrates the kind of computing environment in which Grapevine was constructed and operates.

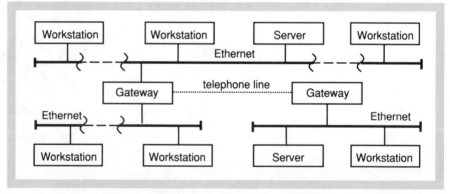

Figure A2.1 An example of a small internet.

A large internet of this style exists within the Xerox Corporation research and development community. This internet extends from coast-to-coast in the USA to Canada, and to England. It contains over 1500 computers on more than 50 local networks.

Most computing is done in personal *workstation* computers [Thacker et al. 1981]; typically each workstation has a modest amount of local disk storage. These workstations may be used at different times for different tasks, although generally each is used only by a single individual. The internet connecting these workstations is a collection of Ethernet local networks [Metcalfe and Boggs 1976], gateways, and long-distance links (typically telephone lines at data rates of 9.6 to 56 kbps). Also connected to the internet are *server* computers that provide shared services to the community, such as file storage or printing.

Protocols already exist for communicating between computers attached to the internet [Shoch 1978]. These protocols provide a uniform means for addressing any computer attached to any local network in order to send individual packets or to establish and use byte streams. The individual packets are typically small (up to 532 bytes), and are sent unreliably (though with high probability of success) with no acknowledgement. The byte stream protocols provide reliable, acknowledged, transmission of unlimited amounts of data [Boggs et al. 1980].

A2.1.2 Services and clients

Our primary consideration when designing and implementing Grapevine was its use as the delivery mechanism for a large, dispersed computer mail system. A computer mail system allows a group of human users to exchange messages of digital text. The sender prepares a message using some sort of text editing facility and names a set of recipients. He then presents the message to a delivery mechanism. The delivery mechanism moves the message from the sender to an internal buffer for each recipient, where it is stored along with other messages for that recipient until he wants to receive them. We call the buffer for a recipient's messages an *inbox*. When ready, the recipient can read and process the messages in his inbox with an appropriate text display program. The recipient names supplied by the sender may identify *distribution lists*: named sets of recipients, each of whom is to receive the message. We feel that computer mail is both an important application of distributed computing and a good test bed for ideas about how to structure distributed systems.

Buffered delivery of a digital message from a sender to one or more recipients is a mechanism that is useful in many contexts: it may be thought of as a general communication protocol, with the distinctive property that the recipient of the data need not be available at the time the sender wishes to transmit the data. Grapevine separates this message delivery function from message creation and interpretation, and makes the delivery function available for a wider range of uses. Grapevine does not interpret the contents of the messages it transports. Interpretation is up to the various message manipulation programs that are software *clients* of Grapevine. A client program implementing a computer mail user interface will interpret messages as interpersonal, textual memos. Other clients might interpret messages as print files, digital audio, software, capabilities, or database updates.

Grapevine also offers *authentication, access control,* and *resource location* services to clients. For example, a document preparation system might use Grapevine's resource location service to find a suitable printing server attached to the internet (and then the message delivery service to transfer a document there for printing) or a file server might use Grapevine's authentication and access control services to decide if a read request for a particular file should be honored.

Grapevine's clients run on various workstations and server computers attached to the internet. Grapevine itself is implemented as programs running on server computers dedicated to Grapevine. A client accesses the services provided by Grapevine through the mediation of a software package running on the client's computer. The Grapevine computers cooperate to provide services that are distributed and replicated.

A2.2 Design goals

We view distributed implementation of Grapevine both as a design goal and as the implementation technique that best meets the other design goals. A primary motivation for the Grapevine project was implementing a useful distributed system in order to understand some system structures that met a real set of requirements. Once we chose message delivery as the functional domain for the project, the following specific design goals played a significant role in determining system structure.

Grapevine makes its services available to many different clients. Thus, it should make no assumptions about message content. Also, the integrity of these services should not in any way depend on correctness of the clients. Though the use of an unsatisfactory client program will affect the service given to its user, it should not affect the service given to others. These two goals help determine the distribution of function between Grapevine and its clients.

Two goals relate to Grapevine's reliability properties. First, a user or client implementor should feel confident that if a message is accepted for delivery then it will either be made available to its intended recipients or returned with an indication of what went wrong. The delivery mechanism should meet this goal in the face of user errors (such as invalid names), client errors (such as protocol violations), server problems (such as disk space congestion or hardware failures), or communication difficulties (such as internet link severance or gateway crashes). Second, failure of a single Grapevine server computer should not mean the unavailability of the Grapevine services to any client.

The typical interval from sending a message to its arrival in a recipient's inbox should be a few minutes at most. The typical interactive delay perceived by a client program when delivering or receiving a message should be a few seconds at most. Since small additions to delivery times are not likely to be noticed by users, it is permissible to improve interactive behaviour at the expense of delivery time.

Grapevine should allow decentralized administration. The users of a widespread internet naturally belong to different organizations. Such activities as admission of users, control of the names by which they are known, and their inclusion in distribution lists should not require an unnatural degree of cooperation and shared conventions among administrations. An administrator should be able to implement his decisions by interacting directly with Grapevine rather than by sending requests to a central agency.

Grapevine should work well in a large size range of user communities. Administrators should be able to implement decentralized decisions to adjust storage and computing resources in convenient increments when the shape, size, or load patterns of the internet change.

Grapevine should provide authentication of senders and recipients, message delivery secure from eavesdropping or content alteration, and control on use and modification of its databases.

A2.3 Overview

A2.3.1 Registration database

Grapevine maintains a *registration database* that maps names to information about the users, machines, services, distribution lists, and access control lists that those names signify. This database is used in controlling the message delivery service; is accessed directly for the resource location, access control, and authentication services; and is used to configure Grapevine itself. Grapevine also makes the values in the database available to clients to apply their own semantics.

There are two types of entries in the registration database: *individual* and *group*. We call the name of an entry in the registration database an *RName*.

A group entry contains a set of RNames of other database entries, as well as additional information that will be discussed later. Groups are a way of naming collections of RNames. The groups form a naming network with no structural constraints. Groups are used primarily as distribution lists: specifying a group RName as a recipient for a message causes that message to be sent to all RNames in that group, and in contained groups. Groups also are used to represent access control lists and collections of like resources.

An individual entry contains an *authenticator* (a password), a list of *inbox sites*, and a *connect site*, as well as additional information that will be discussed later. The inbox site list indicates, in order of preference, the Grapevine computers where the individual's messages may be buffered. The way these multiple inboxes are used is discussed in Section 4.2. The connect site is an internet address for making a connection to the individual. Thus, an individual entry specifies ways of authenticating the identity of and communicating with – by message delivery or internet connection – the named entity. Individuals are used to represent human users and servers, in particular the servers that implement Grapevine. Usually the connect site is used only for individuals that represent servers. Specifying an individual RName (either a human or a server) as a recipient of a message causes the message to be forwarded to and buffered in an inbox for that RName.

A2.3.2 Functions

Following is a list of the functions that Grapevine makes available to its clients. Responses to error conditions are omitted from this description. The first three functions constitute Grapevine's *delivery service*.

Accept message:
[sender, password, recipients, message-body] → ok
    The client presents a message body from the sender for delivery to the recipients. The sender must be RName of an individual and the password must authenticate that individual (see below). The recipients are individual and group RNames. The individuals correspond directly to message recipients while the groups name distribution lists. After Grapevine acknowledges acceptance of the message the client can go about its other business. Grapevine then expands any groups specified as recipients to produce the complete set of individuals that are to receive the message and delivers the message to an inbox for each.

Message polling:
[individual] → {empty, nonempty}
    Message polling is used to determine whether an individual's inboxes contain messages that can be retrieved. We chose not to authenticate this function so it would respond faster and load the Grapevine computers less.

Retrieve messages:
[name, password] → sequence of messages → ok
    The client presents an individual's name and password. If the password authenticates the individual then Grapevine returns all messages from the corresponding inboxes. When the client indicates 'ok', Grapevine erases these messages from those inboxes.

Grapevine's authentication, access control, and resource location services are implemented by the remaining functions. These are called the *registration service*, because they are all based on the registration database.

Authenticate:
[individual, password] → {authenticate, bogus}
    The authentication function allows any client to determine the authenticity of an individual. An individual/password combination is authentic if the password matches the one in the individual's registration database entry.†

Membership:
[name, group] → {in, out}

---

† This password-based authentication scheme is intrinsically weak. Passwords are transmitted over the internet as clear-text and clients of the authentication service see individuals' passwords. It also does not provide two-way authentication: clients cannot authenticate servers. The Grapevine design includes proper encryption-based authentication and security facilities that use Needham and Schroeder's protocols [1978] and the Federal Data Encryption Standard [National Bureau of Standards 1977]. These better facilities, however, are not implemented yet.

Grapevine returns an indication of whether the name is included in the group. Usually the client is interpreting the group as an access control list. There are two forms of the membership function. One indicates direct membership in the named group; the other indicates membership in its closure.

Resource location:

[group] → members

[individual] → connect site

[individual] → ordered list of inbox sites

The first resource location function returns a group's membership set. If the group is interpreted as a distribution list, this function yields the individual recipients of a message sent to the distribution list; if the group is interpreted as the name of some service, this function yields the names of the servers that offer the service. For a group representing a service, combining the first function with the second enables a client to discover the internet addresses of machines offering the service, as described in Section 5. The third function is used for message delivery and retrieval as described in Section 4.

Registration database update and inquiry:

There are various functions for adding and deleting names in the registration database, and for inspecting and changing the associated values.

A2.3.3 Registries

We use a partitioned naming scheme for RNames. The partitions serve as the basis for dividing the administrative responsibility, and for distributing the database among the Grapevine computers. We structure the name space of RNames as a two-level hierarchy. An RName is a character string of the form *F.R* where *R* is a *registry* name and *F* is a name within that registry. Registries can correspond to organizational, geographic, or other arbitrary partitions that exist within the user community. A two-level hierarchy is appropriate for the size and organizational complexity of our user community, but a larger community or one with more organizational diversity would cause us to use a three-level scheme. Using more levels would not be a fundamental change to Grapevine.

A2.3.4 Distribution of function

As indicated earlier, Grapevine is implemented by code that runs in dedicated Grapevine computers, and by code that runs in clients' computers. The code running in a Grapevine computer is partitioned into two parts, called the *registration server* and the *message server*. Although one registration server and one message server cohabit each Grapevine computer, they should be thought of as separate entities. (Message servers and registration servers communicate with one another purely by internet protocols.) Several Grapevine computers are scattered around the internet, their placement being dictated by load and topology. Their registration servers work together to implement the registration service. Their message servers work together to implement the delivery service. As we will see in Sections 4 and 5, message and registration services are each clients of the other.

The registration database is distributed and replicated. Distribution is at the grain of a registry; that is, each registration server contains either entries for all RNames in a registry or no entries for that registry. Typically no registration server contains all registries. Also, each registry is replicated in several different registration servers. Each registration server supports, by publicly available internet protocols, the registration functions described above for names in the registries that it contains. Any server that contains the data for a registry can accept a change to that registry. That server takes the responsibility for propagating the change to the other relevant servers.

Any message server is willing to accept any message for delivery, thus providing a replicated mail submission service. Each message server will accept message polling and retrieval requests for inboxes on that server. An individual may have inboxes on several message servers, thus replicating the delivery path for the individual.

If an increase in Grapevine's capacity is required to meet expanding load, then another Grapevine computer can be added easily without disrupting the operation of existing servers or clients. If usage patterns change, then the distribution of function among the Grapevine computers can be changed for a particular individual, or for an entire registry. As we shall see later this redistribution is facilitated by using the registration database to describe the configuration of Grapevine itself.

The code that runs in clients' machines is called the *GrapevineUser package*. There are several versions of the GrapevineUser package: one for each language or operating environment. Their function and characteristics are sufficiently similar, however, that they may be thought of as a single package. This package has two roles: it implements the internet protocols for communicating with particular Grapevine servers; and it performs the resource location required to choose which server to contact for a particular function, given the data distribution and server availability situation of the moment. GrapevineUser thus makes the multiple Grapevine servers look like a single service. A client using the GrapevineUser package never has to mention the name or internet address of a particular Grapevine server. The GrapevineUser package is not trusted by the rest of Grapevine. Although an incorrect package could affect the services provided to any client that uses it, it cannot affect the use of Grapevine by other clients. The implementation of Grapevine, however, includes engineering decisions based on the known behaviour of the GrapevineUser package, on the assumption that most clients will use it or equivalent packages.

A2.3.5 Examples of how Grapevine works

With Figure A2.2 we consider examples of how Grapevine works. If a user named *P.Q* were using workstation 1 to send a message to *X.Y*, then events would proceed as follows. After the user had prepared the message using a suitable client program, the client program would call the delivery function of the GrapevineUser package on workstation 1.

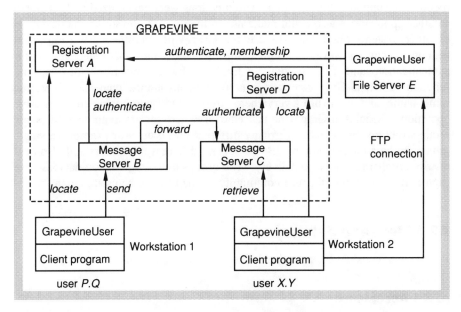

Figure A2.2 Distribution of function.

GrapevineUser would contact some registration server such as *A* and use the Grapevine resource location functions to locate any message server such as *B*; it would then submit the message to *B*. For each recipient, *B* would use the resource location facilities, and suitable registration servers (such as *A*) to determine that recipient's best inbox site. For the recipient *X.Y*, this might be the message server *C*, in which case *B* would forward the message to *C*. *C* would buffer this message locally in the inbox for *X.Y*. If the message had more recipients, the message server *B* might consult other registration servers and forward the message to multiple message servers. If some of the recipients were distribution lists, *B* would use the registration servers to obtain the members of the appropriate groups.

When *X.Y* wishes to use workstation 2 to read his mail, his client program calls the retrieval function of the GrapevineUser package in workstation 2. GrapevineUser uses some registration server (such as *D*) that contains the *Y* registry to locate inbox sites for *X.Y*, then connects to each of these inbox sites to retrieve his messages. Before allowing this retrieval, *C* uses a registration server to authenticate *X.Y*.

If *X.Y* wanted to access a file on the file server *E* through some file transfer program (FTP) the file server might authenticate his identity and check access control lists by communicating with some registration server (such as *A*).

A2.3.6 Choice of functions

The particular facilities provided by Grapevine were chosen because they are required to support computer mail. The functions were generalized and separated so other applications also could make use of them. If they want to, the designers of other systems are invited to use the Grapevine facilities. Two important benefits occur, however, if Grapevine becomes the *only* mechanism for authentication and for grouping individuals by organization, interest, and function. First, if Grapevine performs all authentications, then users have the same name and password everywhere, thus simplifying many administrative operations. Second, if Grapevine is used everywhere for grouping, then the same group structure can be used for many different purposes. For example, a single group can be an access control list for several different file servers and also be a distribution list for message delivery. The groups in the registration database can capture the structure of the user community in one place to be used in many ways.

A2.4 Message delivery

We can now consider the message delivery service in more detail.

A2.4.1 Acceptance

To submit a message for delivery a client must establish an internet connection to a message server; any operational server will do. This resource location step, done by the GrapevineUser package, is described in Section 5. Once such a connection is established, the GrapevineUser package simply translates client procedure calls into the corresponding server protocol actions. If that particular message server crashes or otherwise becomes inaccessible during the message transmission, then the GrapevineUser package locates another message server (if possible) and allows the client to restart the message submission.

The client next presents the RName and password of the sender, a *returnTo* RName, and a list of recipient RNames. The message server authenticates the sender by using the registration service. If the authentication fails, the server refuses to accept the message for delivery. Each recipient RName is then checked to see if it matches an RName in the registration database. All invalid recipient names are reported back to the client. In the infrequent case that no registration server for a registry is accessible, all RNames in that registry are presumed for the time being to be valid. The server constructs a *property list* for the message containing the sender name, returnTo name, recipient list, and a *postmark*. The postmark is a unique identification of the message, and consists of the server's clock reading at the time the message was presented for delivery together with the server's internet address. Next, the client machine presents the *message body* to the server. The server puts the property list and message body in reliable storage, indicates that the message is accepted for delivery, and closes the connection. The client may cancel delivery anytime prior to sending the final packet of the message body, for example, after being informed of invalid recipients.

Only the property list is used to direct delivery. A client might obtain the property values by parsing a text message body and require that the parsed text be syntactically separated as a 'header', but this happens before Grapevine is involved in the delivery. The property list stays with the message body throughout the delivery process and is available to the receiving client. Grapevine guarantees that the recipient names in the property list were used to control the delivery of the message, and that the sender RName and postmark are accurate.

A2.4.2 Transport and buffering

Once a message is accepted for delivery, the client may go about its other business. The message server, however, has more to do. It first determines the complete list of individuals that should receive the message by recursively enumerating groups in the property list. It obtains from the registration service each individual's inbox site list. It chooses a destination message server for each on the basis of the inbox site list ordering and its opinion of the present accessibility of the other message servers. The individual names are accumulated in *steering lists*, one for each message server to which the message should be forwarded and one for local recipients. The message server then forwards the message and appropriate steering list to each of the other servers, and places the messages in the inboxes for local recipients. Upon receiving a forwarded message from another server, the same algorithm is performed using the individuals in the incoming steering list as the recipients, all of which will have local inboxes unless the registration database has changed. The message server stores the property list and body just once on its local disk and places references to the disk object in the individual's inboxes. This sharing of messages that appear in more than one local inbox saves a considerable amount of storage in the server.†

With this delivery algorithm, messages for an individual tend to accumulate at the server that is first on the inbox site list. Duplicate elimination, required because distribution lists can overlap, is achieved while adding the message into the inboxes by being sure never to add a message if that same message, as identified by its postmark, was the one previously added to that inbox. This duplicate elimination mechanism fails under certain unusual circumstances such

---

† As another measure to conserve disk storage, messages from an inbox not emptied within seven days are copied to a file server and the reference in the inbox are changed to point at these archived copies. Archiving is transparent to clients: archive messages are transferred back through the message server when messages from the inbox are retrieved.

as servers crashing or the database changing during the delivery process, but requires less computation than the alternative of sorting the list of recipient individuals.

In some circumstances delivery must be delayed, for example, all of an individual's inbox sites or a registry's registration servers may be inaccessible. In such cases the message is queued for later delivery.

In some circumstances delivery will be impossible: for example, a recipient RName may be removed from the registration database between validation and delivery, or a valid distribution list may contain invalid RNames. Occasionally delivery may not occur within a reasonable time, for example, a network link may be down for several days. In such cases the message server mails a copy of the message to an appropriate RName with a text explanation of what the problem was and who did not get the message. The appropriate RName for this error notification may be the returnTo name recorded in the message's property list or the owner of the distribution list that contained the invalid name, as recorded in a group entry in the registration database. Even this error notification can fail, however, and ultimately such messages end up in a *dead letter* inbox for consideration by a human administrator.

A2.4.3 Retrieval

To retrieve new messages for an individual, a client invokes the GrapevineUser package to determine the internet addresses of all inbox sites for the individual, and to poll each site for new messages by sending it a single *inbox check* packet containing the individual's RName. For each positive response, GrapevineUser connects to the message server and presents the individual's name and password. If these are authentic, then the message server permits the client to inspect waiting messages one at a time, obtaining first the property list and then the body. When a client has safely stored the messages, it may send an acknowledgement to the message server. On receipt of this acknowledgement, the server discards all record of the retrieved messages. Closing the retrieval connection without acknowledgement causes the message server to retain these messages. For the benefit of users who want to inspect new messages when away from their personal workstation, the message server also allows the client to specify that some messages from the inbox be retained and some be discarded.

There is no guarantee that messages will be retrieved in the order they were presented for delivery. Since the inbox is read first-in, first-out and messages tend to accumulate in the first inbox of an individual's inbox site list, however, this order is highly likely to be preserved. The postmark allows clients who care to sort their messages into approximate chronological order. The order is approximate because the postmarks are based on the time as perceived by individual message servers, not on any universal time.

A2.4.4 Use of replication in message delivery

Replication is used to achieve a highly available message delivery service. Any message server can accept any message for delivery. Complete replication of this acceptance function is important because the human user of a computer mail client may be severely inconvenienced if he cannot present a message for delivery when he wants to. He would have to put the message somewhere and remember to present it later. Fortunately, complete replication of the acceptance function is cheap and simple to provide. Message transport and buffering, however, are not completely replicated. Once accepted for delivery, the crash of a single message server can delay delivery of a particular message until the server is operational again, by temporarily trapping the message in a forwarding queue or an inbox.† Allowing multiple inboxes for an individual replicates the delivery path. Unless all servers containing an individual's inbox sites are inaccessible at once, new messages for that individual can get through. We could have replicated messages in several of an individual's inboxes, but the expense and complexity of doing so does not seem to be justified by the extra availability it would provide. If the immediate delivery of a message is important then its failure to arrive is likely to be noticed outside the system; it can be sent again because a delivery path for new messages still exists.

A2.5 The registration database

The registration database is used by Grapevine to name registration servers, message servers, and indeed, registries themselves. This recursive use of the registration database to represent itself results in an implementation that is quite compact.

A2.5.1 Implementing registries

One registry in the database is of particular importance, the registry named GV (for Grapevine). The GV registry is replicated in every registration server; all names of the form *.gv exist in every registration server. The GV registry controls the distribution and replication of the registration database, and allows clients to locate appropriate registration servers for particular RNames.

Each registration server is represented as an individual in the GV registry. The connect site for this individual is the internet address where clients of this registration server can connect to it. (The authenticator and inbox site list in the entry are used also, as we will see later.)

The groups of the GV registry are the registries themselves; *reg* is a registry if and only if there exists a group *reg.gv*. The members of this group are the RNames of the registration servers that contain the registry. The GV registry is

---

† The servers are programmed so that any crash short of a physical disk catastrophe will not lose information. Writing a single page to the disk is used as a primitive atomic action.

represented this way too. Since the GV registry is in every registration server, the membership set for *gv.gv* includes the RNames of all registration servers.

A2.5.2 Message server names

Each message server is represented as an individual in the MS registry (for message servers). The connect site in this entry is the internet address where clients of this message server can connect to it. (The authenticator and inbox site list in the entry are used also, as we will see later.) It is message server RNames that appear in individuals' inbox site lists.

A group in the MS registry, *Maildrop.ms*, contains as members some subset (usually, but not necessarily, all) of the message server RNames. This group is used to find a message server that will accept a message for delivery.

A2.5.3 Resource location

The registration database is used to locate resources. In general, a service is represented as a group in the database; servers are individuals. The members of the group are the RNames of the servers offering the service; the connect sites of the individuals are the internet addresses for the servers. To contact an instance of the service, a client uses the GrapevineUser package to obtain the membership of the group and then to obtain the connect site of each member. The client then may choose among these addresses, for example, on the basis of closeness and availability.

The GrapevineUser package employs such a resource location strategy to find things in the distributed registration database. Assume for a moment that there is a way of getting the internet address of some operational registration server, say *Cabernet.gv*. GrapevineUser can find the internet addresses of those registration servers that contain the entry for RName *f.r* by connecting to *Cabernet.gv* and asking it to produce the membership of *r.gv*. GrapevineUser can pick a particular registration server to use by asking *Cabernet.gv* to produce the connect site for each server in *r.gv* and attempting to make a connection until one responds. If *f.r* is a valid name, then any registration server in *r.gv* has the entry for it. At this point GrapevineUser can extract any needed information from the entry of *f.r*, for example, the inbox site list.

Similarly, GrapevineUser can obtain the internet addresses of message servers that are willing to accept messages for delivery by using this resource location mechanism to locate the servers in the group *MailDrop.ms*. Any available server on this list will do.

In practice, these resource location algorithms are streamlined so that although the general algorithms are very flexible, the commonly occurring cases are handled with acceptable efficiency. For example, a client may assume initially that *any* registration server contains the database entry for a particular name; the registration server will return the requested information or a *name not found* error if this registration server knows the registry, and otherwise will return a *wrong server* error. To obtain a value from the registration database a client can try any registration server; only in the case of a *wrong server* response does the client need to perform the full resource location algorithm.

We are left with the problem of determining the internet address of some registration server in order to get started. Here it is necessary to depend on some more primitive resource location protocol. The appropriate mechanism depends on what primitive facilities are available in the internet. We use two mechanisms. First, on each local network is a primitive *name lookup server*, which can be contacted by a broadcast protocol. The name lookup server contains an infrequently updated database that maps character strings to internet addresses. We arrange for the fixed character string *GrapevineRServer* to be entered in this database and mapped to the internet addresses of some subset of the registration servers in the internet. The GrapevineUser package can get a set of addresses of registration servers using the broadcast name lookup protocol, and send a distinctive packet to each of these addresses. Any accessible registration server will respond to such packets, and the client may then attempt to connect to whichever server responds. Second, we broadcast a distinctive packet on the directly connected local network. Again, any accessible registration server will respond. This second mechanism is used in addition to the first because, when there is a registration server on the local network, the second method gives response faster and allows a client to find a local registration server when the name lookup server is down.

Part II Grapevine as a distributed system

A2.6 Updating the registration database

The choice of methods for managing the distributed registration database was largely determined by the requirement that Grapevine provide highly available, decentralized administrative functions. Administrative functions are performed by changing the registration database. Replication of this database makes high availability of administrative functions possible. An inappropriate choice of the method for ensuring the consistency of copies of the data, however, might limit this potential high availability. In particular, if we demanded that database updates be atomic across all servers, then most servers would have to be accessible before any update could be started. For Grapevine, the nature of the services dependent on the registration data allows a looser definition of consistency that results in higher availability of the update function. Grapevine guarantees only that the copies of a registration database entry eventually will have the same new value following an update to one of them. If all servers containing copies are up and can communicate with one another, convergence will occur within a few minutes at most. While an update is converging, clients may detect inconsistency by reading the value of an entry from several servers.

A2.6.1 Representation

The value for each entry in the registration database is represented mainly as a collection of lists. The membership set of a group is one such list. Each list is represented as two sublists of items, called the *active* sublist and the *deleted* sublist. An item consists of a string and a timestamp. A particular string can appear only once in a list, either in the active or the deleted sublist. A timestamp is a unique identifier whose most significant bits are a time and least significant bits an internet address. The time is that perceived by the server that placed the item in the list; the address is that server's. Because a particular server never includes the same time in two different timestamps, all timestamps from all servers are totally ordered.†

For example, Figure A2.3 presents the complete entry for a group named *LaurelImp↑.pa* from the registration database as it appeared in early April 1981.

Prefix:	*[1-Apr-81 12:46:45, 3#14], type = group, LaurelImp↑.pa*
Remark:	*(stamp=[22-Aug-80 23:42:14, 3#22]) Laurel Team*
Members:	*Birrell.pa Brotz.pa, Horning.pa, Levin.pa, Schroeder.pa*
Stamp-list:	*[23-Aug-80 17:27:45, 3#22], [23-Aug-80 17:42:35, 3#22], [23-Aug-80 19:04:54, 3#22], [23-Aug-80 19:31:01, 3#22], [23-Aug-80 20:50:23, 3#22]*
DelMembers:	*Butterfield.pa*
Stamp-list:	*[25-Mar-81 14:15:12, 3#14]*
Owners:	*Brotz.pa*
Stamp-list:	*[22-Aug-80 23:43:09, 3#14]*
DelOwners:	*none*
Stamp-list:	*null*
Friends:	*LaurelImp↑.pa*
Stamp-list:	*[1-Apr-81 12:46:45, 3#14]*
DelFriends:	*none*
Stamp-list:	*null*

Figure A2.3 A group from the registration database.

There are three such lists in this entry: the membership set labeled *members* and two access control lists labeled *owners* and *friends* (see Section 6.5 for the semantics of these). There are five current members followed by the corresponding five timestamps, and one deleted member followed by the corresponding timestamp. The owners and friends lists each contain one name and no deletions are recorded from either.

---

†   The item timestamps in the active sublist are used to imply the preference order for the inbox site list in an individual's entry; older items are preferred. Thus, deleting then adding a site name moves it to the end of the preference ordering.

A registration database entry also contains a version timestamp. This timestamp, which has the same form as an item timestamp, functions as an entry's version number. Whenever anything in an entry changes the version timestamp increases in value, usually to the maximum of the other timestamps in the entry. When interrogating the database, a client can compare the version timestamp on which it based some cached information with that in the database. If the cached timestamp matches then the client is saved the expense of obtaining the database value again and recomputing the cached information. The version timestamp appears in the prefix line in Figure A2.3.

A2.6.2 Primitive operations

Grapevine uses two primitive operations on the lists in a registration database entry. An *update* operation can add or delete a list item. To add/delete the string *s* to/from a list, any item with the matching string in either of the sublists first is removed. Then a timestamp *t* is produced from the server's internet address and clock. Finally the item (*s, t*) is added to the active/deleted sublist. A *merge* operation combines two versions of a complete list to produce a new list with the most recent information from both. Each string that appears in either version will appear precisely once in the result. Each string will be in the active or deleted sublist of the result according to the largest timestamp value associated with that string in either version. That largest timestamp value also provides the timestamp for the string in the result. Keeping the sublists sorted by string value greatly increases the speed with which the merge can be performed. The update and merge operations are atomic in each particular server.

A2.6.3 Propagation

The administrative interface to Grapevine is provided by client software running in an administrator's computer. To make a change to the data of any registry, a client machine uses the resource location facilities of the GrapevineUser package to find and connect to some registration server that knows about that registry. That registration server performs an update operation on the local copy of an entry. Once this update has been completed the client can go about its other business. The server propagates the change to the replicas of the entry in other servers. The means used to propagate the change is Grapevine's delivery service itself, since it gives a guarantee of delivery and provides buffering when other servers are temporarily inaccessible. As described in Section 5.1, the members of the group that represent a registry are the registration servers that contain a copy of the data for that registry. Thus, if the change is to an entry in the *reg* registry, the accepting server sends a *change message* to the members, other than itself, of the distribution list *reg.gv*. A change message contains the name of the affected entry and the entire new value for the entry. Registration servers poll their inboxes for new messages every 30 seconds. When a change message is received by a server it uses merge operations to combine the entry from the change message with its own copy.

With this propagation algorithm, the same final state eventually prevails everywhere. When a client makes multiple updates to an entry at the same server, a compatible sequence of entry values will occur everywhere, even if the resulting change messages are processed in different orders by different servers. If two administrators perform conflicting updates to the database such as adding and removing the same member of a group, initiating the updates at different servers at nearly the same time, it is hard to predict which one of them will prevail; this appears to be acceptable, since the administrators presumably are not communicating with each other outside the system. Also, since copies will be out of step until the change messages are received and acted upon, clients must be prepared to cope with transient inconsistencies. The algorithms used by clients have to be *convergent* in the sense that an acceptable result will eventually ensue even if different and inconsistent versions of the registration data appear at various stages in a computation. The message delivery algorithms have this property. Similar update propagation techniques have been proposed by others who have encountered situations that do not demand instantaneous consistency [Rothnie et al. 1977, Thomas 1976].

If deleted items were never removed from an entry, continued updates would cause the database to grow. Deleted items are kept in an entry so that out-of-order arrival of change messages involving addition followed by deletion of the same string will not cause the wrong final state. Deleted items also provide a record of recent events for use by human administrators. We declare an upper bound of 14 days upon the clock asynchrony among the registration servers, on message delivery delay, and on administrative hindsight. The Grapevine servers each scan their local database once a day during inactive periods and purge all deleted items older than the bound.

If a change message gets destroyed because of a software bug or equipment failure, there is a danger that a permanent inconsistency will result. Since a few destroyed messages over the life of the system are inevitable, we must provide some way to resynchronize the database. At one point we dealt with this problem by detecting during the merge operation whether the local copy of the entry contained information that was missing from the incoming copy. Missing information caused the server to send the result of the merge in a change message to all servers for the registry. While this 'anti-entropy' mechanism tended to push the database back into a consistent state, the effect was too haphazard to be useful; errors were not corrected until the next change to an entry. Our present plan for handling long-term inconsistencies is for each registration server periodically, say once a night, to compare its copy of the database for a registry with another and to use merges to resolve any inconsistencies that are discovered. The version timestamp in each entry makes this comparison efficient: if two version timestamps are equal then the entries match. Care must be taken that the comparisons span all registration servers for a registry, or else disconnected regions of inconsistency can survive.

A2.6.4 Creating and deleting names

The rule that the latest timestamp wins does not deal adequately with the creation of new names. If two administrators connect to two different registration servers at about the same time and try to create a new database entry with the same name, it is likely that both will succeed. When this database change propagates, the entry with the latest timestamp will prevail. The losing administrator may be very surprised, if he ever finds out. Because the later creation could be trapped in a crashed registration server for some time, an administrator could never be sure that his creation had won. For name creation we want the *earlier* creation to prevail. To achieve this effect, we faced the possibility of having to implement one of the known and substantial algorithms for atomic updates to replicated databases [Gifford 1979a], which seemed excessive, or of working out a way to make all names unique by appending a hidden timestamp, which seemed complex. We instead fell back on observations about the way in which systems of this nature are used. For each registry there is usually some human-level centralization of name creation, if only to deal with questions of suitability of RNames (not having a junior clerk preempt the RName which everyone would associate with the company president). We consider this centralization enough to solve the problem. Note that there is no requirement that a particular *server* be used for name creation: there is no centralization at the machine level.

Deleting names is straightforward. A deleted entry is marked as such and retained in the database with a version timestamp. Further updates to a deleted entry are not allowed. Recreation of a deleted entry is not allowed. Sufficiently old deleted entries are removed from the database by the purging process described in Section 6.3.

A2.6.5 Access controls

An important aspect of system administration is control of who can make which administrative changes. To address this need we associate two access control lists with each group: the *owners list* and the *friends list*. These lists appear in the example entry in Figure A2.3. The interpretation of these access lists is the responsibility of the registration server. For ordinary groups the conventions are as follows: membership in the owners list confers permission to add or remove any group member, owner, or friend; membership in the friends list confers permission to add or remove oneself. The names in the owners and friends lists may themselves be the names of groups. Quite separately, clients of the registration server have freedom to use membership in groups for access control purposes about which the registration server itself knows nothing at all. The owners and friends lists on the groups that represent registries are used to control name creation and deletion within registries; these lists also provide the default access controls on groups whose owners list is empty. While we have spent some time adjusting the specific semantics of the Grapevine access controls, we do not present further details here.

A2.6.6 Other consequences of changes

The registration servers and message servers are normal clients of one another's services, with no special relationship. Registration servers use message server delivery functions and message servers use the registration service to authenticate clients, locate inboxes, etc. This view, however, is not quite complete. If a change is made to the inbox locations of any individual, notice has to be given to all message servers that are removed, so they can redeliver any messages for that individual buffered in local inboxes. Notice is given by the registration server delivering a message to the message servers in question informing them of the change. Correctness requires that the last registration server that changes its copy of the entry emit the message; we achieve this effect by having each registration server emit such a message as the change is made. A message server receiving an inbox removal message simply redelivers all messages in the affected inbox. Redelivery is sufficient to rebuffer the messages in the proper server. In the system as implemented a simplification is made; inbox removal messages are sent to all inbox sites for the affected individual, not just to removed sites. While this may appear to be wasteful, it is most unusual for any site other than the primary one to have anything to redeliver.

Other registration service clients that use the registration database to control resource bindings may also desire notification of changes to certain entries. A general notification facility would require allowing a notification list to be associated with any database entry. Any change to an entry would result in a message being sent to the RNames on its notification list. We have not provided this general facility in the present implementation, but would do so if the system were reimplemented.

A2.7 Finding an inbox site

The structure and distribution of the Grapevine registration database are quite complex, with many indirections. Algorithms for performing actions based on this database should execute reliably in the face of administrative changes to the registration database (including those which cause dynamic reconfiguration of the system) and multiple servers that can crash independently. In their full generality such algorithms are expensive to execute. To counter this, we have adopted a technique of using caches and hints to optimize these algorithms. By *cache* we mean a record of the parameters and results of previous calculations. A cache is useful if accessing it is much faster than repeating the calculation and frequently produces the required value. By *hint* we mean a value that is highly likely to be correct and that is faster to check than to recalculate. To illustrate how caches and hints can work, we describe here in some detail how the message server caches hints about individuals' inbox sites.

The key step in the delivery process is mapping the name of an individual receiving a message to the preferred inbox site. The mapping depends upon the current state of the registration database and the availability of particular message servers. To make this mapping process as efficient as possible, each message server maintains an *inbox site cache* that maps RNames of individuals to a hint for the currently preferred inbox site. Each message server also maintains a *down server list* containing the names of message servers that it believes to be inaccessible at present. A message server is placed on this list when it does not accept connections or fails during a connection. The rules for using the inbox site cache to determine the preferred message server for a recipient *I* are:

1. If an entry for *I* is in the cache and the site indicated for *I* in the cache is not on the down server list, then use that site.
2. Otherwise get the inbox site list for *I* from the registration service; cache and return for use the first site not on the down server list; if the selected site is not first on the list, mark the entry as 'secondary.'

There has to be a rule for removing message servers from the down server list; this happens when the server shows signs of life by responding to a periodic single packet poll.

When a message server is removed from the down server list, the inbox site cache must be brought up to date. Any entry that is marked as 'secondary' and that is not the revived site could be there as a substitute for the revived site; all such entries are removed from the cache. This heuristic removes from the cache a superset of the entries whose preferred inbox site has changed (but not all entries in the cache) and will cause recalculation of the preferred inbox site for those entries the next time they are needed.

We noted earlier that changing an individual's inbox site list may require a message server to redeliver all messages in that individual's inbox, and that this redelivery is triggered by messages from registration servers to the affected message servers. The same changes also can cause site caches to become out of date. Part of this problem is solved by having the inbox redelivery messages also trigger appropriate site cache flushing in the servers that had an affected inbox. Unfortunately any message server potentially has a site cache entry made out of date by the change. Instead of sending a message to *all* message servers, we correct the remaining obsolete caches by providing feedback from one message server to another when incorrect forwarding occurs as a result of an out-of-date cache. Thus, the site cache really does contain hints.

To summarize the cache flushing and redelivery arrangements, then, registration servers remove servers from an inbox site list and send messages to all servers originally on the list. Each responds by removing any entry for the subject individual from its site cache and redelivering any messages found in that individual's inbox. During this redelivery process, the cache entry will naturally be refreshed. Other message servers with out-of-date caches may continue to forward messages here for the subject individual. Upon receiving any message forwarded from another server, then, the target message server repeats the inbox site mapping for each name in the steering list. If the preferred site is indeed this target message server, then the message is added to the corresponding inbox. If not, then the target site does the following:

1. forwards the message according to the new mapping result;
2. sends a cache flush notification for the subject individual back to the server that incorrectly forwarded the message here.

The cache flush notification is a single packet sent unreliably: if it fails to arrive, another one will be provoked in due course. This strategy results in the minimum of cache flush notifications being sent, one to each message server whose cache actually needs attention, sent when the need for attention has become obvious. This mechanism is more economical than the alternative of sending cache flush notifications.gv to all message servers, and even if that were done it would still be necessary to cope with the arrival of messages at old inbox sites.

A2.8 System configuration

As described in Section 5, the configuration of the Grapevine system is controlled by its registration database. Various entries in the database define the servers available to Grapevine and the ways in which the data and functions of Grapevine are distributed among them. We now consider procedures for reconfiguring Grapevine.

A2.8.1 Adding and deleting registry replicas

The set of registration servers that contain some registry is defined by the membership set for the corresponding group in the GV registry. When a change occurs to this membership set, the affected server(s) need to acquire or discard a copy of the registry data. To discover such changes, each registration server simply monitors all change messages for groups in the GV registry, watching for additions or deletions of its own name. A registration server responds to being deleted by discarding the local replica of the registry. With the present implementation, a registration server ignores being added to a registry site list. Responding to a registry addition in the obvious way – by connecting to another registration server for the registry and retrieving the registry data – is not sufficient. Synchronization problems arise that can lead to the failure to send change messages to the added server. Solving these problems may require the use of global locks, but we would prefer a solution more compatible with the looser synchronization philosophy of Grapevine. For the present obtaining a registry replica is triggered manually, after waiting for the updates to the GV registry to propagate and after ensuring that other such reconfigurations are not in progress.

A2.8.2 Creating servers

Installing a new Grapevine computer requires creating a new registration server and a new message server. To create the new registration server named, say, *Zinfandel.gv*, a system administrator first creates that individual (with password) in the registration database, and gives it a connect site that is the internet address of the new computer. Next, *Zinfandel.gv* is added to the membership set of all registries that are to be recorded in this new registration server. To create the new message server named, say *Zinfandel.ms*, the administrator creates that individual with the same connect site, then adds *Zinfandel.ms* to *MailDrop.ms*. Both servers are assigned inbox sites.

Once the database changes have been made, the registration and message servers are started on the new computer. The first task for each is to determine its own name and password so that it may authenticate itself to the other Grapevine servers. A server obtains its name by noting its own internet address, which is always available to a machine, then consulting the database in a different registration server to determine which server is specified to be at that address: the registration server looks for a name in the group *gv.gv*, the message server looks for a name in the group *MailDrop.ms*. Having found its name, the server asks a human operator to type its password; the operator being able to do this correctly is the fundamental source of the server's authority. The server verifies its password by the authentication protocol, again using a registration server that is already in operation, and then records its name and password on its own disk. The new registration server then consults some other registration server to obtain the contents of the GV registry in order to determine which groups in the GV registry contain its name: these specify which registries the new server should contain. It then contacts appropriate other servers to obtain copies of the database for these registries. Because the new server can authenticate itself as an individual in the GV registry, other registration servers are willing to give it entire database entries, including individuals' passwords.

Obtaining the registry replicas for the new registration server suffers from the same synchronization problems as adding a registry replica to an existing server. We solve them the same way, by waiting for the administrative updates to the GV registry to propagate before starting the new computer and avoiding other simultaneous reconfigurations.

A2.8.3 Stopping and restarting servers

Stopping a server is very easy. Grapevine computers can be stopped without disturbing any disk write in progress. The message and registration servers are programmed so that, when interrupted between disk page writes, they can be restarted without losing any permanent information. While a message or registration server is not running, messages for it accumulate in its inboxes in message servers elsewhere, to be read after it restarts.

Whenever a message and registration server restart, each verifies its name and password by consulting other servers, and verifies that its internet address corresponds to the connect site recorded for it in the database; if necessary it changes the connect site recorded in the database. Updating the connect site allows a server to be moved to a new machine just by moving the contents of the disk. After restarting, a registration server acts on all accumulated database change messages before declaring itself open for business.

Using the internet, it is possible, subject to suitable access controls, to load a new software version into a remote running Grapevine computer, stop it, and restart it with the new version.

A2.8.4 Other reconfigurations

One form of reconfiguration of the system requires great care: changing the location of inbox sites for a registration server. Unless special precautions are taken, the registration server may never encounter the change message telling it about a new inbox site, because that message is waiting for it at the new site. A similar problem arises when we change the internet address of a message server that contains a registration server's inbox. Restrictions on where such database changes can be initiated appear to be sufficient to solve these problems, but we have not automated them. Although this resolution of this problem is somewhat inelegant, the problem is not common enough to justify special mechanisms.

Part III Conclusions

A2.9 Present state

The Grapevine system was first made available to a limited number of clients during 1980. At present (Late 1981) it is responsible for most of the mail traffic and distribution lists on the Xerox research internet. There are five dedicated Grapevine computers, each containing a registration server and a message server. The computers are physically distributed among northern and southern California and New York. The registration database contains about 1500 individuals and 500 groups, divided mainly into four major registries; there are two other registries used by nonmail clients of the registration service, plus the GV and MS registries. The total message traffic amounts to some 2500 messages each working day, with an average of four recipients each; the messages average about 500 characters, and are almost exclusively text.

The registration database also is used for authentication and configuration of various file servers, for authentication and access control in connection with maintenance of the basic software and databases that support our internet gateways, and for resource location associated with remote procedure call binding. The registration database is administered almost exclusively by non-technical staff. There are at least three separate computer mail interface programs in use for human-readable mail. Most mail system users add and delete themselves from various distribution lists, removing this tiresome job from administrative staff.

The Grapevine registration and message servers are programmed in Mesa [Mitchell et al. 1979]. They contain some 33 000 lines of custom written code, together with standard packages for run-time support and PUP-level communications. The Grapevine computers are Altos [Thacker et al. 1981] with

128 kbytes of main memory and 5 Mbytes of disk storage. A running Grapevine computer has between 40 and 70 Mesa processes [Lampson and Redell 1980], and can handle 12 simultaneous connections. The peak load of messages handled by a single message server so far exceeds 150 per hour and 1000 messages per day. One server handled 30 000 messages while running for 1000 hours. The maximum number of primary inboxes that have been assigned to a server is 380.

A2.10 Discussion

The fundamental design decision to use a distributed database as the basis for Grapevine's message delivery services has worked out well. The distributed database allowed us to meet the design goals specified in Section 2, and has not generated operational difficulties. The distributed update algorithms that trade atomic update for increased availability have had the desired effect. The temporary inconsistencies do not bother the users or administrators and the ability to continue database changes while the internet is partitioned by failed long-distance links is exercised enough to be appreciated.

In retrospect, our particular implementation of the database for Grapevine was too inflexible. As the use of the system grew, the need for various extensions to the values recorded in individual and group entries has become apparent. Reformatting the existing distributed database to include space for the new values is difficult operationally. In a new implementation we would consider providing facilities for dynamic extension of the value set in each entry. With value set extension, however, we would keep the present update algorithm and its loose consistency guarantees. These guarantees are sufficient for Grapevine's functional domain, and their simplicity and efficiency are compelling. There is a requirement in a message system for some database which allows more flexible descriptions of recipients or distribution lists to be mapped onto message system RNames (such as the white or yellow page services of the telephone system), but in our view that service falls outside of Grapevine's domain. A system which provides more flexibility in this direction is described in Dawes et al. [1981].

Providing all naming semantics by indirection through the registration database has been very powerful. It has allowed us to separate the concept of *naming* a recipient from that of *addressing* the recipient. For example, the fact that a recipient is named *Birrell.pa* says nothing about where his messages should be sent. This is in contrast to many previous message systems. Indirections also provide us with flexibility in configuring the system.

One feature which recurs in descriptions of Grapevine is the concept of a 'group' as a generalization of a distribution list. Our experience with use of the system confirms the utility of use of the single 'group' mechanism for distribution lists, access control lists, services and administrative purposes.

Clients other than computer mail interfaces are beginning to use Grapevine's naming, authentication, and resource location facilities. Their experience suggests that these are an important set of primitives to provide in an internet for constructing other distributed applications. Message transport as a communication protocol for data other than textual messages is a useful addition to our set of communication protocols. The firm separation between Grapevine and its clients was a good decision; it allows us to serve a wide variety of clients and to give useful guarantees to our clients, even if the clients operate in different languages and in different computing environments.

At several points in Grapevine, we have defined and implemented mechanisms of substantial versatility. As a consequence, the algorithms to implement these mechanisms in their full generality are expensive. The techniques of caches and hints are powerful tools that allow us to regain acceptable efficiency without sacrificing 'correct' structure. The technique of adding caches and hints to a general mechanism is preferable to the alternative style of using special case short cut mechanisms whose existence complicates algorithmic invariants.

Grapevine was built partly to demonstrate the assertion that a properly designed replicated system can provide a very robust service. The chance of all replicas being unavailable at the same time seems low. Our experience suggests that unavailability due to hardware failure follows this pattern. No more than one Grapevine computer at a time has ever been down because of a hardware problem. On the other hand, some software bugs do not exhibit this independence. Generally all servers are running the same software version. If a client's action provokes a bug that causes a particular server to fail, then in taking advantage of the service replication that client may cause many servers to fail. A client once provoked a protocol bug when attempting to present a message for delivery. By systematically trying again at each server in *MailDrop.ms*, that client soon crashed all the Grapevine computers. Another widespread failure occurred as a result of a malformed registration database update propagating to all servers for a particular registry. We conclude that it is hard to design a replicated system that is immune from such coordinated software unreliability.

Our experience with Grapevine has reinforced our belief in the value of producing 'real' implementations of systems to test ideas. At several points in the implementation, reality forced us to rethink initial design proposals: for example, the arrangements to ensure long-term consistency of the database in the presence of lost messages. There is no alternative to a substantial user community when investigating how the design performs under heavy load and incremental expansion.

References

Acetta, M., Baron, R., Bolosky, W., Golub, D., Rashid, R., Tevanian, A. and Young, M. 1986. 'Mach: a new kernel foundation for UNIX development', *Proceedings of USENIX 1986 Summer Conference*, pp. 93–112.   (cited on page 287)

Adobe Systems Incorporated 1986. *PostScript Language Reference Manual*, Reading, Mass.: Addison-Wesley.   (cited on page 49)

ANSA 1987. *ANSA Reference Manual Release 0.03 (Draft)*, Alvey Advanced Network Systems Architecture Project, 24 Hills Road, Cambridge CB2 1JP, UK.
(cited on pages 9, 10)

Aspinall, D. 1984. 'CYBA-M', in Chambers [1984], pp. 267–76.   (cited on page 7)

Bach, M.J. 1986. *The Design of the Unix Operating System*, Englewood Cliffs, New Jersey: Prentice-Hall.   (cited on pages 101, 102)

Bacon, J. and Hamilton, K.G. 1988. 'Distributed computing with RPC: the Cambridge approach', *Proc. IFIP Conference on Distributed Computing*, Amsterdam, Oct. 1987: North-Holland, in press.   (cited on pages 86, 203)

Baran, P. 1964. 'On distributed communication networks', *IEEE Trans. on Comm. Syst., vol. CS-12*, pp. 1–9.   (cited on page 229)

Barnes, G.H. et al. 1968. 'The Illiac IV computer', *IEEE Trans. on Computers, vol. C-17, no. 8*, pp. 746 on.   (cited on page 7)

Bayer, R. and McCreight, E. 1972. 'Organization and maintenance of large ordered indexes', *Acta Informatica, vol. 1*, pp. 173–89.   (cited on page 145)

Bayer, R., Graham, R.M. and Seegmuller, G., (editors) 1978. *Operating Systems: an Advanced Course, Lecture Notes in Computer Science, vol. 60*, Springer-Verlag.
(cited on pages 351, 352)

Ben-Ari, M. 1982. *Principles of Concurrent Programming*, Prentice-Hall International.
(cited on pages 100, 108)

Berkeley 1981. *A 4.2BSD Interprocess Communication Primer*, in Unix Software Distribution, University of California at Berkeley.   (cited on page 101)

Bernstein, P.A., Shipman, D.W. and Rothnie, J. B. 1980. 'Concurrency control in a system for distributed databases (SDD-1)', *ACM Trans. on Database Systems, vol. 5, no. 1*, pp. 18–51.   (cited on page 185)

Birrell, A.D. and Needham, R.M. 1980. 'A universal file server', *IEEE Trans. on Software Engineering, vol. SE-6, no. 5*, pp. 450–3.　　　　(cited on pages 119, 278)

Birrell, A.D. and Nelson, B.J. 1984. 'Implementing remote procedure calls', *ACM Trans. on Computer Systems, vol. 2*, pp. 39–59.　　　(cited on pages 85, 87, 106, 253, 311)

Birrell, A.D., Levin, R., Needham, R.M. and Schroeder, M.D. 1982. 'Grapevine: an exercise in distributed computing', *Commun. of the ACM, vol. 25, no. 4*, pp. 260–73.
(cited on pages 11, 33, 302)

Boddington, A. 1988. 'The bug in the machine', *The Guardian*, London, 11 Feb..
(cited on page 232)

Boggs, D.R., Shoch, J.F., Taft, E.A. and Metcalfe, R.M. 1980. 'Pup: an internetwork architecture', *IEEE Trans. on Communications, vol. COM-28, no. 4*, pp. 612–24.
(cited on pages 58, 323)

Bouknight, S., Denenberg, S.A., McIntyre, D.E., Randell, J.M., Sameh, A.H. and Slotnick, D.L. 1981. 'The Illiac IV system', in Siewiorek et al. [1981].
(cited on page 7)

Bourne, S. 1982. *The Unix System*, Reading, Mass.: Addison-Wesley.
(cited on pages 5, 124)

Brinch Hansen, P. 1970. 'The nucleus of a multiprogramming system', *Commun. of the ACM, vol. 13, no. 4*, pp. 238–41.　　　　　　　　　(cited on page viii)

Brotz D.K. 1981. *Laurel Manual*, Technical Report CSL-81-6, Xerox PARC, Palo Alto, Calif.　　　　　　　　　　　　　　　　　　　　　(cited on page 312)

Brown, M.R., Kolling, K. and Taft, E.A. 1985. 'The Alpine file system', *ACM Transactions on Computer Systems, vol. 3, no. 4*, pp. 261–293.
(cited on pages 129, 278, 311)

Brownbridge, D.R., Marshall, L.F. and Randell, B. 1982. 'The Newcastle connection, or UNIXes of the world unite!', *Software – Practice and Experience, vol. 12*, pp. 1147–62.　　　　　　　　　　　　　　　　　　　　(cited on page 31)

Card, S.K., Moran, T.P. and Newell, A. 1983. *The Psychology of Human Computer Interaction*, Lawrence Erlbaum Associates.　　　　　(cited on pages 11, 35)

CCITT 1981. *Character Terminal Access to Public Packet-Switched Data Networks – X.3, X.28, X.29*, International Telecommunications Union, Place des Nations, 1211 Geneva, Switzerland.　　　　　　　　　　　　　　　(cited on page 33)

CCITT 1984. *Draft Recommendations X.MHS (X.400 series) Message Handling Systems*, International Telecommunications Union, Place des Nations, 1211 Geneva, Switzerland.　　　　　　　　　　　　　(cited on pages 34, 61, 306, 307)

CCITT 1985a. *Red Book, vol. VIII, Data Communications Networks, Message handling Systems, Recommendation X.409, Presentation Transfer Syntax and Notation*, International Telecommunications Union, Place des Nations, 1211 Geneva, Switzerland.　　　　　　　　　　　　　　　　　　(cited on page 62)

CCITT 1985b. *Red Book, vol. VIII, Data Communications Networks, Message handling Systems, Recommendation X.410, Remote Operations and Reliable Transfer Server*, International Telecommunications Union, Place des Nations, 1211 Geneva, Switzerland.　　　　　　　　　　　　　　　　　　(cited on page 61)

Ceri, S. and Pelagatti, G., 1985. *Distributed Databases – Principles and Systems*, McGraw-Hill. (cited on pages 177, 185, 201, 204)

Chambers, F.B., Duce, D.A. and Jones, G.P. (editors), 1984. *Distributed Computing*, London: Academic Press. (cited on page 8)

Champine, G.A. 1977. 'Six approaches to distributed databases', *Datamation*, May 1977. (cited on page 18)

Cheriton, D.R. 1984. 'The V kernel: a software base for distributed systems', *IEEE Software, vol. 1 no. 2*, pp. 19–42. (cited on pages 43, 76, 107)

Cheriton, D.R. and Zwaenpoel, W. 1985. 'Distributed process groups in the V kernel', *ACM Trans. on Computer Systems, vol. 3, no. 2*, pp. 77–107. (cited on page 43)

Clark, D.W., Lampson, B.W., McDaniel, G.A., Ornstein, S.M. and Pier, K.A. 1981. *The Dorado: a High-performance Personal Computer*, Technical Report CSL 81-1, Xerox PARC, Palo Alto, Calif. (cited on page 12)

Corbato, F.J., Merwin-Dagget, M. and Daley, R.C. 1962. 'An experimental time-sharing system', *Proc. AFIPS Spring Joint Computer Conference, vol. 21*, pp. 1335–44. (cited on page 5)

Cosserat, D.C. 1974. 'A data model based on the capability protection mechanism', *Proceeedings of the IRIA International Workshop on Protection in Operating Systems*, pp. 35–54. (cited on page 236)

Darlington, J. and Reeves, M.J. 1981. 'Alice: a multiprocessor reduction machine for applicative languages', *Proc. ACM/MIT Conference on Functional languages and Computer Architecture*, Portsmouth, Mass. (cited on page 7)

Date, C.J. 1983. *An Introduction to Database Systems, vol. II*, Reading, Mass.: Addison-Wesley. (cited on page 204)

Davies, D.W. 1981. 'Protection', pp. 211–42 in Lampson et al. [1981]. (cited on page 253)

Dawes, N., Harris, S., Magoon, M., Maveety, S. and Petty, D. 1981. 'The design and service impact of COCOS – an electronic office system', in *Computer Message Systems*, (Ed. R.P. Uhlig) North-Holland, New York. pp. 373–85. (cited on page 345)

Denning, D. 1982. *Cryptography and Data Security*, Reading, Mass.: Addison-Wesley. (cited on page 247)

Dennis, J.B. 1974. 'First version of a dataflow procedure language', *Programming Symposium Proceedings (Colloque sur la Programmation)*, Paris April 9–11. Lecture Notes in Computer Science, no. 19. Springer-Verlag. (cited on page 7)

Digital Equipment Corporation 1987. *Digital Technical Journal*, no. 5, Sept. 1987. (cited on page 2)

DOD 1980. 'DOD standard internet protocol', *ACM Computer Communication Review, vol. 10, no. 4*, pp. 12–51. (cited on page 33)

Donahue, J. 1985. 'Integration mechanisms in Cedar', *Proc. ACM SIGPLAN 85 Symposium on Programming Languages and Environments*. (cited on page 44)

Duce, D.A. (editor) 1984. *Distributed Computing Systems Programme*, London: Peter Peregrinus.   (cited on page 8)

Estrin, D. 1985. 'Non-discretionary controls for inter-organization networks', *Proceedings of the 1985 Symposium on Security and Privacy, IEEE Computer Society Press*, pp. 56–61.   (cited on page 230)

Eswaran, K.P., Gray, J.N., Lorie, R.A. and Traiger, L.L. 1976. 'The notions of consistency and predicate locks in a database system', *Commun. of the ACM, vol. 19, no. 11*, pp. 624–33.   (cited on page 174)

Farber, D.J. and Larson, K.C. 1972. 'The system architecture of the distributed computer system – the communications network', Proc. Symposium on Computer Networks, Polytechnic Institute of Brooklyn.   (cited on page 73)

Farmer, W.D. and Newhall, E.E. 1969. 'An experimental distributed switching system to handle bursty computer traffic', *Proc. ACM Symposium on Problems in Optimization of Data Communication Systems*, ACM, pp. 1–33.   (cited on page 73)

Fitzgerald, R. and Rashid, R.F. 1986. 'The integration of virtual memory management and interprocess communication in Accent', *ACM Transactions on Computer Systems, vol. 4, no. 2*, pp. 147–77.   (cited on page 287)

Frazer, J.G. 1922. *The Golden Bough, A Study in Magic and Religion*, Macmillan, pp. 321–45.   (cited on page 231)

French, R.E., Collins, R.W. and Loen, L.W. 1978. 'System/38 machine storage management', in *IBM System/38 Technical Developments*, IBM General Systems Division, pp. 63–6.   (cited on page 291)

Gealy, M. 1987. 'Experience with Clearinghouse in large internetworks', short abstract in *Report on the Second European SIGOPS Workshop: 'Making Distributed Systems Work'*, ACM Operating Systems Review, vol. 21, no. 1, pp. 53–3.

(cited on page 302)

Gifford, D.K. 1979a. 'Weighted voting for replicated data', in *Proc. 7th Symposium on Operating Systems Principles*, ACM, December 1979, pp. 150–62.

(cited on pages 217, 339)

Gifford, D.K. 1979b. 'Violet: an experimental decentralized system', *ACM Operating Systems Review, vol. 13, no. 5*, (also in Lampson et al. [1981]).   (cited on page 176)

Gifford, D.K., Needham, R.M. and Schroeder, M.D. 1988. 'The Cedar file system', *Commun. of the ACM, vol. 31, no. 3*, pp. 288–98.   (cited on page 121)

Goldberg, A. and Robson, D., 1983. *Smalltalk 80: The Language and its Implementation*, McGraw-Hill.   (cited on page 11)

Graham, G.S. and Denning, P.J. 1972. 'Protection – principles and practice', *Proc. AFIPS Spring Joint Computer Conference*, pp. 417–29.   (cited on page 237)

Gray, J. 1978. 'Notes on database operating systems', in Bayer et al. [1978], pp. 394–481.   (cited on pages 166, 204)

Grosch, H.R.J. 1953. 'High speed arithmetic: the digital computer as a research tool', *J. Optical Society of America, vol. 4, no. 4*, pp. 306–10.   (cited on page 8)

Halsall, F. 1988. *Data Communications and Computer Networks and OSI (2nd Edn)*, Wokingham, England: Addison-Wesley.   (cited on page 60)

Hillis, D. 1985. *The Connection Machine*, Cambridge, Mass.: MIT Press.
(cited on page 7)

Hinden, R., Haverty, J. and Sheltzer, A. 1983. 'The DARPA internet: interconnecting heterogeneous networks with gateways', *IEEE Computer, vol. 16, no. 9*, pp. 38–49.
(cited on page 58)

Hoare, C.A.R. 1974. 'Monitors: an operating system structuring concept', *Commun. of the ACM, vol. 17, no. 10*, pp. 549–57.   (cited on page 108)

Hoare, C.A.R. 1978. 'Communicating sequential processes', *Commun. of the ACM, vol. 21*, pp. 667–77.   (cited on page 40)

Hockney, R.W and Jesshope, C.R. 1986. *Parallel Computers*, Bristol: Adam Hilger.
(cited on page 7)

Hopper, A. and Needham, R.M. 1988. 'The Cambridge Fast Ring networking system', *IEEE Trans. on Computers*, in press.   (cited on page 72)

Hopper, A., Temple, S. and Williamson, R.C. 1986. *Local Area Network Design*, Wokingham, England: Addison-Wesley.   (cited on page 72)

IEEE 1983. Special issue on local area networks, *IEEE Journal on Selected Areas in Communications, SAC vol. 1, no. 5*.   (cited on page 58)

IEEE 1985a. *Local Area Network – CSMA/CD Access Method and Physical Layer Specifications*, American National Standard, ANSI/IEEE Std. 802.3.
(cited on pages 58, 68)

IEEE 1985b. *Local Area Network – Token Ring Access Method and Physical Layer Specifications*, American National Standard, ANSI/IEEE Std. 802.5.
(cited on pages 58, 73)

IEEE 1985c. *Local Area Network – Logical Link Control*, American National Standard, ANSI/IEEE Std. 802.2.   (cited on page 58)

IEEE 1985d. *Draft IEEE Standard 802.1 (Part A): Overview and Architecture*, IEEE Computer Society.   (cited on page 58)

Iliffe, J.K. 1968. *Basic Machine Principles*, London: Macdonald and New York: American Elsevier.   (cited on page 236)

Iliffe, J.K. 1982. *Advanced Computer Design*, Prentice-Hall International.
(cited on page 7)

INMOS Ltd 1983. *Occam Programming Manual*, Prentice-Hall International.
(cited on page 40)

Israel, J.E., Mitchell, J.G. and Sturgis, H.E. 1978. 'Separating data from function in a distributed file system', in *Operating Systems: Theory and Practice*, (Ed. Lanciaux, D.), North-Holland, Amsterdam, pp. 17–27. (cited on pages 179, 204, 206, 275, 277)

Johnson, R. and Wick, J. 1982. 'An overview of the Mesa processor architecture', *Proc. Symposium on Architectural Support for Programming Languages and Operating Systems* (April 1982), in SIGPLAN Notices, vol. 17, no. 4.   (cited on page 11)

Jones, A.K. 1978. 'Protection mechanisms and enforcement of security policies', in Bayer et al. [1978], pp. 228–50.   (cited on page 229)

Jones, M.B. and Rashid, R.T. 1986. 'Mach and Matchmaker: kernel and language support for object-oriented distributed systems', *ACM Sigplan Notices, vol. 21, no. 11*, pp. 67–77.   (cited on pages 92, 287)

Jones, A.K. et al. 1977. 'Software management of CM*: a multiple microprocessor', *Proc. AFIPS National Computer Conference*,   (cited on page 7)

Kahn, D. 1967. *The Codebreakers*, New York: MacMillan.   (cited on page 247)

Kahn, D. 1980. 'Cryptology goes public', *IEEE Commun. Mag., vol. 18*, pp.19–28.
                                                                       (cited on page 230)

Knuth, D.E. 1973. *The Art of Computer Programming,* vol. 3, *Sorting and Searching*, Reading, Mass.: Addison-Wesley.   (cited on page 145)

Kronenberg, N.P., Lercy, H.M. and Strecht, W.D. 1985. 'VAX clusters: a closely-coupled distributed system', *ACM Operating Systems Review, vol. 19, no. 5*, p. 1.
                                                                       (cited on page 2)

Kung, H.T. and Robinson, J.T. 1981. 'Optimistic methods for concurrency control', *ACM Trans. on Database Systems, vol. 6, no. 2*, pp. 213–26.   (cited on page 181)

Lamport, L. 1978. 'Time, clocks and the ordering of events in a distributed system', *Commun. of the ACM, vol. 21, no. 7*, pp. 558–65.   (cited on page 201)

Lampson, B.W. 1969. 'Dynamic protection structures', *Proc. AFIPS Fall Joint Computing Conference*, pp. 27–38.   (cited on page 237)

Lampson, B.W. 1981a. 'Remote procedure calls', in Lampson et al. [1981], pp. 365–8.
                                                                       (cited on page 108)

Lampson, B.W. 1981b. 'Atomic transactions', in Lampson et al. [1981], pp. 254–9.
                                                                       (cited on pages 152, 166, 315)

Lampson, B.W. 1981c. 'Ethernet, Pup and Violet', in Lampson et al. [1981], pp. 265–73.
                                                                       (cited on pages 13, 176, 275)

Lampson, B.W. and Pier, K.A. 1980. 'A processor for a high-performance personal computer', *Proc. 7th IEEE Symposium on Computer Architecture*, pp.146–60.
                                                                       (cited on page 12)

Lampson, B.W. and Redell, D. 1980. 'Experience with processes and monitors in Mesa', *Commun. of the ACM, vol. 23, no. 2*, pp. 105–17.   (cited on pages 40, 344)

Lampson, B.W. and Sproull, R.F. 1979. 'An open operating system for a single-user machine', *Proc. 7th Symp. on Operating Systems Principles*, pp. 98–106.
                                                                       (cited on page 40)

Lampson, B.W., Paul, M. and Siegert, H.J. (editors) 1981. *Distributed systems – Architecture and Implementation*, Springer-Verlag (and second edition 1983).
                                                                       (cited on page 2)

Leach, P.J., Levine, P. H., Douros, B.P., Hamilton, J.A., Nelson, D.L. and Stumpf, B.L. 1983. 'The architecture of an integrated local network', *IEEE Journal on Selected Areas in Communications, vol. SAC-1, no. 5*, pp. 842–56.
                                                                       (cited on pages 127, 203, 293, 297)

LeLann, G. 1981. 'Motivations, objectives and characterization of distributed systems', in Lampson et al. [1981], pp. 1–9. (cited on page 9)

Leslie, I., Needham, R.M., Burren, J., Cooper, C. and Adams, C. 1984. 'The architecture of the Universe network', *ACM Computer Communication Review, vol. 14, no. 2.* (cited on page 57)

Levin, R. and Schroeder, M.D. 1979. 'Transport of electronic messages through a network', *Teleinformatics 79,* Amsterdam, North-Holland, pp. 29–33. (cited on page 322)

Levine, P. 1987. 'The Domain system', short abstract in *Report on the Second European SIGOPS Workshop: 'Making Distributed Systems Work'*, ACM Operating Systems Review, vol. 21, no. 1, p. 54. (cited on page 299)

Lindsay, B., Haas, L.M., Mohan, C., Wilms, P. and Yost, R.A. 1983. 'Computation and communication in R*: a distributed database manager', in *Proceedings of the 9th ACM Symposium on Operating System Principles* (Bretton Woods, NH, October 11–13), ACM SIGOPS Operating Systems Review, vol. 17, no. 5, pp. 1–2. (cited on page 192)

Liskov, B. 1979. 'Primitives for distributed computing', *Proc. 7th ACM Symposium on Operating System Principles*, Pacific Grove, Calif., pp. 33–43. (cited on page 269)

Liskov, B. and Guttag, J. 1986. *Abstraction and Specification in Program Development*, The MIT Press, McGraw-Hill. (cited on page 87)

Liskov, B. and Scheifler, R.W. 1982. 'Guardians and actions: linguistic support for robust, distributed programs', *ACM Trans. Programm. Lang. and Systems vol. 5, no. 3*, pp. 381–404. (cited on pages 89, 269)

Liskov, B., Moss, E., Schaffert, C., Sheifler, R. and Snyder, A. 1981. *CLU Reference Manual*, Lecture Notes in Computer Science 114, Springer-Verlag. (cited on pages 87, 270)

Loveluck, J.M. 1982. 'The PERQ workstation and the distributed computing environment', *ICL Technical Journal*, November 1982. (cited on page 12)

McKusick, M.K., Joy, W.N., Leffler, S.J. and Fabry, R.S. 1984. 'A fast file system for UNIX', *ACM Trans. on Comp. Systems, vol. 2, no. 3*, pp. 181–97. (cited on pages 147, 148)

Madnick, S.E. and Alsop, J.W. 1969. 'A modular approach to file system design', *Proc. AFIPS Spring Joint Computer Conference, vol. 34*, pp. 1–14. (cited on page 116)

Mason, W.A. 1987. 'Distributed processing: the state of the art', *Byte, vol. 12, no. 13, (November 1987)*, pp. 291–315. (cited on page 287)

Metcalfe, R.M. and Boggs, D. R. 1976. 'Ethernet: distributed packet switching for local computer networks', *Commun. of the ACM, vol. 19*, pp. 395–403 (also in Siewiorek et al. [1981]). (cited on pages 67, 323)

Mitchell, J.G. 1982. 'File servers for local area networks', Lecture notes for course on Local Area Networks, University of Kent, Canterbury, England, pp. 83–114. (cited on pages 121, 179)

Mitchell, J.G. 1985. 'File servers', in *Local Area Networks: an Advanced Course*, Lecture Notes in Computer Science, no. 184, Springer-Verlag, pp. 221–59.
(cited on pages 13, 129, 275, 278)

Mitchell, J.G. and Dion, J., 1982. 'A comparison of two network-based file servers', *Commun. of the ACM, vol. 25, no. 4*, pp. 233–45.
(cited on pages 11, 13, 275, 278, 281, 282)

Mitchell, J.G., Maybury, W. and Sweet, R. 1979. *Mesa Language Reference Manual (Version 5.0)*, Technical Report CSL-79-3, Xerox PARC, Palo Alto, Calif.
(cited on pages 11, 85, 344)

Moss, J.E.B. 1981. *Nested Transactions: An Approach to Reliable Distributed Computing*, Technical Report MIT/LCS/TR-260, Lab. for Computer Science, MIT.
(cited on page 263)

Mueller, E., Moore, J. and Popek, J. 1983. 'A nested transaction system for LOCUS', *Proceedings of the Ninth Symposium on Operating System Principles*, pp. 71–89.
(cited on page 262)

Mullender, S.J. 1985. *Principles of Distributed Operating System Design*, Mathematisch Centrum, Amsterdam (Doctoral Thesis).   (cited on pages 2, 127, 166, 184, 283)

Mullender, S.J. and Tannenbaum, A.S. 1985. 'A distributed file server based on optimistic concurrency control', *ACM Operating Systems Review, vol. 19, no. 5*, pp. 51–62 (Proc. of 10th Symposium on Operating Systems, Orcas Island, Washington USA, Dec. 1985).   (cited on pages 76, 169, 283)

Mullender, S.J. and Tanenbaum, A.S. 1986. 'The design of a capability-based distributed operating system', *Computer Journal, vol. 29, no. 4*, pp. 289–300.
(cited on pages 29, 245, 283)

National Bureau of Standards (United States) 1977. Data encryption standard, *Federal Information Processing Standards No. 46*, Washington DC.
(cited on pages 248, 326)

Needham, R.M. 1985. 'Protection', in *Local Area Networks: an Advanced Course*, Lecture Notes in Computer Science, no. 184, Springer-Verlag, pp. 261–81.
(cited on page 228)

Needham, R.M. and Herbert, A.J. 1982. *The Cambridge Distributed Computing System*, Wokingham, England: Addison-Wesley.
(cited on pages 2, 28, 127, 143, 242, 278, 282)

Needham, R.M. and Schroeder, M.D. 1978. 'Using encryption for authentication in large networks of computers', *Commun. of the ACM, vol. 21*, pp. 993–9.
(cited on pages 249, 326)

Oppen, D.C. and Dalal, Y.K. 1983. 'The Clearinghouse: a decentralized agent for locating named objects in a distributed environment', *ACM Trans. on Office Systems, vol. 1*, pp. 230–53.   (cited on page 302)

Organick, E.I. 1972. *The MULTICS System: an Examination of its Structure*, Cambridge, Mass.: MIT Press.   (cited on pages 5, 291)

Peterson, J.L. and Silberschatz, A. 1985. *Operating System Concepts*, Addison-Wesley.
(cited on page 41)

Pfaff, G.E. (editor), 1985. *User Interface Management Systems*, Eurographics Seminars, Springer-Verlag.   (cited on page 35)

Pierce, J. 1972. 'How far can data loops go?', *IEEE Trans. on Communications, vol. COM-20*, pp. 527–30.   (cited on page 73)

Popek, G. and Walker, B. (editors) 1985. *The LOCUS Distributed System Architecture*, Cambridge, Mass.: MIT Press.   (cited on pages 2, 31, 203, 240, 262)

Popek, G., Walker, B., Chow, J., Edwards, D., Kline, C., Rudison, G. and Thiel, G. 1981. 'LOCUS: a network transparent, high reliability distributed system', *Proceedings of the Eighth SOSP*, Pacific Grove, California, pp. 169–77.   (cited on page 262)

Postel, J.B. 1980. 'Internetwork protocol approaches', *IEEE Trans. on Communication, vol. COM-28, no. 5*, pp. 604–11.   (cited on page 58)

Rashid, R.F. 1985. 'Network operating systems', in *Local Area Networks: an Advanced Course*, Lecture Notes in Computer Science, no. 184, Springer-Verlag, pp. 314–40.
                                                         (cited on pages 242, 287, 292)

Rashid, R.F. 1986. 'From RIG to Accent to Mach: the evolution of a network operating system', *Proceedings of the ACM/IEEE Computer Society Fall Joint Conference*, ACM, Nov. 1986.   (cited on pages 44, 287, 292)

Rashid, R. and Robertson, G. 1981. 'Accent: a communications oriented network operating system kernel', *ACM Operating Systems Review, vol. 15, no. 5*, pp. 64–75.
                                                              (cited on pages 44, 287)

Reddaway, S.F. 1973. 'DAP – a distributed array processor', ACM Symposium on Computer Architecture, December 1973.   (cited on page 7)

Reed, D.P. 1983. 'Implementing atomic actions on decentralized data', *ACM Trans. on Computer Systems, vol. 1, no.1*, pp. 3–23.   (cited on pages 166, 169, 185, 207)

Richards, M., Aylward, A.R., Bond, P., Evans, R. and Knight, B. 1979. 'TRIPOS – a portable operating system for minicomputers', *Software – Practice and Experience, vol. 9*, pp. 513–26.   (cited on pages 28, 279)

Ritchie, D.M. and Thompson, K. 1974. 'The UNIX time-sharing system', *Commun. of the ACM, vol. 17, no. 7*, pp. 365–75.   (cited on page 100)

Rivest, R.L., Shamir, A. and Adelman, L. 1978. 'A method of obtaining digital signatures and public key cryptosystems', *Comm. ACM, vol. 21, no. 2*, pp. 120–26.
                                                                   (cited on page 252)

Roberts, W.T. 1985. *A comparison of two remote procedure call mechanisms*, Computer Science Report, Queen Mary College, London.   (cited on page 106)

Rothnie, J.B., Goodman, N. and Bernstein, P.A. 1977. *The redundant update methodology, of SDD-1: a system for distributed databases (the fully redundant case)*, Computer Corporation of America.   (cited on page 338)

Rozier, M. and Martins, L. 1987. 'The Chorus distributed operating system: some design issues', in *Distributed Operating Systems. Theory and Practice*, (ed. Y. Paker et al.), NATO ASI Series, vol. F28, Springer-Verlag, pp. 261–87.   (cited on page 46)

Salmon, R. and Slater, M., 1987. *Computer Graphics Systems and Concepts*, Wokingham, England: Addison-Wesley.   (cited on page 35)

Saltzer, J.H. and Schroeder, M.D. 1975. 'The protection of information in computer systems', *Proceedings of the IEEE, vol. 63, no. 9*, pp. 1278–1308.
(cited on page 229)

Saltzer, J.H., Reed, D.P. and Clarke, D. 1984. 'End-to-end arguments in system design', *ACM Trans. on Computer Systems, vol. 2, no. 1*, pp. 3–21.   (cited on page 64)

Sansom, R.D., Julin, D.P. and Rashid, R.F. 1986. *Extending a capability based system into a network environment*, Technical Report CMU-CS-86-116, Carnegie-Mellon University.   (cited on pages 245, 253, 291)

Scheifler, R.W. and Gettys, J. 1986. 'The X window system', *ACM Transactions on Graphics, vol. 5, no. 2*, pp. 76–109.   (cited on pages 37, 49)

Schroeder, M.D., Birrell, A.D. and Needham, R.M. 1984. 'Experience with Grapevine: the growth of a distributed system', *ACM Trans. on Computer Systems, vol. 2, no. 1*, pp. 3–23.   (cited on pages 302, 307, 312)

Selfridge, O. and Schwartz, J. 1980. 'Telephone technology and privacy', *Technology Review, vol. 82*, pp. 56–65.   (cited on page 230)

Sequent Computer Systems 1986. *Balance Technical Summary*, MAN-0 110-00, Sequent Computer Systems, Beaverton, Oregon.   (cited on page 7)

Shapiro, M. 1986a. 'SOS: a distributed object-oriented operating system', short abstract in *Report on the Second European SIGOPS Workshop: 'Making Distributed Systems Work'*, ACM Operating Systems Review, vol. 21, no. 1, p. 60.   (cited on page 46)

Shapiro, M. 1986b. 'Structure and encapsulation in distributed systems: the proxy principle', *in Proc. 6th IEEE Intl. Conf. on Distributed Computing Systems*, Cambridge, Mass., May 1986, pp.198–204.   (cited on page 46)

Shoch, J.F. 1978. 'Internetwork naming, addressing and routing', *in Proc. 17th IEEE Computer Society International Conf., September 1978*, pp. 72–79.
(cited on page 323)

Shoch, J.F. and Hupp, J.A. 1980. 'Measured performance of an Ethernet local network', *Commun. of the ACM, vol. 23, no. 12*, pp. 711–21.   (cited on page 70)

Shoch, J.F. and Hupp, J.A. 1982. 'The 'Worm' programs – early experience with a distributed computation', *Commun. of the ACM, vol. 25, no. 3*, pp. 172–80.
(cited on page 234)

Shoch, J.F., Dalal, Y.K. and Redell, D.D. 1982. 'The evolution of the Ethernet local area network', *IEEE Computer, vol. 15, no. 8*, pp. 10–28.   (cited on page 67)

Shoch, J.F., Dalal, Y.K., Redell, D.D. and Crane, R.C. 1985. 'The Ethernet', in *Local Area Networks: an Advanced Course*, Lecture Notes in Computer Science, no. 184, Springer-Verlag, pp. 1–33.   (cited on page 67)

Siewiorek, D., Bell, C.G. and Newell, A. (editors) 1981. *Computer Structures: Readings and Examples* (2nd Edition), New York: McGraw-Hill.   (cited on pages 8, 236)

Smith, D.C., Irby, C., Kimball, R. and Verplank, B. 1982. 'Designing the Star user interface', *Byte, April 1982*, pp. 242–82.   (cited on page 11)

Smith, E.T. and Anderson, D. B. 1986. 'Flamingo: object-oriented abstractions for user interface management', *Proc. Winter 1986 Usenix Conference*, pp. 72–8.
(cited on page 292)

Spector, A.Z. 1982. 'Performing remote operations efficiently on a local computer network', *Commun. of the ACM, vol. 25, no. 4*, pp. 246–60. (cited on pages 97, 106)

Spector, A.Z., Butcher, J., Daniels, D., Duchamp, D., Eppinger, J.L., Fineman, C.E., Heddaya, A., Schwarz, P. 1985. 'Support for distributed transactions in the TABS prototype', *IEEE Trans. Soft. Eng., vol. SE-11, no. 6*, pp. 520–29.
(cited on page 292)

Stallings, W. 1984. 'Local area networks', *Computing Surveys, vol. 16, no.1*, pp. 3–42.
(cited on page 67)

Stallings, W. 1985. *Data and Computer Communications*, Macmillan.
(cited on page 60)

Stallings, W. 1987. *Local Area Networks: An Introduction*, Macmillan.
(cited on page 67)

Stern, H.L. 1987. 'Comparison of windowing systems', *Byte, vol. 12, no. 13, (November 1987)*, pp. 265–72.   (cited on pages 37, 49)

Sturgis, H.E., Mitchell, J.G. and Israel, J. 1980. 'Issues in the design and use of a distributed file system', *ACM Operating Systems Review, vol. 14, no. 3*, pp. 55–69.
(cited on pages 139, 275)

Sun Microsystems 1987a. *Sun Network File System (NFS) Reference Manual*, Sun Microsystems, Mountain View, Calif.   (cited on pages 16, 211)

Sun Microsystems 1987b. *Sun Network-extensible Window System (NeWS) Technical Overview and Reference Manual*, Sun Microsystems, Mountain View, Calif.
(cited on pages 37, 49)

Svoboda, L. 1984. 'File servers for network-based distributed systems', *Computing Surveys, vol. 16, no. 4*, pp. 353–98.   (cited on page 207)

Swinehart, L., McDaniel, G. and Boggs, D.R. 1979. 'WFS: a simple shared file system for a distributed environment', *Proc. of the Seventh Symposium on Operating Systems Principles, Asilomar, California, Dec 1979*, pp. 9–17.   (cited on page 275)

Tanenbaum, A.S. 1981a. *Computer Networks*, Englewood Cliffs, New Jersey: Prentice-Hall.   (cited on pages 60, 65, 248, 253)

Tanenbaum, A.S. 1981b. 'Network protocols', *Computing Surveys, vol. 13, no. 4*, pp. 453–89.   (cited on page 60)

Tanenbaum, A.S. 1987. *Operating Systems: Design and Implementation*, Englewood Cliffs, New Jersey: Prentice-Hall.   (cited on pages viii, 136)

Tanenbaum, A.S. and van Renesse, R. 1985. 'Distributed operating systems', *Computing Surveys, vol. 17, no. 4*, pp. 419–70.   (cited on pages 25, 283)

Teitelman, W. 1983. *The Cedar programing environment: a midterm report and examination*, Technical Report CSL-83-11 Xerox PARC, Palo Alto, Calif.

(cited on page 92)

Teitelman, W. 1984. 'A tour through Cedar', *IEEE Software, vol. 1, no. 2*, pp. 44–73.

(cited on page 44)

Teitelman, W. and Masinter, D., 1981. 'The Interlisp programming environment', *Computer vol. 14, no. 4*, pp. 25–33.   (cited on page 11)

Thacker, C.P., McCreight, E.M., Lampson, B.W., Sproull, R.F. and Boggs, D.R. 1981. 'Alto: a personal computer', in Siewiorek et al. [1981]. (cited on pages 11, 322, 344)

Thomas, R.H. 1976. *A solution to the update problem for a multiple copy database which used distributed control*, Technical Report No. 3340, Bolt, Beranek and Newman, Cambridge, Mass.   (cited on page 338)

Thomas, R.H. 1979. 'A majority consensus approach to concurrency control in multiple copy databases', *ACM Trans. on Database Systems, vol. 4, no. 2*, pp. 180–209.

(cited on pages 185, 215)

Thompson, K. 1978. 'UNIX implementation', *Bell Systems Technical Journal, vol. 57, no. 6, part 2*, pp. 1931–46.   (cited on page 142)

Thornton, J.E. 1970. *Design of a Computer: The CDC 6600*, Scott, Freeman and Co., see also Siewiorek et al. [1981].   (cited on page 7)

Treleaven, P.P., Brownbridge, D.R. and Hopkins, R.P. 1982. 'Data-driven and demand-driven computer architecture', *Computing Surveys, vol. 14, no. 1*, pp. 93–143.

(cited on page 7)

Ullman, J.D. 1984. *Principles of Database Systems*, Computer Science Press.

(cited on page 145)

Walker, B., Popek, G., English, R., Kline, C. and Theil, G.H. 1983. 'The Locus distributed operating system', *Proc. of the 9th. ACM Symposium on Operating System Principles*, Oct. 1983, pp. 49–70.   (cited on page 262)

Weihl, W. and Liskov, B. 1985. 'Implementation of resilient, atomic data types', *ACM Trans. on Prog. Lang. and Systems, vol. 7, no. 2*, pp. 244–69.   (cited on page 269)

Wilbur, S. and Bacarisse, B. 1987. 'Building distributed systems with remote procedure call', *IEE Software Engineering Journal, vol. 2, no. 5*, pp. 148–59.(cited on page 86)

Wilkes, M.V. and Needham, R.M. 1979. *The Cambridge CAP Computer and its Operating System*, New York: North-Holland.   (cited on pages 236, 279)

Wirth, N. 1982. *Programming in Modula-2*, Springer-Verlag.   (cited on page 109)

Wulf, W.A. et al. 1972. 'C.mmp: a multi-processor', *Proc. AFIPS Fall Joint Computer Conference 1972, vol. 41, no. 2*, pp. 765–777.   (cited on page 7)

Wulf, W.A., Cohen, E.S., Corwin, W.M., Jones, A.K, Levin, R., Pearson, C. and Pollack, F.J. 1974. 'Hydra: the kernel of a multiprocessor operating system', *Commun. of the ACM, vol. 17, no. 6*, pp. 337–345.   (cited on page 7)

Xerox Corporation 1981. *Courier: the remote procdure call protocol*, Xerox Systems Integration Standards, Stamford, Connecticut: Xerox Corporation. (cited on page 85)

Xerox, Digital and Intel 1981. 'The Ethernet, Version 1.0', *ACM Computer Communications Review, vol. 11, no. 2*, pp. 17–65.   (cited on page 68)

Young, M., Tevanian, A., Rashid, R., Golub, D., Eppinger, J., Chew, J., Bolosky, W., Black, D., Acetta, M. and Baron, R. 1987. *The duality of memory and communication in the implementation of a multiprocessor operating system*, Technical Report CMU-CS-87-140, Carnegie–Mellon University.
(cited on page 287)

Index

Page numbers marked with an asterisk are main entries

360